The New
Pâtissiers

Olivier Dupon

The New Pâtissiers

Thames & Hudson

With 335 illustrations, 320 in colour

Above 'Shades of Yellow: Orange Poppy Seed Cake, Yuzu White Chocolate Ganache, Lemon Zat' by Janice Wong (see recipe on p. 212).

p. 7 Tempered chocolate being cut to shape by Julie Sharp (see recipe on p. 162).

p. 8 'Popcorn Cheesecake, Blackcurrant Meringue, Raspberry and Solliès Sorbet' by Marike van Beurden (see recipe on p. 174).

First published in the United Kingdom in 2013 by
Thames & Hudson Ltd, 181A High Holborn, London WC1V 7QX

The New Pâtissiers © 2013 Olivier Dupon
dossier37.tumblr.com

Designed by Karolina Prymaka

British Library Cataloguing-in-Publication Data
A catalogue record for this book is available from the British Library

ISBN 978-0-500-51692-8

Printed and bound in China through Asia Pacific Offset Ltd

To find out about all our publications, please visit **www.thamesandhudson.com**. There you can subscribe to our e-newsletter, browse or download our current catalogue, and buy any titles that are in print.

Contents

Note to the Reader

The temperatures given in this book are for fan-assisted (fan-forced/convection) electric ovens. Celsius/Fahrenheit conversions have been calibrated for each recipe and for each technique, such as syrup-making or deep-frying. Since ovens vary, manufacturers' instructions should be checked for guidance. In addition, a portable oven thermometer should be used to monitor temperatures accurately.

Quantities for ingredients are given in metric and imperial measures, and in standard cups and spoons. One set of measures should be followed but not a mix, as the quantities are not interchangeable. High-calibre pâtisserie-making requires great precision, so it is *strongly recommended* that readers follow metric measures, as supplied by the pâtissiers themselves (their varying metric measurements for liquids – e.g. grams/millilitres – have been retained, as have their slight variations in general methodology and instructions throughout). Imperial and cup/spoon conversions do not give the same level of precision, though quantities have been specified here in fractions that are as precise as possible, with notes of 'sc.' (scant) or 'gen.' (generous), for increased accuracy in the event these must be used.

1 tsp = 5 ml, 1 tbsp = 15 ml, 1 cup = 236.5 ml. Cups vary in size from country to country, but the customary US cup measurement has been used here. Australian standard tablespoons are 20 ml, so Australian readers should substitute 3 tsp in place of 1 tbsp. Gelatine quantities have been calculated on the basis of 2 g per sheet of gold gelatine and 2.5 g per sheet of silver gelatine, as weights may vary according to brand. Bracketed terms are intended for American readers. British spellings, e.g. colouring for coloring, or mould for mold, have been used throughout.

Full-fat (whole) milk and medium (US large) eggs are used in the recipes, unless otherwise stated. NB Pregnant women, the elderly, the infirm and the very young should avoid recipes using raw or lightly cooked eggs. Some recipes also contain alcohol, nuts and nut products, as well as other possible allergens and ingredients for which caution may be required.

Ingredients have been listed before quantities for ease of reference. Requirements for specific utensils have also been listed, though kitchen equipment regarded as standard, such as food processors and microwaves, has not been included. Several recipes require a spray gun; a new spray-painting gun from a hardware store may be substituted for a professional food spray gun, if necessary. Finally, each recipe has been graded on a scale of difficulty from 1 to 5, with 5 being the most difficult.

Introduction

I remember sitting in a beautiful restaurant – the setting: a restored, historic Florentine mansion – reflecting on the delicious meal that had been served thus far, when our desserts arrived. Have you ever thought, 'It cannot get any better than this', and then it does? The strawberry, melon, sugar, jelly and mousse composition was such a delight for the eye as well as the palate that it turned out to be the highlight of the soirée, astonishingly surpassing what had preceded it. To this day, I don't remember anything specific about the meal, except for the dessert. With that in mind, I approached *The New Pâtissiers* with the intention of finding and sharing recipes from some of the great pastry and dessert chefs of our time; recipes that would excite, intrigue and challenge most of us, and that above all would be memorable.

This book offers a chance to replicate at home cakes, tarts, biscuits, entremets, desserts, petits fours, pastries, confectionery, chocolate, ice creams and sorbets courtesy of some of the best kitchen professionals in the world. I hope it provides you with a unique opportunity to test your culinary skills and knowledge, to discover unfamiliar or unusual pastry ingredients, to experiment with genius pairings and to expand your repertoire.

Finding some of the ingredients could end up feeling like a treasure hunt on the internet or in specialized gourmet stores, but the chefs and I have made sure we have also included some more conventional recipes for you to choose from. Please do not feel intimidated by the sophisticated equipment that a few recipes require. If you are a serious cookery aficionado, you may already own that KitchenAid® or Thermomix®, or you might decide to splash out on a gadget that could turn out to be a great investment for your kitchen, or else you may be able to borrow from kitchen-savvy friends or family.

The book is divided into four categories, offering four different ways to set a culinary mood for any occasion: New Classics presents chefs who revisit traditional recipes and give them contemporary relevance; Art on a Plate delivers the sort of artistic and sophisticated compositions I so memorably experienced in Florence; Experimental Exotica will help you think again about possibilities in cooking – edible wood or parsnips for dessert?; finally, Wonderland Confections introduces a few favourite pastry designers who have the ability to turn cakes into spectacular, one-of-a-kind, sugar-paste marvels. Bon appetit!

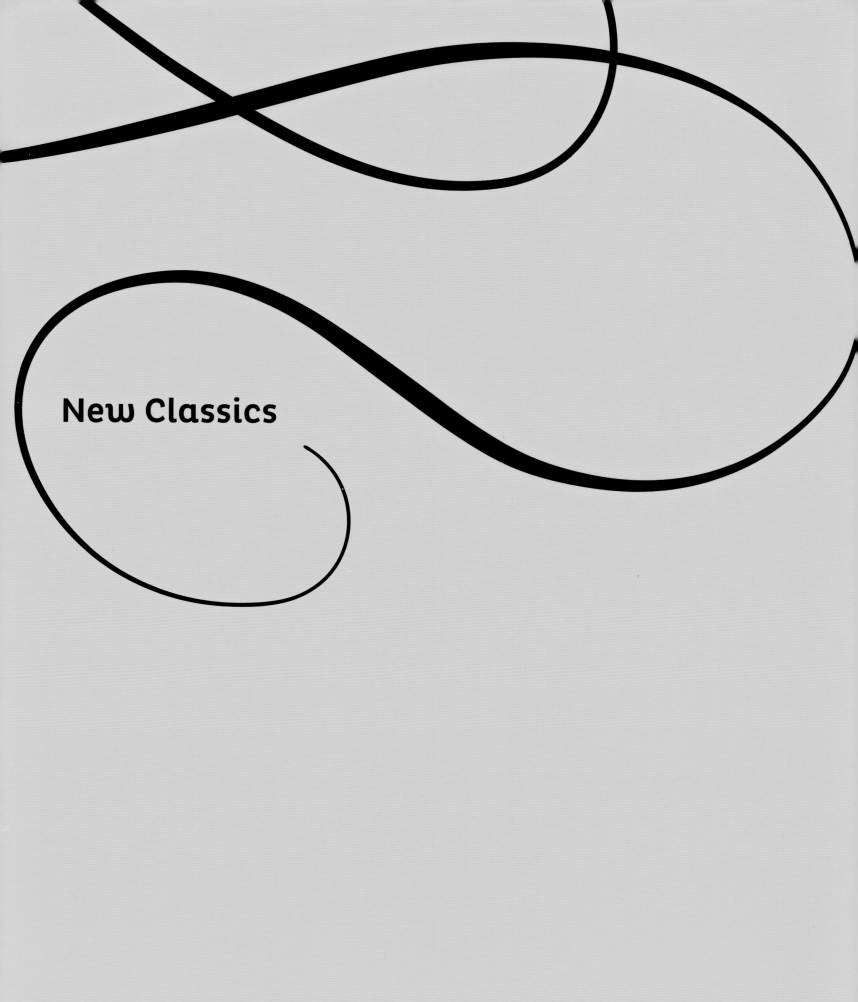

New Classics

The chefs in this section offer a new pastry heritage in the making. By revisiting favourite textures and tastes, they take the best from traditional recipes and methodology to reinvigorate classics and come up with the sweet staples of the future. An unwavering allegiance to quality, flavour and style ensures that each petit-gâteau not only looks delicious but also gives the word 'palatable' a whole new emphasis. These cakes will trigger sensual memories as familiar aromas and flavours are experienced again in note-perfect modern renditions. Some of the chefs run their own pâtisserie shops and cafés, and these also reflect the ethos of 'co-existence of past, present and future', whether with a sleek, cutting-edge mode of décor, a cool, contemporary interior or a throwback style to a latter-day charm. Welcome to your new tea-time favourites.

Andrea Reiss
....
AUSTRALIA

When asked how she would convince a 'salt tooth' to take an interest in pastry, Andrea Reiss does not shy away from a direct answer. 'It's nonsense,' she declares. 'Sweetness is a necessary part of our psyche.' This Melbourne-based pastry chef/ entrepreneur has her head planted firmly on her shoulders when it comes to her craft. 'I dislike the media's current approach that pastry chefs are the rock stars of the kitchen. When ego is involved, it hinders the creative process. Also I rarely use the word "passion" to describe anything I do. Passion makes it sound glamorous, when the day-to-day is very far from that. Cleanliness, neatness and organization are as key for a kitchen as they are for a shop front.'

Andrea reflects on a thread of simplicity and classicism that runs through all the places she has worked since 2004: 'They've been heavily "foundation"-based, meaning that the basics of pastry-making have been the key to being able to manipulate ingredients. And the more natural the overall process, the more confident I feel about presenting the work.'

It is with this same ethos that Andrea and her business associate, Stephen Sam, converted a South Melbourne warehouse into a one-stop pâtisserie/bou-langerie/café, which now employs some forty members of staff. Chez Dré drew a loyal following from its initial opening in 2011, with customers often comment-ing, 'This is the closest to Paris that you can get!' The compliment is testament to Andrea's conviction that success is not about following trends; rather, it's about carving out one's own niche, while still paying homage to classicism – in Andrea's case, with simplicity, clean design, delicate flavours, attention to detail and a sense of feminine strength.

'The more natural and organic the ingredients, the more possible it is to deliver a final product that will have true impact on the customer, not just a "wow" factor.' Andrea adds, 'I like the idea of people coming back to the familiar, but with a twist every time. The changing seasons are definitely a huge inspiration, and I often refer back to what we've produced and see how I can make it different, using crossover items and adding an element of something new.' This is stand-out authenticity with a difference.

http://chezdre.com.au

PASSION FRUIT TART

When Andrea visited L'École du Grand Chocolat Valrhona in southeastern France, creative director and executive chef Frédéric Bau introduced her to a brand-new flavour combination. 'I love the tartness and sourness of passion fruit cream,' Andrea enthuses, 'and it marries so well with the rich sweetness of dark chocolate.'

MAKES 25   DIFFICULTY 3½/5   PREPARATION TIME 24 hours (including setting time for inserts)
SPECIFIC EQUIPMENT Circle cutter (12 cm/4¾ in. diameter); 25 x tart moulds (each 8 cm/3⅛ in. diameter, 2 cm/¾ in. high); digital candy thermometer; 2 x piping (pastry) bags with size 9 nozzles; Silpat® mats

INGREDIENTS

For the Chocolate Sweet Paste

Cocoa powder 20 g | sc. ¾ oz | gen. 2¾ tbsp
Plain (all-purpose) flour 350 g | gen. 12¼ oz | 2⅓ cups
Salt 2 g | gen. ¼ tsp
Unsalted butter 200 g | 7 oz
Caster (superfine) sugar 140 g | sc. 5 oz | sc. ⅔ cup
1 whole egg
1 egg yolk

For the Passion Fruit Cream

Passion fruit juice 285 g | gen. 9½ fl oz | gen. 1⅛ cups
Caster (superfine) sugar 270 g | 9½ oz | sc. 1¼ cups
Whole eggs 188 g | sc. 6¾ oz | gen. ¾ cup
Egg yolks 158 g | 5½ oz | ⅔ cup
Custard powder 26 g | sc. 1 oz | gen. 6 tsp
Unsalted butter 188 g | sc. 6¾ oz (cut into cubes, room temperature)

For the Chocolate-Passion Fruit Ganache

Passion fruit purée 65 g | gen. 2¼ fl oz | ¼ cup
Milk chocolate couverture buttons 140 g | sc. 5 oz
Unsalted butter 25 g | gen. ¾ oz (cut into cubes, room temperature)

For the Macaron Shell

Water 60 g | 2 fl oz | gen. 4 tbsp
Caster (superfine) sugar 200 g | 7 oz | sc. 1 cup
Egg whites [1] 80 g | gen. 2¾ oz | ⅓ cup
Yellow food colouring (to achieve desired colour)
Blanched almond meal 200 g | 7 oz | 2⅓ cups
Pure icing (confectioner's) sugar 200 g | 7 oz | 1¼ cups
Freeze-dried passion fruit powder 3 g | ½ tsp (optional)
Egg whites [2] 80 g | gen. 2¾ oz | ⅓ cup
Black sesame seeds (to garnish)

INSTRUCTIONS

Chocolate Sweet Paste

1 Sift the cocoa powder, flour and salt together.
2 Cream the butter and sugar in a mixer with a paddle attachment.
3 Add the whole egg and egg yolk (the mixture will look split).
4 Add the sifted ingredients, mixing until the dough comes together.
5 Scrape the dough out of the bowl onto plastic wrap, then press down and flatten to a thickness of about 2 cm (¾ in.); this will make the dough easier to roll out.
6 Wrap tightly and place in the fridge for a minimum of 3 hours.
7 Take out of the fridge and leave to rest at room temperature for approximately 20 minutes before rolling out to a thickness of 2–3 mm (⅛ in.).
8 Cut into circles with the cutter, then line the tart moulds.
9 Blind bake at 155°C (300°F) for about 20 minutes.
10 Take the tart shells out of the oven and allow to cool completely.

Passion Fruit Cream

1 Bring the passion fruit juice to the boil in a medium-sized saucepan.
2 At the same time, whisk the sugar, eggs, egg yolks and custard powder together very thoroughly.
3 Pour a small amount of the passion fruit juice over the mixture to temper the eggs, then pour the mixture back into the saucepan.
4 Bring to the boil, stirring continually with a whisk, then cook for 2 minutes (the mixture will be very thick).
5 Pour into a stainless steel bowl and cool to 35–40°C (95–104°F).
6 Mix with a hand mixer, adding the cubes of butter until completely emulsified.
7 Transfer into a clean container and place a piece of plastic wrap directly touching the mix so that a skin does not develop.
8 Store in the fridge overnight.

Chocolate-Passion Fruit Ganache

1 Boil the passion fruit purée.
2 Pour the boiled purée over the milk chocolate couverture buttons.
3 Cool to 35°C (95°F), add the cubes of butter and mix with an immersion blender.
4 Pour into a container and cover with plastic wrap directly touching the mix.
5 Leave to set overnight at room temperature.
6 Once set, put into a piping (pastry) bag ready to fill the macarons.

Macaron Shell

1 Make an Italian meringue by forming a syrup with the water and caster (superfine) sugar and boiling to 121°C (250°F); begin whisking egg whites [1] in a mixer; slowly pour the boiling syrup onto the whisking egg whites, and continue to whisk until stiff and glossy and cooled to about 35°C (95°F); finally, add a small amount of yellow food colouring.
2 Sift the almond meal, icing (confectioner's) sugar and freeze-dried passion fruit powder (if desired, to add more flavour) onto egg whites [2], then mix.
3 Take the Italian meringue off the mixer and fold in the almond/sugar mix.
4 Once the two mixes are incorporated, use a piping (pastry) bag to form 2.5 cm (1 in.) rounds onto Silpat® mats, then sprinkle with black sesame seeds.
5 Leave to dry for 20 minutes, then bake in a 130°C (250°F) oven for 15–18 minutes.
6 Cool on wire racks, then pair up and fill with a little chocolate-passion fruit ganache.

ASSEMBLING

Components/Garnishes 25 small squares of tempered dark chocolate; melted dark chocolate; gold leaf

Fill the tart shells with passion fruit cream, smoothing any excess away. Place in the freezer to set for about 1 hour. Take out of the freezer and place a square of chocolate towards the rim of each tart. Dunk the edge of each macaron into some melted dark chocolate in order to secure it to the square of chocolate on the tarts, then garnish with a small amount of gold leaf. Leave in the fridge to defrost. Serve at room temperature.

CARAMEL DOME

'Caramel is one of those flavours that always seems to be in fashion,' notes Andrea, 'but in the past few years the addition of salt has really taken off.' In this recipe the sweetness of sugar, the bitterness of chocolate and the tanginess of sea salt all balance to create a smooth, appealing mouth sensation.

MAKES 12 **DIFFICULTY** 3½/5 **PREPARATION TIME** 12+ hours (including freezing time) **SPECIFIC EQUIPMENT** Digital candy thermometer; 2 x baking trays (each 20 x 30 cm; 7¾ x 11¾ in.); circle cutter (7 cm/2¾ in.); 12 x Flexipan® tartlet moulds (each 5.8 cm/2¼ in. diameter, 2 cm/¾ in. deep, 35 ml/gen. 1 fl oz volume); 12 x Flexipan® dome-shaped moulds (each 7 cm/2¾ in. diameter, 4 cm/1⅝ in. deep, 105 ml/3½ fl oz volume)

INGREDIENTS

For the Chocolate-Almond Base

Dark chocolate (55%) 150 g | gen. 5¼ oz
Marzipan 300 g | 10½ oz
Egg whites [1] 50 g | 1¾ oz | sc. 3½ tbsp
Whole eggs 125 g | sc. 4½ oz | gen. ½ cup
Egg yolks 75 g | gen. 2½ oz | 5 tbsp
Egg whites [2] 275 g | 9¾ oz | gen. 1 cup
Caster (superfine) sugar 100 g | 3½ oz | sc. ½ cup
Plain (all-purpose) flour 80 g | gen. 2¾ oz | gen. ½ cup
Cocoa powder 40 g | sc. 1½ oz | sc. ⅖ cup

For the Caramel Crémeux

Caster (superfine) sugar [1] 80 g | gen. 2¾ oz | gen. ⅓ cup
Milk 210 g | 7 fl oz | gen. ⅘ cup
Whipping cream (35% fat) 210 g | gen. 7¼ fl oz | gen. ¾ cup
1 vanilla pod (bean) (split, scraped, seeds reserved)
Egg yolks 120 g | 4¼ oz | ½ cup
Fine sea salt 2 g | sc. ½ tsp
Caster (superfine) sugar [2] 50 g | 1¾ oz | sc. ¼ cup
Gelatine (gold) 8 g | 4 sheets (softened in ice cold water, with excess water squeezed out)

For the Caramel Mousse

Whipping cream (35% fat) [1] 280 g | 9¾ fl oz | gen. 1 cup
Caster (superfine) sugar 85 g | 3 oz | sc. ⅖ cup
Whipping cream (35% fat) [2] 90 g | 3¼ fl oz | ⅓ cup
Gelatine (gold) 3 g | 1½ sheets (softened in ice cold water, with excess water squeezed out)
White chocolate 85 g | 3 oz

For the Caramel Glaze

Caster (superfine) sugar 430 g | sc. 1 lb | 2 cups
Whipping cream (35% fat) 350 g | 12¼ fl oz | sc. 1½ cups
Water 250 g | gen. 8¾ fl oz | gen. 1 cup
Cornflour (cornstarch) 15 g | ½ oz | 1½ tbsp
Gelatine (gold) 15 g | 7½ sheets (softened in ice cold water, with excess water squeezed out)
Dark chocolate (60–65%) 60 g | gen. 2 oz

INSTRUCTIONS

Chocolate-Almond Base

1 Melt the chocolate to 40°C (104°F) and set aside.
2 Mix the marzipan and egg whites [1] in a food processor until a smooth paste forms, then slowly add the whole eggs and egg yolks.
3 At the same time, make a meringue with egg whites [2] and the sugar.
4 Sift the flour and cocoa powder together.
5 Pour the marzipan mix into a stainless steel bowl and fold in the meringue.
6 Add the sifted ingredients, and fold the melted chocolate in last.
7 Spread the mixture over the two baking trays, lined with silicone baking paper.
8 Cook in a 180°C (350°F) oven for 9 minutes, leave to cool, then cut into discs with the circle cutter.

Caramel Crémeux

1 Make a dry caramel with sugar [1].
2 At the same time, warm the milk, cream and vanilla seeds, then use to deglaze the caramel.
3 Bring to the boil, then take off the heat.
4 Whisk the egg yolks, salt and sugar [2], then slowly cook, stirring continuously to 75°C (167°F) before removing from the heat.
5 Slowly add the caramel to the egg yolk mixture, stirring well.
6 Add the gelatine, then strain into a stainless steel bowl and leave to cool.
7 Once cool, pour into the small Flexipan® tartlet moulds and freeze.
8 Once frozen, unmould and return to the freezer.

Caramel Mousse

1 Whip cream [1] to a soft peak, then set aside in the fridge.
2 Make a dry caramel with the sugar.
3 Warm cream [2] in a separate saucepan, and use to deglaze the caramel.
4 Bring to the boil and add the gelatine.
5 Strain, then pour the mixture over the white chocolate and stir.
6 Cool to 35–40°C (95–104°F), fold in the whipped cream [1], then refrigerate until very thick.

Caramel Glaze

1 Make a dry caramel with the sugar.
2 At the same time, warm the cream and use to deglaze the caramel.
3 Boil until all the caramel has dissolved.
4 Mix the water and cornflour (cornstarch), then whisk into the caramel mix.
5 Cook for about 30 seconds, then add the gelatine and stir to dissolve.
6 Strain and cool to 45°C (113°F), then add the chocolate.
7 Emulsify using an immersion blender, then set aside; use the glaze at about 25–28°C (77–82°F).

ASSEMBLING

Component Tempered dark chocolate

Place some caramel mousse in the dome-shaped Flexipan® moulds, then push in a frozen caramel crémeux insert. Cover with more mousse and smooth over with a palette knife. Place a chocolate-almond base disc on top, then place in the freezer until frozen hard. The next day, pop out of the mould and put onto a wire rack. Cover with several layers of caramel glaze. Break pieces of tempered dark chocolate to place around the bottom. Leave in the fridge to defrost and come up to room temperature.

WHITE CHOCOLATE AND STRAWBERRY CHEESECAKE

'Cheesecake is a classic mousse, and every pastry chef seems to have a version,' comments Andrea. 'It goes well with so many flavours, which is why I love it. So don't limit yourself to strawberry. You can use mango or raspberry jelly, for example, and decorate accordingly.'

MAKES 15 **DIFFICULTY** 2/5 **PREPARATION TIME** 6 hours (not including freezing time for the strawberry jelly inserts)
SPECIFIC EQUIPMENT 15 x petit gâteau rings (each 7 x 6 cm/2¾ x 2⅜ in., 4.5 cm/1¾ in. high); 15 x Flexipan® oval moulds
(each 5.7 x 3.5 cm/2¼ x 1⅜ in., 1.2 cm/½ in. deep); piping (pastry) bag with size 10 nozzle

INGREDIENTS

For the Sablé-Gianduja Base

Unsalted butter 200 g | 7 oz
Pure icing (confectioner's) sugar 200 g | 7 oz | 1¼ cups
Blanched almond meal 100 g | 3½ oz | gen. 1 cup
Whole eggs 85 g | 3 oz | sc. ⅔ cup
Plain (all-purpose) flour [1] 100 g | 3½ oz | ⅔ cup
Salt 3 g | ½ tsp
Plain (all-purpose) flour [2] 290 g | 10¼ oz | sc. 2 cups
Gianduja milk chocolate (hazelnut-flavoured) 380 g | sc. 13½ oz (melted to 35°C/95°F)

For the Strawberry Jelly

Strawberry purée 400 g | 14¼ fl oz | 1½ cups
Caster (superfine) sugar 60 g | gen. 2 oz | gen. ¼ cup
Gelatine (gold) 10 g | 5 sheets (softened in ice cold water, with excess water squeezed out)

For the White Chocolate Cheesecake Mousse

Whipping cream (35% fat) 266 g | gen. 9¼ fl oz | 1 cup
Caster (superfine) sugar 25 g | gen. ¾ oz | sc. 2 tbsp
Cream cheese 200 g | 7 oz | sc. 1 cup (room temperature)
White chocolate 160 g | sc. 5¾ oz (melted to 40°C/104°F)

INSTRUCTIONS

Sablé-Gianduja Base

1 Cream the butter, sugar, almond meal, eggs, flour [1] and salt in a food processor or stand mixer (e.g. KitchenAid®) with a paddle attachment.
2 Add flour [2] and combine.
3 Take the resulting sablé out of the food processor/stand mixer.
4 Divide the sablé between two sheets of silicone baking paper and roll it between the sheets until it is 2–3 mm (⅛ in.) thick.
5 Allow to rest in the fridge for about 1 hour.
6 Set the oven to 155°C (300°F), then bake the sablés on trays for 25–30 minutes until golden and dry.
7 Allow to cool, then make into crumbs in the food processor.
8 Add melted Gianduja chocolate to the crumbs, which will stick together.
9 Push a layer of crumb into the petit gâteau rings placed on silicone baking paper.
10 Reserve in the fridge until ready to use.

Strawberry Jelly

1 Bring half the strawberry purée and all of the sugar to the boil.
2 Add the gelatine to the mixture.
3 Add the remaining purée.
4 Pour into the Flexipan® oval moulds.
5 Leave to set in the freezer.
6 Once frozen, unmould, then return to the freezer.

White Chocolate Cheesecake Mousse

1 Whip the cream and store in the fridge.
2 Mix the sugar and cream cheese until smooth in a food processor with a paddle attachment.
3 Pour in the melted white chocolate and incorporate.
4 Fold in the whipped cream.
5 Pour the mixture into the piping (pastry) bag, ready for the cakes to be assembled.

ASSEMBLING

Garnishes Fresh strawberries; chocolate decorations

Take the petit gâteau rings, with sablé-Gianduja base in the bottom, out of the fridge. Fill halfway up with cheesecake mousse. Push a frozen strawberry jelly insert into the centre. Cover with cheesecake mousse to the top of the ring. Flatten the top with a palette knife, then freeze overnight. Remove the rings and leave the cakes in the fridge to defrost and come up to room temperature. Present with fresh strawberries and chocolate decorations.

Arnaud Delmontel

FRANCE

Too often we have to choose between a beautiful but flavourless cake or a delicious but unattractive one. Not in Arnaud Delmontel's company. This French pastry chef ensures his creations meet both criteria of taste and design by crafting impeccably modern, instantly mouthwatering fares. 'We work our products – their packaging designed according to seasonal collections – like a fashion house,' he explains. 'We also follow what's happening worldwide, picking up on trends that can twist and modernize our traditional signature, as with our *uzu bûche*, a good example of how we've merged a French classic with Japanese exotica.'

With three bakeries/pastry shops in Paris, Arnaud, his wife and their extensive team work closely together, embracing the value of debate. 'We each compile ideas, then collectively decide which will be tested, according to the market and our personal preferences. Next comes the tasting, and this is when our differences in perception appear. We discuss everything at length until I settle the argument.' Arnaud happily identifies with the concept of a fraternal pastry society, but his own gift for leadership and entrepreneurship complements his creativity and love and respect for his craft.

'I enjoy working with flour from the Beauce region; much nicer to handle than ordinary flour. I also source honey exclusively from black bees from a producer in the Alps,' he notes. 'My love for the handmade and for quality ingredients dates way back. When I was working at the Hôtel des Neiges in Courchevel, kneading the dough with my own hands imprinted a fulfilling sensation in me forever. I owe most of who I am today as a chef to my apprenticeship tutor, M. Pradier, and to the pastry legends Gaston Lenôtre and Paul Bocuse.' Arnaud's experiences in various prestigious restaurants and kitchens – including that of Palais Matignon, while acting as the French prime minister's private head pastry chef – have exposed him to countless challenges, though nothing could have prepared him for the comment of an American fan after she ate one of his desserts: 'I just had a gastric orgasm!'

Arnaud's entremets and petits-gâteaux are always stylishly and precisely presented – a clean offering that allows the sophistication of the filling and layers to shine. This chef knows never to overdo the wrapping of a superb present.

www.arnaud-delmontel.com

OPERA ESTRAGON

This entremet is one of Arnaud's favourites. 'Textures are contrasted between the crunchy and the unctuous: "ça craque … ça crème." The tarragon is sweet and sour, so, when used sparingly, it can transform a dessert. With the red berries, the full benefit of sweet and sour is achieved.'

MAKES 1 cake (20 x 20 cm/7¾ x 7¾ in.); to be served in 12 portions   **DIFFICULTY** 4/5   **PREPARATION TIME** 4 hours (not including 24 hours' infusing time for the tarragon ganache)   **SPECIFIC EQUIPMENT** Baking tray (at least 20 x 40 cm/7¾ x 15¾ in.); digital candy thermometer; frame or cake tin (pan) with bottom (20 x 20 x 5 cm/7¾ x 7¾ x 2 in.)

INGREDIENTS

For the Dacquoise

Egg whites 250 g | gen. 8¾ oz | 1 cup
Granulated white sugar 63 g | sc. 2¼ oz | sc. ⅓ cup
Red food colouring (to achieve desired colour)
Icing (confectioner's) sugar 63 g | sc. 2¼ oz | ⅖ cup
Plain (all-purpose) flour 50 g | 1¾ oz | ⅓ cup
Almond meal 188 g | sc. 6¾ oz | sc. 2¼ cups

For the Almond 'Croquant'

Unsalted butter 45 g | 1½ oz (soft)
Icing (confectioner's) sugar 55 g | sc. 2 oz | ⅓ cup
Plain (all-purpose) flour 15 g | ½ oz | 1¼ tbsp
Almond flakes 60 g | gen. 2 oz | sc. ¾ cup

For the Red Berry Crémeux

Red berry mix purée 100 g | 3½ fl oz | ⅖ cup
Whole egg 38 g | gen. 1¼ oz | 2½ tbsp
Egg yolks 60 g | gen. 2 oz | ¼ cup
Granulated white sugar 50 g | 1¾ oz | ¼ cup
Gelatine (gold) 5 g | 2½ sheets (softened in ice cold water, with excess water squeezed out)
Unsalted butter 38 g | gen. 1¼ oz

For the Tarragon Ganache

Whipping cream (35% fat) 375 g | gen. 13 fl oz | 1½ cups
Fresh tarragon 12 g | sc. ½ oz | ¼ cup
White chocolate couverture (e.g. Ivoire 35% by Valrhona) 450 g | 1 lb (chopped)

For the Opera Glazing

Ivory pâte à glacer (white glazing compound, e.g. Ivory [Ivoire] compound coating by Cacao Barry, or Original White by Carma; if this cannot be obtained, substitute 50 g/1¾ oz premium white cooking compound, e.g. Plaistowe by Nestlé, and follow the same method) 50 g | 1¾ oz
White chocolate couverture (e.g. Ivoire 35% by Valrhona) 100 g | 3½ oz
Vegetable oil 12.5 g | ½ fl oz | 1 tbsp
Red food colouring (to achieve desired colour)

INSTRUCTIONS

Dacquoise

1 Pre-heat the oven to 200°C (400°F).
2 Beat the egg whites until soft peaks form, then slowly add the granulated sugar.
3 Continue beating until the sugar has completely dissolved and the mixture is smooth and shiny.
4 Add enough food colouring to make the desired shade of pink.
5 Fold the icing (confectioner's) sugar, flour and almond meal into the mixture.
6 Spread out onto the silicone baking paper-lined tray of at least 20 x 40 cm (7¾ x 15¾ in.), as you will need to cut two 20 x 20 cm (7¾ x 7¾ in.) squares of dacquoise to make the finished cake.
7 Bake for 10–15 minutes, or until slightly crisp on top.

Almond 'Croquant'

1 Pre-heat the oven to 180°C (350°F).
2 Mix the soft butter with the sugar in the bowl of a stand mixer.
3 Add the flour and combine.
4 Spread out to form a square of at least 20 x 20 cm (7¾ x 7¾ in.) on a silicone baking paper sheet.
5 Sprinkle the almond flakes evenly on top.
6 Bake for 15–17 minutes.
7 Leave to cool, then cut out the 20 x 20 cm (7¾ x 7¾ in.) square.

Red Berry Crémeux

1 Bring the red berry mix purée to the boil.
2 Separately blend the whole egg and egg yolks with the sugar.
3 Pour in some of the purée and combine.
4 Pour this mixture back into the remainder of the purée and heat to 87°C (188°F), mixing well.
5 Remove from the heat, add in the gelatine and butter, and stir until well combined.
6 Leave to cool in a container sealed with plastic wrap for 2–4 hours, or until thick.

Tarragon Ganache

1 Heat together the cream and the tarragon.
2 Remove from the heat and allow to infuse for 24 hours.
3 After the infusion period, remove the tarragon and bring to the boil.
4 Pour over the chopped chocolate, stir until combined and smooth, then leave to cool.

Opera Glazing

1 Melt the pâte and the chocolate together in a bain-marie.
2 Add in the oil and enough food colouring to make the desired shade of pink, then mix.

ASSEMBLING

Components Blackcurrants (140 g/sc. 5 oz/1 cup)

The assembling starts upside down. Thinly spread some of the tarragon ganache to form a layer of approximately 0.5 cm (¼ in.) in the bottomed frame or cake tin (pan). Add the first layer of dacquoise. Add the red berry crémeux, which you will need to whisk to make smooth. Carefully add the almond 'croquant'. Spread out the remainder of the ganache and incorporate the blackcurrants. Finish with the second layer of dacquoise. Freeze, unmould, turn over and top with the opera glazing. Slice as desired before the cake is fully defrosted. You could also garnish each slice with edible silver leaf.

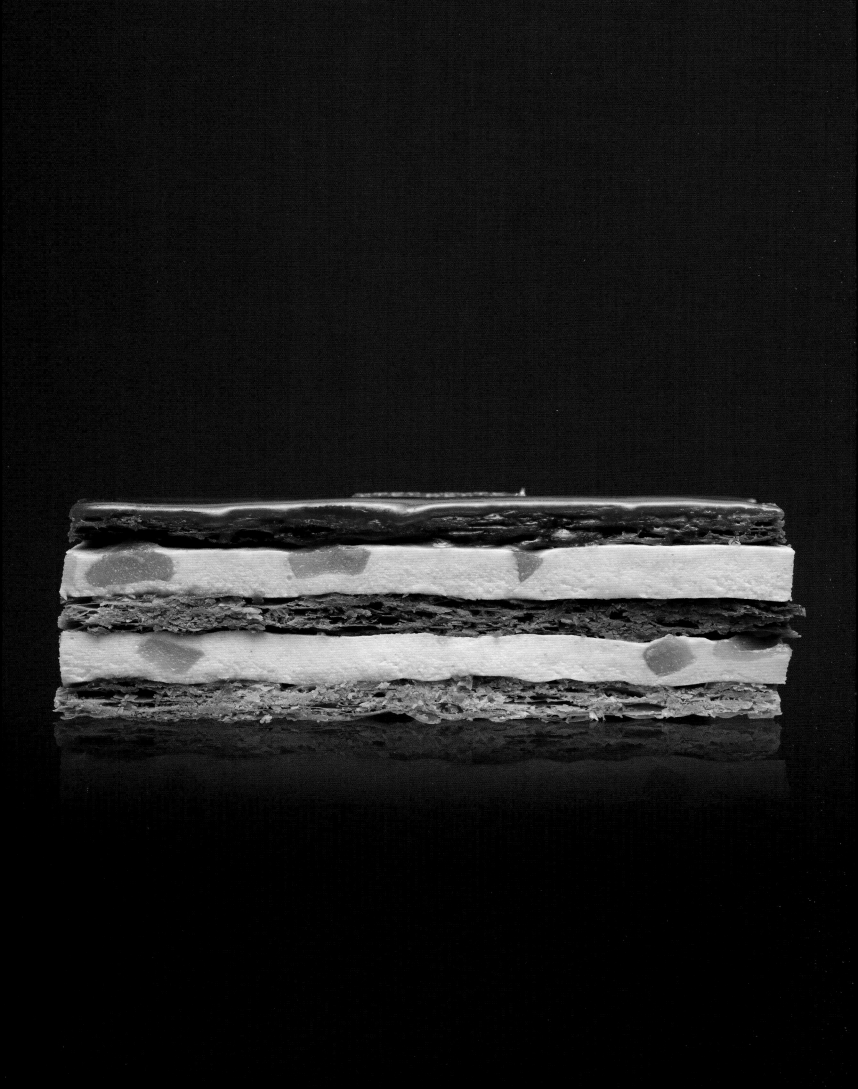

MILLE-FEUILLES PEAR/CARAMEL

'Next to the poire Belle-Hélène and the poire au vin, we could have the poire caramel,' suggests Arnaud. 'Pear and caramel suit an autumnal puff pastry entremet. They make a subtly refined, light and tasty combination.'

MAKES 1 mille-feuilles (20 x 20 x 5 cm/7¾ x 7¾ x 2 in.); serves 10 **DIFFICULTY** 3/5 **PREPARATION TIME** 3½ hours (not including cooling time for the caramel glaze or draining time for the cooked pears) **SPECIFIC EQUIPMENT** Digital candy thermometer

INGREDIENTS

For the Caramel Glaze
(must be prepared in advance due to cooling time)
Granulated white sugar 200 g | 7 oz | 1 cup
Glucose syrup 20 g | ¾ fl oz | sc. 1½ tbsp
Whipping cream (crème fleurette; 35% fat)
100 g | gen. 3½ fl oz | sc. ½ cup
Unsalted butter 50 g | 1¾ oz

For the Cooked Pears
(must be prepared in advance due to draining time)
Fresh whole pears (ideally Bosc) 500 g | 1 lb 1½ oz
Brown sugar 200 g | 7 oz | 1 cup
Pear alcohol (or pear brandy) 70 g | sc. 2½ fl oz | sc. 4¾ tbsp

For the Pear Mousse
Pear purée 750 g | 26¾ fl oz | 3 cups
Egg yolks 250 g | gen. 8¾ oz | 1 cup
Granulated white sugar 150 g | gen. 5¼ oz | ¾ cup
Gelatine (gold) 20 g | 10 sheets (softened in ice cold water, with excess water squeezed out)
Whipping cream (35% fat) 450 g | 15¾ fl oz | gen. 1¾ cups (softly whipped)

For the Puff Pastry
To be bought ready-made, high-quality

INSTRUCTIONS

Caramel Glaze
1   Melt one-third of the sugar with the glucose syrup, then add the rest of the sugar and cook at 190°C (374°F) until caramelized.
2   At the same time, bring the cream to the boil.
3   Dissolve the caramel by stirring in the boiled cream.
4   Remove from the heat and stir in the butter.
5   Pass the mixture through a sieve (strainer) and leave to set in the fridge for 24 hours.

Cooked Pears
1   Core, peel and chop the pears into small pieces.
2   Place the pieces, with the sugar and alcohol, in a large shallow pan.
3   Cook for 25 minutes on a medium heat.
4   Remove from the heat, place in a sieve (strainer) and allow to drain for 24 hours.

Pear Mousse
1   Place the pear purée, egg yolks and sugar in a saucepan, and heat to 87°C (189°F) while stirring.
2   Add the gelatine, stirring to dissolve.
3   Leave to cool.
4   Once cool, gently stir until smooth and fold in the softly whipped cream.
5   Spread the mousse on a silicone baking paper-lined tray to a thickness of 1.5 cm (⅝ in.). NB You may need to spread the mousse on two trays in order to cut two 20 x 20 cm (7¾ x 7¾ in.) squares from the mousse once set.
6   Scatter evenly with the cooked pears (from above recipe).
7   Leave to set in the freezer for 2 hours.

Puff Pastry
1   Bake according to instructions until dry, crisp and a rich, deep gold. NB There should be sufficient to cut three 20 x 20 cm (7¾ x 7¾ in.) squares.

ASSEMBLING

Slice the puff pastry into three squares and the mousse into two squares, all of equal size (20 x 20 cm/7¾ x 7¾ in.). Layer one square of pastry with a square of mousse, repeat, then top with a square of pastry. Glaze with the caramel gently re-heated in a bain-marie until thick and viscous, then smooth the surface.

Bernard Heberle

....

JAPAN

Life can work in mysterious ways. Bernard Heberle, owner of the Abondance pastry shop in Hamamatsu, Japan, only recently discovered that he was following in the footsteps of one of his forefathers. 'When I told my parents I wanted to be a pastry chef, they were very surprised but eventually supportive,' he relates. 'One of the reasons for their reaction was that my grandfather had also worked as a pastry chef, but it was some sort of taboo in the family and there's still a lot of secrecy around the subject.' Could it be that pastry genes run in the family?

Bernard had long been fascinated by the alchemy involved in desserts, but as a young man he also wanted to travel. So after graduating from a bakery apprenticeship in his native Alsace, where 'pastry turned out to be more colourful in every sense of the word', and after holding various high-level positions, he embarked on a five-star Royal Viking Line cruise ship as chef and toured the world twice.

Having worked on and off in France, Switzerland and the Netherlands, the pastry globetrotter eventually settled in Japan, where his wife, Hasegawa Toyoka, now helps him operate Abondance. Of his business he notes, 'I'm trying to work as much as possible in accordance with the seasons; a meandering sort of progress in which the final call is up to the customer. Japanese people enjoy new products, and you need to impress them every time.' Bernard notes that this can be challenging, but also interesting. 'My creativity relies on my inspiration, while keeping in mind a few self-imposed rules, such as only using three colours or two major flavours.' His mantra? 'Keep things simple and beautiful.'

Bernard opposes processed, ready-made, 'instant' products that are full of chemicals and is a strong advocate for preserving pastry on an artisanal/human level. He also strives constantly to maintain a balance between tradition and innovation. 'I love *yuzu*, for example, an Asian citrus, but I won't allow myself to use it in my shop because we are a French pastry shop,' he admits. 'A good pastry chef needs to be rigorous, sensitive and full of passion, as well as mentally and physically strong. To be a pastry chef, one has to be a kind of poet.'

www.abondance.jp

LAVANDE FRAMBOISE

'This cake originated out of travel – the encounter between two French regions, Provence and Alsace; the alliance of south and north. It wasn't an easy pairing at first, but,' quips Bernard, 'it turned out just fine, thanks to trials and inspiration!'

MAKES 10 **DIFFICULTY** 3½/5 **PREPARATION TIME** 2½ hours (not including setting time once assembled)
SPECIFIC EQUIPMENT Digital candy thermometer; Silpat® mat; serrated icing scraper; piping (pastry bag); 20 x half-sphere moulds (each 4 cm/1⅝ in. wide, 1 cm/⅜ in. high); 10 x small rings (each 5.5 cm/2⅛ in. diameter, 4.5 cm/1¾ in. high)

INGREDIENTS

For the Sponge Cake (Génoise)
Whole eggs 80 g | gen. 2¾ oz | gen. ⅓ cup (lightly whisked)
Granulated white sugar 60 g | gen. 2 oz | gen. ¼ cup
Glucose syrup 3 g | ¼ tsp
Plain (all-purpose) flour 85 g | 3 oz | gen. ½ cup (sifted)
Milk 10 g | gen. ¼ fl oz | 2 tsp (tepid)
Unsalted butter 12 g | sc. ½ oz (melted)

For the Pâte à Cigarette
Unsalted butter 20 g | sc. ¾ oz (soft)
Icing (confectioner's) sugar 20 g | sc. ¾ oz | 2 tbsp
Egg whites 20 g | sc. ¾ oz | sc. 1½ tbsp
Plain (all-purpose) flour 20 g | sc. ¾ oz | 4 tsp (sifted)
Red food colouring (to achieve desired colour)

For the Biscuit Joconde
Egg whites 55 g | sc. 2 oz | sc. ¼ cup
Granulated white sugar 8 g | ¼ oz | 2 tsp
Almond meal 62 g | gen. 2 oz | sc. ¾ cup
Icing (confectioner's) sugar 62 g | gen. 2 oz | 6 tbsp
Whole eggs 58 g | 2 oz | ¼ cup
Plain (all-purpose) flour 16 g | ½ oz | sc. 1½ tbsp (sifted)
Unsalted butter 12 g | sc. ½ oz (melted at 40°C/104°F)

For the Raspberry Mousse
Italian meringue 20 g | sc. ¾ oz | sc. 3½ tbsp
Double (heavy) whipping cream (38% fat)
40 g | sc. 1½ fl oz | sc. 2¼ tbsp
Raspberry purée [1] 10 g | gen. ¼ fl oz | sc. 1½ tsp
Gelatine (gold) 0.68 g | ⅓ sheet (softened in ice cold water, with excess water squeezed out)
Raspberry purée [2] 20 g | sc. ¾ fl oz | gen. 1 tbsp

For the Lavender Supreme
Dried lavender 0.4 g | 1 tsp
Milk 130 g | sc. 4½ fl oz | ½ cup
Double (heavy) whipping cream (38% fat) [1]
20 g | gen. ½ fl oz | 1 tbsp
Granulated white sugar [1] 20 g | sc. ¾ oz | 5 tsp
Egg yolks 60 g | gen. 2 oz | ¼ cup
Gelatine (gold) 5 g | 2½ sheets (softened in ice cold water, with excess water squeezed out)
Double (heavy) whipping cream (38% fat) [2]
360 g | gen. 12½ fl oz | sc. 1½ cups
Granulated white sugar [2] 20 g | sc. ¾ oz | 5 tsp

INSTRUCTIONS

Sponge Cake (Génoise)
1   Heat the lightly whisked eggs, the sugar and the glucose syrup to 40°C (104°F) in a bain-marie, then whisk in a stand mixer until pale and aerated.
2   Sprinkle in the sifted flour, stirring to avoid lumps, then add the tepid milk and melted butter.
3   Spread the mixture on a silicone baking paper-lined tray to a thickness of 3 mm (⅛ in.).
4   Bake at 210°C (400°F) for 5 minutes.
5   Remove from the oven and immediately transfer to a wire rack to cool as fast as possible.

Pâte à Cigarette
1   Mix the butter, add the sugar, then the egg whites and lastly the flour.
2   Once the mixture is homogeneous, pass it through a fine sieve (strainer).
3   Add red food colouring, mixing to combine.
4   Reserve in the fridge.

Biscuit Joconde
1   Beat the egg whites with the granulated sugar.
2   In a separate bowl, mix the almond meal and icing (confectioner's) sugar, then gradually add the whole eggs, emulsifying the mixture.
3   Pour the egg white mixture into the almond meal mixture, then add the sifted flour and the melted butter.
4   Spread the pâte à cigarette (from above recipe) on the Silpat® mat on a tray, create a stripe pattern with the serrated icing scraper, then carefully spread the biscuit joconde over the pâte.
5   Tap the tray to get rid of air bubbles, then bake at 240°C (475°F) for 4 minutes.

Raspberry Mousse
1   Prepare an Italian meringue (see overleaf).
2   Beat the cream until stiff, but not too firm.
3   Heat purée [1] to 50°C (122°F), add the gelatine and purée [2], then fold in the meringue and beaten cream.
4   Pipe the mousse into the half-sphere moulds and freeze.

Lavender Supreme
1   Bring the lavender, milk and cream [1] to the boil, allow to infuse for 10 minutes, then strain.
2   Add sugar [1] and the egg yolks, and pasteurize at 85°C (185°F).
3   Add the gelatine and strain once more.
4   Cool the mixture as fast as possible to 20°C (68°F).
5   Meanwhile, whip cream [2] with sugar [2].
6   Fold the whipped cream/sugar mixture into the cooled lavender mixture.

ASSEMBLING

Garnishes Chantilly cream; fresh raspberries, cut in half; flowering mint leaves

Line the inside of the rings with strips of biscuit joconde (2 cm/¾ in. high). Cut out the sponge cake and place it in the bottom of the rings. Pipe lavender supreme to halfway up, insert a full sphere (two halves) of raspberry mousse and immediately cover with the rest of the lavender supreme. Flatten the tops of the rings with a palette knife, then reserve in the fridge to set. Unmould, pipe Chantilly cream on top in a rosette pattern, and finish with fresh, halved raspberries and a flowering mint leaf.

TARTE CITRON DOUCE AMÈRE

This recipe won Bernard an award at the Lemon Festival of Menton in France. 'It's no ordinary lemon tart,' he notes, 'thanks to its special approach. It uses the whole fruit, and the harmony between the lemon, sugar and rum transports one on a delicious journey through Creole flavours.'

MAKES 6 **DIFFICULTY** 2/5 **PREPARATION TIME** 2 hours (not including 24 hours' recommended resting time for the pastry)
SPECIFIC EQUIPMENT Digital candy thermometer; piping (pastry) bag with wide plain nozzle; 6 x small tart moulds (each 6.3 cm/2½ in. diameter, 1.6 cm/⅝ in. high); brûlée torch **NOTE: THIS TART IS NOT SUITABLE FOR YOUNG CHILDREN DUE TO ITS ALCOHOL CONTENT AND STRONG LEMON FLAVOUR**

INGREDIENTS

For the Sweet Crust Pastry
(best to prepare a day ahead to let it rest)
Unsalted butter 30 g | 1 oz (soft)
Icing (confectioner's) sugar 22 g | ¾ oz | gen. 2 tbsp
Whole egg 12 g | sc. ½ oz | sc. 1 tbsp
Plain (all-purpose) flour 46 g | gen. 1½ oz | sc. ⅓ cup (sifted)
Almond meal 9 g | sc. ½ oz | 1½ tbsp (sifted)

For the Sweet-Sour Lemon Cream
1 lemon (organic)
Granulated white sugar 70 g | 2½ oz | ⅓ cup
Whole eggs 53 g | gen. 1¾ oz | ¼ cup
Unsalted butter 45 g | 1½ oz (melted at 35°C/95°F)
Brown rum 13 g | sc. ½ fl oz | sc. 1 tbsp

For the Italian Meringue
Granulated white sugar 100 g | 3½ oz | ½ cup
Water 25 g | gen. ¾ fl oz | 5 tsp
Egg whites 50 g | 1¾ oz | sc. 3½ tbsp

INSTRUCTIONS

Sweet Crust Pastry
1 Mix the butter and sugar together well (but do not over-aerate), then add the egg, then add the sifted flour and almond meal.
2 Work the dough until homogeneous, then reserve in the fridge, wrapped in plastic wrap.

Sweet-Sour Lemon Cream
1 Wash the lemon thoroughly, then cut into small pieces, removing all the pips.
2 Pulverize the lemon pieces in a food processor.
3 Add the sugar and eggs, add the melted butter, and lastly add the rum.
4 Mix until the texture is homogeneous, then reserve in the fridge.

Italian Meringue
1 Heat the sugar and water.
2 When the syrup reaches 113°C (235°F), start to whisk the egg whites on high in a stand mixer.
3 When the syrup reaches 121°C (250°F), pour it on the egg whites and whisk until thick and glossy.
4 Reserve in the piping (pastry) bag.

ASSEMBLING

Take the sweet crust pastry out of the fridge and roll it out to a thickness of 3 mm (⅛ in.) between two sheets of silicone baking paper on a cold, flat surface (for easier handling you may wish to divide the pastry into six small balls and roll these individually). Prick the pastry lightly with a fork (the pricked side is to face the bottom of the moulds). Return to the fridge to firm up. Once firm, line the tart moulds with the pastry, then reserve again in the fridge for at least 1 hour. Pour sweet-sour lemon cream into each pastry-lined mould and bake at 170°C (325°F) for 30 minutes. Before removing the tarts from the oven, lightly blowtorch them to accentuate the bitterness of the lemon. Leave to cool, then unmould. Pipe a spiral of Italian meringue on top and caramelize this immediately with the brûlée torch.

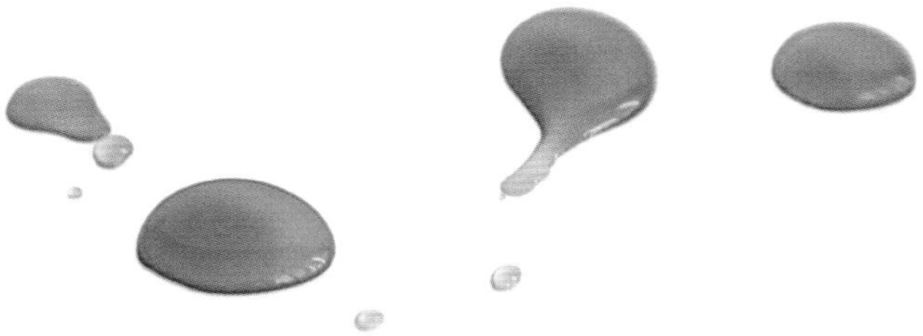

Christophe Roussel
....

FRANCE

In the zesty, modern work of French pastry chef Christophe Roussel, it is as if traditional pâtisserie staples have been injected with a new lease of life. The spirit of Willy Wonka hovers over his creations, with their playfulness, abundance of colours and catchy names (see the Electro'Choc® chocolate bar). If there was any doubt about comparisons with Roald Dahl's fictional character, one has only to visit Christophe's aptly named Atelier Gourmand. Located in La Baule on the north-western coast of France, the Atelier is an effervescent 400-square-metre kitchen/creative hub, where a team of seventeen constantly brainstorms and experiments with chocolate and pastry.

Teamwork is inscribed in Christophe's ethos and in that of his wife, Julie (the Duo Créatif Avec Julie outlet in Paris celebrates her pivotal role in the couple's business ambitions). 'Most of the time, I start by brainstorming with my wife,' Christophe reports. 'Afterwards I like to do a pencil drawing. Then I think about the flavours, the structure and the different textures that the final product could have.' He notes, 'I like sharing my ideas and my trials with the team. It's a two-way contribution: they taste the new pastry and give their feedback, and it teaches them about the flavours and textures I like.'

Christophe's professional experiences have shaped his calling. 'Working in restaurants – especially Relais et Châteaux in Uruguay and Méridien Resort on St Martin's Island – helped me discover a lot of new ingredients, which I still incorporate in my work to play with the notion of "exoticism",' he says. 'Fruit, chocolate, spices such as ginger, vanilla and cardamom ... these ingredients are packed with flavour and they take you on an exhilarating journey.'

Every year Christophe launches an average of forty new chocolate and pastry recipes. 'I started to make pastry twenty-five years ago,' he reflects. 'Now I go for more simplicity. I want to create tasty, sound products, which means no extra ingredients added to the recipes. And I want to experiment with textures, thereby providing a burst of emotion for the consumer.' It's a scrumptious combustion that our inner Charlie Bucket just cannot resist.

www.christophe-roussel.fr

VARIATION PROVENÇALE

The flavour combination of lavender and apricot has always worked well in macarons; add two colours that also work well together, and Christophe was inspired to try and create an individual dessert. His 'Variation Provençale' is a nod to the Religieuse cake, which is made by stacking choux pastries on top of one another.

MAKES 24 **DIFFICULTY** 4/5 **PREPARATION TIME** 3 hours **SPECIFIC EQUIPMENT** Digital candy thermometer; 3 x piping (pastry) bags with size 10 nozzles; Flexipan® round moulds with 8 inserts (each 6 cm/2⅜ in. diameter, 3.5 cm/1⅜ in. high); circle cutter (6 cm/2⅜ in.); straight-sided baking tray (at least 37 x 25 cm/14½ x 9¾ in. and 1 cm/⅜ in. high)

INGREDIENTS

For Two Flavours of Macarons
(24 x lavender and 24 x apricot)
Water 60 g | 2 fl oz | ¼ cup
Granulated white sugar 240 g | 8½ oz | 1⅛ cups
Egg whites [1] 100 g | 3½ oz | ⅖ cup
Egg white powder 1.5 g | gen. ½ tsp
Egg whites [2] 85 g | 3 oz | ⅓ cup
TPT 250 g/gen. 8¾ oz/gen. 1½ cups icing (confectioner's) sugar + 250 g/gen. 8¾ oz/sc. 3 cups almond meal
For lavender macarons Purple food colouring and lavender food aroma to taste (or other flavouring, such as almond, if lavender-allergic)
For apricot macarons Apricot food colouring and apricot food aroma to taste

For the Apricot Mousse
Apricot pulp/purée 250 g | 9 fl oz | 1 cup
Juice of ¼ of a lemon
Gelatine (gold) 6 g | 3 sheets (softened in ice cold water, with excess water squeezed out)
Whipping cream (35% fat) 150 g | sc. 5½ fl oz | gen. ½ cup
Apricot spirit (e.g. eau de vie d'abricot Wolfberger) 10 g | gen. ¼ fl oz | 2 tsp
Italian meringue *

* Italian Meringue
Caster (superfine) sugar 64 g | 2¼ oz | gen. ¼ cup
Water 15 g | ½ fl oz | 1 tbsp
Egg whites 42 g | sc. 1½ oz | sc. 3 tbsp

For the Apricot Compote
Apricots (fresh or frozen) 300 g | 10½ oz
Apricot pulp 150 g | gen. 5¼ oz | gen. ½ cup
Honey (or invert sugar) 40 g | sc. 1½ fl oz | 2 tbsp
¼ vanilla pod (bean) (split, scraped, both pod/bean and seeds reserved)
Granulated white sugar 40 g | sc. 1½ oz | gen. 3 tbsp
Gelatine (gold) 10 g | 5 sheets (softened in ice cold water, with excess water squeezed out)
Apricot spirit (e.g. eau de vie d'abricot Wolfberger) 10 g | gen. ¼ fl oz | 2 tsp

For the Lavender Choux
For the Lavender French Pastry Cream Filling
Milk 500 g | 17 fl oz | gen. 2 cups
Granulated white sugar 85 g | 3 oz | sc. ½ cup
2 whole eggs
Cornflour (cornstarch) 24 g | gen. ¾ oz | sc. 2½ tbsp
Lavender food aroma (or other flavour, e.g. almond) (to taste)
Whipping cream (35% fat) 150 g | sc. 5½ fl oz | gen. ½ cup

INSTRUCTIONS

Two Flavours of Macarons
1 Heat the water and sugar to dissolve, then boil the resulting syrup to 118°C (244°F).
2 In a stand mixer, beat egg whites [1] with the egg white powder until stiff, gradually adding the boiling syrup to make an Italian meringue.
3 Whisk until the mixture cools to 42°C (108°F).
4 Beat egg whites [2] and add to the TPT, then combine with the Italian meringue.
5 Divide the mixture into two-thirds and one-third.
6 Flavour and colour the larger amount with the lavender aroma (or flavour of your choice) and purple food colouring.
7 Flavour and colour the smaller amount with the apricot aroma and apricot food colouring.
8 Pipe the lavender mixture onto silicone baking paper-lined trays to form 48 shells (which will be 24 whole macarons) of 6.2 cm (2⅜ in.) diameter, leaving space between each shell to allow for spreading; allow to rest for 10 minutes.
9 Pipe the apricot mixture onto silicone baking paper-lined trays to form 48 shells (24 whole macarons) of 4 cm (1⅝ in.) diameter, leaving space between each shell to allow for spreading; allow to rest for 20 minutes.
10 Bake at 150°C (300°F) – the lavender shells for 14–16 minutes, the apricot shells for 10–12 minutes – to achieve a crisp exterior and chewy interior.
11 Cool on wire racks.

Apricot Mousse
1 Heat the apricot pulp/purée with the lemon juice.
2 Remove from the heat, add the gelatine, stir to dissolve, then leave to cool.
3 Whip the cream.
4 Stir the apricot spirit into the apricot mixture, then fold in the Italian meringue* and cream.
5 Pour the mixture into the Flexipan® moulds and leave in the freezer until solid.
6 Once solid, slice each mousse into three even discs.

* Italian Meringue
1 Dissolve the sugar in the water and boil to 124°C (255°F).
2 At the same time, use a stand mixer to beat the egg whites stiffly.
3 Gradually pour the boiling syrup onto the beaten egg whites.
4 Whisk until the mixture is stiff and glossy.

Apricot Compote
1 Heat the apricots, pulp, honey (or invert sugar), and vanilla pod (bean) and seeds together.
2 Add the sugar and gelatine, and stir until dissolved.
3 Remove from the heat, remove the vanilla pod (bean) and add the apricot spirit.
4 Pour into the shallow baking tray to make a layer 1 cm (⅜ in.) high.
5 Leave to set in the fridge, then cut out 24 discs of 6 cm (2⅜ in.) diameter – the same diameter as the apricot mousse discs. NB Reserve left-over compote for the assembling stage.

Lavender Choux
Lavender French Pastry Cream Filling
1 Bring the milk to the boil with half the sugar.
2 Mix the rest of the sugar with the eggs and the cornflour (cornstarch).
3 Pour some of the hot milk onto the egg mixture before pouring everything back into the milk pan and cooking for 3 minutes while whisking.
4 Add the flavouring of your choice, then allow to cool.
5 Whip the cream and fold into the cooled custard.
6 Reserve in the fridge.

Milk 250 g | 8½ fl oz | gen. 1 cup

Unsalted butter 125 g | sc. 4½ oz (diced)

Salt 5 g | sc. ¼ oz | gen. ¼ tbsp

Granulated white sugar 7.5 g | ¼ oz | gen. ½ tbsp

Plain (all-purpose) flour 162 g | 5¾ oz | gen. 1 cup

Whole eggs 230 g | 8 oz | 1 cup

For Choux Icing

Fondant (e.g. Fondant Blanc Extra by Produits Marguerite, or Fondant Pâtissier by Caullet) 200 g | 7 oz | ⅔ cup

Glucose syrup 50 g | 1¾ fl oz | sc. 3 tbsp

Lavender food aroma (to taste)

Purple food colouring (to achieve desired colour)

Choux Pastry

7 Bring the milk, butter, salt and sugar to the boil.

8 Remove from the heat and immediately add the flour.

9 Blend the flour well, then place back on the heat to dry the pastry for 1 minute.

10 Gently mix the pastry in a stand mixer (e.g. KitchenAid®) and add the eggs gradually.

11 Fill a piping (pastry) bag with the mixture and pipe 24 choux onto a silicone baking paper-lined tray.

12 Bake at 170°C (325°F) for 30–35 minutes.

Choux Icing

13 Mix the fondant with the glucose syrup.

14 Mix in aroma and food colouring.

15 Spread on top of each choux.

ASSEMBLING

Components Almond paste (e.g. Pâte d'Amande de Provence by Valrhona); apricot jam

Spread a thin layer of the reserved apricot compote onto the flat side of a lavender macaron shell, top with a disc of apricot mousse, followed by a disc of apricot compote, then 'close' the sandwich with the other lavender macaron shell. Top with an apricot macaron filled with a mixture of 50% almond paste and 50% apricot jam. Finish with an icing-glazed choux filled with lavender or your preferred flavour of French pastry cream. Hold the elements of the dish together with a decorative bamboo stick.

TARTE PIÈGE À FRUITS
Christophe designed this tart with freshness and prominence of flavours in mind. He achieved his results by using fresh fruit, rather than cooked fruit, set in a jelly syrup.

MAKES 15 **DIFFICULTY** 2/5 **PREPARATION TIME** 1½ hours (not including 4 hours' cooling time for the vanilla crémeux)
SPECIFIC EQUIPMENT 15 x tart moulds (each 8 cm/3⅛ in. diameter); digital candy thermometer; 15 x Flexipan® moulds (each 6 cm/2⅜ in. diameter, 2 cm/¾ in. high)

INGREDIENTS

For the Pâte Sablée, or Sweet Tart Pastry
Salted butter 240 g | 8½ oz (softened)
Whole eggs 90 g | sc. 3¼ oz | ⅖ cup
Icing (confectioner's) sugar 160 g | sc. 5¾ oz | 1 cup
Almond or hazelnut meal 55 g | sc. 2 oz | sc. ⅔ cup
Vanilla extract 2 g | ½ tsp
Bread flour (French type 55/white hard-wheat flour)
470 g | 1 lb | 3⅓ cups

For the Vanilla Crémeux
Whipping cream (35% fat) 250 g | 8¾ fl oz | 1 cup
1 vanilla pod (bean) (split, scraped, both pod/bean and seeds reserved)
Egg yolks 60 g | gen. 2 oz | ¼ cup
Granulated white sugar 30 g | 1 oz | 2½ tbsp
Gelatine (gold) 2 g | 1 sheet (softened in ice cold water, with excess water squeezed out)

For the Exotic Fruit Jelly with Agar Agar
Fresh fruits that do not exude too much water
(e.g. dices of kiwi, blueberries, apricot slices, small whole strawberries, raspberries, etc.)
Mango purée 250 g | 9 fl oz | 1 cup
Passion fruit purée 125 g | 4½ fl oz | ½ cup
Water 125 g | sc. 4¼ fl oz | ½ cup
Granulated white sugar 40 g | sc. 1½ oz | gen. 3 tbsp
Agar agar 3 g | 1 tsp
Xanthan gum 1.5 g | ¼ tsp

INSTRUCTIONS

Pâte Sablée, or Sweet Tart Pastry
1 Mix all the ingredients together, except for the flour.
2 Add the flour last.
3 Mix until the dough just comes together.
4 Shape into a disc, wrap in plastic wrap and place in the fridge for at least 30 minutes.
5 Roll out on a lightly floured surface.
6 Place the pastry in the tart moulds.
7 Bake blind at 150°C (300°F) for 30–40 minutes.

Vanilla Crémeux
1 Heat the cream with the vanilla pod (bean) and seeds at 70°C (158°F) for 5 minutes, then remove the vanilla pod (bean).
2 At the same time, beat the egg yolks, add the sugar and continue to beat until the mixture is pale.
3 Pour in some of the vanilla-infused cream and combine.
4 Pour this mixture back into the remainder of the cream and heat at 82–84°C (180–183°F), while mixing well.
5 Add the gelatine, then mix with an immersion blender or hand whisk.
6 Leave to cool for 4 hours in a container sealed with plastic wrap.

Exotic Fruit Jelly with Agar Agar
1 Put some of the fresh fruit in each Flexipan® mould (sparing some for the garnish).
2 Bring the mango and passion fruit purées and the water to the boil.
3 Sprinkle in the sugar, agar agar and xanthan gum.
4 Stir well to dissolve.
5 Bring back to the boil.
6 Rapidly pour the jelly on top of the fruit.
7 Leave to set in the fridge before removing from the moulds.

ASSEMBLING

Garnishes Fresh berries

Pipe or spread enough vanilla crémeux (25 g/gen. ¾ oz/1¾ tbsp) to cover the bottom of each tart shell. Leave to set in the freezer for 10–15 minutes. Carefully place the fruit jelly on top. Decorate with fresh berries – a raspberry, a bunch of redcurrants, a blackberry, etc. You could also add a small macaron (the photo opposite shows a lime/basil version chosen to contrast with the colouring of the tart and to harmonize with its flavours).

Gontran Cherrier

FRANCE

The new generation of bakers has no finer representative than French maverick Gontran Cherrier. Young, free-spirited and ambitious, Gontran is a chef who is making the most of the opportunities offered by modern technology and media to propel his vision worldwide.

A fourth-generation baker, he trained at his parents' bakery, graduated from the best speciality schools and refined his skills at prestigious restaurants. It was during his time as head pastry chef at L'Arpège with Alain Passard and the Lucas Carton with Alain Senderens that he began to define what has become his signature style: the rejuvenation of tradition through unconventional marriages, such as mustard ice cream or coffee and confit tomato sorbet. 'I like to start with something familiar, which I then systematically alter by adding unexpected attributes. I like surprises!' he exclaims, adding, 'As I'm primarily a baker and Viennese pastry maker, citrus fruits are my favourites. They efficiently counterbalance all types of flour: grapefruit goes with buckwheat, lemon with rye and orange with spelt.'

Having published several books, starred in 'Gontran Cuisine' on the Cuisine+ TV channel and begun his world conquest in not-so-slow-motion by opening shops in Paris, Tokyo and Singapore, this celebrity baker embodies the future of baking, while still adhering to traditional values. 'I often get stopped by customers on the street, who ask me to make little breads with an ingredient they love,' he says. 'It really touches me because these requests mostly come from older people. It's almost as if a child begged you for a chocolate tartine. It's all about *gourmandise*!'

Gontran's ever-growing success owes a lot to his desire to please others. It is also due to his love for using global inspiration to invent products for markets that do not yet know they are about to become addicted. 'I design coloured buns with specific garnishes for my Paris stores; in Japan, we've created boxes in which we combine the traditional Japanese snowball with a marshmallow and a *pâte de fruit*; in Singapore, I created a pandan croissant and a pineapple tarte tatin for Chinese New Year,' he says. What unites the stores is that they each allow customers to experience a multi-sensory nirvana. Move over Amélie: Gontran Cherrier is the new global ambassador for the (edible) 'French touch'.

www.gontrancherrierboulanger.com | **http://gontran-cherrier.jp** | **www.tiongbahrubakery.com**

PEACH TART, ORGEAT JELLY AND FRESH ROSEMARY

'I created this recipe for the first time when I was staying at a friend's house for the holidays,' recalls Gontran. 'The flavour of ripe white peaches became combined with that of rosemary, and they immediately made me salivate. The orgeat jelly is just a complementary link between the two.'

MAKES 8–10   **DIFFICULTY** 2/5   **PREPARATION TIME** 3 hours   **SPECIFIC EQUIPMENT** 8–10 x tartlet moulds (each 8 cm/3⅛ in. diameter)

INGREDIENTS

For the Orgeat (French Barley Water) Jelly
Orgeat syrup 100 g | 3½ fl oz | gen. ¼ cup
Water 100 ml | 3½ fl oz | sc. ½ cup
Gelatine (gold) 4 g | 2 sheets (softened in ice cold water, with excess water squeezed out)

For the Sweet Pastry
Icing (confectioner's) sugar 115 g | 4 oz | sc. ¾ cup
Unsalted butter [1] 100 g | 3½ oz (soft)
Whole egg 50 g | 1¾ oz | sc. ¼ cup
Plain (all-purpose) flour 190 g | sc. 6¾ oz | 1¼ cups
Salt 4 g | sc. ¼ tbsp
Unsalted butter [2] (to line tartlet moulds)

For the Cream
Unsalted butter 70 g | 2½ oz (soft)
Granulated white sugar 70 g | 2½ oz | ⅓ cup
Almond meal 70 g | 2½ oz | ⅘ cup
Whole eggs 70 g | 2½ oz | gen. ¼ cup
Plain (all-purpose) flour 10 g | sc. ½ oz | 2 tsp

INSTRUCTIONS

Orgeat (French Barley Water) Jelly
1. Mix the syrup and water over a medium heat.
2. As soon as the liquid is tepid, add in the gelatine and whisk well until combined.
3. Pass through a fine sieve (strainer) into a small dish.
4. Reserve in the fridge for about 3 hours.

Sweet Pastry
1. Whisk the sugar and soft butter together, then add the egg.
2. Add the flour and salt, and work the mixture by hand until a homogeneous dough is formed.
3. Reserve in the fridge for 1 hour, wrapped in plastic wrap.
4. Pre-heat the oven to 210°C (400°F).
5. Roll out the dough between two sheets of silicone baking paper on a cold, flat surface to a thickness of 3 mm (⅛ in.), then cut discs of 12–15 cm (4¾–6 in.) diameter.
6. Line the tartlet moulds (previously coated with butter) with the discs.
7. Bake blind at 210°C (400°F) for 10 minutes, then leave to cool on a wire rack.

Cream
1. Mix the soft butter and sugar together until creamed to a paste-like texture.
2. Add the almond meal, eggs and finally flour, stirring constantly to achieve a homogeneous mix.
3. Reserve in the fridge.

ASSEMBLING

Components/Garnishes 5 white peaches; fresh rosemary

Spread the sweet pastry with the cream and bake in the pre-heated oven at 210°C (400°F) for 15–20 minutes, then leave to cool on a wire rack. Add little pieces of the jelly, once set, either by cutting directly from the whole jelly or by flaking the jelly with a fork. Cut the peaches into small slices and arrange them evenly on the tartlets. Chop a few stalks of rosemary very finely and sprinkle over the tarts. Finally, top each tart with a small sprig of rosemary.

PEACH, PISTACHIO AND ROSE WATER TART

'This is an interpretation of a traditional Iranian recipe, which usually comes in the form of a salad with roasted and crushed pistachios,' says Gontran. 'In other Iranian savoury dishes, pistachio, rose and orange zest are combined... Maybe an idea for a future dessert recipe!'

MAKES 1 tart (serves 8–12) **DIFFICULTY** 2/5 **PREPARATION TIME** 2 hours **SPECIFIC EQUIPMENT** Tart mould (55 cm/21⅝ in. long, 11 cm/4⅜ in. wide)

INGREDIENTS

For the Sweet Pastry

Icing (confectioner's) sugar 115 g | 4 oz | sc. ¾ cup

Unsalted butter [1] 100 g | 3½ oz (soft)

Whole egg 50 g | 1¾ oz | sc. ¼ cup

Plain (all-purpose) flour 190 g | sc. 6¾ oz | 1¼ cups

Salt 4 g | sc. ¼ tbsp

Unsalted butter [2] (to line tart mould)

For the Cream

Unsalted butter 70 g | 2½ oz (soft)

Pistachio paste 30 g | 1 oz | 2 tbsp

Granulated white sugar 70 g | 2½ oz | ⅓ cup

Almond meal 70 g | 2½ oz | ⅘ cup

Whole eggs 70 g | 2½ oz | gen. ¼ cup

Plain (all-purpose) flour 10 g | sc. ½ oz | 2 tsp

INSTRUCTIONS

Sweet Pastry

1 Whisk the sugar and soft butter together, then add the egg.

2 Add the flour and salt.

3 Work the mixture by hand until a homogeneous dough is formed.

4 Reserve in the fridge for 1 hour, wrapped in plastic wrap.

5 Pre-heat the oven to 210°C (400°F).

6 Roll out the dough between two sheets of silicone baking paper on a cold, flat surface to a thickness of 3 mm (⅛ in.).

7 Prick the dough with a fork, then line the tart mould (previously coated with butter).

8 Bake blind at 210°C (400°F) for 10 minutes, then leave to cool on a wire rack.

Cream

1 Mix the soft butter, pistachio paste and sugar together until creamed to a paste-like texture.

2 Add the almond meal, eggs and finally flour, stirring constantly to achieve a homogeneous mix.

3 Reserve in the fridge.

ASSEMBLING

Components/Garnishes 5 white peaches; pistachio nuts, without the shell (60 g/gen. 2 oz/½ cup); rose water (the best quality possible); almond milk ice cream, or orange sorbet

Cut the peaches into quarters, and each quarter into half. Crush the pistachios. Spread the cream onto the sweet pastry, then place the peaches in rows on top and sprinkle with the crushed pistachios. Bake in the pre-heated oven at 210°C (400°F) for 15–20 minutes, then leave to cool on a wire rack. Once the tart is cold, sprinkle some rose water all over it. Serve with ice cream or sorbet.

STRAWBERRY AND CUCUMBER TART WITH BASIL

'The idea behind this odd combination came to me randomly,' Gontran recalls. 'I was preparing a selection of skewers for a customer. I already knew about the association between strawberry and basil, but needed a neutral-flavoured yet texturally rich garnish to complement the two. Cucumber seemed to be the perfect match.'

MAKES 1 tart (28 cm/11 in. diameter); serves 10–12 **DIFFICULTY** 2/5 **PREPARATION TIME** 1¾ hours
SPECIFIC EQUIPMENT Tart mould (28 cm/11 in. diameter); mandolin

INGREDIENTS

For the Sweet Pastry

Icing (confectioner's) sugar 115 g | 4 oz | sc. ¾ cup
Unsalted butter [1] 100 g | 3½ oz (soft)
Whole egg 50 g | 1¾ oz | sc. ¼ cup
Plain (all-purpose) flour 190 g | sc. 6¾ oz | 1¼ cups
Salt 4 g | sc. ¼ tbsp
Unsalted butter [2] (to line tart mould)

For the Cream

Unsalted butter 70 g | 2½ oz (soft)
Granulated white sugar 70 g | 2½ oz | ⅓ cup
Almond meal 70 g | 2½ oz | ⅘ cup
Whole eggs 70 g | 2½ oz | gen. ¼ cup
Lemon zest 7 g | ¼ oz | gen. 1 tsp
Cream cheese 105 g | sc. 3¾ oz | sc. ½ cup
Plain (all-purpose) flour 10 g | sc. ½ oz | 2 tsp

INSTRUCTIONS

Sweet Pastry

1 Whisk the sugar and soft butter together, then add the egg.
2 Add the flour and salt, and work the mixture by hand until a homogeneous dough is formed.
3 Reserve in the fridge for 1 hour, wrapped in plastic wrap.
4 Pre-heat the oven to 210°C (400°F).
5 Roll out the dough between two sheets of silicone baking paper on a cold, flat surface to a thickness of 3 mm (⅛ in.).
6 Prick the dough with a fork, then line the tart mould (previously coated with butter).
7 Bake blind at 210°C (400°F) for 10 minutes, then leave to cool on a wire rack.

Cream

1 Mix the soft butter and sugar together until creamed to a paste-like texture.
2 Add the almond meal, then the eggs.
3 Add the lemon zest, cream cheese and finally the flour, stirring constantly to achieve a homogeneous mix.
4 Reserve in the fridge.

ASSEMBLING

Components/Garnishes 2 punnets of strawberries; 1 medium-sized cucumber; 1 bunch of fresh basil

Spread the cream onto the sweet pastry and bake in the pre-heated oven at 210°C (400°F) for 15–20 minutes (the centre of the tart should almost be raw). Leave to cool on a wire rack. Prepare the strawberries by removing the stems and cutting the fruit in half. Finely slice the cucumber with a mandolin (it is very important to keep the skin). Neatly place the strawberries and cucumber strips over the tart so as to give volume to the composition. Decorate with a mix of whole and torn basil leaves and some nice basil stems.

Luca Ori

ITALY

Not only do you need to have a calling, you also need to put in a lot of effort to translate your dreams into a career. Italian pastry chef Luca Ori is living proof. He has seen himself as a chef for as long as he can remember. 'I have a photo of myself at the age of three or four, at nursery school, with a chef's hat. I think subconsciously something was already there.' He went on to study first at the Giuseppe Magnaghi hotelier institute in Salsomaggiore, then at Luigi Biasetto's atelier in Padua. By interning and working with some of the best names in the business (including Paul Wittamer in Brussels), Luca soon learned the ropes of the pastry trade – so well, in fact, that after an intense evaluation process he was appointed one of the few members of the Accademia Maestri Pasticceri Italiani.

Behind the mantra that pâtisserie is a serious business – pastry recipes usually go hand in hand with compulsory formulae and the conservation of tradition – Luca gives a glimpse of another side of himself and of the industry: the fun side. 'If I think about what other job I could have done, craft is the common denominator. I have to use my hands, work a "live" product; anything that allows me to create. Of course, from a rational point of view, sales are the driving force, but deep down fun prevails. It's what lets you keep on playing.' Ask Luca what makes him passionate about pastry, and his answer is invariably: 'The game.'

His Parma-based shop, aptly named Le Delizie di Ori, appeals to our weakness for delicacies as much as to our appreciation for handcrafted, healthy food. An Ali Baba cavern-type gourmet café, it offers delicious dishes made exclusively with natural ingredients. Luca also runs his own academy, where both amateurs and professionals can brainstorm, exchange ideas and experiment. 'Trying to understand the rationale for certain things has led me to learn and to travel,' he says. 'I've never been content with pat explanations, such as "It's always been done like this". I've always wanted to get to the bottom of things, and this is what I advocate at the academy.' This is the antithesis of snap-judgment fast thinking ... and Luca gives us the opposite of fast food.

www.ledeliziediori.it

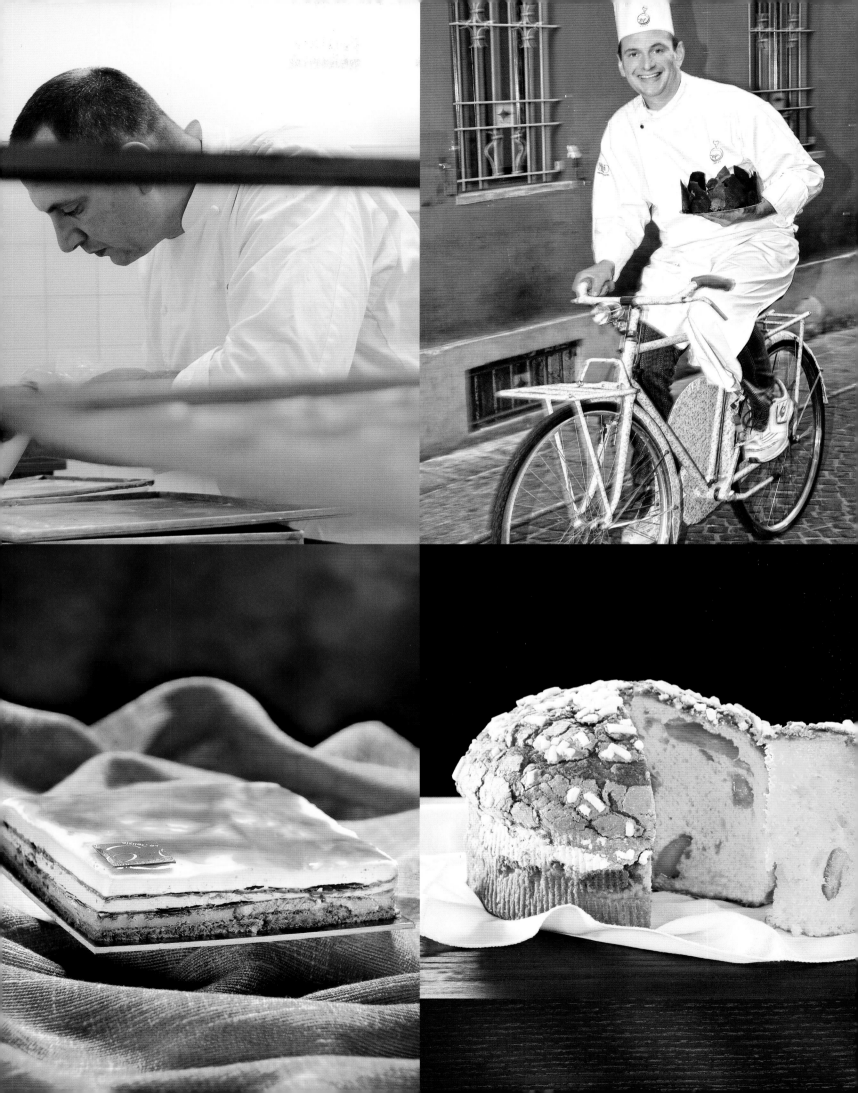

JAM TART WITH MARASCA CHERRY AND ZUCCHELLA PLUM JAM

'This is your typical jam tart, but with a richer, more noble pastry,' says Luca. 'The jam is also interesting. It has quite a well-defined taste because of the kind of fruit and cooking process used. The tart is ideal as a mid-afternoon snack or for children's parties.'

MAKES 2 tarts (each 20 x 2 cm; 7¾ x ¾ in.); serve 6–8   **DIFFICULTY** 2/5   **PREPARATION TIME** 4 hours
SPECIFIC EQUIPMENT 2 x ring moulds or pie tins (pans), preferably non-stick (each 20 x 2 cm/7¾ x ¾ in.)

INGREDIENTS

For the Marasca Cherry and Zucchella Plum Jam

Marasca (Maraschino) cherries 300 g | 10½ oz (washed and pitted)

Zucchella plums (fibrous fruit, typical of northern Italy: *Prunus domestica* L. subsp. *domestica* 'Zucchella') 700 g | 1½ lb (washed and pitted)

Caster (superfine) sugar 600 g | gen. 1 lb 5 oz | 2⅔ cups

Juice and zest of 1 lemon

For the Short Pastry

Unsalted butter 300 g | 10½ oz (room temperature)

Icing (confectioner's) sugar [1] 100 g | 3½ oz | sc. ⅔ cup

Yolks of boiled eggs 140 g | sc. 5 oz | ½ cup (well strained)

Rum (50% alcohol) 10 g | gen. ¼ fl oz | 2 tsp

Plain (all-purpose) flour 380 g | sc. 13½ oz | 2½ cups

Salt 6 g | ¼ oz | 1 tsp

Ground cinnamon 5 g | sc. ¼ oz | 2 tsp

Almond meal 60 g | gen. 2 oz | sc. ¾ cup

Icing (confectioner's) sugar [2] (to taste)

INSTRUCTIONS

Marasca Cherry and Zucchella Plum Jam

1   Bring the cherries, plums and sugar to the boil in a casserole dish, stirring often.

2   Once at a boil, reduce the heat and leave to simmer for 1½ hours, stirring from time to time.

3   Add the lemon juice and zest.

4   Check the density by putting some jam on a plate and tilting it; the jam should not 'run' too fast.

5   Once at the correct density, pour the hot jam straight into clean (sterile), dry jars, close tight and place upside down to create a vacuum. NB Ensure the rims of the jars are perfectly clean, otherwise the vacuum – and thus conservation – may be compromised.

6   Once the jars are completely cold, turn them the right way round.

Short Pastry

1   Mix the butter and sugar [1] until pale, either by hand or in a stand mixer (e.g. KitchenAid®) with a flat beater.

2   Add the boiled egg yolks and rum, and mix until incorporated.

3   Add the flour, salt, cinnamon and almond meal sifted together.

4   Knead the mixture, then wrap the dough in plastic wrap and refrigerate for a couple of hours.

5   Roll the pastry on a cold, flat surface to a thickness of 4–5 mm (³⁄₁₆ in.).

6   Prick the whole surface of the pastry with a fork, then line each mould up to its edge, paying attention not to leave air bubbles between the pastry and the mould.

7   Spread the jam, then overlay strips of pastry in a criss-cross design.

8   Bake at 160°C (325°F) for a minimum of 30 minutes.

9   Leave to cool, then remove from the moulds.

10 Dust the rim of each tart with sugar [2] (not shown in the photo opposite).

LA VIOLA DI PARMA

'"La Viola di Parma" is a simple, country-style cake that my grandmother used to make, slightly re-interpreted here to have an affinity with violets, the favourite flowers of Maria Luigia, Duchess of Parma from 1816 to 1847,' explains Luca. 'It is a very soft cake – ideal to be served warm, with a light sabayon on the side.'

MAKES 2 cakes (serve 20–24)   **DIFFICULTY** 3½/5   **PREPARATION TIME** 2 days   **SPECIFIC EQUIPMENT** Stand mixer with dough hook, or kneading machine; 2 x cake rings (each 22 cm/8⅝ in. diameter, 4 cm/1⅝ in. high)

INGREDIENTS

For the First Dough

Water [1] 150 g | 5¼ fl oz | ⅔ cup
Caster (superfine) sugar 225 g | sc. 8 oz | 1 cup
Sourdough starter, refreshed 3 times 225 g | sc. 8 oz | 1 cup
(a portion may be obtained from a local baker or purchased from a wholefood store or online)
Strong flour (W370/380) 600 g | gen. 1 lb 5 oz | gen. 4¼ cups
Egg yolks 250 g | gen. 8¾ oz | 1 cup
Water [2] 50 g | 1¾ fl oz | 3½ tbsp
Unsalted butter 275 g | 9¾ oz (room temperature)
1 vanilla pod (bean) (split, scraped, seeds reserved)
Lemon zest 1 g | ⅛ tsp (grated)
Aroma of violet 1 g | gen. ⅛ tsp

For the Second Dough and Baking

First dough (from above recipe)
Strong flour (W370/380) 400 g | 14 oz | 2⅘ cups
Caster (superfine) sugar 50 g | 1¾ oz | sc. ¼ cup
Unsalted butter 75 g | gen. 2½ oz (room temperature)
Egg yolks 75 g | gen. 2½ oz | 5 tbsp
Salt 12 g | sc. ½ oz | 2 tsp
White chocolate 150 g | gen. 5¼ oz (grated)
Strong flour (for dough)
Melted, unsalted butter (for dough)
Caster (superfine) sugar (for dough)

INSTRUCTIONS

First Dough

1 Make a syrup with water [1] and the sugar.
2 Knead the ready-to-use sourdough starter (after 3 refreshments, it will have doubled its volume in about 4 hours), the flour, some of the egg yolk and the syrup.
3 Let the gluten develop until the dough is smooth, then add, in this order, the water [2], butter, remainder of the egg yolk, vanilla seeds, lemon zest and aroma of violet, being careful not to add the next ingredient until the previous one has been incorporated.
4 Once the dough is smooth and elastic, leave it in a warm area, ideally at 23–24°C (73–75°F), to rise for 14 to 15 hours.

Second Dough and Baking

1 Knead the first dough (now tripled in volume) and mix with the flour to make a smooth and elastic dough.
2 Add, in this order, the sugar, butter and egg yolks, being careful to keep the dough elastic, with the gluten well developed.
3 Add the salt, and finally the grated chocolate.
4 Let the dough rest for 30 minutes.
5 Once rested, divide it into portions, each weighing 550 g (just over 1 lb).
6 Roll each portion around to form a ball, adding as much flour as necessary to make it manageable.
7 Let the balls rest for another 30 minutes in a warm area, ideally at 27°C (81°F).
8 Press the dough into the cake rings, using hands greased with melted butter, and leave in a warm area, ideally at 23–24°C (73–75°F), to rise for about 12 hours.
9 Brush with melted butter, lightly sprinkle with caster (superfine) sugar and prick the surface with a fork.
10 Bake at 170°C (325°F) for 40 minutes, or until a skewer comes out clean.

ASSEMBLING

Components/Garnishes Clarified melted butter; candied violets

Once cooked, brush the surface with clarified melted butter and decorate with candied violets (typical of traditional Parma).

Martin Isaksson

SWEDEN

Chocolate lovers rejoice, especially if you are in or visiting Sweden, or indeed Japan. Head pastry chef Martin Isaksson and his team of twenty-five, including nine pastry chefs, will warmly welcome you to their four bright, modern stores across Stockholm, as well as their Tokyo outpost. With an upbeat motto in mind – 'you don't imperatively need to eat pastry products, but if you do it's to make yourself feel good' – Martin delights in presenting chocolate in every possible form, so anyone can find their cocoa match.

Martin and his wife Ellinor founded the Chokladfabriken (the Chocolate Factory), an all-encompassing business comprising factories and stores, in 1997. It has been one of his most satisfying achievements to date, along with competing as part of Sweden's national culinary team from 2000 to 2004. Everything on offer in the stores contains chocolate that is of the highest quality and from the most reputable international suppliers, including Valrhona, Callebaut, Felchlin, Chocovic and Cru Sauvage. 'With chocolate and fruit you can do almost anything, and it doesn't hurt that I love them both!' quips Martin.

The Chokladfabriken is an enterprise that has succeeded in pairing excellence with friendliness, as seen in its educational initiatives and the fact that the factories welcome visitors. Most of the recipes are a careful reappropriation of traditional dishes, but with clever updates and a modern and clean presentation, which is potentially the most Scandinavian attribute of Martin's creations. He himself states, 'I don't believe we are that typically Swedish because we don't offer traditional Swedish pastry. I like to get inspired by other pastry cultures, and I think this has become very common in the Swedish culinary scene. It's all about taking the flavours of Sweden, but not working them in the expected, typical way.'

Martin has acquired his free-minded approach over twenty-five years of practice. To demonstrate his customers' loyalty, he likes to recount the story of a little girl who came to visit. 'She was around six or seven years old, and she used all her savings – in coins – to buy a Christmas gift for her father, who liked our products. That really touched me.' Given the chance, we would also gladly empty our wallets, but this time it would be to treat ourselves!

www.chokladfabriken.com

TRIO OF CHOCOLATE

A specialist in chocolate, Martin explains, 'I wanted to create a dessert that plays with three different chocolates and three different textures.' He has invented a chocolate lover's dream, with all the expressions of the cocoa bean in one sleek dish.

MAKES 10   **DIFFICULTY** 3/5   **PREPARATION TIME** 2 hours (not including baking or setting times for the various layers, which includes up to 4 hours for the white chocolate bavarois)   **SPECIFIC EQUIPMENT** 10 x ovenproof glasses (each 7 cm/2¾ in. diameter, 250 ml/8¾ fl oz volume); digital candy thermometer

INGREDIENTS

For the Milk Chocolate Brûlée
Milk (3% fat) 85 g | 3 fl oz | gen. ⅓ cup
Whipping cream (35% fat) 210 g | gen. 7¼ fl oz | gen. ¾ cup
1 vanilla pod (bean) (split, scraped, seeds reserved)
Milk chocolate couverture (e.g. Maracaibo 49% by Felchlin) 95 g | gen. 3¼ oz
Egg yolks 75 g | gen. 2½ oz | 5 tbsp
Caster (superfine) sugar 30 g | 1 oz | 2¼ tbsp

For the White Chocolate Bavarois
Milk 150 g | gen. 5 fl oz | gen. ½ cup
Caster (superfine) sugar 40 g | sc. 1½ oz | 3 tbsp
½ vanilla pod (bean) (split, scraped, seeds reserved)
Egg yolks 80 g | gen. 2¾ oz | ⅓ cup
Granulated white sugar 20 g | sc. ¾ oz | 5 tsp
White chocolate 60 g | gen. 2 oz
Gelatine (gold) 3 g | 1½ sheets (softened in ice cold water, with excess water squeezed out).
Whipping cream (35% fat) 150 g | sc. 5½ fl oz | gen. ½ cup (whipped)

For the Cocoa Jelly
Water 10 g | gen. ¼ fl oz | 2 tsp
Double (heavy) whipping cream (40% fat) 70 g | 2½ fl oz | gen. ¼ cup
Caster (superfine) sugar 25 g | gen. ¾ oz | sc. 2 tbsp
Dark chocolate (e.g. Manjari 64% by Valrhona) 50 g | 1¾ oz
Gelatine (gold) 2 g | 1 sheet (softened in ice cold water, with excess water squeezed out)

INSTRUCTIONS

Milk Chocolate Brûlée
1   Combine the milk, cream and vanilla seeds together over heat.
2   Bring to the boil, then pour on top of the chocolate.
3   Stir to combine and leave to cool.
4   Whisk the egg yolks and sugar.
5   Combine the egg mixture with the chocolate mixture.
6   Pour into the ovenproof glasses.
7   Bake in a bain-marie in the oven at 90°C (195°F) for 50 minutes.
8   Leave to cool.

White Chocolate Bavarois
1   Combine the milk, caster (superfine) sugar and vanilla seeds together over heat, and bring to the boil.
2   Blend the egg yolks with the granulated sugar, temper into the milk mixture and continue heating and stirring to 84°C (183°F).
3   Strain over the chocolate and stir until homogeneous.
4   Add the gelatine and stir until well blended.
5   Let the resulting 'anglaise' sauce cool down.
6   Gently fold in the whipped cream.
7   Pour the bavarois on top of the cooled brûlées (from above recipe).
8   Freeze for at least 4 hours before coating with the cocoa jelly (recipe below).

Cocoa Jelly
1   Combine the water, cream and sugar together over heat.
2   Bring to the boil, then pour on top of the chocolate.
3   Mix with an immersion blender until smooth.
4   Add the gelatine and stir until completely melted.
5   Use to coat the frozen white chocolate bavarois (from above recipe).

ASSEMBLING

Garnish Mixed berries

Reserve the completed trios of chocolate in the fridge until ready to serve. Once ready, garnish with mixed berries.

MOCCA FRAGILITET
'This is a traditional pastry,' says Martin, 'combining classic French and Swedish style.'
It is also a distinctive composition of two other bold elements: crunch and strong mocha.

MAKES 1 cake (serves approx. 25) **DIFFICULTY** 3/5 **PREPARATION TIME** 2 hours
SPECIFIC EQUIPMENT 5 x baking trays; piping (pastry) bag with size 10 nozzle; digital candy thermometer

INGREDIENTS

For the Meringue

Egg whites 500 g | 1 lb 1½ oz | 2 cups
Caster (superfine) sugar 750 g | 1 lb 10½ oz | sc. 3½ cups
Almond paste 500 g | 1 lb 1½ oz | 1¾ cups
Milk (3% fat) 125 g | sc. 4½ fl oz | gen. ½ cup
Almond flakes 100 g | 3½ oz | 1 cup

For the Mocha Cream

Egg yolks 240 g | 8½ oz | 1 cup
Whipping cream (35% fat) 192 g | 6¾ fl oz | ¾ cup
Caster (superfine) sugar 216 g | gen. 7½ oz | 1 cup
Instant coffee 12 g | sc. ½ fl oz | 3 tbsp
Unsalted butter 360 g | sc. 12¾ oz (softened, in cubes)
Dark chocolate couverture (70%) 80 g | gen. 2¾ oz (melted)
Gelatine (gold) 4 g | 2 sheets (softened in ice cold water, with excess water squeezed out)

INSTRUCTIONS

Meringue

1 On the reverse side of silicone baking paper, draw five squares of 27 x 27 cm (10⅝ x 10⅝ in.).
2 Whisk the egg whites and sugar to a firm meringue.
3 Mix the almond paste with the milk until smooth, then fold into the meringue.
4 Divide between the five silicone baking paper-lined trays, piping each mixture to a thickness of no more than 1 cm (⅜ in.) within the pre-sketched outlines.
5 Sprinkle almond flakes on top of one of the trays before baking.
6 Bake all the trays at 190°C (375°F) for 15 minutes. NB Baking the trays separately will give a better result with regular ovens.

Mocha Cream

1 Heat everything except the butter, chocolate and gelatine to 84°C (183°F).
2 Take off the heat and pour into a cool bowl.
3 Mix in the softened butter, then add the chocolate.
4 Add the gelatine and allow it to melt into the mixture.
5 Leave the mixture to cool.

ASSEMBLING

Garnish Cocoa powder

Alternate the five layers of meringue sheets with four layers of mocha cream, starting with plain meringue and finishing with the almond-coated meringue, then freeze. While still frozen, trim the edges of the cake to create a 25 x 25 cm (9¾ x 9¾ in.) square. Cut this into 5 x 5 cm (2 x 2 in.) squares. Decorate with a cocoa powder pattern on top, leave to defrost in the fridge, then serve.

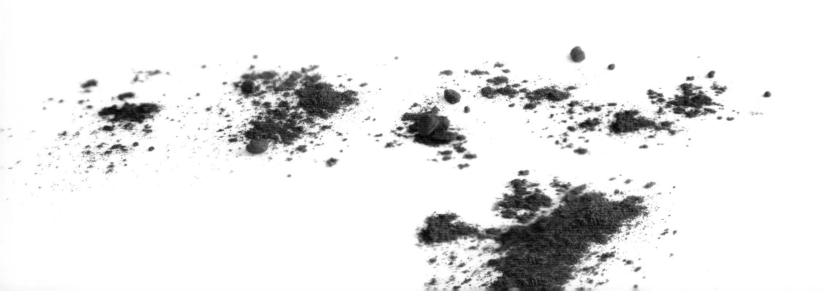

COCONUT/LIME CAKE
'This represents another of my favourite combinations,' notes Martin. 'Coconut and milk chocolate, enlivened with the fresh tang of lime, harmonize in this delicious cake.'

MAKES 1 cake (20 cm/7¾ in. diameter); serves 10–12   **DIFFICULTY** 4/5   **PREPARATION TIME** 4 hours (not including up to 4 hours' freezing/setting time prior to assembling)   **SPECIFIC EQUIPMENT** Digital candy thermometer; panna cotta mould (18 cm/7 in. diameter, 1.5 cm/⅝ in. high); 2 x deep cake tins (pans) (each 20 cm/7¾ in. diameter); spray gun; cake ring (20 cm/7¾ in.)

INGREDIENTS

For the Lime Panna Cotta
Lime purée 53 g | sc. 2 fl oz | sc. ¼ cup (or lime juice with 10% caster/superfine sugar)
Zest of ½ a lime
Milk (3% fat) 60 g | 2 fl oz | ¼ cup
Double (heavy) whipping cream (40% fat) 60 g | gen. 2 fl oz | ¼ cup
Caster (superfine) sugar 45 g | 1½ oz | 3½ tbsp
Gelatine (gold) 1.5 g | ¾ sheet (softened in ice cold water, with excess water squeezed out)

For the Coconut Dacquoise
Egg whites 340 g | 12 oz | 1⅖ cups
Caster (superfine) sugar 115 g | 4 oz | ½ cup
Desiccated (shredded) coconut 50 g | 1¾ oz | ⅔ cup
Blanched almond meal 35 g | 1¼ oz | ⅖ cup
Icing (confectioner's) sugar 85 g | 3 oz | gen. ½ cup

For the Milk Chocolate Mousse
Caster (superfine) sugar 94 g | gen. 3¼ oz | ⅖ cup
Water 94 g | 3¼ fl oz | gen. ⅓ cup
Whole eggs 83 g | 3 oz | gen. ⅓ cup (lightly whisked)
Egg yolks 75 g | gen. 2½ oz | 5 tbsp (lightly whisked)
Whipping cream (35% fat) [1] 195 g | gen. 6¾ fl oz | ¾ cup
Gelatine (gold) 6 g | 3 sheets (softened in ice cold water, with excess water squeezed out)
Milk chocolate 563 g | gen. 1 lb 3¾ oz
Whipping cream (35% fat) [2] 488 g | 17 fl oz | 2 cups

For the Spray Gun Chocolate Mixture
Dark chocolate (70%) 100 g | 3½ oz
Cocoa butter 100 g | 3½ oz

INSTRUCTIONS

Lime Panna Cotta
1 Mix all the ingredients, except for the gelatine, and allow to simmer for 10 minutes on a low heat.
2 Remove from the heat and cool to about 50°C (122°F) before adding the gelatine.
3 Once the gelatine has melted, pour the mixture into the 18 cm (7 in.) mould.
4 Freeze for at least 4 hours.

Coconut Dacquoise
1 Whisk the egg whites and caster (superfine) sugar to a firm meringue.
2 Blend together the coconut, almond meal and icing (confectioner's) sugar.
3 Fold the dry ingredients gently into the meringue.
4 Spread the dacquoise into the two silicone baking paper-lined cake tins (pans) and bake in a 180°C (350°F) oven for about 15–20 minutes.
5 Remove from the cake tins (pans), cool on wire racks and reserve.

Milk Chocolate Mousse
1 Heat the sugar, water and lightly whisked eggs and egg yolks in a bain-marie to 84°C (183°F), stirring constantly.
2 Pour into a stand mixer and whisk until airy.
3 Bring cream [1] to the boil, then add the gelatine.
4 Blend the cream/gelatine mixture with the chocolate, and stir until melted.
5 Whip cream [2].
6 Fold the chocolate mixture into the egg mixture, followed by the whipped cream.

Spray Gun Chocolate Mixture
1 Melt both ingredients in a bain-marie.
2 Remove from the heat as soon as melted.
3 Put in a spray gun when the mixture is still liquid but not hot.

ASSEMBLING

Components/Garnishes Butter; slices of lime

Lightly grease the cake ring with butter, line it with silicone baking paper and sit it on a tray. Put one coconut dacquoise disc in the ring. Fill the ring two-thirds of the way up with milk chocolate mousse. Push the frozen panna cotta down into the mousse. Put the other dacquoise disc on top of the panna cotta. Fill the ring with mousse, but make sure you save some separately in the fridge. Freeze the cake. Once the cake has frozen, make some 'spikes' on top with the reserved mousse and freeze again. Once frozen, unmould and spray the cake with the chocolate mixture. Decorate with slices of lime. You could also add tempered chocolate decorations. Defrost the cake in the fridge before serving.

Nadège Nourian

CANADA

Queen Street, West Toronto, is where one can find most trendy shops and galleries; it is therefore befitting to have at No. 780 Nadège Nourian's trendsetting pâtisserie, which has set new standards in the industry and in the experience of cake-shopping. Her jewel-bright wares are highly contemporary and stylishly presented in the pristine boutique. The vibrancy of the colours pops out against the crisp white shelves, the goods like kaleidoscopic gems displayed in elegant cases. *Elle* magazine was quick to catch on and commissioned Nadège to create her 'Avida Dollars' cake for a feature on Surrealism.

Nadège (the pâtisserie is simply called by its founder's first name) undoubtedly delivers a creative vision that is striking in its maturity, the graphic design aspect being second to none. The numerous pastries, lines of packaged treats, broad chocolate range and savoury goods are high-end gourmet standard, and the service is perfectly fine-tuned. The store has the ambience of luxury retail, combined with genuine warmth. And let's not forget that it is very affordable.

'I would say my creative style is modern and elegant, mixing international flavours with French flair. I love experimenting with unusual ingredients, using spices or alcohol, mixing savoury and sweet. For example, I've created a Guinness macaron and a gin and tonic marshmallow,' notes Nadège. 'Technology has of course developed the industry, but it will never replace technique. We shouldn't lose the artisan aspect or a signature style.'

Born in Lyon, Nadège is a fourth-generation pastry chef, who, prior to settling in Toronto in 2009, worked with Meilleurs Ouvriers de France pâtisserie and in Michelin-starred restaurants. 'I grew up in the industry. I remember when I first started experimenting with pastry, I was making chocolate truffles with my grandmother, and she looked up and said "You must be very proud" to my deceased grandfather,' Nadège touchingly recalls.

Encouraged by her success, in 2011 she opened her second shop, on Yonge Street in Toronto, and in 2012 launched her e-boutique. 'When you're in a position to open a second location, it means the demand for your product is there, but more importantly it tells you that people appreciate what you do.' It sounds as if this is a mini-empire in the making. 'I would love to open in Tokyo.' High-street pastry shops, prepare to up your game...

www.nadege-patisserie.com

AVIDA DOLLARS

'Elle Canada asked me to create a cake to illustrate a piece they were doing on Surrealism,' recalls Nadège. '"Avida Dollars" is my interpretation of Surrealism via the flashy red colour, the shape and the chocolate decoration representing Salvador Dalí's moustache.'

MAKES 10 small cakes   **DIFFICULTY** 5/5   **PREPARATION TIME** 5 hours   **SPECIFIC EQUIPMENT** Digital candy thermometer; 10 x mini half-sphere silicone moulds (each 4.2 cm/1⅝ in. diameter, 2.1 cm/⅞ in. high); acetate sheet; piping (pastry) bag; 20 x half-sphere silicone moulds (each 7 cm/2¾ in. diameter, 3.5 cm/1⅜ in. high); spray gun

INGREDIENTS

For the Orange Madeleine

Invert sugar 11g | ½ fl oz | gen. 1¼ tsp
Caster (superfine) sugar 28g | 1 oz | 2 tbsp
Whole egg 33g | gen. 1 oz | gen. 2 tbsp
Zest of 1 orange
Strong flour 33g | gen. 1 oz | gen. 2¾ tbsp
Baking powder 1g | ¼ tsp
Salt 1g | gen. ⅛ tsp
Unsalted butter 33g | gen. 1 oz

For the Crunchy Orange

Unsalted butter 68g | sc. 2½ oz
Caster (superfine) sugar 68g | sc. 2½ oz | sc. ⅓ cup
Slivered almonds 52g | 1¾ oz | ½ cup
Soft flour 14g | ½ oz | gen. 1 tbsp
Salt 2g | gen. ¼ tsp
Zest of 1 orange

For the Soft Jelly Mulled Wine

Merlot or other low-tannin, light-bodied red wine
116g | 4 fl oz | ½ cup
Star anise 1g | 2 small
Whole cloves 1g | ½ tsp
Zest of 1 orange
Cinnamon 6g | ¼ oz | 2 sticks
Light brown sugar 30g | 1 oz | sc. 2½ tbsp
Gelatine (gold) 4g | 2 sheets (softened in ice cold water, with excess water squeezed out)

For the Cinnamon Mousse

Milk 193g | 6½ fl oz | gen. ¾ cup
Whipping cream (35% fat) [1] 193g | 6¾ fl oz | ¾ cup
Cinnamon 22g | ¾ oz | 7½ sticks
Egg yolks 93g | 3¼ oz | ⅖ cup
Caster (superfine) sugar 78g | 2¾ oz | ⅓ cup
Gelatine (gold) 6g | 3 sheets (softened in ice cold water, with excess water squeezed out)
Whipping cream (35% fat) [2] 207g | 7¼ fl oz | gen. ¾ cup

For the Red Outer Coating

White chocolate 300g | 10½ oz
Cocoa butter 300g | 10½ oz
Red food colouring for chocolate 4g | 2½ tsp

For the Chocolate 'Moustaches'

Dark chocolate couverture (70%) 120g | 4¼ oz (tempered)

INSTRUCTIONS

Orange Madeleine

1 Mix the sugars, egg and orange zest.
2 Sift the flour, baking powder and salt together, and slowly add to the egg mixture while whisking.
3 Melt the butter at 45°C (113°F), add to the rest of the ingredients and mix.
4 Divide the mixture between the 10 mini half-sphere silicone moulds.
5 Pre-heat the oven to 210°C (400°F), then turn down to 170°C (325°F) when the madeleines go in.
6 Bake for 6–10 minutes, or until baked through, then remove from the moulds and reserve.

Crunchy Orange

1 Cream the butter and sugar.
2 Add all the remaining ingredients and combine.
3 Spread the mixture very thinly onto a silicone baking paper-lined tray.
4 Bake in the oven at 150°C (300°F) until golden brown.

Soft Jelly Mulled Wine

1 Heat the wine in a small saucepan but remove from the heat before it boils.
2 Put all the ingredients except for the gelatine into the wine, then cover for 20 minutes to allow the flavours to infuse.
3 Strain the wine, discarding the solids.
4 Stir the gelatine into the wine.
5 Divide between the cleaned, re-used 10 mini half-sphere silicone moulds.
6 Place in the freezer to set.

Cinnamon Mousse

1 Put the milk and cream [1] into a small pan and bring to the boil.
2 Crack the cinnamon sticks, add to the cream mixture to infuse for 20 minutes, then strain and discard the solids.
3 Whisk the egg yolks and sugar in a bowl until pale.
4 Temper the egg yolk/sugar mixture with the cream mixture and cook to 85°C (185°F), stirring constantly.
5 Add the gelatine and stir to dissolve.
6 Put the mixture into a bowl on ice and stir until cooled to 25°C (77°F).
7 Whip cream [2] and fold into the mixture.

Red Outer Coating

1 Melt the chocolate and cocoa butter together in a bain-marie, then add the food colouring. NB The mixture is to be applied with a spray gun; it must be used at 50°C (122°F) in order to be sprayable (liquid, but not too hot).

Chocolate 'Moustaches'

1 Spread the tempered chocolate on the acetate sheet.
2 Cut out some triangles, 2 cm (¾ in.) at the base x 10 cm (4 in.) high .
3 Roll the sheet a little to create a curve before the chocolate sets.

ASSEMBLING

Component Melted chocolate

Pipe a little bit of mousse into ten of the 7 cm (2¾ in.) half-sphere silicone moulds, add a frozen soft jelly, add some more mousse, add pieces of the crunchy orange, top with more mousse, smooth level, then store in the freezer until set. In the other ten half-sphere silicone moulds, pipe a little bit of mousse, add a madeleine, add more mousse, add pieces of crunchy orange, top with more mousse, smooth level and place in the fridge until the first moulds are frozen. Unmould the first ten frozen half-spheres and put them on top of the refrigerated half-spheres. Store the assembled spheres in the freezer until set. Once set, unmould, ensuring that the madeleine half of each sphere is on the bottom. Apply a little bit of melted chocolate to the underside of the spheres to create a base. Spray the spheres with the red outer coating. Place in the fridge to defrost. Before serving, arrange three chocolate 'moustaches' around each sphere, tucking the bases underneath.

MACARON MOJITO

'I always think mixologists and pastry chefs are very close and connected in their work,' comments Nadège, 'so I decided to play with cocktails and to change the state of famous drinks. I created edible cocktails as mojito macaron, gin and tonic marshmallow and Cosmopolitan entremets. With this macaron, the mint is strong at first and the rum is very subtle but still quite present.'

MAKES approx. 25 **DIFFICULTY** 3/5 **PREPARATION TIME** 2 hours
SPECIFIC EQUIPMENT Digital candy thermometer; piping (pastry) bag with size 11 nozzle

INGREDIENTS

For the Macaron Shell

Blanched almond meal 150 g | gen. 5¼ oz | 1¾ cups
Icing (confectioner's) sugar 150 g | gen. 5¼ oz | sc. 1 cup
Egg whites [1] 52 g | 1¾ oz | 3½ tbsp
Green natural food colouring 0.6 g | approx. 10 drops
Egg whites [2] 52 g | 1¾ oz | 3½ tbsp
Water 38 g | 1¼ fl oz | 2½ tbsp
Caster (superfine) sugar 150 g | gen. 5¼ oz | sc. ¾ cup

For the Mojito Ganache

Fresh mint 19 g | sc. ¾ oz | 1 cup
Whipping cream (35% fat) 125 g | 4½ fl oz | ½ cup
White chocolate couverture (e.g. Ivoire 35% by Valrhona) 236 g | gen. 8¼ oz
White rum (e.g. Habana Club) 25 g | gen. ¾ fl oz | 5 tsp

INSTRUCTIONS

Macaron Shell

1 Sift the almond meal and icing (confectioner's) sugar together.
2 Add egg whites [1] and the food colouring.
3 Mix until the texture becomes smooth, then reserve.
4 Put egg whites [2] into the bowl of a stand mixer.
5 Put the water and caster (superfine) sugar into a small pan and heat.
6 When the syrup reaches 110°C (230°F), start to whisk egg whites [2].
7 When the syrup reaches 118°C (244°F), pour it onto the fluffy egg whites.
8 Keep mixing until the meringue holds and cools to 50°C (122°F).
9 Fold the first mix into the meringue until it is smooth and shiny.
10 Pipe the resulting macaron mixture into 4 cm (1⅝ in.) circles; this will make approximately 50 macaron shells.
11 Allow to dry at room temperature for 15 minutes.
12 Bake at 150°C (300°F) for 15 minutes.
13 Reserve.

Mojito Ganache

1 Wash the fresh mint.
2 Bring the cream to the boil, add the mint and leave to infuse for 20 minutes.
3 Strain the cream thoroughly.
4 Melt the white chocolate to 45°C (113°F).
5 Pour the cream onto the white chocolate and blend.
6 Add the rum.
7 Reserve in a cool place until set.

ASSEMBLING

Pipe the set ganache onto half the macaron shells (about 25). Cover with the remaining macaron shells. Put into a container in the fridge for a day before consuming.

LA MANCHA

'"La Mancha" was created as part of a cake collection inspired by different parts of the world that I travel to,' explains Nadège. 'It represents a fusion of the classic flavours of Spain and Canada.'

MAKES 10   **DIFFICULTY** 4 /5   **PREPARATION TIME** 3 hours (not including freezing time)
SPECIFIC EQUIPMENT Digital candy thermometer; 20 x mini-muffin silicone moulds
(each 4.2 cm/1⅝ in. diameter); 10 x sapphire (or dome)-shaped silicone moulds
(each 7 x 7 cm/2¾ x 2¾ in.); piping (pastry) bag

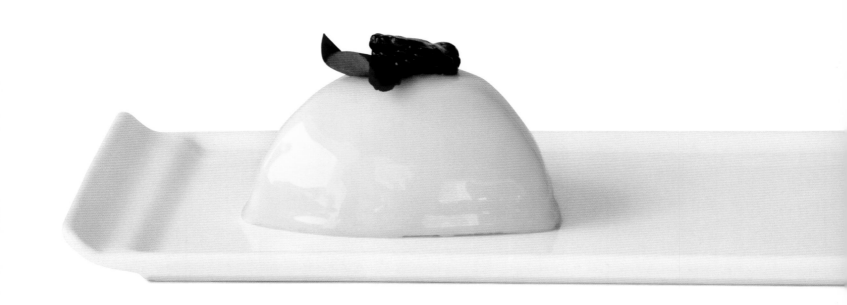

INGREDIENTS

For the Blackberry Gelée

Blackberry purée 138 g | 5 fl oz | ½ cup

Gelatine (gold) 2 g | 1 sheet (softened in ice cold water, with excess water squeezed out)

For the Saffron Crème

Egg yolks 20 g | sc. ¾ oz | sc. 1½ tbsp

Caster (superfine) sugar 15 g | ½ oz | gen. 1 tbsp

Saffron (from La Mancha region) 3 pistils

Whipping cream (35% fat) 83 g | 3 fl oz | ⅓ cup

Gelatine (gold) 1 g | ½ sheet (softened in ice cold water, with excess water squeezed out)

For the Sablé Breton

Salted butter 102 g | 3½ oz

Caster (superfine) sugar 102 g | 3½ oz | sc. ½ cup

Egg yolks 52 g | 1¾ oz | 3½ tbsp

Pastry flour type 55 144 g | 5 oz | sc. 1 cup

For the Honey Mousse

Clover honey (from Ontario) 110 g | sc. 4 fl oz | ⅓ cup

Crème pâtissière* 220 g | 7¾ oz | gen. ¾ cup

Whipping cream (35% fat) 657 g | 23 fl oz | sc. 2⅔ cups

*** Crème Pâtissière**

Egg yolks 126 g | sc. 4½ oz | ½ cup

Caster (superfine) sugar 197 g | sc. 7 oz | gen. ⅘ cup

Poudre à crème (custard powder/instant pudding powder) 63 g | sc. 2¼ oz | ⅖ cup

Milk 107 g | gen. 3½ fl oz | sc. ½ cup

Unsalted butter 79 g | gen. 2¾ oz

Gelatine (gold) 1 g/½ sheet, softened in ice cold water, with excess water squeezed out (optional)

INSTRUCTIONS

Blackberry Gelée

1 Warm the blackberry purée to 20°C (68°F) and, separately, the gelatine to 50°C (122°F).
2 Mix the gelatine and the purée together.
3 Measure 14 g (½ fl oz/1 tbsp) into each cavity of ten of the mini-muffin silicone moulds.
4 Store in the freezer until set.

Saffron Crème

1 Whisk the egg yolks and sugar In a bowl until pale.
2 Put the saffron and cream into a small pan and bring to the boil.
3 Temper the egg yolk/sugar mixture with the cream and cook in a bain-marie to 85°C (185°F), stirring constantly.
4 Add the gelatine and stir to dissolve.
5 Put the mixture into a bowl on ice and stir.
6 Measure 12 g (sc. ½ fl oz/sc. 1 tbsp) into each cavity of the remaining ten mini-muffin silicone moulds.
7 Store in the freezer until set.

Sablé Breton

1 Soften the butter in the microwave.
2 Cream the butter and caster (superfine) sugar together.
3 Add the egg yolks and then the flour.
4 Mix until the dough is homogeneous.
5 Roll the dough to a thickness of 1 cm (⅜ in.).
6 Rest the dough in the freezer until firm.
7 Cut discs of 5 cm (2 in.) diameter.
8 Bake the sablé in the oven at 150°C (300°F) for 10 minutes, then reserve.

Honey Mousse

1 Mix the honey with the crème pâtissière.
2 Whip the cream until fluffy.
3 Fold the whipped cream into the honey crème pâtissière.

*** Crème Pâtissière**

1 Whisk the egg yolks and sugar in a bowl until pale, then mix in the poudre à crème dissolved in the milk.
2 Cook all the ingredients, except the butter (and the gelatine, if using), in a pan, stirring frequently until very thick.
3 Allow to boil for 1 minute.
4 Remove from the heat, then stir in the butter (and gelatine, if using) until combined.
5 Store in the fridge until cold.

ASSEMBLING

Garnishes Purple pansies; blackberries

In each sapphire (or dome)-shaped silicone mould, pipe a little bit of mousse. Add a frozen saffron crème, then pipe some more mousse on top. Add a frozen blackberry gelée, then pipe more mousse up to 1 cm (⅜ in.) from the top of the mould. Put a sablé disc on top, use a palette knife to level with the mould, then place in the freezer until set. At least 40 minutes before serving, unmould and reserve in the fridge. Decorate with a pansy and half a blackberry on top.

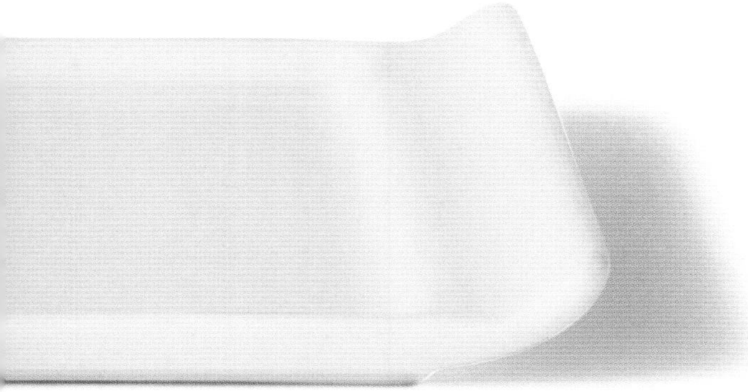

Nathaniel Reid

USA

A young Nathaniel Reid learned the value of resilience the hard way. 'I was working in a restaurant as a prep cook and within a few months had advanced to the sauté station. When the pastry chef resigned, I applied for the position. With a great deal of perseverance, having had multiple rejections from the chef, I was eventually given a trial job,' he recalls. 'I prepared pastries in the morning, with a lot of trial and error; attended school during the day; and worked the sauté station at night. After I'd proven my skills, the chef promoted me to the permanent position of pastry chef.'

Nathaniel, whose passion for food was instilled in him from an early age by his parents, has now been named one of the Top 10 Pastry Chefs of America, an accolade conferred by *Dessert Professional* magazine, America's leading publication for the pastry, ice cream and chocolate industries. Numerous additional achievements crowd his résumé, including obtaining the Grand Diploma in Culinary and Pastry Arts from Le Cordon Bleu Paris; winning the US Pastry Chef of the Year competition; and taking first place in the 'Best Chocolate/Confection' category at the Pastryscoop.com Golden Scoop Awards.

Since 2002, Nathaniel's pastry style has evolved into a sophisticated signature, but he is keen to share his knowledge. 'When I began my career, chef Chris Desens gave me a helping hand by awarding me a scholarship for culinary school. In 2010 he invited me back to Missouri to teach a class. It was an amazing opportunity to teach these young people from my home state about my profession that I love so much and that has rewarded me so well. I hope that I was able to open the students' eyes to what is possible with pastry and that it can open a door to the world. It was incredibly inspiring to witness their excitement.' The experience has fuelled a dream to one day 'start a scholarship to help the next generation of chefs achieve their dreams'.

Nathaniel's enthusiasm for food extends to its powerful link with memory. 'Caramel: it's the essence of pastry, it's provocative and it evokes great memories.' He also notes: 'Presentation will make clients purchase a pastry for the first time, but taste will make them buy it again and again.' As he muses: 'Eating a good pastry should be a memory that lasts a lifetime.'

www.chefnathanielreid.com

PARADISE | PASSION FRUIT AND BANANA CRÉMEUX, STRAWBERRY GELÉE, ALMOND SPONGE

When Nathaniel was working in Florida, he received deliveries of beautiful, locally grown strawberries and passion fruit at the same time. 'I decided to use the fruits together in a pastry,' he says, 'with the seasons as inspiration.'

MAKES 10   **DIFFICULTY** 3½/5   **PREPARATION TIME** 4½ hours (not including overnight setting time for the white chocolate chantilly and strawberry gelée)   **SPECIFIC EQUIPMENT** 3 x bottomless frames (each 32 x 14.5 cm/12⅝ x 5¾ in.); digital candy thermometer; acetate sheet; piping (pastry) bag

INGREDIENTS

For the White Chocolate Chantilly
1 vanilla pod (bean) (split, scraped, seeds reserved)
Whipping cream (35% fat) [1] 83 g | 3 fl oz | ⅓ cup
White chocolate (33%) 68 g | sc. 2½ oz
Whipping cream (35% fat) [2] 83 g | 3 fl oz | ⅓ cup (cold)

For the Strawberry Gelée
Strawberry purée 225 g | 8 fl oz | sc. 1 cup
Granulated white sugar 20 g | sc. ¾ oz | 5 tsp
Fresh raspberries 25 g | gen. ¾ oz | ⅕ cup
Gelatine (gold) 5 g | 2½ sheets (softened in ice cold water, with excess water squeezed out)

For the Almond Sponge
Icing (confectioner's) sugar 39 g | sc. 1½ oz | 4 tbsp
Blanched almond meal 81 g | gen. 2¾ oz | sc. 1 cup
Egg yolks 43 g | 1½ oz | sc. 3 tbsp
Whole eggs 70 g | 2½ oz | gen. ¼ cup
Egg whites 148 g | 5¼ oz | sc. ⅔ cup
Granulated white sugar 96 g | sc. 3½ oz | sc. ½ cup
Plain (all-purpose) flour 65 g | gen. 2¼ oz | sc. ½ cup

For the Passion Fruit and Banana Crémeux
Passion fruit purée 98 g | 3½ fl oz | ⅖ cup
Mango purée 59 g | 2 fl oz | ¼ cup
Banana purée 20 g | sc. ¾ fl oz | gen. 1 tbsp
Coconut purée 12 g | sc. ½ fl oz | 1¾ tsp
Whipping cream (35% fat) 109 g | 4 fl oz | sc. ½ cup
Granulated white sugar 59 g | 2 oz | gen. ¼ cup
Egg yolks 94 g | gen. 3¼ oz | ⅖ cup
Gelatine (gold) 3 g | 1½ sheets (softened in ice cold water, with excess water squeezed out)

For the Yellow Chocolate Waves
White chocolate 200 g | 7 oz
Yellow fat-dispersible colourant (to achieve desired colour)

For the Clear Glaze
Granulated white sugar 100 g | 3½ oz | ½ cup
Pectin NH 10 g | sc. ½ oz | 4 tsp
Water 250 g | gen. 8¾ fl oz | gen. 1 cup
Lemon juice 10 g | gen. ¼ fl oz | 2 tsp

INSTRUCTIONS

White Chocolate Chantilly
1 Add the vanilla seeds to cream [1], bring to the boil, then strain.
2 Pour the warm cream over the white chocolate and stir until the chocolate has fully melted.
3 Slowly add the cold cream [2] to the emulsion.
4 Store in the fridge overnight.

Strawberry Gelée
1 Place an empty frame, bottom sealed with plastic wrap, on a silicone mat in the freezer.
2 Bring half the strawberry purée with the sugar and raspberries to the boil.
3 Add the gelatine to the hot purée mixture.
4 Add the remaining strawberry purée and mix.
5 Cool the gelée down, pour it into the frozen frame, now placed on a silicone baking paper-lined tray, and freeze. NB Ensure that the gelée is well frozen before the cake is assembled, and that the cake remains in the freezer for one night before cutting, as it takes gelatine a day to gel to its full strength.

Almond Sponge
1 Combine the icing (confectioner's) sugar, almond meal, egg yolks and whole eggs in a mixing bowl for about 4 minutes, or until pale and airy.
2 In a separate bowl, make a meringue with the egg whites and granulated sugar.
3 Fold the meringue into the first mixture, then fold in the flour.
4 Prepare two sponges by spreading 263 g (9¼ oz/gen. 2½ cups) of sponge mix into each of two bottomless frames placed on silicone baking paper-lined trays.
5 Bake in a 185°C (350°F) oven for 9–11 minutes.
6 Remove from the oven and immediately transfer to a wire rack to cool as fast as possible, then unmould and set aside.

Passion Fruit and Banana Crémeux
1 Warm all the fruit purées and the cream together.
2 Whisk the sugar and egg yolks together thoroughly.
3 Temper the warm cream mixture into the egg yolk mixture.
4 Cook to 80°C (176°F).
5 Add the gelatine.
6 Cool to 30°C (86°F).

Yellow Chocolate Waves
1 Temper the chocolate, then add the colourant to the melted chocolate.
2 Spread thinly onto the acetate sheet over an area of at least 25 x 50 cm (9¾ x 19½ in.).
3 Cut into shapes measuring approximately 12.5 cm (5 in.) in length and 4.5 cm (1¾ in.) in height (to the tip of each wave).
4 Reserve in a cool area.

Clear Glaze
1 Mix the sugar and pectin together.
2 Heat the water and lemon juice to 45°C (113°F).
3 Whisk the sugar/pectin mixture into the water/lemon juice.
4 Bring to the boil, then boil for 3–5 minutes.
5 Strain and allow to cool.

ASSEMBLING

Components/Garnishes Desiccated (shredded) coconut; fresh raspberries; icing (confectioner's) sugar

Pour half of the passion fruit and banana crémeux into a frozen frame, bottom sealed with plastic wrap and placed on a tray. Place a layer of almond sponge on top. Pour on half of the remaining crémeux. Add the frozen strawberry gelée. Next pour the remainder of the crémeux on top. Finish by placing the second almond sponge on top. Put the cake in the freezer. Once frozen, unmould and turn the cake over. Trim all the edges of the cake and cut into 12.5 x 3 cm (5 x 1⅛ in.) bars. Glaze the top of each bar with clear glaze, then sprinkle fine desiccated (shredded) coconut on top. Dust three raspberries with icing (confectioner's) sugar and place on top. Whip the white chocolate chantilly and pipe three drops in between the raspberries. Garnish with yellow chocolate waves. Allow to defrost in the fridge before serving. NB The gelée needs to be cold to keep its shape.

DALLIANCE | HAZELNUT POUND CAKE, CANDIED/CONFIT ORANGE, VANILLA CARAMEL MOU

Of the inspiration for this cake, Nathaniel recalls, 'I competed in the International Pâtisserie Grand Prix in 2009. One of the requirements was to make a pound cake. I had an idea to bake the cake with a silicone insert in the centre, which, when removed after baking, left a well to be filled with soft caramel.'

MAKES 3 cakes (serve 6–9) **DIFFICULTY** 3½/5 **PREPARATION TIME** 6–7 hours **SPECIFIC EQUIPMENT** 3 x round silicone discs (each 8 x 1 cm/3⅛ x ⅜ in.), or an 8 cm (3⅛ in.) biscuit cutter; 3 x cake rings (each 10 x 6 cm/4 x 2⅜ in.); digital candy thermometer; silicone mat

INGREDIENTS

For the Hazelnut Pound Cake
Hazelnut meal 144 g | 5 oz | 1¼ cups
Candied/confit orange 40 g | sc. 1½ oz | 5 tbsp (chopped)
Cornflour (cornstarch) 60 g | gen. 2 oz | sc. 6½ tbsp (sifted)
Almond meal 56 g | 2 oz | ⅔ cup
Dark brown sugar 200 g | 7 oz | 1 cup
Whole eggs 160 g | sc. 5¾ oz | sc. ¾ cup
Egg yolks 48 g | sc. 1¾ oz | gen. 3 tbsp
Egg whites 72 g | 2½ oz | sc. 5 tbsp
Granulated white sugar 20 g | sc. ¾ oz | 5 tsp
Fine sea salt 1 g | gen. ⅛ tsp
Unsalted butter 50 g | 1¾ oz (melted)
Lemon zest 3 g | sc. ½ tsp
Orange zest 5 g | sc. ¼ oz | 1 tsp

For the Citrus Syrup
Water 100 g | 3½ fl oz | sc. ½ cup
Granulated white sugar 100 g | 3½ oz | ½ cup
Lemon juice 50 g | 1¾ fl oz | gen. 3¼ tbsp
Grand Marnier 25 g | gen. ¾ fl oz | gen. 1½ tbsp

For the Soft Vanilla Caramel
Whipping cream (35% fat) 150 g | sc. 5½ fl oz | gen. ½ cup
Lightly salted butter 8 g | ¼ oz
Invert sugar 15 g | gen. ½ fl oz | ¾ tbsp
½ vanilla pod (bean) (split, scraped, both pod/bean and seeds reserved)
Granulated white sugar 112 g | 4 oz | gen. ½ cup
Glucose syrup 90 g | 3¼ fl oz | ¼ cup

For the Pralines
(the praline preparation process is time-consuming, so ready-made chopped pralines may be preferred)
Blanched hazelnuts 250 g | gen. 8¾ oz | sc. 1½ cups
Granulated white sugar 125 g | sc. 4½ oz | ⅝ cup
Water 38 g | 1¼ fl oz | 2½ tbsp
Cocoa butter 5 g | sc. ¼ oz

INSTRUCTIONS

Hazelnut Pound Cake
1 Toast the hazelnut meal, then cool.
2 Dust the candied/confit orange with some of the sifted cornflour (cornstarch).
3 Combine the toasted hazelnut meal, the almond meal and the remaining cornflour (cornstarch) together.
4 Whisk the dark brown sugar, whole eggs and egg yolks together until thick.
5 Whisk the egg whites, granulated white sugar and sea salt together to make a soft meringue.
6 Fold the meringue into the egg mixture, then fold in the dry ingredients.
7 Slowly fold in the melted butter.
8 Next fold in the lemon zest, orange zest and candied/confit orange.
9 Place a round silicone disc, if using, into the bottom of each cake ring.
10 Divide the batter evenly between the three cake rings, pouring into the space between the silicone discs and the outer metal rings, and covering the discs. If not using silicone discs, divide the mixture evenly between the three cake rings.
11 Bake at 155°C (300°F) for 30–35 minutes.

Citrus Syrup
1 Bring the water and sugar to the boil.
2 Take off the heat, then add the lemon juice and Grand Marnier.
3 When the pound cakes (from above recipe) come out of the oven, remove the outer rings, leaving the discs in place, if using, and soak the cakes on all sides in the warm citrus syrup. NB If not using discs to create wells for the caramel (recipe below), a similar result can be achieved by pressing an 8 cm (3⅛ in.) circle cutter into a whole citrus-infused cake and removing enough cake to create a 1 cm (⅜ in.) deep hole.

Soft Vanilla Caramel
1 Warm the cream, butter and invert sugar together.
2 Add the vanilla pod (bean) and seeds to a saucepan containing the granulated sugar and glucose syrup.
3 Caramelize the sugar/glucose mix slowly, without allowing it to colour.
4 Deglaze the caramelized sugars with the warm cream, strain, then reheat to 115°C (239°F).
5 Remove the silicone inserts from the pound cakes, if using. Pour the caramel into the indentations left by the inserts/biscuit cutter, then leave to cool for about 1 hour.

Pralines
1 Warm the hazelnuts slowly in a low oven to 80°C (175°F).
2 Cook the sugar and water in a saucepan to 118°C (244°F).
3 Add the warmed hazelnuts to the syrup and stir.
4 Keep stirring until the sugar crystallizes.
5 Continue to cook and stir until the sugar melts and becomes an attractive caramel colour.
6 Stir in the cocoa butter, then pour the hazelnuts out onto the silicone mat.
7 Once the nuts have cooled, chop them finely, reserving three whole caramelized hazelnuts for decoration.

ASSEMBLING

Components/Garnishes Warmed apricot jam (without apricot pieces); whole caramelized hazelnuts

Brush the sides of the pound cakes with warmed apricot jam. Apply chopped pralines to the sides of the cakes. Decorate each with a whole caramelized hazelnut.

AMBER | PECAN CARAMEL, SABLÉ BRETON, CARAMELIZED PECAN

'The sweet smell of brown sugar and pecan praline cooking in New Orleans, Louisiana, instantly gave me the urge to recreate the city's famous candy into a pastry,' notes Nathaniel.

MAKES 10   **DIFFICULTY** 3½/5   **PREPARATION TIME** 5–6 hours (not including overnight resting time for the sablé breton)
SPECIFIC EQUIPMENT Piping (pastry) bag with size 10 nozzle; 10 x cake rings (each 8.5 cm/3⅜ in. diameter); digital candy thermometer; 10 x dome-shaped silicone moulds (each 8 cm/3⅛ in. diameter)

INGREDIENTS

For the Sablé Breton

Egg yolks 51g | 1¾ oz | sc. 3½ tbsp
Granulated white sugar 102g | 3½ oz | ½ cup
Unsalted butter 102g | 3½ oz (softened)
Plain (all-purpose) flour 144g | 5 oz | sc. 1 cup
Baking powder 10g | sc. ½ oz | 2½ tsp
Fine sea salt 1.5g | gen. ¼ tsp

For the Caramel Mousse

Whipping cream (35% fat) [1] 86g | 3 fl oz | ⅓ cup
Unsalted butter 8g | ¼ oz
Fine sea salt a pinch
½ vanilla pod (bean) (split, scraped, both pod/bean and seeds reserved)
Granulated white sugar [1] 40g | sc. 1½ oz | gen. 3 tbsp
Glucose syrup 52g | 1¾ fl oz | sc. 3 tbsp
Egg yolks 38g | gen. 1¼ oz | 2½ tbsp
Water 15g | ½ fl oz | 1 tbsp
Granulated white sugar [2] 15g | ½ oz | 1¼ tbsp
Gelatine (gold) 4g | 2 sheets (softened in ice cold water, with excess water squeezed out)
Whipping cream (35% fat) [2] 177g | gen. 6¼ fl oz | sc. ¾ cup

For the Pecan Caramel

Granulated white sugar [1] 30g | 1 oz | 2½ tbsp
Toasted pecans 50g | 1¾ oz | ⅓ cup
Whipping cream (35% fat) 60g | gen. 2 fl oz | ¼ cup
Dark brown sugar 15g | ½ oz | gen. 1 tbsp
Granulated white sugar [2] 15g | ½ oz | 1¼ tbsp
Unsalted butter 40g | sc. 1½ oz

For the Caramelized Pecans

Granulated white sugar 50g | 1¾ oz | ¼ cup
Water 50g | 1¾ fl oz | 3½ tbsp
Invert sugar 15g | gen. ½ fl oz | ¾ tbsp
Chopped pecans 150g | gen. 5¼ oz | 1¼ cups

For the Caramel Glaze

Whipping cream (35% fat) 360g | gen. 12½ fl oz | sc. 1½ cups
Granulated white sugar 430g | sc. 1 lb | gen. 2 cups
Cornflour (cornstarch) 24g | gen. ¾ oz | sc. 2½ tbsp
Water 360g | gen. 12½ fl oz | 1½ cups
Gelatine (gold) 12g | 6 sheets (softened in ice cold water, with excess water squeezed out)

INSTRUCTIONS

Sablé Breton

1   Whisk the egg yolks and sugar until thick.
2   Slowly whisk the softened butter into the yolk/sugar mixture.
3   Sift the flour, baking powder and sea salt together.
4   Add the dry ingredients to the yolk/sugar mixture and mix together.
5   Pipe the resulting sablé breton into the cake rings, set on a silicone baking paper-lined tray.
6   Leave to rest overnight in the fridge.
7   Bake in a 150°C (300°F) oven for 22–24 minutes.
8   Unmould and allow to cool.

Caramel Mousse

1   Warm cream [1] with the butter and sea salt.
2   Place the vanilla pod (bean) and seeds in a saucepan with granulated sugar [1] and the glucose syrup.
3   Slowly caramelize the sugar and glucose.
4   Deglaze the caramel with the warm cream mixture, strain and cool.
5   Place the egg yolks, water and granulated sugar [2] in a bain-marie and whisk until thick.
6   Add the gelatine to the egg yolk mixture, stirring until dissolved.
7   Remove the mixture from the bain-marie and whisk with a mixer until cooled to 35°C (95°F).
8   Whip cream [2] to soft peaks.
9   Fold the egg yolk mixture into the caramel, then fold in the whipped cream.
10 Pipe 40 g (sc. 1½ oz/¼ cup) of the resulting mousse into each dome-shaped silicone mould (half-filling the mould), then freeze.

Pecan Caramel

1   Make a dry caramel with granulated sugar [1], then pour over the toasted pecans.
2   Once the pecans have cooled, process the mixture into a smooth paste.
3   Combine the pecan paste, cream, brown sugar, granulated sugar [2] and butter in a saucepan.
4   Cook to 103°C (217°F), then cool.

Caramelized Pecans

1   Bring the granulated sugar, water and invert sugar to the boil.
2   Pour the hot syrup over the chopped pecans.
3   Allow to rest for 10 minutes.
4   Strain the excess syrup off the pecans, then place them on a baking tray.
5   Caramelize the pecans in the oven at 190°C (375°F) for 6–8 minutes, then cool.

Caramel Glaze

1   Warm the cream in a saucepan.
2   In another saucepan make a dry caramel with the granulated sugar.
3   Deglaze the caramel with the warm cream.
4   Mix the cornflour (cornstarch) and water together, add to the caramel, and boil for 1 minute.
5   Add the gelatine.
6   Cool the resulting glaze and use at 25°C (77°F).

ASSEMBLING

Garnish Gold leaf

Pipe pecan caramel onto the top centre of each sablé breton. Sprinkle a few caramelized pecan pieces on top. Unmould the frozen caramel mousses, place them on a wire rack and coat them with the caramel glaze. Immediately place the mousses on the pecan caramel base. Decorate around the base of each glazed mousse dome with caramelized pecans. Adorn with a piece of gold leaf. Reserve in the fridge until ready to serve.

Pasquale Marigliano

ITALY

Creating pâtisserie is not dissimilar to composing music: the enchantment of a melody that sits on a complex arithmetic of notes; a dependence on optimal ratios and base elements of the highest quality; the way in which strongly calibrated, classical foundations can allow magic to happen. No surprise, then, that Italian pastry chef and chocolate master Pasquale Marigliano was learning solfège when he became interested in pastry. 'My dream was to become a concert pianist,' he recalls, 'but my interest in pastry was also strong. When at 19 I relocated to Paris, the capital of confectionery, I never looked back. I revelled in exploring all the nuances of a culture that heralds gastronomy as a true philosophy.'

On his return to his homeland, having learned from the best confectioners (Fauchon, Lenôtre), Pasquale was able to blend the best of French technique with the best of Italian tradition. 'I drew up my own taste philosophy, which I share with customers via my store. For example, through the "Petites Passions" – a series of novel petits fours that revisit Neapolitan flavours, such as the "Annurca" mini baba made with local apples, the "Mosaic" made with apricots from the Vesuvius region, or the "Capresine" made with Amalfi Coast lemons – I try to celebrate our traditions and culinary values, while cautiously adopting new trends.'

Pasquale points out that his creative style is 'minimalist, linear and ordered'. This does not, however, eclipse the fact that he has a highly sensual approach. 'Mixing, touching, smelling and tasting are essential to my experimentation,' he notes. His wife, Catherine, is also quick to stress that her husband is a born artist, who can consequently never be fully satisfied … despite the fact that he has won the Tre Torte prize and the Italian Confectioners' Championship, and was awarded second place out of five hundred Italian pastry shops by the food guide, Gambero Rosso.

'Quantity has supplanted quality to the detriment of our wellbeing,' Pasquale laments. 'Mass consumption has reduced food to the necessity of nourishment, whereas food should be about the heritage, culture and merits of a society and its natural environment.' This advocate of 'terroir' and first-class confectionery has undoubtedly succeeded in creating hymns for our gratified palates.

www.pasqualemarigliano.com

LA SINFONIA D'ESTATE

'This recipe is a mosaic of soft, warm colours like summertime,' says Pasquale.
'Flavours sparkle and textures are crisp when tasted, just like an air of celebration.'

MAKES 1 cake (to be served in 12 portions)   **DIFFICULTY** 3 /5   **PREPARATION TIME** 1¼ hours
SPECIFIC EQUIPMENT Digital candy thermometer; square frame (18 x 18 cm/7 x 7 in., 4.5 cm/1¾ in. high)

INGREDIENTS

For the Sponge

Egg yolks 80 g | gen. 2¾ oz | ⅓ cup
Whole eggs 50 g | 1¾ oz | sc. ¼ cup
Granulated white sugar [1] 50 g | 1¾ oz | ¼ cup
Egg whites 120 g | 4¼ oz | ½ cup
Granulated white sugar [2] 70 g | 2½ oz | ⅓ cup
Potato flour 30 g | 1 oz | 3 tbsp
Plain (all-purpose) flour 50 g | 1¾ oz | ⅓ cup

For the Syrup

Water 50 g | 1¾ fl oz | 3½ tbsp
Granulated white sugar 30 g | 1 oz | 2½ tbsp
Apricot liqueur (40% alcohol) 10 g | gen. ¼ fl oz | 2½ tsp

For the Crunchy Base

Milk chocolate 30 g | 1 oz
Pailleté feuilletine (chopped crêpes dentelles/
French crispy pancakes) 80 g | gen. 2¾ oz | 1 cup
Hazelnut paste 45 g | 1½ oz | 3 tbsp
Hazelnut praline 45 g | 1½ oz | 3 tbsp

For the Sparkling Wine and Apricot Juice Crème Anglaise

Egg yolks 40 g | sc. 1½ oz | gen. 2½ tbsp
Granulated white sugar 70 g | 2½ oz | ⅓ cup
Lemon juice 15 g | ½ fl oz | 3 tsp
Apricot nectar 70 g | sc. 2½ fl oz | 4½ tbsp
Dry sparkling wine 100 g | 3½ fl oz | ½ cup
Gelatine 200 Bloom (gold) 6 g | 3 sheets (softened in ice cold
water, with excess water squeezed out)
Whipping cream (35% fat) 175 g | gen. 6¼ fl oz | sc. ¾ cup

INSTRUCTIONS

Sponge

1 Mix the egg yolks and whole eggs with sugar [1] until they become pale.
2 At the same time, beat the egg whites with sugar [2] in a stand mixer.
3 Combine both mixtures, then fold in the potato flour and plain (all-purpose) flour sifted together.
4 Spread out two squares, a little larger than the frame size, to a thickness of 1 cm (⅜ in.), on silicone baking paper-lined trays, then bake at 200°C (400°F) for 7–10 minutes.
5 Once cooked, transfer immediately onto a wire rack to cool.
6 Reserve at room temperature (about 20°C/68°F).

Syrup

1 Bring the water and sugar to the boil.
2 Cool, then add the liqueur.

Crunchy Base

1 Melt the milk chocolate and mix into the pailleté feuilletine.
2 Add the hazelnut paste and praline, and stir well.
3 Reserve at room temperature (about 20°C/68°F).

Sparkling Wine and Apricot Juice Crème Anglaise

1 Mix the egg yolks, sugar, lemon juice, apricot nectar and half the dry sparkling wine.
2 Cook in a bain-marie to 82–84°C (179–183°F), stirring constantly.
3 Remove from the heat and add the gelatine.
4 Stir well, then cool to 32°C (90°F).
5 Whip the cream and fold into the cooled mixture, together with the rest of the dry sparkling wine. NB The crème must be used immediately.

ASSEMBLING

Components/Garnishes Finely sliced semi-confit apricots (300 g/10½ oz/sc. 1 cup); clear glazing (syrup/pectin mix); fresh apricots; fresh blueberries; tempered chocolate pieces; apricot jam

In the silicone baking paper-lined frame, placed on a tray, spread half the crunchy base in a layer, add one square of sponge cut to fit, then a second layer of the remaining crunchy base. Spread with a 1.5 cm (⅝ in.) layer of crème anglaise, then cover with a layer of half the finely sliced semi-confit apricots. Next place the second square of sponge and spoon over enough of the syrup to moisten the sponge. Add a second 1 cm (⅜ in.) layer of crème anglaise, followed by the remaining sliced semi-confit apricots. Leave to set in the fridge, then spread the clear glaze onto the fruit. Refrigerate to set before unmoulding (this process can be accelerated by placing the mould in the freezer until set). Unmould the square, slice it in half, then into a total of 12 bars, trimming as necessary to create sharp edges. Decorate with fresh apricots, fresh blueberries, tempered chocolate pieces and a smear of apricot jam on the plate.

STRUFFOLI À LA CRÈME DE LIMONCELLO

'This dish illustrates my philosophy,' says Pasquale. 'Through the use of a lemon liqueur and my quirky take on an original recipe, it is a homage to antique Neapolitan tradition and to the wealth of the region and country. *Struffoli* share the same position as *pastiera* or *sfogliatella* as the ultimate Neapolitan Christmas cake. It takes a bit of time to make, but the recipe is fairly easy and it is so worth it!'

MAKES 1 cake (serves 12) **DIFFICULTY** 2/5 **PREPARATION TIME** 3 hours, over 2 days
SPECIFIC EQUIPMENT Straight-blade knife; digital candy thermometer; mould of your choice

INGREDIENTS

For the Struffoli

Plain (all-purpose) flour 500 g | 1 lb 1½ oz | 3⅓ cups
Granulated white sugar 80 g | gen. 2¾ oz | ⅖ cup
Baking powder 5 g | sc. ¼ oz | 1¼ tsp
Salt 10 g | sc. ½ oz | gen. ½ tbsp
½ vanilla pod (bean) (split, scraped, seeds reserved)
Zest of 1 orange
Zest of 1 lemon
Unsalted butter (ideally 82% fat) 50 g | 1¾ oz
5 whole eggs
Oil for deep-frying

For the Limoncello Cream

Whipping cream (35% fat) 250 g | 8¾ fl oz | 1 cup
Glucose syrup 100 g | 3½ fl oz | gen. ¼ cup
1 vanilla pod (bean) (split, scraped, seeds reserved)
White chocolate 300 g | 10½ oz
Limoncello liqueur 50 ml | 1¾ fl oz | 3½ tbsp

INSTRUCTIONS

Struffoli

Day 1

1 Mix all the ingredients, except for the oil, making sure to add the eggs one by one.
2 Knead the dough until homogeneous.
3 Cover the dough with plastic wrap and leave to rest in the fridge for 12 hours.

Day 2

4 Remove the dough from the fridge and roll it out on a cold, flat surface.
5 Cut the dough into strips and roll each by hand into batons 1 cm (⅜ in.) in diameter, while constantly sprinkling with flour.
6 Use a straight-blade knife to cut each baton further into small, round pieces 1 cm (⅜ in.) in diameter.
7 Sift to get rid off any excess flour.
8 Heat the oil to 180°C (356°F) and plunge the dough pieces into it.
9 Gently toss and remove from the oil after 3–4 minutes, or as soon as the pieces are golden.
10 Leave to drain and cool on absorbent paper.

Limoncello Cream

Day 1

1 Bring the cream, glucose syrup and vanilla seeds to the boil.
2 Separately, melt the white chocolate in a bain-marie.
3 Off the heat, emulsify the first mixture in small batches with the melted chocolate.
4 Pour in the liqueur last, and stir.
5 Place in the fridge for 12 hours.

ASSEMBLING

Garnishes Grated orange zest; grated lemon zest

Once the struffoli are at room temperature, add the limoncello cream and mix. Pour into a mould of your choice. Decorate with grated orange and lemon zest. Reserve at 18°C (64°F) or below until set. Unmould, serve and eat within 48 hours.

TORTA VESUVIO

'The "Torta Vesuvio" is a nod to the famous volcano, Mount Vesuvius,' says Pasquale. 'The cake contains crispy bits of crêpes dentelles and hazelnuts, which are traditional staples of the Naples region.'

MAKES 1 cake (serves 10–12)   **DIFFICULTY** 3/5   **PREPARATION TIME** 4½ hours (not including cooling and freezing time)
SPECIFIC EQUIPMENT Round cake tin (pan) (18 cm/7 in. diameter, 7 cm/2¾ in. high); digital candy thermometer; spray gun

INGREDIENTS

For the Cocoa Sponge Cake

Whole eggs 120 g | 4¼ oz | gen. ½ cup
Granulated white sugar 80 g | gen. 2¾ oz | ⅖ cup
Egg yolks 80 g | gen. 2¾ oz | ⅓ cup
Flour (180w) 70 g | 2½ oz | ½ cup
Bitter cocoa powder 8 g | ¼ oz | 1 tbsp
Potato flour 10 g | sc. ½ oz | 1 tbsp
Unsalted butter [1] 30 g | 1 oz (melted)
Unsalted butter [2] (to grease cake tin/pan)

For the Crunchy Base

Pailleté feuilletine (chopped crêpes dentelles/ French crispy pancakes) 80 g | gen. 2¾ oz | 1 cup
Milk chocolate 30 g | 1 oz (melted)
Hazelnut paste 45 g | 1½ oz | 3 tbsp
Hazelnut praline 45 g | 1½ oz | 3 tbsp

For the Hazelnut Bavarian Cream

Milk 90 g | 3 fl oz | 6 tbsp
Gelatine (gold) 5 g | 2½ sheets (softened in ice cold water, with excess water squeezed out)
Egg yolks 50 g | 1¾ oz | sc. 3½ tbsp
Granulated white sugar 30 g | 1 oz | 2½ tbsp
Hazelnut praline 70 g | 2½ oz | 4¼ tbsp
Whipping cream (35% fat) 240 g | sc. 8½ fl oz | 1 cup

For the Chocolate Cream

Egg yolks 40 g | sc. 1½ oz | gen. 2½ tbsp
Granulated white sugar 40 g | sc. 1½ oz | gen. 3 tbsp
Milk 50 g | sc. 1¾ fl oz | sc. 3½ tbsp
Whipping cream (35% fat) 50 g | 1¾ fl oz | ⅕ cup
Dark chocolate couverture (64%) 50 g | 1¾ oz (melted)

For the Rum Syrup

Water 50 g | 1¾ fl oz | 3½ tbsp
Granulated white sugar 30 g | 1 oz | 2½ tbsp
½ vanilla pod (bean) (split, scraped, seeds reserved)
Rum (70% alcohol) 10 g | gen. ¼ fl oz | 2 tsp

For the Spray Gun Chocolate Mixture

Dark chocolate couverture (55%) 70 g | 2½ oz
Cocoa butter 30 g | 1 oz

INSTRUCTIONS

Cocoa Sponge Cake

1 Beat the eggs with the sugar for 7 minutes.
2 Gradually add the egg yolks and beat for 3 minutes.
3 Gently mix in the previously sifted 180w flour, cocoa powder and potato flour, and lastly the melted butter.
4 Grease the cake tin (pan) with butter.
5 Pour in the mixture.
6 Bake for 18–20 minutes at 180°C (350°F).
7 Remove from the oven and immediately transfer to a wire rack to cool as fast as possible.

Crunchy Base

1 Combine the pailleté feuilletine with the melted milk chocolate.
2 Add the hazelnut paste and praline, mixing well.

Hazelnut Bavarian Cream

1 Bring the milk to the boil and add the gelatine, stirring to dissolve.
2 Whisk the egg yolks with the sugar until pale.
3 While whisking, add in the hazelnut praline, then gradually the milk/gelatine mixture.
4 Leave to cool until the mixture reaches 27°C (81°F).
5 Whip the cream, then fold into the cooled mixture.

Chocolate Cream

1 Whisk the egg yolks with the sugar until pale.
2 At the same time, boil the milk and cream, then gradually pour onto the yolk mixture while whisking.
3 Cook in a bain-marie, stirring constantly until the mixture reaches 82°C (180°F).
4 Add to the melted chocolate and gently mix together (you can add a pinch of salt, if desired).
5 Leave in the fridge to set.

Rum Syrup

1 Bring the water, sugar and vanilla seeds to the boil.
2 Leave to cool, then add the rum.

Spray Gun Chocolate Mixture

1 Melt both ingredients and temper them at 30°C (86°F).
2 Use the mixture to spray the cake while the mixture is still liquid but not hot.

ASSEMBLING

Slice the sponge cake in half to form two equal discs, each 1 cm (⅜ in.) high. Place one disc into the silicone baking paper-lined cake tin (pan). Cover with a layer of the crunchy base, 1.2 cm (½ in.) thick. Spread a layer of hazelnut Bavarian cream on top. Soak the second sponge cake disc with the rum syrup, then place on top of the hazelnut cream layer. Spread another layer of hazelnut cream. Freeze, then unmould. Make quenelles of chocolate cream and place in a circle on top of the cake. Freeze. Use a spray gun to lightly coat the cake with the chocolate mixture (one coating from a distance of 20 cm/approx. 8 in.). Return to the fridge to defrost. Finally, decorate as desired before serving.

Ronny Latva

SWEDEN

If you ask Ronny Latva what other career he could have pursued, he does not take long to reply: 'Gardener! I love trees, and nature in general.' We could perhaps have anticipated his answer since R.C. Chocolat, the company he launched with Charlotta Söör in 2002 in Sigtuna, Sweden, is dedicated to improving the art of chocolate- and dessert-making through the use of top-quality ingredients and methods that are as natural as possible.

Along with Calle Jeurling, the pair have recently pushed their ambitions even further by creating a new business. 'Through Quinto Cacao, we do direct and fair trade with cocoa farmers to improve their lives and to make being a cocoa farmer worthwhile,' explains Ronny. 'Unfortunately, today's reality is that it's more lucrative to grow other things, so high-quality fermented cocoa is harder to find.' In the pipeline is the construction of a chocolate factory, where Ronny will be able to oversee the roasting and preparation of the Quinto beans and make whatever adjustments are necessary to obtain the purest flavour. The goal? 'To make Quinto Cacao successful so we can buy lots of beans; and, as we become more important, to spread our vision and make a difference.'

With this project, Ronny has become a chef who manages one of his own core ingredients, with the ultimate aim of controlling the entire production chain from raw material to the treats available on store shelves. It is no surprise that Ronny graduated from the Cordon Bleu with top honours, coinciding with his shift from culinary to pastry chef. 'There's no fast track to knowledge,' he asserts. 'It takes time and hard work. With a few exceptions, the best pastry chefs I know are those who started as culinary chefs.'

Ronny's own creations are traditional, with just the right amount of modern fancy. 'Our customers want something extra. We can make a tart that's perfect in taste, but they won't buy it if it's not uniquely decorated.' He advocates an absolute respect for ingredients and balance of flavours, as well as dedication and a good sense of humour. 'Ozzy Osbourne was served our éclairs on a flight and he was so happy that he ordered chocolate to take home to his family,' says Ronny. 'Well, after all, he is the "prince of darkness", isn't he?'

www.rcchocolat.se | www.quinto.se

BLACK PISTACHIO

This cake is Ronny's solution to showcase the harmony between chocolate and fragrant pistachio. The blackberry panna cotta, hidden inside, adds a vibrant contrast.

MAKES 1 cake (serves 10–12) **DIFFICULTY** 4/5 **PREPARATION TIME** 10 hours **SPECIFIC EQUIPMENT** Cake ring (22 cm/8⅝ in. diameter); cake tin (pan) (20 cm/7¾ in. diameter); digital candy thermometer; spray gun

INGREDIENTS

For the Pistachio Base

Blanched almond meal 100 g | 3½ oz | gen. 1 cup
Icing (confectioner's) sugar 100 g | 3½ oz | sc. ⅔ cup
Pistachio paste 62 g | gen. 2 oz | ¼ cup
Egg whites [1] 62 g | gen. 2 oz | ¼ cup
Egg whites [2] 62 g | gen. 2 oz | ¼ cup
Granulated white sugar 25 g | gen. ¾ oz | 2 tbsp

For the Blackberry Yoghurt Panna Cotta

Blackberry purée 200 g | 7 fl oz | ¾ cup
Granulated white sugar 70 g | 2½ oz | ⅓ cup
1 vanilla pod (bean) (split, scraped, both pod/bean and seeds reserved)
Gelatine (gold) 7 g | 3½ sheets (softened in ice cold water, with excess water squeezed out)
Plain yoghurt 200 g | 7¼ fl oz | sc. 1 cup

For the Dark Chocolate Mousse

Whipping cream (35% fat) 550 g | 19¼ fl oz | 2⅓ cups
Dark chocolate (e.g. Florencio 71% by Quinto Cacao) 385 g | 13½ oz
Granulated white sugar 154 g | sc. 5½ oz | gen. ¾ cup
Water 66 g | gen. 2¼ fl oz | gen. ¼ cup
Egg yolks 242 g | 8½ oz | 1 cup

For the Spray Mixture
(to be made only once the cake is assembled and frozen)

Milk chocolate 87 g | 3 oz
Dark chocolate couverture (70%) 87 g | 3 oz
Cocoa butter 175 g | 6 oz

INSTRUCTIONS

Pistachio Base

1 Mix the almond meal, icing (confectioner's) sugar and pistachio paste with egg whites [1].
2 Whisk egg whites [2] with the granulated sugar to firm peaks.
3 Gently fold the two mixtures together.
4 Spread thinly on a silicone baking paper-lined tray to make a round disc base the diameter of the 22 cm (8⅝ in.) cake ring.
5 Bake at 180°C (350°F) for about 15 minutes, or until golden, then allow to cool and set aside.

Blackberry Yoghurt Panna Cotta

1 Bring the blackberry purée, sugar, and vanilla pod (bean) and seeds to the boil.
2 Remove from the heat.
3 Add the gelatine and stir.
4 Add the yoghurt and stir.
5 Remove the vanilla pod (bean), then pour the mixture into the silicone baking paper-lined 20 cm (7¾ in.) cake tin (pan).
6 Put in the freezer, then, once frozen, unmould and return to the freezer.

Dark Chocolate Mousse

1 Lightly whip the cream and refrigerate.
2 Melt the chocolate in a bain-marie and set aside.
3 Bring the sugar and water to the boil.
4 When the syrup reaches 110°C (230°F), start whisking the egg yolks in a stand mixer until thick and pale.
5 When the syrup reaches 120°C (248°F), add it to the egg yolks a little at a time and whisk until the mixture reaches room temperature.
6 Fold in the melted chocolate, and lastly fold in the lightly whipped cream.

Spray Mixture

1 Melt all the ingredients in a bain-marie and remove from the heat as soon as melted.
2 Put in a spray gun when the mixture is still liquid but not hot.

ASSEMBLING

Components/Garnishes Melted dark chocolate (70%) (perhaps around 150 g/gen. 5¼ oz); fresh blackberries; shelled pistachios

Place the pistachio base inside the 22 cm (8⅝ in.) cake ring fully lined with silicone baking paper. Pour the chocolate mousse inside to half-fill the ring. Press the frozen panna cotta into the mousse. Put more mousse on top and level with a palette knife. Place the cake in the freezer. When frozen, take it out and remove it from the cake ring. Spray all over with the chocolate/cocoa butter mixture, then put back in the fridge. Decorate with melted chocolate and add fresh blackberries and shelled pistachios. You could also add a few pre-bought macarons. Allow 5 hours in the fridge to defrost. Serve at approximately 10°C (50°F).

CHOCOLATE TART

This is Ronny's answer as to how to combine creamy, soft and crispy textures all at the same time, on the same plate.

MAKES 1 tart (serves 6)   **DIFFICULTY** 2/5   **PREPARATION TIME** 4½ hours (including resting time for the dough)
SPECIFIC EQUIPMENT Tart mould (22 cm/8⅝ in. diameter); digital candy thermometer

INGREDIENTS

For the Pâte Sucrée

Unsalted butter 125 g | sc. 4½ oz
Granulated white sugar 50 g | 1¾ oz | ¼ cup
Zest of ½ a lemon
1 whole egg
¼ vanilla pod (bean) (split, scraped, seeds reserved)
Soft flour type 55 (cake flour) 200 g | 7 oz | 1⅓ cups
Salt a pinch

For the Chocolate Filling

Milk 210 g | 7 fl oz | gen. ⅘ cup
Whipping cream (35% fat) 210 g | gen. 7¼ fl oz | ⅘ cup
Honey 40 g | sc. 1½ fl oz | sc. 2 tbsp
Egg yolks 85 g | 3 oz | ⅓ cup
Dark chocolate (e.g. Florencio 71% by Quinto Cacao) 200 g | 7 oz
Milk chocolate (e.g. Milk Chocolate 38% by Quinto Cacao) 100 g | 3½ oz

INSTRUCTIONS

Pâte Sucrée

1   Work the butter, sugar and lemon zest in a stand mixer with a paddle attachment until a creamy texture is achieved.
2   Mix the egg and vanilla seeds, then incorporate little by little into the butter mixture.
3   Sift the flour and salt and add to the mixture, but do not work the dough too long (you do not want the gluten to start working).
4   Let the dough rest in the fridge for 2 hours, wrapped in plastic wrap.
5   Roll out the dough to a thickness of approximately 2.5 mm (⅛ in.), put it in the tart mould and let it rest in the fridge for 1 hour.
6   Blind bake at 180°C (350°F) until golden brown.
7   Remove the blind-baking weights and allow the tart shell to cool before removing from the mould.

Chocolate Filling

1   Heat the milk, cream, honey and egg yolks to 80°C (176°F), stirring constantly.
2   Pour over the dark and milk chocolate, and mix with an immersion blender, or stir thoroughly with a balloon whisk, until a mayonnaise-like consistency is achieved.
3   Pour into the tart shell and chill in the fridge.

ASSEMBLING

Garnishes Fresh raspberries

Carefully arrange fresh raspberries on top of the tart. You can also decorate with tempered chocolate ribbons. Serve at room temperature.

Sébastien Gaudard

FRANCE

No matter how many garnishes and embellishments are added, the most important thing customers want is to taste a pastry that is 'simply good'. This refreshing back-to-basics mantra is fully put to practice by French chef Sébastien Gaudard. 'I believe one of my best character traits that has led me to where I am today is my sincerity, coupled with simplicity. The titles of my desserts keep their promises: they genuinely say it all and spell out what you'll get.'

We can probably trace Sébastien's purist philosophy back to his beginnings, since he was almost literally born in his parents' pâtisserie shop in Pont-à-Mousson. 'While my friends were playing with Play-Doh, I was obsessed with almond paste,' he laughs. He trained under his father, Daniel Gaudard, then took up apprenticeships with Georges Vergne in Audincourt and Gérard Bannwarth in Mulhouse before landing in Paris and experiencing a life-changing encounter with the pastry master, Pierre Hermé, at the gastronomy temple of Fauchon.

Although Sébastien has worked in high-end, decoration-driven pastry environments, he has never stopped avowing his allegiance to authenticity. This can also be explained by his interest in design. 'The look of the pastry has to inform the customer about what the pastry is. A strawberry fruit should herald a strawberry mousse, for instance,' he states. 'I've always been inspired by the creative approach of my designer friends. A shape must above all address a need, a function; then, if it's also aesthetically pleasing, a good design equation has been successfully accomplished.'

No surprise that Sébastien notes he could have been an architect or a designer. The interior of his own shop, La Pâtisserie des Martyrs on rue des Martyrs in Paris, is reminiscent of the cheerfully refined olden days, with celestial blue and white cabinetry, hand-blown clear glass pendant lights and gold-trimmed display shelves laden with classic pastries such as rum babas, mille-feuilles, strawberry tarts and Saint-Honoré cakes. A stroll down memory lane, if you are French or familiar with French pastry culture; if you are not, then a stylish dip into an ever-vibrant gastronomic heritage.

www.sebastiengaudard.fr

SAINT-HONORÉ
This classic French puff pastry is named after Honoratus (St Honoré), Bishop of Amiens, patron saint of bakers and pastry chefs. 'The cake has to be eaten the same day it is made,' notes Sébastien.

MAKES 1 cake (serves 6)   **DIFFICULTY** 3½/5   **PREPARATION TIME** 3½ hours
SPECIFIC EQUIPMENT Piping (pastry) bag with size 9 and 4 round nozzles and special Saint-Honoré nozzle (size 9); digital candy thermometer

INGREDIENTS

For the Crème Chantilly

Whipping cream (35% fat) 480 g | gen. 16¾ fl oz | sc. 2 cups (to be used at 4°C/39°F)
Granulated white sugar 24 g | gen. ¾ oz | 2 tbsp

For the Crème Pâtissière

Milk 372 g | sc. 12¾ fl oz | gen. 1½ cups
Whipping cream (35% fat) 123 g | sc. 4½ fl oz | ½ cup
⅓ vanilla pod (bean) (split, scraped, both pod/bean and seeds reserved)
Granulated white sugar 99 g | 3½ oz | ½ cup
Cornflour (cornstarch) 39 g | sc. 1½ oz | sc. 4 tbsp
Egg yolks 108 g | gen. 3¾ oz | sc. ½ cup
Unsalted butter 24 g | gen. ¾ oz

For the Crème Légère

Crème pâtissière (from above recipe) 700 g | 24½ fl oz | 3 cups
Crème Chantilly (from previous recipe) 140 g | 5 fl oz | 1¼ cups
(Note: the ratio is to add 20% of the crème pâtissière's weight in crème Chantilly)

For the Pâte à Choux

Milk 60 g | 2 fl oz | ¼ cup
Water 60 g | 2 fl oz | ¼ cup
Granulated white sugar 2.5 g | sc. ¾ tsp
Salt 2.5 g | sc. ½ tsp
Unsalted butter 55 g | sc. 2 oz
Bread flour (French type 55 or type 00/white hard-wheat flour) 55 g | sc. 2 oz | sc. ½ cup (sifted)
Whole eggs 125 g | sc. 4½ oz | gen. ½ cup

For the Cake Base and Choux Balls

Ready-made, high-quality puff pastry
Pâte à choux (from above recipe)
Crème légère (from previous recipe)

For the Boiled Sugar

Granulated white sugar 250 g | gen. 8¾ oz | 1¼ cups
Water 75 g | 2½ fl oz | 5 tbsp
Glucose syrup 75 g | gen. 2½ fl oz | gen. 4 tbsp

INSTRUCTIONS

Crème Chantilly

1 Whip the cream and sugar together in a frozen bowl until light and airy.
2 Reserve in the fridge (this cream will be used both for the crème légère below and for the assembling stage).

Crème Pâtissière

1 Bring the milk and cream to the boil.
2 Add the vanilla pod (bean) and seeds.
3 Separately whisk together the sugar, cornflour (cornstarch) and egg yolks, then temper into the hot mixture.
4 Bring the entire mixture back to a simmer for 30 seconds, whisking continuously.
5 Remove from the heat and whisk in the butter.
6 Pour into a shallow dish and cover with plastic wrap.
7 Refrigerate for 2 hours (this cream will be used for the crème légère below).

Crème Légère

1 Remove the vanilla pod (bean) from the crème pâtissière.
2 Whisk the crème pâtissière in a bowl until smooth (if necessary, add a little milk to make up to 700 g/24½ fl oz/3 cups and to ease whisking).
3 Gently fold in the crème Chantilly (the remainder of this cream will be used at assembling stage).

Pâte à Choux

1 Bring the milk, water, sugar, salt and butter to the boil.
2 Incorporate the sifted flour with a spatula.
3 Dehydrate the dough on a medium heat, then place it in the bowl of a stand mixer.
4 Incorporate the eggs, little by little, using the flat beater attachment at speed setting 3.
5 Place in a piping (pastry) bag with a size 9 round nozzle and cool in the fridge before use.

Cake Base and Choux Balls

1 Use a rolling pin to roll out the puff pastry on a hard-floured surface.
2 Stretch each of the sides of the pastry.
3 Cut out a disc according to the desired size: 22 cm (8⅝ in.) diameter for 6 servings; 18 cm (7 in.) diameter for 4 servings; 9 cm (3½ in.) diameter for 1 serving.
4 Pipe a ring of pâte à choux 1 cm (⅜ in.) from the edge of the pastry disc; for the 'serves 6 or 4' sizings, also draw a fine, light spiral of pâte à choux inside the ring, starting from the centre.
5 From the remainder of the choux pastry, prepare choux balls (diameter 2 cm/¾ in.) on silicone baking paper. NB At this stage, one can freeze the various elements and remove them from the freezer when needed.
6 Bake the pastry with the choux ring and the choux balls at 190–200°C (375–400°F) for 25–30 minutes until dry and brown (once the choux have risen, from time to time open the door just a little to let the steam out).
7 Once baked, remove from the oven and leave to cool.
8 Once cool, pierce the choux ring every 2 cm (¾ in.) and pipe with crème légère using nozzle 4; also pipe the crème légère into the choux balls, wiping off any excess.

Boiled Sugar

1 Boil all the ingredients to 158°C (316°F).

ASSEMBLING

Garnishes Roasted almond flakes

Glaze the top part of the choux balls by plunging them into the boiled sugar (at 158°C/316°F), then flip them onto a lightly greased tray. A few minutes later, plunge the bottom half of the choux in the boiled sugar, then stick them to the outer edge of the pastry ring, one ball next to the other. Once the sugar has completely cooled, garnish the inside of the cake with crème légère up to half of the choux height. Complete with crème Chantilly up to the level of the choux. Decorate the top by piping crème Chantilly with a Saint-Honoré-type nozzle. Finally sprinkle a few roasted almond flakes on top (not shown in the photo opposite).

OTHELLO

'For this cake,' says Sébastien, 'it is essential that one chooses a chocolate intense in cocoa flavour so that the sweetness of the meringue will marry perfectly with the pleasant bitterness of the chocolate.'

MAKES 12   **DIFFICULTY** 2/5   **PREPARATION TIME** 2½ hours   **SPECIFIC EQUIPMENT** Piping (pastry) bag with size 8 nozzle

INGREDIENTS

For the Chocolate Ganache

Dark chocolate (70%) 240 g | 8½ oz
Honey (preferably acacia/wattle) 10 g | ¼ fl oz | ½ tbsp
Milk 50 g | sc. 1¾ fl oz | sc. 3½ tbsp
Whipping cream (30–35% fat) 260 g | gen. 9 fl oz | 1 cup
Unsalted butter 90 g | sc. 3¼ oz (room temperature)

For the Meringue

Unsalted butter (to coat tray)
4 egg whites approx. 120 g | 4¼ oz | ½ cup
Granulated white sugar 240 g | 8½ oz | 1⅕ cups
1 vanilla pod (bean) (split, scraped, seeds reserved)

For the Chocolate Shavings

Dark chocolate (70%) 200 g | 7 oz

INSTRUCTIONS

Chocolate Ganache

1   Put the chocolate in a bowl and chop it into little bits with a serrated knife.
2   Add the honey.
3   Bring the milk and cream to the boil in a saucepan.
4   Add the milk/cream mixture to the chocolate mixture in four separate steps, stirring well with a wooden spoon between each addition so that the texture is shiny and smooth at every stage.
5   Once a mayonnaise-like texture is achieved, add the butter and mix with an electric mixer until combined.
6   Allow to set, then reserve at room temperature.

Meringue

1   Pre-heat the oven to 120°C (250°F).
2   Use either a brush or cloth to coat a baking tray with butter.
3   Beat the egg whites and a quarter of the sugar at room temperature.
4   Add the vanilla seeds to the egg white/sugar mixture.
5   Slowly add the second quarter of sugar.
6   Finish with the remaining half of sugar, continually whisking.
7   Place a silicone baking paper sheet on the butter-coated tray and pipe 24 small, rounded (not peaked) meringues to a diameter of approximately 5 cm (2 in.).
8   Place in the oven for 60–75 minutes, first at 120°C (250°F), then reduced to 90°C (195°F) after 20 minutes.
9   Ensure the meringues are cooked through.

Chocolate Shavings

1   Chop the chocolate and process it in a mixer to get a rough powder.

ASSEMBLING

Reserve 200 g (7 oz/sc. 1 cup) of ganache. Use the rest in a piping (pastry) bag to garnish every other meringue shell, then assemble the two halves of meringue together, macaron-style. Place in the fridge for 10 minutes, then use a brush to coat the meringue balls with the reserved ganache. Roll by hand in the chocolate shavings. Reserve in the fridge until ready to serve.

Sébastien Ordioni

FRANCE

When it comes to gastronomy, cultural heritage is important to all societies but probably nowhere more so than in France. So when Frédérique Watremet decided to open Le Macaron Bleu, a pastry shop in the world-renowned Champagne region, she was sure to employ a head chef who could balance the perfect execution of traditional recipes with the subtle introduction of modern tweaks. She found Sébastien Ordioni, who had been working at three-starred restaurants, including establishments run by Gérard Boyer and Arnaud Lallement. Sébastien says it was with them that he learned the necessary work ethics and love of a job well done.

'I don't look for inspiration in foreign cuisine,' he notes, 'other than cheesecake or tiramisu. It's not what our clientele are looking for. They like traditional French pastry – above all, staples from French regions – and that is what I strive to perfect through little personal interpretations.' And it works. Le Macaron Bleu was recently awarded first prize for the best regional Galette des Rois cake; no mean feat when you consider that this Epiphany tradition is a serious business in France.

Sébastien suspects that cooking might run in the genes: his twin brother is also a pastry chef, to their parents' delight (they themselves used to be in the catering business). Sébastien's simple and unpretentious style, combined with the best ingredients, plus of course the secret extra touches that he will not reveal, amount to a winning formula. 'I've been baking pastries and desserts for twenty years – one starts young in this line of work – and my signature has evolved towards lighter and purer concoctions, with an emphasis on healthy choices: less sugar, salt and saturated fat. When I used to work for starred restaurants, the pastry that was on offer was avant-garde compared to what one could find in stores. Those same pastries are now very similar to what reputable pastry shops are providing today. I'm proud to have contributed to this democratization.'

Macaron tower cakes are his customers' favourite, not just for their bravura extravagance but also for their quality. 'A few customers have compared our macarons to those of Ladurée, and they told us ours are better,' quips Sébastien. Just one of the many reasons why people are flocking to Le Macaron Bleu ... and everybody knows that the customer is always right.

http://lemacaronbleu.fr

CHOCOLAT FRAMBOISE

'This cake combines my experiences as a pastry chef in both a restaurant and a shop,' says Sébastien, adding, 'The powerful and pure presence of dark chocolate sits on a soft layer that brings a respite of freshness to the palate.'

MAKES 1 cake (serves 10–12) **DIFFICULTY** 4/5 **PREPARATION TIME** 4½ hours (not including freezing and defrosting time)
SPECIFIC EQUIPMENT Digital candy thermometer; round mould (16 cm/6¼ in. diameter); cake ring (18 cm/7 in. diameter, 4.5 cm/1¾ in. high)

INGREDIENTS

For the Raspberry Crémeux

Whipping cream (35% fat) 83 g | 3 fl oz | ⅓ cup
Milk 42 g | sc. 1½ fl oz | sc. 3 tbsp
Egg yolks 33 g | gen. 1 oz | gen. 2 tbsp
Granulated white sugar 13 g | sc. ½ oz | 1 tbsp
Gelatine (gold) 2 g | 1 sheet (softened in ice cold water,
with excess water squeezed out)
White chocolate couverture 50 g | 1¾ oz
Fresh raspberries 83 g | 3 oz | ⅔ cup

For the Almond/Chocolate Base
(quantity for a 20 x 20 cm/7¾ x 7¾ in. tray)

Icing (confectioner's) sugar 82 g | gen. 2¾ oz | ½ cup
Almond meal 62 g | gen. 2 oz | sc. ¾ cup
Plain (all-purpose) flour 30 g | 1 oz | 2½ tbsp
Cocoa powder 17.5 g | gen. ½ oz | 2½ tbsp
Egg whites 106 g | 3¾ oz | gen. ⅖ cup
Granulated white sugar 56 g | 2 oz | gen. ¼ cup

For the Chocolate Mousse

30° Baumé syrup (ratio: 40 g/sc. 1½ fl oz/sc. 3 tbsp water to
59 g/2 oz/gen. ¼ cup granulated white sugar)
52 g | 1¾ fl oz | 3 tbsp
Egg yolks 31 g | 1 oz | 2 tbsp
Dark chocolate couverture (70%) 88 g | gen. 3 oz
(melted at 40°C/104°F)
Whipping cream (35% fat) 175 g | gen. 6¼ fl oz | sc. ¾ cup
(whipped)

For the Dark Chocolate Glaze
(to be made only once the cake is assembled and frozen)

Granulated white sugar 87 g | 3 oz | sc. ½ cup
Water 27 g | sc. 1 fl oz | sc. 2 tbsp
Black food colouring 2½ drops
Whipping cream (35% fat) 57 g | 2 fl oz | sc. ¼ cup
Glucose syrup 30 g | gen. 1 fl oz | gen. 1½ tbsp
Cocoa powder 32 g | gen. 1 oz | ⅓ cup
Gelatine (gold) 3.75 g | gen. 1¾ sheets (softened in
ice cold water, with excess water squeezed out)

INSTRUCTIONS

Raspberry Crémeux

1. Bring the cream and milk to the boil.
2. At the same time, whisk the egg yolks with the sugar until pale.
3. Pour the cream mixture onto the egg yolk mixture.
4. Cook to 82°C (180°F) in a bain-marie, stirring constantly.
5. Add the gelatine and stir until dissolved.
6. Pour onto the white chocolate and allow to melt while stirring.
7. Pour into the 16 cm (6¼ in.) mould, then evenly position the raspberries over the surface.
8. Leave to set in the freezer.

Almond/Chocolate Base

1. Mix the icing (confectioner's) sugar with the almond meal.
2. Add in the flour and cocoa powder.
3. Whisk the egg whites with the granulated sugar.
4. Fold the egg white mixture into the dry mixture.
5. Spread onto a silicone baking paper-lined tray and bake at 210°C (400°F) for 11 minutes.
6. Leave to cool, then remove the baking paper.
7. Cut out a disc 16 cm (6¼ in.) in diameter.

Chocolate Mousse

1. Heat the 30° Baumé syrup to 110°C (230°F).
2. Pour onto the egg yolks and whisk with an electric beater until completely cool.
3. Pour onto the melted dark chocolate and stir.
4. Gently fold in the whipped cream, then reserve.

Dark Chocolate Glaze

1. Heat the sugar, water and food colouring to 110°C (230°F).
2. Separately bring the cream and glucose syrup to the boil, then stir in the cocoa powder off the heat.
3. Combine both mixtures off the heat, then add the gelatine and stir until dissolved.
4. Process with an immersion blender for 1 minute . NB Do not blend for longer, as the mixture will become bubbly as it cools and you will not be able to obtain the desired smooth, shiny surface.

ASSEMBLING

Place the almond/chocolate disc at the bottom of the cake ring. Pour the chocolate mousse to half-way. Place the disc of frozen raspberry crémeux in the centre. Fill with the remainder of the chocolate mousse and smooth the surface. Leave to set in the freezer. Unmould the cake and coat entirely with the dark chocolate glaze, sitting the cake on a wire rack over a bowl so that any excess glaze drains off. Decorate as you wish (perhaps fresh raspberries or chocolate decorations). Defrost in the fridge before serving.

CHARLOTTE FRAMBOISE AUX BISCUITS ROSES DE REIMS

'This is my personal take on "Home Sweet Home",' confides Sébastien. 'The tartness of lemon and raspberries faces off the *biscuit de Reims*, a traditional sponge biscuit from my native region and city.'

MAKES 1 cake (serves 8–10) **DIFFICULTY** 3½ /5 **PREPARATION TIME** 4½ hours **SPECIFIC EQUIPMENT** Piping (pastry) bag with 1.5 cm (⅝ in.) diameter nozzle; digital candy thermometer; silicone mould (16 cm/6¼ in. diameter), or round cake tin (pan); cake ring (20 cm/7¾ in. diameter)

INGREDIENTS

For the Biscuits Roses de Reims

Egg whites 75 g | gen. 2½ oz | 5 tbsp
Granulated white sugar 63 g | sc. 2¼ oz | sc. ⅓ cup
Red food colouring (to achieve desired colour)
Egg yolks 50 g | 1¾ oz | sc. 3½ tbsp (lightly beaten)
Plain (all-purpose) flour 63 g | sc. 2¼ oz | sc. ½ cup (sifted)
Icing (confectioner's) sugar (to taste)

For the Lemon Sabayon

Egg yolks 40 g | sc. 1½ oz | gen. 2½ tbsp
Granulated white sugar 37 g | gen. 1¼ oz | 3 tbsp
Zest of 1 lemon
Lemon juice 31 g | 1 fl oz | 2 tbsp
Gelatine (gold) 1.5 g | ¾ sheet (softened in ice cold water, with excess water squeezed out)

For the Raspberry Mousse

Raspberry purée 175 g | 6¼ fl oz | sc. ¾ cup
Granulated white sugar 53 g | gen. 1¾ oz | ¼ cup
Gelatine (gold) 5.5 g | 2¾ sheets (softened in ice cold water, with excess water squeezed out)
Whipping cream (35% fat) 263 g | gen. 9¼ fl oz | 1 cup (whipped)

For the Nappage Blond Glaze

Apricot jam (without fruit pieces)
Water (optional)

INSTRUCTIONS

Biscuits Roses de Reims

1   On the reverse side of silicone baking paper, draw two rectangles 8 cm (3⅛ in) high and 32 cm (12⅝ in.) wide, and one circle 18 cm (7 in.) diameter.
2   Whisk the egg whites with a small amount of the granulated sugar.
3   After about 3 minutes, beat in the rest of the sugar to form a meringue, then add the food colouring to create a delicate pink.
4   Carefully mix in the lightly beaten egg yolks, then gently fold in the sifted flour.
5   Pipe fingers of the mixture 8 cm (3⅛ in.) high within the pre-drawn rectangles, leaving a 3 mm (⅛ in.) gap between each finger.
6   Sprinkle with icing (confectioner's) sugar, then leave to rest for 20 minutes before baking.
7   Pipe a round base 18 cm (7 in.) diameter within the pre-drawn circle.
8   Bake the fingers and the base for 8–10 minutes at 175°C (350°F), taking care to avoid browning.
9   Remove from the oven and immediately transfer to a wire rack to cool as fast as possible.

Lemon Sabayon

1   Whisk the egg yolks, sugar and lemon zest until pale.
2   Add in the lemon juice.
3   Cook in a bain-marie to 70°C (158°F), stirring constantly.
4   Add in the gelatine, and stir to dissolve.
5   Using an electric beater, whisk on medium speed until cool.
6   Pour into the 16 cm (6¼ in.) silicone mould or silicone baking paper-lined cake tin (pan), then freeze.

Raspberry Mousse

1   Mix the raspberry purée and sugar, and heat gently.
2   Add the gelatine and stir to dissolve.
3   Fold the mixture into the whipped cream once it begins to thicken as it cools, but before it sets.

Nappage Blond Glaze

1   Warm the jam in a saucepan on a low heat. You may add a spoonful of water if necessary to achieve the desired consistency (neither too viscous nor too liquid).

ASSEMBLING

Garnishes Fresh raspberries and strawberries

Slice the bottom off each row of sponge fingers (lose about 2 cm/¾ in.) to form a straight base. Line the inside of the cake ring with the sponge fingers. Place the base at the bottom of the ring. Pour in half the raspberry mousse. Unmould the disc of frozen lemon sabayon and place it in the centre. Pour in the remainder of the raspberry mousse and smooth with a palette knife. Cover the whole of the top with fresh raspberries and strawberries, and leave to set in the fridge. Use a brush to glaze the fruit with the nappage blond. Alternatively you could dust the top with sifted icing (confectioner's) sugar and add fresh pistachios and tempered, patterned chocolate decorations.

Shigeru Nojima
....

JAPAN

Luxury in the hotel industry is always defined by the quality of the customer service. The ability to listen, to understand and to anticipate a client's expectations is rare, but The Peninsula Hotel group is one of the best there is at doing just that. Chef Shigeru Nojima arrived as executive pastry chef at The Peninsula Tokyo in 2007, having previously worked as pastry chef at the Park Hyatt Tokyo. His current position entails responsibility for all the pastry on offer at The Peninsula. 'One third of our products are standard seasonal items,' he explains. 'We change the restaurant dessert menus every month and The Peninsula Boutique & Café menus six times a year, which includes the creation of eight to ten new products. Of course, in addition, we have all the other seasonal/occasional items.'

Shigeru is a model of perfectionism and dedication. 'I became a pâtissier in my early twenties,' he recalls, 'and, as I gained more experience, it turned out that my products reflected customer preferences.' His ingenuity is matched by the ingrained Japanese obsession with perfection, as seen in the art of gift-giving and wrapping. 'I receive a lot of feedback from guests who've purchased or tasted my sweets,' he shares. 'One time a woman told me she bought one of my cakes and took it to her son in Osaka. That inspired me to make a chocolate cake that comes in an original wooden box. This makes it easier for guests to travel with my sweets.'

Each of his desserts combines classical French aspects with a clever Japanese twist, be it in the form of local ingredients or whimsical details. 'I'm satisfied with all my products but I'm never fully happy, as I feel there's always room for improvement,' he says. 'My decision-making tends to be quick because, if I have too much time to dwell on how to make something even better, it could take me years to achieve the final product!'

This is the typical modesty of the best. Shigeru won silver when he represented Japan at the 2003 Coupe du Monde de la Pâtisserie in Lyon, France – an outstanding achievement, which he has translated into his daily operations. 'I owe my success to everyone around me, while the primary things I rely on are my hands and my experience.' A simple explanation for an extraordinary talent.

www.peninsula.com/Tokyo

ALYA

'I wanted to create something with various textures. When these ingredients melt in your mouth, the balance of acidity makes this one of the most unusual experiences for your palate,' muses Shigeru. 'I made this cake for the Coupe du Monde de la Pâtisserie competition in 2003. It brings back a lot of memories for me.'

MAKES 1 cake (to be served in 12 portions)   **DIFFICULTY** 3½/5   **PREPARATION TIME** 6 hours (not including 2 days for the lemon confiture)
SPECIFIC EQUIPMENT Piping (pastry) bag; bottomless metal rectangular frame #1 (36 cm/14 in. long, 10 cm/4 in. wide, 4 cm/1½ in. high); digital candy thermometer; Silpat® mat, or silicone baking paper-lined tray; bottomless metal rectangular frame #2 (36 cm/14 in. long, 8 cm/3⅛ in. wide, 4 cm/1⅝ in. high)

INGREDIENTS

For the Lemon Confiture
1 whole lemon peel and juice
Granulated white sugar 60 g | gen. 2 oz | gen. ¼ cup

For the Noisette Sponge
Turkish hazelnut meal 70 g | 2½ oz | sc. ¾ cup
Sicilian almond meal 40 g | sc. 1½ oz | sc. ½ cup
Icing (confectioner's) sugar 70 g | 2½ oz | gen. ⅔ cup
Egg whites [1] 35 g | 1¼ oz | sc. 2½ tbsp
Whole eggs 80 g | gen. 2¾ oz | gen. ⅓ cup
Plain (all-purpose) flour 20 g | sc. ¾ oz | 4 tsp
Cultured butter 55 g | sc. 2 oz (soft)
Egg whites [2] 45 g | 1½ oz | 3 tbsp
Granulated white sugar 25 g | gen. ¾ oz | 2 tbsp

For the Nougat Noisette
Turkish hazelnuts 40 g | sc. 1½ oz | gen. ⅖ cup
Granulated white sugar [1] 20 g | sc. ¾ oz | 5 tsp
Unsalted butter 20 g | sc. ¾ oz
Glucose syrup 7.5 g | ¼ fl oz | sc. 1 tsp
Pectin 0.4 g | ⅛ tsp
Granulated white sugar [2] 5.5 g | ¼ oz | 1¼ tsp
Whipping cream (35% fat) 5.5 g | ¼ fl oz | sc. 1 tsp

For the Crème Miel
Fir honey [1] 40 g | sc. 1½ fl oz | sc. 2 tbsp
Whipping cream (35% fat) [1] 200 g | 7 fl oz | ⅘ cup
Egg yolks 53 g | gen. 1¾ oz | sc. ¼ cup
Fir honey [2] 21 g | ¾ fl oz | 1 tbsp
Gelatine (gold) 3 g | 1½ sheets (softened in ice cold water, with excess water squeezed out)
Whipping cream (35% fat) [2] 60 g | gen. 2 fl oz | ¼ cup

For the Chantilly
Gelatine 1 g | ½ sheet (softened in ice cold water, with excess water squeezed out)
Whipping cream (35% fat) 60 g | gen. 2 fl oz | ¼ cup
Icing (confectioner's) sugar 10 g | sc. ½ oz | 1 tbsp

For the Chocolate Mousse
Granulated white sugar [1] 15 g | ½ oz | 1¼ tbsp
Fir honey 15 g | ½ fl oz | 2 tsp
Whipping cream (35% fat) [1] 125 g | 4½ fl oz | ½ cup
Dark chocolate (70%) 185 g | 6½ oz
Egg yolks 50 g | 1¾ oz | sc. 3½ tbsp
Granulated white sugar [2] 15 g | ½ oz | 1¼ tbsp
Whipping cream (35% fat) [2] 295 g | gen. 10¼ fl oz | 1⅓ cups

For the Chocolate Glaçage
Whipping cream (35% fat) 150 g | sc. 5½ fl oz | gen. ½ cup
Trimoline (invert sugar) 22 g | gen. ¾ fl oz | gen. 1 tbsp
Granulated white sugar 18 g | gen. ½ oz | 1½ tbsp
Cocoa powder 9 g | gen. ¼ oz | gen. 1 tbsp
Gelatine (gold) 4.5 g | 2¼ sheets (softened in ice cold water, with excess water squeezed out)
Fir honey 22 g | ¾ fl oz | 1 tbsp
Hazelnut praline 18 g | gen. ½ oz | gen. 1 tbsp
Dark chocolate (56%) 56 g | 2 oz

INSTRUCTIONS

Lemon Confiture
1 Slice the lemon peel and blanch two to three times.
2 Add the sugar and lemon juice and boil until the peel begins to soften.
3 Leave overnight at room temperature.
4 The next day, bring to the boil and cook until the white part of the lemon peel is transparent and softened (or until the Brix scale reads 56%).
5 Leave overnight in the fridge (or until the Brix scale reads 56%), then purée.

Noisette Sponge
1 Mix the hazelnut meal, almond meal, icing (confectioner's) sugar, egg whites [1] and whole eggs in a stand mixer, making sure the mixture is well aerated.
2 Add the flour, then the soft butter.
3 Whisk egg whites [2] and granulated sugar to form a meringue, then fold into the first mixture.
4 Put all the ingredients in a piping (pastry) bag and pipe out onto a silicone baking paper-lined tray to a thickness of 1.2 cm (½ in.), to the same dimensions as bottomless frame #1.
5 Bake at 190°C (375°F) for 15 minutes, leave to cool, then cut to shape/size to fit the frame.

Nougat Noisette
1 Place the hazelnuts in a baking tray and bake at 190°C (375°F) for 10–15 minutes until lightly toasted, then remove from the oven and, while still hot, wrap in a tea towel (dish towel) and rub back and forth until the skins come off; once cool, chop coarsely.
2 Mix the granulated sugar [1], butter and glucose syrup in a saucepan and heat to 80°C (176°F).
3 Add the pectin and granulated sugar [2], and bring to the boil.
4 Add the cream and bring to the boil again, then add the chopped hazelnuts.
5 Spread the mixture out onto a Silpat® mat or silicone baking paper-lined tray.
6 Bake at 160°C (325°F) for 20 minutes, leave to cool, then break into pieces.

Crème Miel
1 Caramelize honey [1], add cream [1], then re-heat.
2 Temper into the egg yolks, then stir in honey [2] and the gelatine.
3 Cook in a bain-marie to 75°C (167°F), then chill on ice until thickened.
4 Whip cream [2] and fold into the mixture.
5 Pour into frame #2, the bottom sealed with plastic wrap, then freeze.

Chantilly
1 Melt the gelatine, then stir into the cream.
2 Mix in the icing (confectioner's) sugar, then whip everything together until stiff.
3 Reserve in the fridge.

Chocolate Mousse
1 Caramelize sugar [1], add the honey, then cream [1], and bring to the boil.
2 Melt the chocolate in a bain-marie, add the egg yolks and sugar [2], and stir well to combine.
3 Temper in the first mixture, then cool to 35°C (95°F).
4 Whip cream [2] and fold into the mixture, then reserve in the fridge.

Chocolate Glaçage
1 Boil the cream and trimoline, then slowly blend in the rest of the ingredients.
2 Mix well with an immersion blender.
3 After removing from the heat, allow to sit at room temperature until cooled to 35°C (95°F).
4 Stir until smooth and shiny.

ASSEMBLING

Pipe the lemon confiture in swirls onto the frozen crème miel and freeze again. Spread the Chantilly cream onto the frozen crème miel/lemon confiture and freeze again. Place the noisette sponge base into frame #1, then pour a layer of chocolate mousse on top. Spread the nougat noisette pieces evenly on top of the mousse. Pipe a new thin layer of mousse to cover the nougat. Next place the frozen crème miel/lemon confiture/Chantilly cream on top. Pipe or pour on more mousse and smooth the top with a palette knife, level with the top of the frame. Freeze (ideally in a blast chiller). Unmould and coat the top with the chocolate glaçage. Allow to defrost, decorate as desired, and cut into slices to serve.

CHESTNUT CAKE

'I love Japanese chestnuts,' exclaims Shigeru, 'and I thought it would be nice to find a way to include something Japanese in my sweets concept. Both adults and children love them, too. They're a seasonal item, so they're very popular.'

MAKES 2 cakes (serve 6-8) **DIFFICULTY** 2/5 **PREPARATION TIME** 1½ hours
SPECIFIC EQUIPMENT 2 x round Kugelhopf cake tins (pans) (12 cm/4¾ in. diameter, 6.5 cm/2½ in. high)

INGREDIENTS

For the Chestnut Cake

Lubeca marzipan almond paste 45 g | 1½ oz | 2¾ tbsp
Bottled/canned Japanese chestnuts 80 g | gen. 2¾ oz | ½ cup (strained)
Granulated white sugar 75 g | gen. 2½ oz | gen. ⅓ cup
Unsalted butter 90 g | sc. 3¼ oz
Whole eggs 130 g | 4½ oz | gen. ½ cup
Soft flour (cake flour) 40 g | sc. 1½ oz | gen. ¼ cup
Bread flour 20 g | sc. ¾ oz | gen. 1½ tbsp
Baking powder 1.2 g | gen. ¼ tsp
Chestnut compote 60 g | 2 fl oz | ¼ cup
Whipping cream (35% fat) 30 g | 1 fl oz | sc. 1¾ tbsp (room temperature)

For the Ganache

Milk 45 g | 1½ fl oz | 3 tbsp
Whipping cream (35% fat) 30 g | 1 fl oz | sc. 1¾ tbsp
Trimoline (invert sugar) 15 g | gen. ½ fl oz | ¾ tbsp
Dark chocolate (56%) 75 g | gen. 2½ oz (chopped)
Dark chocolate (70%) 15 g | ½ oz (chopped)
Unsalted butter 20 g | sc. ¾ oz

INSTRUCTIONS

Chestnut Cake

1   Knead the marzipan paste, strained chestnuts and sugar with a beater.
2   Gradually add the butter and mix until smooth.
3   Gradually add the whole eggs and mix.
4   Sift the soft flour (cake flour), bread flour and baking powder together, then add to the mixture, followed by the chestnut compote.
5   Stir in the cream and spoon the finished mixture into the two cake tins (pans).
6   Bake at 190°C (375°F) for 25-40 minutes, or until cooked when tested.

Ganache

1   Bring the milk, cream and trimoline to the boil.
2   Remove from the heat, add the chopped dark chocolates and stir to melt.
3   When all the chocolate has melted, add the butter and stir to combine.

ASSEMBLING

Garnishes Dried fruits and nuts

Coat the chestnut cakes with the ganache, then decorate with dried fruits and nuts.
NB Best eaten on the same day.

COFFEE, CHOCOLATE AND HAZELNUT PARFAIT

'When I was a child, I loved parfaits,' confides Shigeru. 'I wanted to make a version that not only children would love, but that adults would enjoy as well when dining at a luxury hotel. My kids still love eating parfaits, and when we eat them together they have the biggest smiles. I wanted customers to feel that sense of happiness, too, when eating my parfaits.'

MAKES 10 **DIFFICULTY** 3½/5 **PREPARATION TIME** 4½ hours (not including overnight steeping/setting time for the coffee jelly, coffee panna cotta and hazelnut ice cream) **SPECIFIC EQUIPMENT** Digital candy thermometer; ice cream machine; 10 x ice cream sundae glasses

INGREDIENTS

For the Coffee Jelly

Filter coffee (ideally, blend of Brazilian, Colombian, Guatemalan and Tanzanian) 500 ml | 17½ fl oz | gen. 2 cups
Granulated white sugar 100 g | 3½ oz | ½ cup
Gelatine (gold) 10 g | 5 sheets (softened in ice cold water, with excess water squeezed out)
Cognac 14 g | ½ fl oz | sc. 1 tbsp

For the Coffee Panna Cotta

Milk 500 g | 17 fl oz | gen. 2 cups
Whipping cream (35% fat) 190 g | sc. 6¾ fl oz | ¾ cup
Coffee beans (blend of Brazilian, Colombian, Guatemalan and Tanzanian) 125 g | sc. 4½ oz | 1⅔ cups
Granulated white sugar 75 g | gen. 2½ oz | gen. ⅓ cup
Gelatine (gold) 6 g | 3 sheets (softened in ice cold water, with excess water squeezed out)

For the Hazelnut Ice Cream

Turkish hazelnuts 140 g | sc. 5 oz | gen. 1½ cups
Milk 500 g | 17 fl oz | gen. 2 cups
Whipping cream (35% fat) 500 g | 17½ fl oz | 2 cups
½ Tahitian vanilla pod (bean) (split, scraped, both pod/bean and seeds reserved)
Granulated white sugar 210 g | sc. 7½ oz | 1 cup
Ice cream stabilizer 3 g | sc. 1 tsp
Egg yolks 175 g | 6 oz | sc. ¾ cup
Salt a pinch

For the Chocolate Ice Cream

Milk 500 g | 17 fl oz | gen. 2 cups
Whipping cream (35% fat) 50 g | 1¾ fl oz | ⅕ cup
¼ Tahitian vanilla pod (bean) (split, scraped, both pod/bean and seeds reserved)
Cocoa powder 12.5 g | sc. ½ oz | 4 tsp
Trimoline (invert sugar) 50 g | 1¾ fl oz | 2½ tbsp
Ice cream stabilizer 2.5 g | sc. 1 tsp
Granulated white sugar 75 g | gen. 2½ oz | gen. ⅓ cup
Egg yolks 80 g | gen. 2¾ oz | ⅓ cup
Dark chocolate (53%) 125 g | sc. 4½ oz (chopped)
Dark chocolate (66%) 25 g | gen. ¾ oz (chopped)

For the Chocolate Sauce

Water 25 g | gen. ¾ fl oz | 5 tsp
Milk 120 g | 4 fl oz | ½ cup
Whipping cream (35% fat) 35 g | gen. 1 fl oz | sc. 2 tbsp
Cocoa powder 7.5 g | ¼ oz | 1 tbsp
Granulated white sugar 15 g | ½ oz | 1¼ tbsp
Dark chocolate (70%) 35 g | 1¼ oz (chopped)

For the Crunchy Chocolate

Pailleté feuilletine (chopped crêpes dentelles/ French crispy pancakes) 90 g | sc. 3¼ oz | 1 cup
Toasted almonds 30 g | 1 oz | ⅓ cup (finely chopped)
Milk chocolate 90 g | sc. 3¼ oz

INSTRUCTIONS

Coffee Jelly

1 Boil the filter coffee to 80°C (176°F).
2 Add the sugar and gelatine, and stir until dissolved.
3 Add the cognac.
4 Refrigerate to set overnight.

Coffee Panna Cotta

1 Mix the milk, cream and coffee beans, and leave to steep overnight in the fridge.
2 The next day bring the mixture to the boil, then strain.
3 Add the sugar and gelatine, and stir well until completely dissolved.
4 Chill on ice until thickened, then reserve in the fridge.

Hazelnut Ice Cream

1 Place the hazelnuts in a baking tray and bake at 190°C (375°F) for 10–15 minutes until lightly toasted, then remove from the oven and, while still hot, wrap in a tea towel (dish towel) and rub back and forth until the skins come off; once cool, chop them.
2 Mix the milk, cream, chopped hazelnuts, and vanilla pod (bean) and seeds, and bring to the boil.
3 Cool and leave to steep overnight in the fridge.
4 The next day strain the solids, add a small amount of the sugar and the ice cream stabilizer, and bring to the boil again.
5 Whisk together the egg yolks, the remainder of the sugar and the salt until pale, then temper with the boiling mixture and cook to 85°C (185°F).
6 Cool quickly and churn in an ice cream machine according to the manufacturer's instructions.

Chocolate Ice Cream

1 Mix the milk, cream, vanilla pod (bean) and seeds, cocoa powder and trimoline, and bring to the boil.
2 Mix in the ice cream stabilizer and half the sugar, and bring to the boil again.
3 Whisk the egg yolks and the other half of the sugar until pale, then temper with the boiling mixture and cook to 85°C (185°F).
4 Remove the vanilla pod (bean), stir in the chopped dark chocolates and, once melted, leave to cool.
5 Churn in an ice cream machine according to the manufacturer's instructions.

Chocolate Sauce

1 Mix the water, milk and cream, and bring to the boil.
2 Add the cocoa powder mixed with the sugar, and stir until dissolved.
3 Add the chopped chocolate, stirring until melted.
4 Chill and reserve in the fridge.

Crunchy Chocolate

1 Mix the pailleté feuilletine and the finely chopped almonds.
2 Melt the milk chocolate and stir into the almond mixture.
3 Spread on a silicone baking paper-lined tray and put aside to set.
4 When cool, break into chunks.

ASSEMBLING

Components/Garnishes Fresh fruit; tempered dark chocolate sheets; chocolate-coated finger biscuits or wafers (optional)

Place your choice of fruit in each ice cream sundae glass, then add the panna cotta and jelly. Add the hazelnut ice cream and chocolate ice cream, then pour on the chocolate sauce. Decorate with crunchy chocolate, broken pieces of tempered dark chocolate and a biscuit or wafer, if using.

Siang Yee

At a crossroads between Western pastry techniques and Asian influences meet Singapore-based Siang Yee, who has steadily built a small but ever-growing empire with her sister and business manager, Siang Oon. Together, the pair have established a strong reputation for their three complementary businesses: The Patissier, their pastry shop showcasing the best of Siang Yee's repertoire; The Patissier's Design Concierge service, the ultimate tailoring experience whereby customers can order the cake of their dreams; and, last but not least, Petite Patisserie, the aim of which is to turn frozen mousse cakes that are free from artificial preservatives but have a long shelf life into the new Ben & Jerry's-style sensation – no mean feat for a self-described 'petite' person.

'After I graduated with a business degree,' Yee recalls, 'I told my parents I wanted to open a pastry shop. They were quite shocked and my sister asked me, "Are you sure? The equipment is huge, the hours are long, and you are so tiny!"' But Yee was sure. Following a traineeship at the legendary Raffles Hotel, she moved to London, where she graduated from the Cordon Bleu pastry course. Since then she has adapted her signature baking to an ever-more demanding Singaporean market by anticipating what her customers will want.

She designs collections around a key ingredient or technique: cakes based on mascarpone one year and meringue the next. 'I've found that the Singaporean palate has evolved over time. Customers have become more sophisticated and they require cakes that are more complex in taste and texture.' Yee doesn't have favourites: 'I like playing with new ingredients all the time, even ingredients that I don't particularly like. For example, I don't eat tofu but I created a lemongrass crème brûlée tofu cake.'

While she is part designer ('the appearance is vital') and part scientist ('cake-making is a precise science'), Yee primarily cherishes craft, as seen in her interest in origami and flower arranging. 'They have helped me appreciate quiet beauty,' she says, 'while my love of food – all types of food – has helped me to be more experimental in my cake creations.' Cultural fusion has never tasted so sweet.

www.thepatissier.com

MANGO BASIL

'This recipe was inspired by my love for Thai cuisine,' notes Siang Yee. Initially she experimented with traditional herbs and spices, such as lemongrass and peppercorns, but they did not work well with mango. She then opted for a herb with a floral scent – basil – and found a match made in heaven.

MAKES 1 cake (serves 6) **DIFFICULTY** 3/5 **PREPARATION TIME** 2 hours (not including freezing/setting time)
SPECIFIC EQUIPMENT Piping (pastry) bag with size 10 nozzle; cake ring (15 cm/6 in. diameter, at least 6 cm/2⅜ in. high)

INGREDIENTS

For the Mango Mousse
Honey 50 g | 1¾ fl oz | sc. 2½ tbsp
Mango purée 170 g | 6 fl oz | ⅔ cup
Basil leaves 1.5 g | ½ tbsp (extremely finely chopped)
Gelatine (gold) 4 g | 2 sheets (softened in ice cold water, with excess water squeezed out)
Whipping cream (35% fat) 170 g | 6 fl oz | ⅔ cup (whipped to a soft peak)

For the Sponge
2 whole eggs
Granulated white sugar 70 g | 2½ oz | ⅓ cup
Plain (all-purpose) flour 50 g | 1¾ oz | ⅓ cup
Icing (confectioner's) sugar (to taste)

For the Glaze
Mango purée 100 g | 3½ fl oz | ⅖ cup
Water 65 ml | gen. 2¼ fl oz | gen. ¼ cup
Glucose syrup 16 g | gen. ½ fl oz | sc. 1 tbsp
Granulated white sugar 16 g | ½ oz | sc. 1½ tbsp
Gelatine (gold) 6 g | 3 sheets (softened in ice cold water, with excess water squeezed out)

INSTRUCTIONS

Mango Mousse
1 Combine the honey with the mango purée, and bring to the boil.
2 Add the basil leaves, followed by the gelatine, and stir gently.
3 Leave to cool, then fold in the whipped cream.

Sponge
1 Separate the egg whites from the egg yolks.
2 Beat the egg whites with the granulated sugar until soft peaks form.
3 Fold in the egg yolks and flour.
4 To create the outer sponge columns, draw two rectangles, each 5 x 24 cm (2 x 9½ in.), on the reverse side of a piece of silicone baking paper placed on a baking tray; within each rectangle, pipe the mixture into vertical 5 cm (2 in.) lines, leaving a gap between each line the same width as the piped sponge; sprinkle with icing (confectioner's) sugar prior to baking.
5 To create the sponge layer inserts, draw a rectangle 14 x 28 cm (5½ x 11 in.) on the reverse side of a piece of waxed paper placed on a baking tray; within the rectangle pipe the rest of the mixture into parallel lines (these lines should merge).
6 Bake both sets of sponges at 200°C (400°F) for 8 minutes, or until golden brown.
7 Remove from the oven and immediately transfer to a wire rack to cool as fast as possible.

Glaze
1 Boil the mango purée, water, glucose syrup and sugar together, then add the gelatine.
2 Stir until the gelatine is completely dissolved, then leave to cool.

ASSEMBLING

Components/Garnishes Fresh mangoes (50 g/1¾ oz/gen. 3 tbsp, cubed and soaked in rum for 15–20 minutes); mango salsa

Sit the cake ring on greaseproof paper, then line the inside of the ring with the strips of sponge columns, trimming as necessary. Cut the sponge layer inserts into two rounds, approximately 13 cm (5 in.) in diameter, to form the base and second layer of the cake; these should both fit inside the ring now lined with sponge columns. Insert the sponge base, layer the mango mousse over it and sprinkle with rum-soaked mango cubes, allowing enough room to insert the second sponge layer so that it sits level with the top of the side columns. Repeat with another layer of mousse on top of the second sponge layer, almost to the top of the ring. Place the cake in the freezer for about 1 hour, or until set. Use a palette knife or similar to spread a layer of glaze evenly on top, then remove the cake from the ring. Serve with a mango salsa on the side. Optionally, you could also add a small disc of sponge dusted with icing (confectioner's) sugar, topped with a dollop of mousse and garnished with fresh berries, red berry purée and gold leaf.

EMPRESS DOWAGER

This cake is a tribute to Siang Yee's mother, who loves berries. Fittingly, it was created for a Mother's Day celebration.

MAKES 1 cake (serves 6)   **DIFFICULTY** 3/5   **PREPARATION TIME** 2 hours   **SPECIFIC EQUIPMENT** Cake ring (15 cm/6 in. diameter); piping (pastry) bag

INGREDIENTS

For the Mousse

Strawberry purée 100 g | 3½ fl oz | ⅖ cup
Icing (confectioner's) sugar 22 g | ¾ oz | gen. 2 tbsp
Gelatine (gold) 3 g | 1½ sheets (softened in ice cold water, with excess water squeezed out)
Whipping cream (35% fat) 190 g | sc. 6¾ fl oz | ¾ cup (whipped)

For the Royaltine

Milk chocolate 40 g | sc. 1½ oz
Praline paste 50 g | 1¾ oz | 3 tbsp
Pailleté feuilletine (chopped crêpes dentelles/French crispy pancakes) 30 g | 1 oz | 5¼ tbsp

For the Sponge

2 whole eggs
Brown sugar 70 g | 2½ oz | ⅓ cup
Plain (all-purpose) flour 50 g | 1¾ oz | ⅓ cup

For the Glaze

Strawberry purée 100 g | 3½ fl oz | ⅖ cup
Water 65 ml | gen. 2¼ fl oz | gen. ¼ cup
Glucose syrup 16 g | gen. ½ fl oz | sc. 1 tbsp
Granulated white sugar 16 g | ½ oz | sc. 1½ tbsp
Gelatine (gold) 6 g | 3 sheets (softened in ice cold water, with excess water squeezed out)

INSTRUCTIONS

Mousse

1   Boil the strawberry purée with the sugar.
2   Remove from the heat.
3   Add the gelatine and whisk to dissolve.
4   Allow the mixture to cool.
5   Fold in the whipped cream.

Royaltine

1   Melt the chocolate with the praline paste in a bain-marie, then fold in the pailleté feuilletine.
2   While warm, spread onto waxed paper at the base of the cake ring.
3   Leave to set in the fridge.

Sponge

1   Separate the egg whites from the egg yolks.
2   Beat the whites with the brown sugar until soft peaks form, then fold in the yolks and the flour.
3   Spread the batter onto a silicone baking paper-lined tray.
4   Bake at 200°C (400°F) for 6–8 minutes, or until golden brown.
5   Remove from the oven and immediately transfer to a wire rack to cool as fast as possible.

Glaze

1   Bring the strawberry purée, water, glucose syrup and sugar to the boil.
2   Add the gelatine and stir until completely dissolved.
3   Leave the mixture to cool.

ASSEMBLING

Components/Garnishes Crushed frozen raspberries (30 g/1 oz/4 tbsp); fresh fruits; dark chocolate sauce; chocolate decoration

Take the cake ring out of the fridge. Cut the sponge into strips 4 cm (1⅝ in.) high and 25 cm (9¾ in.) wide. Spread mousse across each strip, then sprinkle crushed frozen raspberries on top. Roll each strip to resemble a Swiss roll (jelly roll). Spread some mousse around the inside of the cake ring, then place the rolls into the ring. Use a piping (pastry) bag to fill any gaps between the rolls with mousse. Place the ring in the freezer for 30–60 minutes to allow it to set. Then remove the ring from the freezer and gently heat the outside with a burner: the cake should slide out, but may need a slight push. Heat up a palette knife and smooth all around the cake. Decorate the top with the strawberry glaze. Style with fresh fruits, such as red berries, drizzled dark chocolate sauce and a chocolate decoration. After unmoulding and before styling you could also spray the cake with equal quantities of cocoa butter and white chocolate melted together (as shown in the photo opposite).

Art on a Plate

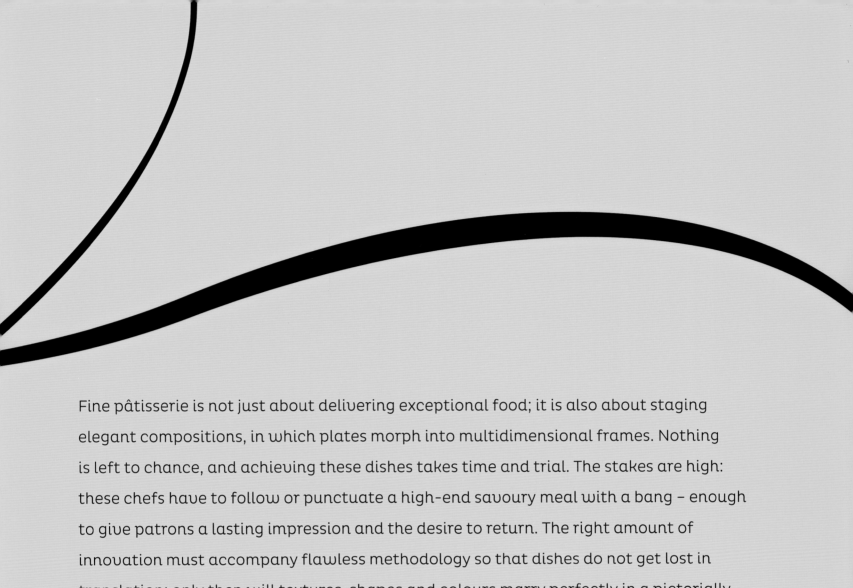

Fine pâtisserie is not just about delivering exceptional food; it is also about staging elegant compositions, in which plates morph into multidimensional frames. Nothing is left to chance, and achieving these dishes takes time and trial. The stakes are high: these chefs have to follow or punctuate a high-end savoury meal with a bang – enough to give patrons a lasting impression and the desire to return. The right amount of innovation must accompany flawless methodology so that dishes do not get lost in translation; only then will textures, shapes and colours marry perfectly in a pictorially harmonious design. The saying 'one eats first with one's eyes' certainly applies here. So keep your eyes wide open, absorb everything and cherish the moment, as it will be the only opportunity you have to dig a spoon into what looks like an abstract painting.

Anna Polyviou

AUSTRALIA

When Australian pastry chef Anna Polyviou produced a dish while competing for the Cacao Barry 'Best Chocolate Plated Dessert', a woman quipped, 'This is better than sex!' Anna's immediate thought was to wonder where the woman was getting her sex from, then she welcomed the compliment.

It was in fact almost by chance that this friendly, engaging personality discovered her talent for pastry-making. 'Halfway through my apprenticeship, I was thrown into a competition that I didn't necessarily want to compete in, but the chefs were desperate for someone,' she recalls. 'I had to learn quickly because the last thing I wanted was to make a fool of myself. It turned out well and, from then on, I decided to compete more, head off overseas, go to university and learn as much as I could, to eventually come back and educate other young pastry chefs.'

Anna has now won multiple awards, including the Nadell Trophy for 'Dessert of the Year' and the Culinary Academy Award of Excellence for pastry. Nevertheless she always gives credit to others, such as her former sous-chef Brookie Stephens, and stresses the importance of 'understanding your team, from the kitchen porters to the suppliers to the restaurant manager; people who support you and are beside you, helping transform your imagination into a creation on a plate'.

She trained with great names, such as Jérôme Landrieu, Jean-Marie Auboine and Kirsten Tibballs, and, following experiences with royal pastry chef Kathryn Boyden, Pierre Hermé in Paris and Julie Sharp (see p. 156) at Claridge's, London (Julie became her mentor and taught her 'how to construct a well-balanced menu with textures, colours and techniques'), Anna eventually settled in Sydney, where she ran Bather's Pavilion in Balmoral, receiving several more awards and media recognition. She also contributes to cookbooks, consults for the Orion cruise line, co-chairs the Sydney Pastry Club and writes for *Australian Baking Business* magazine. All this multi-tasking attests to Anna's expertise and unique style, which appeal to pastry industry connoisseurs, business leaders and patrons alike. So much so that she is now executive pastry chef at the Shangri-La Hotel, Sydney. This five-star destination has been quick to add an extra shining star to its crown.

www.shangri-la.com/sydney/shangrila

TROPIC-ANNA | COCONUT DACQUOISE, FEUILLETINE CRUNCH, PIÑA COLADA CRÈME, TROPICAL COMPOTE

'Nothing beats a cocktail or high tea, so I wanted to have the two in one,' quips Anna. 'I used the flavours of a piña colada and twisted them into "Tropic-Anna", Anna being my name, of course. I used different recipes that I knew worked on their own and could work well together.'

MAKES 20   **DIFFICULTY** 3/5   **PREPARATION TIME** 3 hours   **SPECIFIC EQUIPMENT** Piping (pastry) bag with size 8 nozzle; acetate sheets; circle cutter (5.5 cm/2⅛ in. diameter); circle cutter (3 cm/1⅛ in. diameter)

INGREDIENTS

For the Piña Colada Crème
Coconut purée/cream 300 ml | sc. 10¾ fl oz | sc. 1¼ cups
Caster (superfine) sugar 75 g | gen. 2½ oz | ⅓ cup
Gelatine (gold) 15 g | 7½ sheets (softened in ice cold water, with excess water squeezed out)
Crème fraîche 150 ml | sc. 5⅓ fl oz | gen. ½ cup
Whipping cream (35% fat) 370 ml | 13 fl oz | 1½ cups (semi-whipped)
Malibu rum 50 ml | 1¾ fl oz | sc. ¼ cup

For the Coconut Dacquoise 'Sponge'
(makes 2 x 400 g/14 oz, 400 g/14 oz per tray)
Blanched almond meal 200 g | 7 oz | 2⅓ cups
Plain (all-purpose) flour 60 g | gen. 2 oz | sc. ½ cup
Icing (confectioner's) sugar 240 g | 8½ oz | 1½ cups
Egg whites 300 g | 10½ oz | 1¼ cups
Caster (superfine) sugar 135 g | 4¾ oz | gen. ½ cup
Desiccated (shredded) coconut 100 g | 3½ oz | 1⅓ cups

For the Feuilletine
White chocolate 400 g | 14 oz
Pailleté feuilletine (chopped crêpes dentelles/ French crispy pancakes) 150 g | gen. 5¼ oz | sc. 2 cups

For the White Chocolate Discs
White chocolate 400 g | 1 lb 1½ oz

INSTRUCTIONS

Piña Colada Crème
1 Warm the coconut purée/cream and sugar in a small saucepan.
2 Remove from the heat and add the gelatine.
3 Pour into a bowl and whisk in the crème fraîche.
4 Allow to cool until semi-set.
5 Once semi-set, whisk again by hand and fold through the semi-whipped cream, followed by the Malibu rum.
6 Place in the piping (pastry) bag and reserve in the fridge.

Coconut Dacquoise 'Sponge'
1 Sift together the almond meal, plain (all-purpose) flour and icing (confectioner's) sugar.
2 Whisk the egg whites in a stand mixer until soft peaks form, gradually adding the caster (superfine) sugar.
3 Take the mixture off the machine and gently fold through the sifted dry ingredients, along with the desiccated (shredded) coconut.
4 Spread onto two silicone baking paper-lined trays, 400 g (14 oz) per tray, and bake at 160°C (325°F) for 6 minutes, or until cooked.
5 Remove from the oven and immediately transfer to a wire rack to cool as fast as possible.

Feuilletine
1 Melt the white chocolate and mix in the pailleté feuilletine.
2 Spread evenly onto the dacquoise 'sponges' (from above recipe) once these have cooled.
3 Place into the freezer.

White Chocolate Discs
1 Temper the chocolate.
2 Spread thinly onto acetate sheets.
3 Once semi-set, cut into 20 discs of 5.5 cm (2⅛ in.) diameter and 20 discs of 5.5 cm (2⅛ in.) diameter with a 3 cm (1⅛ in.) hole cut out in the middle.

ASSEMBLING

Components/Garnishes Fresh tropical fruit, such as pineapple, mango, papaya or passion fruit pulp, according to season; sprigs of lemon balm

For each of the 20 cakes, cut out the dacquoise 'sponge' to a diameter of 5.5 cm (2⅛ in.). Place a 5.5 cm (2⅛ in.) white chocolate disc on top. Pipe small rounds of the piña colada crème around the disc, then place a white chocolate disc with the centre cut out on top. In the centre place 0.5 cm (³⁄₁₆ in.) dices of tropical fruit. Garnish each cake with three sprigs of lemon balm.

BREAKFAST VERRINE | VANILLA PANNA COTTA, PAIN PERDU, HONEY CRUNCH GRANOLA, MILK TAPIOCA, STRAWBERRY AND YOGHURT SORBET

'My favourite meal of the day is breakfast,' explains Anna. 'I wrote down different breakfast products that are also sweet, such as French toast (*pain perdu*), granola and yoghurt. I wanted to have different layers within a glass, and I also wanted to outline different textures so as to create something that wasn't simply visually exciting.'

MAKES 8 **DIFFICULTY** 4/5 **PREPARATION TIME** 3–4 hours **SPECIFIC EQUIPMENT** Digital candy thermometer; piping (pastry) bag; 8 x savarin moulds (each 8 cm/3⅛ in. diameter); sorbet machine; 2 x equal-size flat baking trays (each approx. 40 x 25 cm/15¾ x 9¾ in.); 2 x Silpat® mats; 8 x large stemless wine glasses (each 500 ml/17 fl oz volume)

INGREDIENTS

For the Honey Granola
(makes more than required, but a more manageable amount)

Rolled oats 125 g | sc. 4½ oz | sc. 1 cup
Desiccated (shredded) coconut 18 g | gen. ½ oz | sc. ¼ cup
Blanched almonds 43 g | 1½ oz | ½ cup (roughly chopped)
Sunflower seeds 15 g | ½ oz | 2 tbsp
Pumpkin seeds 15 g | ½ oz | 2 tbsp
Brown sugar 25 g | gen. ¾ oz | 2 tbsp
Honey 38 ml | 1¼ fl oz | 2½ tbsp
Sunflower oil 7.5 ml | ¼ fl oz | 1½ tsp
Vanilla paste 15 g | ½ oz | 1 tbsp

For the Strawberry Jelly
Strawberry Essence

Frozen strawberries 500 g | 1 lb 1½ oz | 3½ cups
(roughly chopped)
Granulated white sugar 50 g | 1¾ oz | ¼ cup
Juice of ½ a lemon

Jelly

Water 125 ml | sc. 4½ fl oz | ½ cup
Gelatine (gold) 12 g | 6 sheets (softened in ice cold water, with excess water squeezed out)
Strawberry essence (from above recipe)
250 ml | gen. 8¾ fl oz | gen. 1 cup

For the Vanilla Panna Cotta

Milk 250 ml | gen. 8¾ fl oz | gen. 1 cup
Granulated white sugar 100 g | 3½ oz | ½ cup
1 vanilla pod (bean) (split, scraped, both pod/bean and seeds reserved)
Gelatine (gold) 18 g | 9 sheets (softened in ice cold water, with excess water squeezed out)
Whipping cream (35% fat) 750 ml | 26¼ fl oz | 3 cups
(room temperature)

For the Tapioca Milk Sauce
Tapioca

Water 2 litres | sc. 70½ fl oz | sc. 8½ cups
Tapioca 250 g | gen. 8¾ oz | 1⅓ cups

Anglaise Sauce

Milk 250 ml | gen. 8¾ fl oz | gen. 1 cup
Whipping cream (35% fat) 250 ml | 8¾ fl oz | 1 cup
Granulated white sugar [1] 88 g | gen. 3 oz | sc. ½ cup
½ vanilla pod (bean) (split, scraped, both pod/bean and seeds reserved)
Granulated white sugar [2] 88 g | gen. 3 oz | sc. ½ cup
Egg yolks 100 g | 3½ oz | ⅖ cup

INSTRUCTIONS

Honey Granola

1 Pre-heat the oven to 120°C (250°F).
2 Place the oats, coconut, roughly chopped almonds and seeds in a bowl and mix well.
3 Bring the sugar, honey, oil and vanilla paste to the boil in a large saucepan, then remove from the heat.
4 Add the dry ingredients to the saucepan and stir well, until the dry mixture is coated.
5 Spread evenly on a baking tray and bake for 40 minutes, or until golden brown.

Strawberry Jelly
Strawberry Essence

1 Toss the roughly chopped frozen strawberries, the sugar and the lemon juice together in a bowl, then seal the top with plastic wrap.
2 Place the bowl over a saucepan of boiling water (making a bain-marie) for 3–4 hours, simmering on a low heat.
3 Strain, then use the juice to make the jelly (below).

Jelly

4 Bring the water to the boil in a small saucepan, then remove from the heat and add the gelatine and strawberry essence.
5 Reserve for assembling at room temperature.

Vanilla Panna Cotta

1 Bring the milk, sugar, vanilla pod (bean) and seeds to the boil in a medium saucepan.
2 Add the gelatine to the boiling liquid.
3 Pass through a fine sieve (strainer).
4 Add the cream and use when the panna cotta has started to thicken/is semi-set (this is so that, when the panna cotta is mixed, the vanilla seeds have dispersed evenly through the mixture).
5 Reserve for assembling at room temperature.

Tapioca Milk Sauce
Tapioca

1 Bring the water to the boil, then add the tapioca.
2 Boil the tapioca until transparent, stirring so that it doesn't stick together.
3 Strain and run under cold water until the tapioca is cold.

Anglaise Sauce

4 Bring the milk, cream, sugar [1] and vanilla pod (bean) and seeds to the boil in a medium saucepan.
5 Whisk together sugar [2] and the egg yolks, temper in the hot liquid, then return to the stove and cook until the mixture reaches 85°C (185°F).
6 Strain and cool over ice water.

Putting Together the Tapioca Milk Sauce

7 Stir the cooked tapioca in a bowl, together with 500 g (17½ fl oz/gen. 2 cups) of the anglaise sauce.
8 Place the tapioca milk sauce into a container.
9 Leave to cool.

For the Pain Perdu

Pain Perdu

Strong flour (bread flour) 100 g | 3½ oz | ¾ cup

Salt 2 g | gen. ¼ tsp

Granulated white sugar 10 g | sc. ½ oz | 2½ tsp

Milk 67 ml | gen. 2¼ fl oz | 4½ tbsp

Fresh yeast 7 g | ¼ oz | 1 tsp

1 whole egg (whisked)

Unsalted butter 50 g | 1¾ oz | (very soft)

Soaking Mixture

3 whole eggs

Granulated white sugar 25 g | gen. ¾ oz | 2 tbsp

Milk 75 ml | gen. 2½ fl oz | 5 tbsp

Whipping cream (35% fat) 75 ml | sc. 2¾ fl oz | sc. ⅓ cup

Unsalted butter (to fry pain perdu)

Cinnamon Sugar

Granulated white sugar 50 g | 1¾ oz | ¼ cup

Ground cinnamon 5 g | sc. ¼ oz | 2 tsp

For the Yoghurt Sorbet

Water 175 ml | 6 fl oz | ¾ cup

Granulated white sugar 175 g | 6 oz | sc. 1 cup

Greek yoghurt (natural) 425 g | 15 oz | 1¾ cups

For the Strawberry Sorbet

Granulated white sugar 50 g | 1¾ oz | ¼ cup

Glucose syrup 12 ml | ½ fl oz | sc. 1 tbsp

Sorbet stabilizer 1.5 g | ½ tsp

Water 45 ml | 1½ fl oz | 3 tbsp

Strawberry purée 250 ml | 9 fl oz | 1 cup

For the Pink Bubble Sugar

Granulated isomalt sugar 50 g | 1¾ oz | ¼ cup

Light red food colouring powder speck/tip of pointed knife

Pain Perdu

Pain Perdu

1 Place the flour, salt and sugar in the bowl of a stand mixer with a paddle attachment.
2 Slightly warm the milk in a small saucepan, remove from the heat, then add the yeast.
3 Start mixing the dry ingredients with the milk mixture, then add the whisked egg.
4 Prove for 3 minutes, then place back in the mixer, gradually adding the softened butter.
5 Leave the mix for up to 1 hour in a warm place (ideally 35°C/95°F), so it proves and doubles in volume.
6 Pipe into the savarin moulds and leave to sit for 5 minutes.
7 Bake in the oven at 160°C (325°F) for 12–16 minutes, until lightly coloured.

Soaking Mixture

8 Place the eggs, sugar, milk and cream in a small bowl, and whisk until combined.
9 Put the pain perdu in the soaking mixture and allow to absorb most of the liquid.
10 Fry the pain perdu in a little butter until golden on both sides.

Cinnamon Sugar

11 Combine the sugar and cinnamon.
12 Toss the fried pain perdu in the resulting cinnamon sugar.

Yoghurt Sorbet

1 Boil the water and sugar in a small saucepan, then cool to room temperature.
2 Pour the yoghurt into a bowl.
3 Add the cooled syrup, whisking continuously until combined, then chill.
4 Churn in a sorbet machine according to the manufacturer's instructions.

Strawberry Sorbet

1 Place all the ingredients, except for the strawberry purée, into a small saucepan and boil.
2 Remove from the heat, add the purée, then chill.
3 Strain and churn in a sorbet machine according to the manufacturer's instructions.

Pink Bubble Sugar

1 Pre-heat the oven to 180°C (350°F).
2 Take 10 g (sc. ½ oz/2½ tsp) of the isomalt sugar and mix it with the food colouring powder.
3 Line one flat tray with a Silpat® mat, spread the remaining 40 g (sc. 1½ oz/10 tsp) of isomalt sugar around, then sprinkle the pink isomalt mixture evenly on top.
4 Place the second Silpat® mat on top, then the second flat tray.
5 Bake in the oven for 10 minutes, then allow to cool and use when required (store in a cool, airtight container to avoid the sugar getting moist).

ASSEMBLING

Garnishes Diced fresh strawberries; baby basil leaves

Pour 15 g (½ oz/1 tbsp) of jelly into the bottom of each glass, then set in the fridge. Add 80 g (2¾ oz/gen. 5 tbsp) of panna cotta on top, then set in the fridge. Add another tablespoon of jelly, then set in the fridge. Add a tablespoon of panna cotta, then set in the fridge. Add a tablespoon of jelly, then set in the fridge. Pour a layer of tapioca milk sauce (80–100g/2¾–3½ oz/5–7 tbsp) as high as the first layer of panna cotta, then set in the fridge. Add the pain perdu. Spoon some granola into the hole of the pain perdu and top with a few diced fresh strawberries. Place a quenelle of yoghurt sorbet on top. Top with a ball of strawberry sorbet. Garnish with a piece of pink bubble sugar and some baby basil leaves.

CARROT CAKE WITH PRALINE CRÈME, WALNUT CRUMBLE, CREAM CHEESE FOAM, APRICOT AND CARROT SORBET

'This dessert took over six months to create, as I stopped and started,' says Anna. 'The apricot and carrot sorbet was a mistake; it was supposed to be just carrot, but my staff thought I'd also said "apricot". The cream cheese foam is the icing on the cake.'

MAKES 8   DIFFICULTY 4/5   PREPARATION TIME 5–6 hours   SPECIFIC EQUIPMENT 8 x small round moulds (each 3 cm/1⅛ in. diameter, at least 1 cm/⅜ in. high); digital candy thermometer; 8 x cake rings (each 8 cm/3⅛ in. diameter, 3 cm/1⅛ in. high); acetate sheets; sorbet machine; whipped cream siphon and two cartridges

INGREDIENTS

For the Carrot Cake
Soft flour (cake flour) 100 g | 3½ oz | ⅔ cup
Granulated white sugar 90 g | sc. 3¼ oz | sc. ½ cup
Bicarbonate of soda (baking soda) 4 g | gen. ½ tsp
Baking powder 2.5 g | gen. ½ tsp
Salt 1 g | gen. ⅛ tsp
2 whole eggs
Vegetable oil 60 ml | 2¼ fl oz | ¼ cup
Ground cinnamon 2.5 g | 1 tsp
Grated carrot 75 g | gen. 2½ oz | ¾ cup
Grated apple 38 g | gen. 1¼ oz | gen. ¼ cup
Chopped walnuts 25 g | gen. ¾ oz | ¼ cup
Sultanas 50 g | 1¾ oz | ⅓ cup

For the Carrot Crumbs
Carrot cake scraps (from above recipe)

For the Rice Bubble Sheets
Dark chocolate couverture (e.g. Venezuela 72% by Cacao Barry) 40 g | sc. 1½ oz
Hazelnut praline paste 200 g | 7 oz | ¾ cup
Rice bubbles 10 g | sc. ½ oz | gen. ½ cup
Pailleté feuilletine (chopped crêpes dentelles/French crispy pancakes) 30 g | 1 oz | sc. ½ cup

For the Apricot Insert
Apricot purée 108 ml | gen. 3¾ fl oz | ⅖ cup
Granulated white sugar 9 g | sc. ½ oz | 2 tsp
Gelatine (gold) 5 g | 2½ sheets (softened in ice cold water, with excess water squeezed out)

For the Praline Crème
Milk 130 ml | 4½ fl oz | gen. ½ cup
Whipping cream (35% fat) [1] 120 ml | gen. 4¼ fl oz | ½ cup
½ vanilla pod (bean) (split, scraped, both pod/bean and seeds reserved)
Granulated white sugar 80 g | gen. 2¾ oz | ⅖ cup
Egg yolks 80 g | gen. 2¾ oz | ⅓ cup
Cornflour (cornstarch) 20 g | sc. ¾ oz | 2 tbsp
Hazelnut praline paste 200 g | 7 oz | ¾ cup
Gelatine (gold) 6 g | 3 sheets (softened in ice cold water, with excess water squeezed out)
Whipping cream (35% fat) [2] 250 ml | 8¾ fl oz | 1 cup

For the Caramel Glaze
Milk chocolate couverture (e.g. Ghana 40.5% by Cacao Barry) 250 g | gen. 8¾ oz
Granulated white sugar 100 g | 3½ oz | ½ cup
Glucose syrup 20 ml | ¾ fl oz | sc. 1½ tbsp
Whipping cream (35% fat) 150 ml | sc. 5½ fl oz | gen. ½ cup
Gelatine (gold) 7.5 g | 3¾ sheets (softened in ice cold water, with excess water squeezed out)

INSTRUCTIONS

Carrot Cake
1   Pre-heat the oven to 160°C (325°F).
2   Place the flour, sugar, bicarbonate of soda (baking soda), baking powder and salt in a mixing bowl and use a paddle attachment to beat until combined.
3   Gradually add the eggs and oil until combined into a smooth mixture.
4   Add in the rest of the ingredients and mix until they all just come together.
5   Line a baking tray with silicone baking paper, spread the mixture out and bake for 30–45 minutes.
6   Allow to cool, then cut out eight 8 cm (3⅛ in.) rounds.

Carrot Crumbs
1   Crumble the carrot cake scraps onto a tray.
2   Place in the oven at 45°C (115°F) for 4–5 hours.
3   Blitz with a hand mixer or food processor to form crumbs.

Rice Bubble Sheets
1   Put the chocolate in a microwaveable bowl and melt in the microwave, heating in bursts of 15 seconds so the chocolate doesn't burn.
2   Once melted, whisk in the hazelnut praline paste by hand until combined and smooth.
3   Add in the rice bubbles and pailleté feuilletine, mixing until combined.
4   Roll gently between two silicone baking paper sheets, avoiding breaking the rice bubble mixture, until a thickness of 3 mm (⅛ in.) is achieved.
5   Freeze, so it will be easy to cut out discs for the assembling of the cakes.

Apricot Insert
1   Warm the apricot purée and sugar in a small saucepan.
2   Remove from the heat and add the gelatine.
3   Pass the mixture through a fine sieve (strainer).
4   Dispense into small round moulds, then freeze.

Praline Crème
1   Heat the milk, cream [1], and vanilla pod (bean) and seeds to boiling point in a saucepan.
2   Place the sugar and egg yolks in a bowl, and whisk by hand until creamy.
3   Add the cornflour (cornstarch), then temper with some of the boiling liquid, continuing to whisk until combined.
4   Pour the egg mixture back into the saucepan and continue to whisk and cook out the cornflour (cornstarch) for 4 minutes, until a custard consistency is achieved.
5   Remove from the heat and strain.
6   Whisk in the hazelnut praline paste and the gelatine.
7   Allow the mixture to cool to 40°C (104°F).
8   Semi-whip cream [2], then fold into the mixture.
9   Once the cream has been added, use immediately.

Caramel Glaze
1   Melt the chocolate in a bain-marie.
2   Heat the sugar and glucose syrup in a small saucepan, with a little water, to a golden caramel colour.
3   In another small saucepan, warm up the cream, then add the caramel, whisking continuously until combined, at which point take off the heat.
4   Add the caramel liquid to the melted chocolate.
5   Blitz with an immersion blender until smooth.
6   Add in the gelatine.

For Putting Together the Carrot Cake

Carrot cake (from previous recipe) (thinly sliced)

Rice bubble sheet (from previous recipe)

Praline crème with apricot insert (from previous recipes)

Caramel glaze (from previous recipe)

For the Apricot and Carrot Sorbet

Water 70 ml | 2½ fl oz | 4¾ tbsp

Glucose syrup 30 g | gen. 1 fl oz | gen. 1½ tbsp

Granulated white sugar 60 g | gen. 2 oz | gen. ¼ cup

Sorbet stabilizer 2.5 g | sc. 1 tsp

Lemon juice 20 ml | gen. ½ fl oz | 4 tsp

Apricot purée 200 ml | 7 fl oz | ¾ cup

Carrot juice 100 ml | 3½ fl oz | sc. ½ cup

For the Walnut Crumble

Chopped walnuts 150 g | gen. 5¼ oz | gen. 1¼ cups

Granulated white sugar 100 g | 3½ oz | ½ cup

Water 50 ml | 1¾ fl oz | 3½ tbsp

For the Candy Carrot Strips

1 carrot

Caster (superfine) sugar 200 g | 7 oz | sc. 1 cup

Water 200 ml | 7 fl oz | sc. 1 cup

For the Cream Cheese Foam

Cream cheese 100 g | 3½ oz | sc. ½ cup

Whipping cream (35% fat) 50 ml | 1¾ fl oz | ⅕ cup

Anglaise sauce* 100 ml | 3½ fl oz | sc. ½ cup

* Anglaise Sauce

(these instructions give 300 ml/10½ fl oz/1¼ cups
anglaise sauce, the minimum recipe size to avoid burning)

Milk 125 ml | sc. 4½ fl oz | gen. ½ cup

Whipping cream (35% fat) 125 ml | 4½ fl oz | ½ cup

½ vanilla pod (bean) (split, scraped, both pod/bean
and seeds reserved)

3 egg yolks

Granulated white sugar 50 g | 1¾ oz | ¼ cup

Putting Together the Carrot Cake

1 Line the cake rings with acetate sheet and place them on a wire rack.

2 Place carrot cake on the base of each ring.

3 On a cold, flat surface cut 8 cm (3⅛ in.) diameter discs out of the rice bubble sheet and place on top of the carrot cake base, handling with frozen utensils.

4 Fill each ring halfway with praline crème, then place an apricot insert in the middle.

5 Fill up the rest of the ring with crème.

6 Freeze, then unmould and place on a wire rack ready to glaze.

7 Warm the glaze and pour over the cakes, tapping the rack to get rid of excess glaze.

8 Allow to set.

Apricot and Carrot Sorbet

1 Bring the water, glucose syrup, sugar and sorbet stabilizer to the boil.

2 Remove from the heat, then add in the lemon juice, apricot purée and carrot juice.

3 Strain, chill and churn in a sorbet machine according to the manufacturer's instructions.

Walnut Crumble

1 Put all the ingredients into a small saucepan.

2 Cook until caramelized, stirring constantly so that the mixture doesn't burn.

3 Pour onto a silicone baking paper-lined baking tray and allow to cool completely.

Candy Carrot Strips

1 Use a vegetable peeler to slice the carrot into long strips.

2 Bring the sugar and water to the boil in a small saucepan.

3 Add the carrot strips and simmer.

4 Remove once soft (after up to 10 minutes), and allow to cool in the syrup.

Cream Cheese Foam

1 Warm up the cream cheese and cream in a small saucepan until the mixture breaks down.

2 Remove from the heat, then use an immersion blender to blend the cream cheese, cream and anglaise sauce until smooth, before passing through a fine sieve (strainer) to remove any lumps.

3 Pour into a whipped cream siphon, charge with two cartridges and allow to settle for 30–60 minutes in the cold.

* Anglaise Sauce

1 Place the milk and cream in a small saucepan over a medium heat, add the vanilla pod (bean) and seeds, bring to the boil, then remove from the heat and set aside.

2 Whisk together the egg yolks and sugar in a small bowl until light and creamy.

3 Return the milk/cream/vanilla mixture to the stove, and temper in the egg mixture once the milk/cream/vanilla is re-warmed.

4 Stir constantly over a low heat for around 5 minutes, or until the mixture coats the back of a wooden spoon (do not boil).

5 Remove from the heat, then strain into a bowl over ice water.

6 Once chilled, refrigerate until required.

ASSEMBLING

Garnishes Baby celery leaves

Place each assembled carrot cake on a bed of walnut crumble. Position a quenelle of sorbet on top, and sprinkle the sorbet with carrot crumbs. Position candy carrot strips around the cake. Add a cream cheese foam ball to the side. Garnish with baby celery leaves.

Antonio Bachour

USA

When one juxtaposes Antonio Bachour's plated desserts with photographs of Puerto Rico, its vibrant colours spelling eternal summer, the connection is evident. Born to a family of bakers on the 'enchanted island', Antonio worked his way through several five-star resorts and high-profile restaurants both there and on the US mainland before becoming executive pastry chef at the luxurious St Regis Bal Harbour Hotel in Miami Beach. His signature is creative and unequivocally Caribbean, awash with saturated hues that punctuate clean textures. Each dish is a metaphor for a tropical garden on a plate.

'I start with a new idea, which I write down on paper. I think about the ingredients, research where I can source each product, and eventually I start cooking,' he says. 'The decoration and plating is decided *à la minute*!' This statement encapsulates Antonio's conviction that creativity ultimately runs the show. 'I create three or four new recipes a week,' he notes. As a result, perpetual inventiveness is key. 'Having been in the pastry field for about sixteen years, I believe my style changes on average every three years. What I don't like is that many people now copy or end up doing the same thing. Some dessert menus don't change for years, and that is not good.'

Antonio transforms seasonal ingredients, particularly tropical fruits, into sorbets, jellies and soups, creating a refreshing oasis in the Miami heat – retro marshmallows for grown-ups; delicate 'pearls' and edible flowers in a pumped-up make-up palette. Add the right amount of technology and chemistry, such as Versawhip frozen foam, and you get a very modern and unique freestyle.

There is a catch, however. Before being able to juggle 'the three visions that are artist, scientist and designer, which I now can incorporate into each new dessert', Antonio advises that 'you have to start by working for the toughest kitchens you can find, and don't ever – particularly when you're just getting started – work for somewhere that is "easier" and that is not going to push you or help you to develop any sense of discipline, which then allows you to indulge in creativity'. Antonio's masterpieces are testament to his tightly orchestrated powers of invention.

www.starwoodhotels.com/stregis

PANNA COTTA WITH PEACH SORBET, MORELLO CHERRY AND PEACH PEARL, CHERRY GEL SHEET AND CELLOPHANE OF SUGAR

Antonio was inspired by springtime for this recipe, which pairs peach and cherry for a seasonal celebration. The panna cotta marries well with the punch of the fruits in this modern composition.

MAKES 15   **DIFFICULTY** 4 /5   **PREPARATION TIME** 4 hours   **SPECIFIC EQUIPMENT** 15 x rectangular silicone moulds (each 7 x 2.5 cm/2¾ x 1 in., 3 cm/1⅛ in. deep); sorbet machine; 2 x flat trays; various small-sized circle cutters; squeeze bottle, or syringe; fine-mesh skimmer; digital candy thermometer

INGREDIENTS

For the Panna Cotta

Whipping cream (35% fat) 690 g | gen. 24 fl oz | 2¾ cups
Granulated white sugar 112 g | 4 oz | gen. ½ cup
Gelatine (silver) 7.5 g | 3 sheets (softened in ice cold water, with excess water squeezed out)

For the Peach Sorbet

Water 177 g | 6¼ fl oz | ¾ cup
Glucose powder 70 g | 2½ oz | 7 tbsp
Granulated white sugar 170 g | 6 oz | gen. ¾ cup
Sorbet stabilizer 4 g | 1 tsp
Peach purée 965 g | 34½ fl oz | gen. 3¾ cups

For the Morello Cherry Gel Sheet

Water 100 g | 3½ fl oz | sc. ½ cup
Agar agar 3 g | 1 tsp
Granulated white sugar 20 g | sc. ¾ oz | 5 tsp
Gelatine (silver) 15 g | 6 sheets (softened in ice cold water, with excess water squeezed out)
Morello cherry purée 500 g | gen. 17¾ fl oz | 2 cups

For the Peach Gel Sheet

Water 100 g | 3½ fl oz | sc. ½ cup
Agar agar 3 g | 1 tsp
Granulated white sugar 20 g | sc. ¾ oz | 5 tsp
Gelatine (silver) 15 g | 6 sheets (softened in ice cold water, with excess water squeezed out)
Peach purée 500 g | gen. 17¾ fl oz | 2 cups

For the Cherry Pearls

Cherry purée 275 g | gen. 9¾ fl oz | 1 cup
Water 25 g | gen. ¾ fl oz | 5 tsp
Granulated white sugar 50 g | 1¾ oz | ¼ cup
Agar agar 3 g | 1 tsp
Locust bean gum (carob) 0.4 g | sc. ⅛ tsp
Vegetable oil (cold)

For the Peach Pearls

Peach purée 250 g | 9 fl oz | 1 cup
Water 25 g | gen. ¾ fl oz | 5 tsp
Granulated white sugar 50 g | 1¾ oz | ¼ cup
Agar agar 3 g | 1 tsp
Locust bean gum (carob) 0.4 g | sc. ⅛ tsp
Vegetable oil (cold)

For the Peach Sauce

Peach purée 250 g | 9 fl oz | 1 cup
Icing (confectioner's) sugar 32 g | gen. 1 oz | 3 tbsp
Xanthan gum 8.75 g | gen. ¼ oz | 1¾ tsp

For the Cellophane of Sugar (optional)

Isomalt sugar 200 g | 7 oz | 1 cup

INSTRUCTIONS

Panna Cotta

1   Bring the cream and sugar to the boil.
2   Dissolve the gelatine, then remove from the heat and leave to cool to room temperature.
3   Pour into the silicone moulds and chill for several hours until set.

Peach Sorbet

1   Bring the water, glucose powder, sugar and stabilizer to the boil, then cool in the fridge.
2   When the mixture is cold, add the purée and process in a sorbet machine according to the manufacturer's instructions.

Morello Cherry Gel Sheet

1   Bring the water, agar agar and sugar to the boil.
2   Remove from the heat and add the gelatine.
3   Add the purée to the mixture.
4   Pour into a flat tray lined with plastic wrap.
5   Cool, then leave to set in the fridge.
6   Once set, use circle cutters to cut the gel out into different sized discs.
7   Keep cold.

Peach Gel Sheet

1   Follow the same instructions as for the morello cherry gel sheet, but, once set, cut the peach gel out into rectangular shapes.

Cherry Pearls

1   Combine all the ingredients, except for the vegetable oil, and bring to the boil.
2   Reduce the heat and simmer for 2 minutes.
3   Remove from the heat.
4   Using a squeeze bottle or syringe, drop the mixture into the cold vegetable oil, allowing 5 minutes to set.
5   Use a fine-mesh skimmer to transfer the pearls into cool water to rinse, then remove and drain in a fine-mesh sieve (strainer).

Peach Pearls

1   Follow the same instructions as for the cherry pearls.

Peach Sauce

1   Mix all the ingredients in a blender (e.g. Vitamix®) and reserve in the fridge.

Cellophane of Sugar (optional)

1   Heat the isomalt sugar to 160°C (320°F), then cool a little.
2   Dip a tiny ring or round mould in the sugar and blow thin cellophane bubbles/sheets out of it. NB Take care, as the sugar will be very hot.
3   Reserve.

ASSEMBLING

Garnishes Edible flowers; micro herbs (herb sprouts)

Place a rectangular peach gel on each plate, then unmould a panna cotta and place it on top. Arrange discs of cherry gel around the plate and place cherry pearls on top of the panna cotta. Garnish with peach pearls and peach sauce, some edible flowers and some micro herbs. Finish with peach sorbet and a cellophane of sugar, if using.

COCONUT MARSHMALLOW WITH FROZEN LYO

Despite the childish connotations of marshmallow, it was desserts from El Bulli that inspired Antonio to create this dish.

MAKES 15   **DIFFICULTY** 3/5   **PREPARATION TIME** 24 hours
SPECIFIC EQUIPMENT Tray (minimum 2 cm/¾ in. deep); digital candy thermometer; variously sized ring cutters; Pacojet®, or ice cream machine

INGREDIENTS

For the Coconut Marshmallow

Cornflour (cornstarch) (to dust tray)
Gelatine (gold) 65 g | 32½ sheets (softened in ice cold water, with excess water squeezed out)
Water 375 g | 13¼ fl oz | 1⅔ cups
Glucose syrup 170 g | 6 fl oz | sc. ½ cup
Granulated white sugar 1250 g | 2¾ lb | 6¼ cups
Egg whites 220 g | 7¾ oz | sc. 1 cup (room temperature)
Coconut purée 175 g | 6¼ fl oz | sc. ¾ cup
Rum 25 g | gen. ¾ fl oz | 5 tsp
1 part icing (confectioner's) sugar to 1 part cornflour (cornstarch) (to dust marshmallow)

For the Raspberry Cream

Raspberries 300 g | 10½ oz | 2 cups
Lyophilized raspberries (i.e. freeze-dried, e.g. Lyo Sabores - Texturas) 300 g | 10½ oz | 4½ cups
Granulated white sugar 120 g | 4¼ oz | gen. ½ cup
Glucose syrup 60 g | 2¼ fl oz | sc. 3½ tbsp
Water 140 ml | 5 fl oz | gen. ½ cup
Whipping cream (35% fat) 200 ml | 7 fl oz | ⅘ cup

INSTRUCTIONS

Coconut Marshmallow

1   Line the tray with parchment or foil, and dust with cornflour (cornstarch).
2   Melt the gelatine in a bain-marie, stirring constantly until it completely dissolves.
3   At the same time, heat the water, glucose syrup and sugar together.
4   When this syrup reaches 118°C (244°F), begin to whip the egg whites in a stand mixer.
5   When the syrup reaches 130°C (266°F), begin to pour it in a thin stream into the egg whites. NB Turn the speed to low for this phase; when the pouring is done, turn back to medium-high.
6   Immediately add the melted gelatine, the coconut purée and the rum.
7   Continue whisking on medium-high speed until the mixture becomes thick.
8   Quickly pour onto the tray, to a thickness of 2 cm (¾ in.), liberally dust with the icing (confectioner's) sugar/cornflour (cornstarch) mix, then freeze overnight.
9   The next day, use ring cutters to cut the marshmallow sheet into different sized rings.

Raspberry Cream

1   Wash all the raspberries, then heat them briefly with the sugar, glucose syrup and water.
2   Pour into a Pacojet® beaker and leave to cool.
3   Add the cream and combine.
4   Ensure the surface is level, then deep-freeze at -22°C (-8°F) for 24 hours.
5   Pacotize in the Pacojet®, either in portions or the whole beaker. NB If you do not have a Pacojet®, purée everything in a blender, keep in the fridge for 4 hours, churn in an ice cream machine according to the manufacturer's instructions, then reserve in the freezer.

ASSEMBLING

Garnishes Raspberry sauce; edible flowers; lyophilized raspberries

Put two different sized rings of coconut marshmallow in the centre of each plate. Pour raspberry sauce into and between the rings. Place a quenelle of frozen raspberry cream on top. Garnish with edible flowers, a few lyophilized raspberries and drops of raspberry sauce.

Carmelo Sciampagna

ITALY

Carmelo Sciampagna is a champion, and a precocious one at that. His meteoric professional trajectory began when he was an apprentice of just 14. 'I attended the Accademia Cast Alimenti in Brescia, and then I worked at Iginio Massari's bakery. I never thought about a Plan B. It might seem strange, but I always concentrated on figuring out how to move forward in my pastry career.' He adds with a laugh, 'I would have liked to graduate in food science … it's never too late! From the very beginning I was fascinated by the subject, as I still am today; the fact that with just four basic ingredients – butter, sugar, eggs and flour – an infinity of products can be made.'

Carmelo graduated in hotel and catering services, and early on met a chef who took him under his wing and helped him find work with luxury hotel chains. He ended up working in such far-flung destinations as Thailand, Malaysia, Brazil, Mexico and the Dominican Republic. 'I've always tried to bring together different cultures,' he says, 'to come up with something both unique and universal.'

The result? He has taken national and international chocolate and pastry committees by storm: first place in the Italian chocolate championship; third place in the World Chocolate Masters competition; first prize for making the 'World's Best Dessert'; first prize in the Grand Prix of Italian pastries; and, last but not least, elected a member of the exclusive Accademia Maestri Pasticceri Italiani. No wonder the lucky customers of his shop in Marineo, in the province of Palermo, Sicily, rave about his work.

Carmelo's natural talent, choice of fine ingredients, careful following of what's happening in the confectionery world and proactive research into what his clientele really want leaves little to chance and contributes to his success. 'Once a month I set up a meeting with all the staff. We try to analyze what customers are asking for, and then we make products to be tested in the shop through tastings. We go through a questionnaire and the highest-scored products are put into production,' explains Carmelo. 'Ideally I would like to create a chain of stores and be part of the "Relais Dessert" association.' With such business acumen and hard-to-rival creativity, there is no doubt he will realize his ambitions.

www.pasticceriasciampagna.com

GOLDEN MACARON

'The 24K gold macaron was born out of the idea of making available to our loyal customers a very precious dessert,' says Carmelo. 'A sweet like a jewel both because of its aesthetic and its price... It costs about €80 for 100 g. I'm not sure whether it can be considered the world's most expensive macaron, but it's probably one of the most costly things I've come across on my numerous trips throughout Italy and abroad. A bakery also needs something quirky to make people talk, and that is a side aspect of the business we like to take care of. We prepare the macaron on request only, and we are honestly pretty happy with the orders!'

MAKES 8–10 **DIFFICULTY** 3/5 **PREPARATION TIME** 1½ hours (not including overnight setting time for the ganache)
SPECIFIC EQUIPMENT 2 x piping (pastry) bags; Silpat® mat, or similar placed in a – preferably perforated – baking tray; digital candy thermometer

INGREDIENTS

For the White Chocolate Ganache with Tahitian Vanilla Beans

Whipping cream (35% fat) 128 g | gen. 4½ fl oz | ½ cup
Invert sugar 13 g | sc. ½ oz | ½ tbsp
Glucose syrup 13 g | ½ fl oz | 1½ tsp
Green (unripe) lemon zest 1 g | ⅛ tsp
½ Tahitian vanilla pod (bean) (split, scraped, both pod/bean and seeds reserved)
White chocolate couverture (e.g. Opalys 33% by Valrhona) 208 g | sc. 7½ oz
Cocoa butter 5 g | sc. ¼ oz (or acacia/wattle honey)

For the Macarons

Blanched almond meal 130 g | 4½ oz | 1½ cups
Icing (confectioner's) sugar 225 g | sc. 8 oz | 1⅔ cups
Edible gold powder 5 g | sc. ¼ oz | 2½ tsp
Egg whites 115 g | 4 oz | ½ cup
Caster (superfine) sugar 60 g | gen. 2 oz | gen. ¼ cup
Cream of tartar 1 g | ⅛ tsp

For the Vanilla Sauce

Whipping cream (35% fat) 100 g | gen. 3½ fl oz | sc. ½ cup
Custard* 100 g | 3½ fl oz | sc. ½ cup
½ Tahitian vanilla pod (bean) (split, scraped, seeds reserved)

*** Custard**

Egg yolks 54 g | sc. 2 oz | sc. ¼ cup
Caster (superfine) sugar 13 g | sc. ½ oz | 1 tbsp
Cornflour (cornstarch) 8 g | ¼ oz | sc. 2 tsp
½ Tahitian vanilla pod (bean) (split, scraped, both pod/bean and seeds reserved)
Zest of ½ a small green (unripe) lemon
Milk 75 g | 2½ fl oz | 5 tbsp
Whipping cream (35% fat) 25 g | gen. ¾ fl oz | sc. 1½ tbsp

INSTRUCTIONS

White Chocolate Ganache With Tahitian Vanilla Beans

1 Bring the cream, invert sugar, glucose syrup, lemon zest, and vanilla pod (bean) and seeds to the boil.
2 At the same time, melt the chocolate with the cocoa butter.
3 Pour the hot cream mixture over the melted chocolate mixture in several additions.
4 Remove the vanilla pod (bean), then transfer to a stand mixer with a paddle attachment to complete the emulsion.
5 Leave to set overnight at approximately 17°C (63°F).

Macarons

1 Mix together the almond meal, icing (confectioner's) sugar and gold powder.
2 Separately whisk the egg whites (best if they have been in the fridge for a couple of days) with the caster (superfine) sugar and cream of tartar.
3 Use a flexible spatula to 'macaroner' (or fold) the dry ingredients into the whisked egg white mixture.
4 Use a piping (pastry) bag to create two sizes of macaron shell on a Silpat® mat or similar placed in a baking tray (preferably perforated), then leave to dry for 20 minutes.
5 Bake at 140°C (275°F) for 12–15 minutes.
6 Once baked, leave to cool down on the mat/tray.

Vanilla Sauce

1 Warm the cream and mix vigorously with the custard and the vanilla seeds.
2 Strain before use.

*** Custard**

1 Mix together the egg yolks, sugar, cornflour (cornstarch), vanilla pod (bean) and seeds, and lemon zest.
2 Bring the milk and cream to the boil, then pour them on the egg yolk mixture.
3 Re-heat up to 82°C (180°F), stirring continuously, then strain and cool before use.

ASSEMBLING

Garnishes Edible gold leaves

Pair together the macaron shells of equal size. Cover each shell with edible gold leaves. Pipe the set ganache onto half the shells, then assemble. Serve with vanilla sauce. You could also add some crushed coloured macarons around the plate.

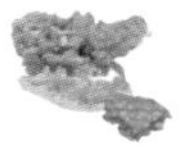

MADE IN SICILY

Cannoli were historically prepared as a treat during carnival season, but they are now a year-round staple throughout Italy. 'This recipe is an evolution of the traditional "cannolo siciliano", says Carmelo.

MAKES 15   **DIFFICULTY** 2/5   **PREPARATION TIME** 3 hours (not including 12 hours' resting time for the cannoli leaves)
SPECIFIC EQUIPMENT Cutting wheel; digital candy thermometer; piping (pastry) bag

INGREDIENTS

For Cannolo Siciliano Leaves
(prepare the day before serving)

Strong pastry flour (360 W) 500 g | 1 lb 1½ oz | 3½ cups
Caster (superfine) sugar 75 g | gen. 2½ oz | ⅓ cup
Cocoa powder (22-24%) 25 g | gen. ¾ oz | 3½ tbsp
Salt 10 g | sc. ½ oz | gen. ½ tbsp
Cinnamon powder 2.5 g | 1 tsp
1 Tahitian vanilla pod (bean) (split, scraped, seeds reserved)
Unsalted butter 75 g | gen. 2½ oz (soft)
Whole eggs 100 g | 3½ oz | sc. ½ cup
White wine 175 g | gen. 6 fl oz | ¾ cup
Sunflower oil (for frying)

For the Fresh Ricotta Cream

Fresh sheep's ricotta 500 g | 1 lb 1½ oz | 2 cups
Caster (superfine) sugar 150 g | gen. 5¼ oz | sc. ¾ cup
½ Tahitian vanilla pod (bean) (split, scraped, seeds reserved)

For the Caramel and Passito di Pantelleria Sauce

Muscovado cane sugar 200 g | 7 oz | 1⅓ cups
Whipping cream (35% fat) 80 g | gen. 2¾ fl oz | ⅓ cup
Passito di Pantelleria wine 150 g | 5¼ fl oz | ⅔ cup

For the Acacia Honey Sauce

Acacia/wattle honey 100 g | 3½ fl oz | 5 tbsp
Whipping cream (35% fat) 50 g | 1¾ fl oz | ⅕ cup

INSTRUCTIONS

Cannolo Siciliano Leaves

1   Combine the flour, sugar, cocoa powder, salt, cinnamon powder and vanilla seeds.
2   Add the rest of the ingredients, mix to combine, then knead for a few minutes.
3   When the dough is ready, wrap in plastic wrap and put in the fridge for 12 hours.
4   Roll to a thickness of approximately 3 mm (⅛ in.), then use the cutting wheel to make 5 x 5 cm (2 x 2 in.) squares.
5   Deep fry in sunflower oil at 180°C (356°F).
6   Leave to drain and cool on absorbent paper.

Fresh Ricotta Cream

1   Mix the ricotta with the sugar and vanilla seeds, then pass through a sieve (strainer).
2   Reserve in the fridge at 2-4°C (35-40°F).

Caramel and Passito di Pantelleria Sauce

1   Melt the sugar and make a caramel.
2   At the same time, heat the cream.
3   Deglaze the caramel with the hot cream, then add the Passito wine. NB Take care, as it will spit.

Acacia Honey Sauce

1   Warm the honey and cream together, stirring well to obtain a homogeneous mixture.
2   Reserve at room temperature, if below 20°C (68°F).

ASSEMBLING

Garnishes Chocolate drops; candied orange cubes; icing (confectioner's) sugar

On each plate, alternate four fried leaves with three layers of ricotta cream piped out in small rounds, forming a small tower shape. Drizzle the caramel and Passito di Pantelleria sauce over the stack. Spread some chocolate drops, candied orange cubes and drops of acacia honey sauce on and around the dessert. Dust with icing (confectioner's) sugar.

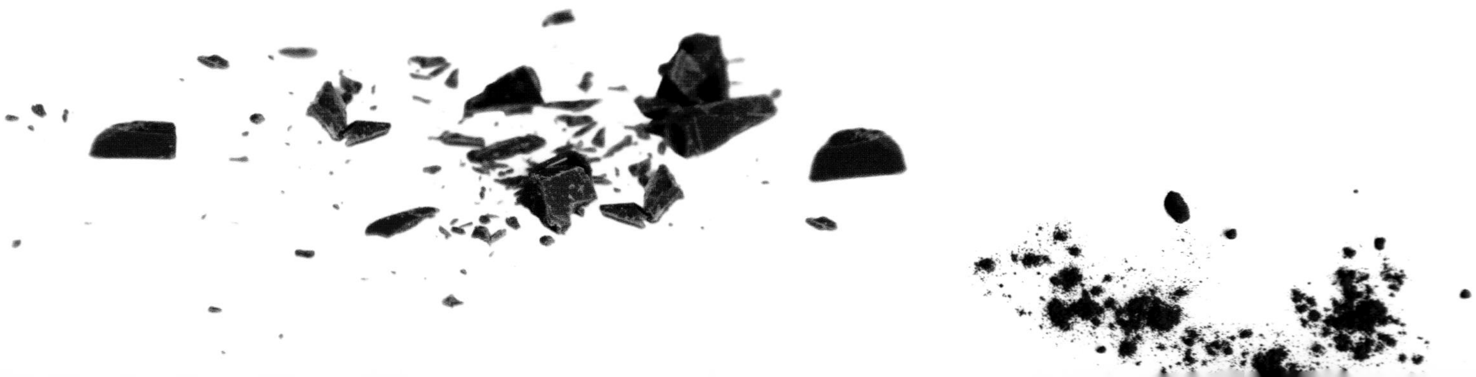

F 2007 This dish helped Carmelo win third place overall at the 2007 World Chocolate Masters, and was named 'World's Best Dessert'. As he explains: 'The name of the cake comes from the F1 Ferrari car of 2007. All the creations that I presented at the competition were a tribute to the Ferrari brand. As you can see, the "support" – it's not really a plate – is a podium similar to the one used in F1 races.'

MAKES 6 **DIFFICULTY** 5/5 **PREPARATION TIME** 5 hours (not including 24 hours' preparation time for the glazes) **SPECIFIC EQUIPMENT** Digital candy thermometer; 6 x rings (each 4 cm/1⅝ in. diameter, 1 cm/⅜ in. high) **NOTE: THIS RECIPE AND THE PHOTO OPPOSITE REPRESENT CARMELO'S SIMPLIFIED VERSION OF HIS 2007 WINNING RECIPE**

INGREDIENTS

For the Glaze with Milk Chocolate and Caramel for the Quenelle with Forest Strawberries (prepare the day before)

Granulated white sugar 30 g | 1 oz | 2½ tbsp
Glucose syrup 62DE 30 g | gen. 1 fl oz | gen. 1½ tbsp
Whipping cream (35% fat) 18 g | gen. ½ fl oz | 1 tbsp
Water 40 g | sc. 1½ fl oz | sc. 3 tbsp
Gelatine 160 Bloom (silver) 2 g | ⅘ sheet (softened in ice cold water, with excess water squeezed out)
Milk chocolate couverture (e.g. Lactée Caramel 31.2% by Cacao Barry) 80 g | gen. 2¾ oz

For the Quenelle with Forest Strawberries without Cream (makes more than required, but a more manageable amount)

Water 92 g | 3¼ fl oz | ⅓ cup
Granulated white sugar 108 g | gen. 3¾ oz | ½ cup
Forest strawberries 100 g | 3½ oz (or, if forest strawberries are difficult to find, replace with raspberries)
Gelatine 160 Bloom (silver) 6 g | 2⅖ sheets (softened in ice cold water, with excess water squeezed out)

For the Glaze with Powdered Cocoa for the Crémeux (prepare the day before)

Water 55 g | sc. 2 fl oz | 3¾ tbsp
Granulated white sugar 25 g | gen. ¾ oz | 2 tbsp
Glucose syrup 62DE 25 g | gen. ¾ fl oz | sc. 1½ tbsp
Whipping cream (35% fat) 50 g | 1¾ fl oz | ⅕ cup
Cocoa powder (22–24%) 25 g | gen. ¾ oz | 3½ tbsp
Gelatine 160 Bloom (silver) 3 g | 1⅕ sheets (softened in ice cold water, with excess water squeezed out)

For the Crémeux with 'Venezuela' Fondant Water

Water 25 g | gen. ¾ fl oz | 5 tsp
Whipping cream (35% fat) 40 g | sc. 1½ fl oz | sc. 2¾ tbsp
Glucose syrup 44DE 10 g | gen. ¼ fl oz | ½ tbsp
Gelatine 160 Bloom (silver) 1 g | ⅖ sheet (softened in ice cold water, with excess water squeezed out)
Dark chocolate couverture (e.g. Venezuela 72% by Cacao Barry) 40 g | sc. 1½ oz (chopped)

INSTRUCTIONS

Glaze with Milk Chocolate and Caramel for the Quenelle with Forest Strawberries

1 Caramelize the sugar and glucose syrup.
2 At the same time, heat the cream with the water, then use this to deglaze the caramel.
3 Remove from the heat and stir in the gelatine.
4 Pour the whole mixture onto the chocolate.
5 Stir until well combined.
6 Reserve in the fridge at 4°C (40°F) until needed for the next stage.

Quenelle with Forest Strawberries without Cream

1 Boil the water with the sugar, then add the strawberries (or raspberries) and boil again.
2 Remove from the heat and add the gelatine.
3 Stir until well combined.
4 Freeze the mixture.
5 Once frozen, blitz in a blender, then transfer to a stand mixer with a whisk attachment and whip to a mousse-like texture.
6 Freeze again.
7 Prepare six quenelles and glaze with the milk chocolate and caramel glaze (from above recipe).
8 Reserve in the fridge at 4°C (40°F) until the final assembling stage.

Glaze with Powdered Cocoa for the Crémeux

1 Boil the water with the sugar and glucose syrup.
2 Add the cream and the cocoa powder, and mix well.
3 Cook at 104°C (219°F).
4 Remove from the heat, add the gelatine and stir until well combined.
5 Reserve in the fridge at 4°C (40°F) until needed for the next stage.

Crémeux with 'Venezuela' Fondant Water

1 Heat the water, cream and glucose syrup to 80°C (176°F).
2 Remove from the heat and add the gelatine.
3 Pour the mixture onto the chopped chocolate.
4 Stir until well combined, then pour into the rings, bottoms sealed with plastic wrap.
5 Freeze.
6 Once frozen, unmould and glaze with the powdered cocoa glaze (from above recipe).
7 Reserve in the fridge at 4°C (40°F) until the final assembling stage.

For the 'Joconde' Type Biscuit with Chocolate and Almonds

Whole eggs 50 g | 1¾ oz | sc. ¼ cup

Icing (confectioner's) sugar 37 g | gen. 1¼ oz | gen. 3½ tbsp

Almond meal (e.g. from Avola, Sicily) 38 g | gen. 1¼ oz | sc. ½ cup

Egg whites 33 g | gen. 1 oz | gen. 2 tbsp

Granulated white sugar 5 g | sc. ¼ oz | 1¼ tsp

Unsalted butter 8 g | ¼ oz (melted)

Cocoa powder (22–24%) 10 g | sc. ½ oz | sc. 1½ tbsp

Weak flour 10 g | sc. ½ oz | sc. 1 tbsp

For the Consommé of Citrus Fruits, Passion Fruit and Cocoa Nibs

Water 410 g | 14½ fl oz | 1¾ cups

Granulated white sugar 150 g | gen. 5¼ oz | ¾ cup

2½ Tahitian vanilla pods (beans) (split, scraped, seeds reserved)

Lemon rinds 3 g | 1 tsp (finely grated)

Ground black pepper a pinch

Ground coriander a pinch

Star anise 3 g | 3 small

Cocoa nibs 30 g | 1 oz | ¼ cup

Lemon juice 5 g | sc. ¼ fl oz | 1 tsp

Orange juice 5 g | sc. ¼ fl oz | 1 tsp

Passion fruit flesh 18 g | gen. ½ oz | gen. 1 tbsp (clean pulp, without seeds)

For the Caramelized Mango with Tahitian Vanilla

Granulated white sugar 70 g | 2½ oz | ⅓ cup

Glucose syrup 62DE 35 g | 1¼ fl oz | sc. 2 tbsp

Water 87 g | 3 fl oz | 6 tbsp

Mango pulp 125 g | sc. 4½ oz | ½ cup (puréed)

2 Tahitian vanilla pods (beans) (split, scraped, seeds reserved)

Mango 100 g | 3½ oz | ¾ cup (cut in small cubes)

'Joconde' Type Biscuit with Chocolate and Almonds

1 Whisk the eggs with the icing (confectioner's) sugar and almond meal.
2 Separately whisk the egg whites with the granulated sugar, and add to the above mixture.
3 Slowly add the melted butter.
4 Sift the cocoa powder and flour, then add.
5 Spread to a thickness of 4–5 mm (³⁄₁₆ in.) on a silicone baking paper-lined tray and bake at 180°C (350°F) for 10 minutes.
6 Leave to cool on a wire rack.
7 Cut into 5 x 5 cm (2 x 2 in.) squares.
8 Reserve in the fridge at 4°C (40°F) until the final assembling stage.

Consommé of Citrus Fruits, Passion Fruit and Cocoa Nibs

1 Boil all the ingredients together, except for the juices and passion fruit flesh.
2 Take off the heat and infuse with the lid on for 15 minutes.
3 Strain, add the juices and passion fruit, then blend to combine.
4 Keep the consommé warm.

Caramelized Mango with Tahitian Vanilla

1 Caramelize the sugar with the glucose syrup.
2 At the same time, heat the water and mango pulp and use to deglaze the caramel.
3 Add the vanilla seeds.
4 Just after completion of decocting (boiling down to extract the flavours), add the mango cubes and remove from the heat.
5 Keep just warm.

ASSEMBLING

For each serving, place some caramelized mango with Tahitian vanilla on the right-hand side of a large plate. Pour consommé of citrus fruits, passion fruit and cocoa nibs into a small glass, and place in the middle of the plate. Then assemble the 'cake', which will sit on the left-hand side of the plate: the 'joconde' type biscuit with chocolate and almonds is the base; then add a cocoa-glazed crémeux; next position on top a milk chocolate and caramel-glazed quenelle of forest strawberries without cream. You could also garnish the 'cake' with edible silver leaf and a vanilla pod (bean).

Douce Steiner
....
GERMANY

At the Hotel/Restaurant Hirschen in Sulzburg, Germany, everything is geared towards the guests' wellbeing: from the elegant yet cosy rooms decorated in romantic style, through the landscaped grounds where most of the fresh ingredients are sourced, to the culinary hubs of the wood-panelled restaurant and the kitchen, where Douce Steiner and her husband Udo concoct modern French feasts.

'I cook with my heart and soul, having developed my love for French pastry in France. I love to play with it and to experiment with combinations,' says Douce. 'Cooking and food are truly a passion. I've never eaten badly, thanks to my parents ... who actually opened the Hirschen and who introduced me to the best French restaurants from an early age. When I was eight, I was already so hooked that I wrote a letter of motivation to a three-starred chef!' A rite of passage that Douce is now replicating with her own daughter, Justine. 'I grew up in a starred restaurant, and now my daughter is being raised in the same environment. For me there was no other world – everything revolved around food – and it may be the same for her.'

In all Douce's cooking, both savoury and sweet, she cherishes noble ingredients, which she transforms into sleek still lifes. 'I love all products, as long as they are perfect and above all seasonal. I love black Périgord truffles, foie gras and caviar, but only at the right time, namely at Christmas. Espelette peppers are also among my favourites, and I use them indiscriminately in my desserts as well.' She adds, 'Have I said that artists must be a little bit mad and live in a different world?!'

Douce's gourmet but charming confections please the most demanding of epicureans. 'I advocate a pure and unadulterated taste; light and modern French cuisine with a lot of flavours to support the product but not destroy it,' she says. 'I respect food so much that we waste nothing. Also modern technology, although it cannot replace technique and artistry, makes it easier to reach perfect consistencies and to work much faster.'

Douce has succeeded in retaining a trademark style both in cooking and serving while steadily innovating, and that is how she ensures the Hirschen's continuing relevance. And maybe, one day, young Justine will take up the baton.

www.douce-steiner.de

WARM CHOCOLATE CAKE IN ORANGE SAUCE WITH PIMENT

D'ESPELETTE CHOCO-SORBET

Douce's invention is a wonderful dessert for the winter that still has freshness due to the acidity of the orange sauce.

MAKES 4–6   **DIFFICULTY** 3/5   **PREPARATION TIME** 2½ hours (not including 2 days' soaking time, plus 12 hours' dehydration time, for the orange slices)   **SPECIFIC EQUIPMENT** Ice cream machine; 4–6 small baking dishes or tart/muffin baking cups (each 9 cm/3½ in. diameter); digital candy thermometer; Silpat® mat, or oiled tray

INGREDIENTS

For the Dehydrated Orange Slices (Garnish)

Orange slices 4–6 (paper thin)

100% syrup (ratio: 100 g/3½ oz/½ cup granulated white sugar
to 100 g/3½ fl oz/½ cup water) (to cover the orange slices)

For the Chocolate Sorbet

Water 250 g | gen. 8¾ fl oz | 1 cup

Granulated white sugar 85 g | 3 oz | sc. ½ cup

Dark chocolate (70%) 100 g | 3½ oz (chopped)

Cocoa powder 25 g | gen. ¾ oz | 3½ tbsp

1 vanilla pod (bean) (split, scraped, both pod/bean
and seeds reserved)

For the Chocolate Cake

Unsalted butter [1] (for baking dishes/cups)

Plain (all-purpose) flour [1] (for baking dishes/cups)

Dark chocolate (70%) 65 g | gen. 2¼ oz

Granulated white sugar 100 g | 3½ oz | ½ cup

2 whole eggs

Plain (all-purpose) flour [2] 35 g | 1¼ oz | 3 tbsp

Unsalted butter [2] 60 g | gen. 2 oz (melted)

For the Orange Sauce

Orange juice 250 ml | gen. 8¾ fl oz | 1 cup

Granulated white sugar 100 g | 3½ oz | ½ cup

Cornflour (cornstarch) 3 g | ¾ tsp

Grand Marnier 43 g | 1½ fl oz | 3 tbsp

Piment d'Espelette/red chilli pepper (to taste)

For the Pulled Dark Chocolate Tuile

Fondant (e.g. Fondant Blanc Extra by Produits Marguerite,
or Fondant Pâtissier by Caullet) 100 g | 3½ oz

Glucose syrup 100 g | 3½ fl oz | gen. ¼ cup

Dark chocolate (100% extra bitter preferred)
30 g | 1 oz (chopped)

INSTRUCTIONS

Dehydrated Orange Slices (Garnish)

1 Soak the slices in 100% syrup for at least 2 days.

2 Bake in an oven at 70°C (160°F) for 12 hours to dry them completely.

Chocolate Sorbet

1 Bring the water and sugar to the boil to make a syrup.

2 Stir in the chopped chocolate, cocoa powder, and vanilla pod (bean) and seeds.

3 When combined, chill completely in the fridge, then remove the vanilla pod (bean).

4 Churn in an ice cream machine according to the manufacturer's instructions.

Chocolate Cake

1 Butter and flour the baking dishes/cups.

2 Melt the chocolate in a bain-marie.

3 Thoroughly mix the sugar with the eggs until creamy, also in a bain-marie, then beat with a whisk and cool on an ice bath.

4 Once cool, add flour [2], butter [2] and the melted chocolate, and mix well.

5 Pour into the baking dishes/cups and, just before serving, bake at 180°C (350°F) for approximately 12 minutes.

Orange Sauce

1 Boil the orange juice with the sugar.

2 Mix the cornflour (cornstarch) with some of the Grand Marnier and stir into the boiling liquid.

3 Leave to cool at room temperature, then mix in the remaining Grand Marnier and season with piment d'Espelette (dilute with a little orange juice, if necessary).

Pulled Dark Chocolate Tuile

1 Mix the fondant and glucose syrup together in a pan, and bring to the boil.

2 Boil to 160°C (325°F), then remove from the heat and stir in the chopped chocolate.

3 Pour onto a Silpat® mat or an oiled tray.

4 At this point the tuile can be pulled and cut with scissors into long thin strips. NB Take care, as the mixture will be very hot.

5 If the mixture begins to cool, put it in the oven for a few minutes to soften (don't over-melt, though, or the mixture will burn).

ASSEMBLING

Components/Garnishes Orange segments; dark chocolate (70%), tempered and cut into squares

Place a few orange segments in the bottom of each dish, then pour in some orange sauce. Add chocolate cake and a quenelle of chocolate sorbet to the side. Add a square of tempered dark chocolate, then a dehydrated orange slice on top. Finish with a pulled dark chocolate tuile.

BLANC MANGER WITH APRICOTS, YOUNG ALMONDS AND FRESH BASIL

Douce conjures up a new taste sensation through the unexpected combination of apricot, almond and basil in this mouthwatering dish.

MAKES 4–6 **DIFFICULTY** 1/5 **PREPARATION TIME** 1 hour (not including 2 weeks' pickling time for the apricots)
SPECIFIC EQUIPMENT Preserving jars; 4–6 x round silicone moulds with edges (each 6 cm/2⅜ in. diameter)

INGREDIENTS

For the Pickled Apricots

Granulated white sugar 100 g | 3½ oz | ½ cup
20 fresh apricots (unripe, stoned and chopped into 8 slices)
Juice of 2 lemons
Pêcher Mignon (peach liqueur) 250 ml | gen. 8¾ fl oz | 1 cup

For the Blanc Manger

Milk 250 ml | gen. 8¾ fl oz | 1 cup
Granulated white sugar 50 g | 1¾ oz | ¼ cup
Marzipan 50 g | 1¾ oz (cut into pieces)
Gelatine (gold) 6 g | 3 sheets (softened in ice cold water, with excess water squeezed out)
Whipping cream (35% fat) 500 ml | 17½ fl oz | 2 cups (lightly whipped)

INSTRUCTIONS

Pickled Apricots

1 Gently heat the sugar in a large, wide saucepan.
2 Place the apricot slices evenly in the saucepan, mix with the lemon juice, then stir in the liqueur.
3 Bring to the boil with the lid on, then immediately take off the heat.
4 Pour into preserving jars, ensuring that the apricot slices are covered with the juice and that the jars are sealed.
5 Place in the fridge for at least 2 weeks.

Blanc Manger

1 Bring the milk, sugar and marzipan pieces to the boil, stirring constantly in order to dissolve the marzipan completely.
2 Pour into a bowl on ice, add the gelatine and stir as the mixture cools.
3 Fold in the lightly whipped cream.
4 Fill the silicone moulds and leave to set in the fridge.
5 Ideally prepare the blanc manger the day before serving so that it is thoroughly cooled and set, and thus will unmould easily.

ASSEMBLING

Components/Garnishes 10 young almonds, peeled and skinned (NB If you cannot find young almonds, crack open your apricot stones, as these contain small seeds; skin the seeds but only use 2–3 per apricot for the dessert, as they are very intense, like bitter almonds); 12 small sprigs of Provençal basil; icing (confectioner's) sugar

Pour some of the apricot juice into the bottom of each dish. Unmould the blanc manger *à la minute* and place on top. Add a generous tablespoon of pickled apricots. Add a few young almonds (or apricot seeds) and several basil sprigs, then dust the whole with icing (confectioner's) sugar.

John Ralley

AUSTRALIA

Every one of his plated desserts looks like an abstract artwork, awash with carefully selected pigments and constructed with finesse. The virtuosity behind the compositions is what catches the eye; one senses that the person who devised these dishes is a true artist at heart. 'I don't really like to listen to what other people say. I do what keeps me happy, and I think of pastry as an art because of the creativity and freedom that comes with the job,' says Sydney-based pastry chef, John Ralley. 'I'm constantly thinking of my next piece, picturing my next creation, never repeating myself. For me the artistic side of pastry takes over the other aspects.'

The way in which John has decorated himself with tattoos and piercings at first gives him a 'bad boy' vibe, but that impression is soon dispelled when one realizes the true meaning behind the ornamentation. John's great flair for visual art is what he achieves both on his body and in his pâtisserie. This talent may also explain why he has a predilection for sugar-sculpting and chocolate-making, having learned from the best, which is to say Hamilton TAFE teacher, Dean Gibson. 'You can create things that most people wouldn't believe,' exclaims John, revelling in the high level of technical skill and artistry required.

'I didn't really have another plan. When I first started in pastry, I discovered a passion and knew this would be my career.' In 2002, he started working for the Gumnut Patisserie in Bowral, New South Wales, and since then he has worked for several renowned restaurants in Australia and the UK. Winning the title of Master Pastry Chef both in 2010 and 2012, and gaining a place on the Australian pastry team in 2011, are just the beginning of what will surely be a meteoric ascent.

'I mostly use classic flavours because I know they work, but I always try to put a modern twist on them. In essence, I like deconstructing classics,' says John. 'And using gadgets, such as vacuum-pack machines, Espuma guns, dehydrators and liquid nitrogen, gives unusual textures to the desserts, which amazes people.' His satisfied diners can certainly attest to that.

www.wildfiresydney.com | www.johnralley.com

STRAWBERRIES AND CREAM

'I saw this consommé done in England,' says John, 'and decided to create my own version by incorporating an old Australian classic.'

MAKES 5–6   **DIFFICULTY** 2/5   **PREPARATION TIME** 2 hours   **SPECIFIC EQUIPMENT** Piping (pastry) bag with size 9 nozzle; 2 x trays (one at least 2 cm/¾ in. deep); circle cutter (4 cm/1⅝ in. diameter)

INGREDIENTS

For the Meringue
Unsalted butter (to coat baking tray)
Egg whites 100 g | 3½ oz | ⅖ cup
Caster (superfine) sugar 100 g | 3½ oz | sc. ½ cup

For the Vanilla Bavarois
Whipping cream (35% fat) [1] 150 ml | sc. 5½ fl oz | gen. ½ cup
1 vanilla pod (bean) (split, scraped, seeds reserved)
3 egg yolks
Granulated white sugar 50 g | 1¾ oz | ¼ cup
Gelatine (gold) 5 g | 2½ sheets (softened in ice cold water, with excess water squeezed out)
Whipping cream (35% fat) [2] 200 ml | 7 fl oz | ⅘ cup

For the Strawberry Consommé
Strawberries 2 punnets
Caster (superfine) sugar 20 g | sc. ¾ oz | 1½ tbsp

INSTRUCTIONS

Meringue
1   Pre-heat the oven to 120°C (250°F).
2   Use a brush or cloth to coat a tray with butter.
3   Beat the egg whites and a quarter of the sugar at room temperature.
4   After a while, slowly add the second quarter of sugar.
5   Finish with the remaining half of the sugar, continually whisking.
6   Place a silicone baking paper sheet on the butter-coated tray and pipe small, rounded (not peaked) meringues to 4 cm (1⅝ in.) diameter.
7   Place in the oven for 60–75 minutes, first at 120°C (250°F), then reduced to 90°C (195°F) after 20 minutes.
8   Ensure the meringues are cooked through.

Vanilla Bavarois
1   Bring cream [1] and the vanilla seeds to the boil in a pan.
2   At the same time, place the egg yolks and sugar in a bowl, and whisk together.
3   When the cream has come to the boil, add this to the yolk mixture, then place back in the pan.
4   Cook out until the mixture coats the back of a spoon.
5   Remove from the heat and add the gelatine.
6   Let the mixture cool for about 20 minutes.
7   Semi-whip cream [2], then fold into the mixture.
8   Place into the deep tray, ensuring a thickness of 2 cm (¾ in.), then leave to set in the fridge.
9   Once set, cut out with the 4 cm (1⅝ in.) circle cutter.

Strawberry Consommé
1   Trim the strawberries, then place into a bowl with the sugar and cover with plastic wrap.
2   Place on top of a saucepan of water on the stove (making a bain-marie).
3   Leave to cook out slowly (30–45 minutes) so that all the juice comes out of the strawberries.
4   When ready, pass through a fine sieve (strainer), discarding the strawberries and retaining the clear consommé.
5   Place in the fridge to cool down.

ASSEMBLING

Components/Garnishes Strawberries, diced into small cubes (1 punnet); micro mint; ready-made strawberry ice cream; edible flowers

Place a vanilla bavarois on the base of each bowl, with a meringue disc on top. Arrange diced strawberries in small piles around the bowl, together with sprigs of micro mint. Place a quenelle of strawberry ice cream on top of the meringue. Pour on consommé to order, and decorate with an edible flower.

LEMON MERINGUE

While he was on a trip to France, John saw a chef making a meringue cylinder. He thought this looked interesting and so decided to create his own version of a lemon meringue.

MAKES 8–10 **DIFFICULTY** 4/5 **PREPARATION TIME** 6 hours (not including baking time for the meringue) **SPECIFIC EQUIPMENT** Digital candy thermometer; acetate sheets; Silpat® mat, or silicone baking paper sheets; piping (pastry) bag; ice cream machine, or Pacojet®

INGREDIENTS

For the Meringue

Granulated white sugar 100 g | 3½ oz | ½ cup
Egg whites 100 g | 3½ oz | ⅖ cup

For the Sablé

Plain (all-purpose) flour 162 g | 5¾ oz | gen. 1 cup
Caster (superfine) sugar 77 g | 2¾ oz | ⅓ cup
Almond meal 94 g | gen. 3¼ oz | gen. 1 cup
Salt 2 g | gen. ¼ tsp
Unsalted butter [1] 94 g | gen. 3¼ oz (soft)
Unsalted butter [2] 65 g | gen. 2¼ oz (melted)

For the Lemon Curd and Lemon Curd Jelly

Unsalted butter 100 g | 3½ oz
Icing (confectioner's) sugar 125 g | sc. 4½ oz | gen. ¾ cup
Lemon juice 100 g | 3½ fl oz | ½ cup
3 whole eggs
Cornflour (cornstarch) 4 g | sc. 1 tsp
Gelatine (gold) 5 g | 2½ sheets (softened in ice cold water, with excess water squeezed out)

For the Lemon Cream

Lemon curd (reserved in bowl, from above recipe)
Whipping cream (35% fat) 150 ml | sc. 5½ fl oz | gen. ½ cup

For the Mascarpone Ice Cream (makes 0.5 litres of ice cream)

Milk 250 ml | gen. 8¾ fl oz | gen. 1 cup
Whipping cream (35% fat) 50 ml | 1¾ fl oz | ⅕ cup
4 egg yolks
Granulated white sugar 75 g | gen. 2½ oz | gen. ⅓ cup
Mascarpone 100 g | 3½ oz | 7½ tbsp

For the White Chocolate 'Snow'

White chocolate 100 g | 3½ oz
Maltodextrin 200 g | 7 oz | sc. 2 cups

INSTRUCTIONS

Meringue

1 Place the sugar in a pan with enough water to soak, then bring up to 118°C (244°F).
2 Place the egg whites in a mixing bowl and begin to whisk.
3 Once the egg whites have formed soft peaks, pour in the sugar on high speed.
4 Cut acetate sheets into six 12 x 12 cm (4¾ x 4¾ in.) squares.
5 When the meringue has a stiff, glossy, firm peak, take it out and smear or pipe it out over the sheets (about 2 mm/1⁄16 in. thick). NB Do not overbeat or else syrup will leak out during cooking, making the acetate more difficult to remove later.
6 Roll each sheet up to form a cylinder (with the meringue inside), then sticky-tape together and place on a silicone baking paper-lined tray.
7 Bake at 70°C (160°F) for about 12 hours, then leave to cool.
8 Remove the acetate and trim any excess to square off the ends of each cylinder.

Sablé

1 Mix all the ingredients, except for the melted butter, until there are no lumps.
2 Add the melted butter to make a paste.
3 Roll out onto a silicone baking paper-lined tray and bake at 180°C (350°F) for about 20 minutes, or until the desired colour is achieved.
4 Place in the fridge to cool down.
5 Once cool, place in a processor, bring to a crumb, then set aside.

Lemon Curd and Lemon Curd Jelly

1 Place the butter, sugar and lemon juice in a pan, stir until melted, then bring to the boil.
2 Whisk the eggs and cornflour (cornstarch) together, then add the previously prepared liquid.
3 Put back on the stove and cook out, stirring constantly until thick.
4 Take the curd off the stove and divide it into two.
5 Place one portion of curd in a bowl in the fridge, to be used for the lemon cream (recipe below).
6 Add the gelatine to the other portion of curd, smear this thinly on a Silpat® mat or silicone baking paper and leave to set in the fridge.

Lemon Cream

1 Reserve 20 g (sc. ¾ oz/1 tbsp) of the non-gelatine lemon curd for plating up, then place the rest in a mixing bowl with the cream and mix until firm.
2 Place into the piping (pastry) bag, ready for piping inside the meringue cylinder.

Mascarpone Ice Cream

1 Bring the milk and cream to the boil.
2 Whisk the egg yolks and sugar in a bowl until very pale.
3 Add the boiled milk and cream, then place back on the heat.
4 Cook to 85°C (185°F), remove from the heat and add the mascarpone.
5 Refrigerate for 4 hours, then churn in an ice cream machine according to the manufacturer's instructions (or freeze for 24 hours and pacotize in a Pacojet®).

White Chocolate 'Snow'

1 Melt the white chocolate.
2 Slowly add the maltodextrin off the heat, while stirring, until the consistency looks like snow.

ASSEMBLING

Garnish Micro lemon balm

Brush reserved lemon curd over each plate. Place portions of sablé where the meringue cylinder and the mascarpone ice cream will be placed. Fill each cylinder with lemon cream. Cut the lemon curd jelly into strips. Place the cylinder on a portion of sablé, lay a jelly strip on top, garnish with micro lemon balm and place white chocolate 'snow' at each end, as if flowing out of the cylinder. Place a quenelle of ice cream on top of the second portion of sablé.

BANANA SPLIT   'I wanted to recreate an old classic,' says John, 'by putting a modern twist on it.'

MAKES 10-12   **DIFFICULTY** 3½/5   **PREPARATION TIME** 3 hours (not including freezing time for the mousse)
SPECIFIC EQUIPMENT Digital candy thermometer; 10-12 x bottomless rectangular frames (each 7 x 3 cm/2¾ x 1⅛ in.); spray gun

INGREDIENTS

For the Hazelnut Dacquoise
Caster (superfine) sugar 50 g | 1¾ oz | sc. ¼ cup
Egg whites 75 g | gen. 2½ oz | 5 tbsp
Hazelnut meal 63 g | sc. 2¼ oz | gen. ½ cup
Icing (confectioner's) sugar 75 g | gen. 2½ oz | sc. ½ cup

For the Caramelized Banana Mousse
Ripe bananas 100 g | 3½ oz
Brown sugar 25 g | gen. ¾ oz | 2 tbsp
Milk 50 ml | 1¾ fl oz | sc. 3½ tbsp
Gelatine (gold) 5 g | 2½ sheets (softened in ice cold water, with excess water squeezed out)
Whipping cream (35% fat) 150 ml | sc. 5½ fl oz | gen. ½ cup

For Putting Together the Banana Split
Hazelnut dacquoise (from previous recipe)
Caramelized banana mousse (from above recipe)
1 large ripe banana (sliced)

For the Caramelized White Chocolate Spray
Caramelized white chocolate 150 g | gen. 5¼ oz
(or plain white chocolate)
Cocoa butter 150 g | gen. 5¼ oz

INSTRUCTIONS

Hazelnut Dacquoise
1   Place the caster (superfine) sugar in a pan with enough water to soak and bring up to 118°C (244°F) to make a syrup.
2   Place the egg whites in the bowl of a stand mixer with a whisk attachment and whisk on high speed, then add the syrup.
3   Whisk until soft peaks form, or until just firm.
4   Fold in the other ingredients by hand.
5   Spread on a silicone baking paper-lined tray, to a thickness of approximately 1 cm (⅜ in.), and bake at 180°C (350°F) for 20 minutes, until golden and crisp.

Caramelized Banana Mousse
1   Caramelize the bananas with the brown sugar.
2   Put the mixture in a processor to make a purée, using the milk.
3   Place the purée in a pan and bring up to 80°C (176°F).
4   Add the gelatine, then allow to cool down.
5   Semi-whip the cream, then fold in the cooled caramelized banana mixture.

Putting Together the Banana Split
1   Cut the hazelnut dacquoise to size and place into the frames, bottoms sealed with plastic wrap.
2   Fill a quarter of each frame with the mousse.
3   Place banana slices in the centre.
4   Fill the rest of each frame with mousse.
5   Freeze until firm.

Caramelized White Chocolate Spray
1   Melt the chocolate and cocoa butter together.
2   Place into the spray gun.
3   Remove the firmed-up banana splits from their frames and place on a tray.
4   Spray evenly with the spray gun.

ASSEMBLING

Components/Garnishes Dry caramel; fresh peeled hazelnuts; tempered dark chocolate plaques, made using 100 g (3½ oz) of dark chocolate (70%); ground hazelnuts; vanilla ice cream

Cook a dry caramel and let it rest. When it starts to set, use tweezers to dip in a hazelnut, then lift it to draw out a tail of caramel. Place a banana split in the centre of each plate. Place three hazelnuts on the mousse, including the one dipped in caramel. Place two tempered chocolate plaques on each side. Brush some caramel on the plate, at either side of the banana split, and some dark chocolate smears. Finally, place ground hazelnuts on the plate and top with a quenelle of vanilla ice cream.

Julie Sharp

....

UK

What would your dream job be? If you love pastry, chocolate and teaching equally, then being development chef and technical adviser for Barry Callebaut, one of the world's leading manufacturers of cocoa and chocolate products, would quite possibly be it. Julie Sharp could not agree more. 'My role within the UK arm consists of educating industry professionals in the use of Cacao Barry products,' she explains. 'The job uses all of my past experiences as a pastry chef and a teacher to help inspire and educate chefs.'

Julie's résumé reads like a roll-call of the best five-star hotels in London (she was executive pastry chef at The Landmark, then at the Mandarin Oriental, culminating in the position of head pastry chef at Claridge's) as well as a few cheerful exotic destinations (executive pastry chef at the Lyford Cay Club, Bahamas; the Chateau Lake Louise, Alberta; and the Sofitel, Melbourne). To say that she is an expert is a given; she is above all a passionate ambassador for her craft. 'Our industry can be very demanding – long hours and poor pay when you're working your way up through the ranks – but I loved it. I like working within a team who are all striving for the same goal. I also love to teach people. I like to see the pleasure and sense of achievement when they've mastered a new technique or have just designed their first pastry or plated dessert.'

Julie abides by a certain classicism – respect for ingredients and techniques. That is not to say that she rejects novelty, but she prefers experimentation that serves tradition rather than bulldozes it. 'I think pastry is an ever-evolving industry. At the moment molecular gastronomy is very popular – it's developed some really interesting concepts, and there are lots of new ingredients that will help create textures and suspensions – but I mostly prefer the more classic route, and I don't like to play around with food too much.' Case in point Julie likes to keep her desserts sweet, not savoury. 'I think most customers want a real dessert to finish their meal,' she states. 'Customers' palates are changing, they are more willing to try new things, but you don't want to confuse them. They like some familiarity.' Doesn't this sound like the sweet voice of reason?

www.cacao-barry.com

ROASTED CARAMEL PEACH

'This dessert is lovely for a summer's evening,' says Julie. 'The roasted peaches are delicious served hot or cold, and if you have any left over they are also nice baked in a tart with frangipani, or folded through a vanilla parfait.'

MAKES 6   **DIFFICULTY** 3/5   **PREPARATION TIME** 3 hours   **SPECIFIC EQUIPMENT** Digital candy thermometer; ice cream machine; immersion blender with a flat disc aeration beater

INGREDIENTS

For the Caramelized Peach

Caster (superfine) sugar [1] 250 g | gen. 8¾ oz | gen. 1 cup
Orange juice 300 g | 10 fl oz | 1¼ cups
1 vanilla pod (bean) (split, scraped, seeds reserved)
6 peaches with skin
Unsalted butter (melted, for brushing peaches)
Caster (superfine) sugar [2] (for coating peaches)

For the Lemon Verbena Sherbet

Lemon verbena (to taste)
Milk 100 g | sc. 3½ fl oz | sc. ½ cup
Water 100 g | 3½ fl oz | sc. ½ cup
Fresh lemon juice 100 g | sc. 3½ fl oz | sc. ½ cup
Granulated white sugar 120 g | 4¼ oz | gen. ½ cup

For the Almond Crumble

Unsalted butter 55 g | sc. 2 oz (softened)
Granulated white sugar 45 g | 1½ oz | sc. ¼ cup
Plain (all-purpose) flour 30 g | 1 oz | 2½ tbsp
Almond meal 30 g | 1 oz | 5 tbsp
Cocoa butter powder (e.g. Mycryo® by Cacao Barry) (to taste)

For the White Chocolate Foam

Milk 450 ml | gen. 15¾ fl oz | sc. 2 cups
8 egg yolks
Granulated white sugar 50 g | 1¾ oz | ¼ cup
White chocolate buttons (e.g. Blanc Satin® 29.2% by Cacao Barry) 150 g | gen. 5¼ oz

INSTRUCTIONS

Caramelized Peach

1   Make a dry caramel from caster (superfine) sugar [1], by heating up a saucepan, then sprinkling thin layers of sugar onto the base of the pan; once this dissolves, sprinkle on some more, trying to stir as little as possible to avoid crystallizing the sugar.

2   Warm up the orange juice, then add the vanilla seeds into it.

3   Slowly add the orange juice to the caramel, stirring over the heat until incorporated. NB Only add small amounts at a time, as it will spit.

4   Brush the outside of the peaches with melted butter, then roll in caster (superfine) sugar [2].

5   Place into a baking tray, then pour over the caramelized orange juice.

6   Bake at 180°C (350°F), basting the peaches every 10 minutes until cooked.

7   Leave the peaches to cool in the caramel.

Lemon Verbena Sherbet

1   Infuse the lemon verbena in the milk at 60°C (140°F) for 20 minutes, then strain.

2   Bring all of the ingredients to the boil, strain and cool down.

3   Churn in an ice cream machine according to the manufacturer's instructions.

Almond Crumble

1   Rub all of the ingredients together, except for the cocoa butter powder, to produce a crumble.

2   Place on a baking tray.

3   Bake at 165°C (325°F) for about 15 minutes, until golden brown.

4   After baking, sprinkle the crumble with cocoa butter powder and mix.

White Chocolate Foam

1   Bring the milk to the boil.

2   Whisk the egg yolks and sugar together until pale, then slowly pour the boiling milk onto the mixture, little by little, continuing to whisk.

3   Return to the saucepan and cook over a low heat to 80°C (176°F), until the sauce starts to thicken.

4   Remove from the heat and add in the white chocolate.

5   Whisk, then strain and cool down.

ASSEMBLING

Garnishes Sprigs of lemon verbena

Remove the skins of the caramelized peaches (as shown in the photo opposite), or leave intact if preferred. Re-warm the peaches in the microwave. Place a peach on one side of a dish and garnish with a sprig of lemon verbena. Place some almond crumble on the dish and stack a quenelle of lemon verbena sherbet on top. Pour the white chocolate sauce into a jug and use an immersion blender with a flat disc aeration beater to create foam. Use a spoon to scoop the foam off and place it between the peach and the sherbet. You could also add a decorative chocolate stick, made by dusting a chocolate splitter with gold creative powder, piping on pre-crystallized (tempered) chocolate and allowing this to set.

CHOCOLATE, RASPBERRY AND LYCHEE PARFAIT

'This dessert is great for dinner parties,' Julie notes. 'It can be done in advance, and all you have to do on the day is plate it up. With the lychee parfait insert your guest will have a surprise in the middle, which is always fun, but remember to take it out of the freezer at least fifteen minutes before serving, so that it can start to thaw out.'

MAKES 10   **DIFFICULTY** 4/5   **PREPARATION TIME** 6–8 hours (including freezing time for the parfaits)   **SPECIFIC EQUIPMENT** Digital candy thermometer; 10 x spherical silicone moulds, e.g. Pavoni® (each 3.5 cm/1⅜ in. diameter), or 20 x half-sphere silicone moulds; spray gun; piping (pastry) bag; 10 x spherical silicone moulds, e.g. Pavoni® (each 5.5 cm/2⅛ in. diameter), or 20 x half-sphere silicone moulds; Silpat® mat; ice cream machine; acetate sheet

INGREDIENTS

For the Lychee Parfait
(makes more than required, but a more manageable amount)

3 egg yolks
1 whole egg
Water 25 g | gen. ¾ fl oz | 5 tsp
Granulated white sugar 60 g | gen. 2 oz | gen. ¼ cup
Whipping cream (35% fat) 225 g | gen. 7¾ fl oz | sc. 1 cup
Lychee purée 300 g | sc. 10¾ fl oz | sc. 1¼ cups
Gelatine (gold) 2 g | 1 sheet (softened in ice cold water, with excess water squeezed out)
Rose water (to taste)

For the Chocolate and Raspberry Parfait
(makes more than required, but a more manageable amount)

2 egg yolks
1 whole egg
Water 25 g | gen. ¾ fl oz | 5 tsp
Granulated white sugar 100 g | 3½ oz | ½ cup
Dark chocolate couverture (e.g. Favorites Mi-Amère 58% by Cacao Barry) 200 g | 7 oz
Gelatine (gold) 1 g | ½ sheet (softened in ice cold water, with excess water squeezed out)
Raspberry purée 250 g | 9 fl oz | 1 cup
Whipping cream (35% fat) 300 g | 10½ fl oz | 1⅓ cups

For the Spraying Chocolate

Dark chocolate couverture (e.g. Favorites Mi-Amère 58% by Cacao Barry) 250 g | gen. 8¾ oz
Cocoa butter 125 g | sc. 4½ oz

For the Caramelized Chocolate

Water 75 g | gen. 2½ fl oz | 5 tbsp
Caster (superfine) sugar 200 g | 7 oz | sc. 1 cup
Dark chocolate couverture (e.g. Fleur de Cao® 70% by Cacao Barry) 80 g | gen. 2¾ oz

For the Lychee Sorbet

Water 250 g | gen. 8¾ fl oz | 1 cup
Caster (superfine) sugar 70 g | 2½ oz | sc. ⅓ cup
Glucose syrup 35 g | 1¼ fl oz | sc. 2 tbsp
Lychee purée 250 g | 9 fl oz | 1 cup
Rose water (to taste)

For the Chocolate Garnish

White cocoa butter (to achieve desired colour)
Red cocoa butter (to achieve desired colour)
Gold creative powder (to dust)
Dark chocolate couverture 150 g | gen. 5¼ oz (tempered)

INSTRUCTIONS

Lychee Parfait

1 Whisk the egg yolks and the egg to full peak in a stand mixer.
2 Boil the water and sugar to 121°C (250°F) (soft ball stage), then pour over the eggs and whisk until cool, forming a sabayon.
3 Whip the cream.
4 Warm a small amount of the purée and melt the gelatine in it, then add to the remaining purée.
5 Add in the rose water.
6 Fold the purée through the sabayon, then fold in the whipped cream.
7 Pipe into the 3.5 cm (1⅜ in.) spherical moulds, freeze, unmould, then place back in the freezer.

Chocolate and Raspberry Parfait

1 Whisk the egg yolks and the egg in a stand mixer.
2 Boil the water and sugar to 121°C (250°F), then pour over the eggs to make a sabayon.
3 Melt the chocolate and carefully stir into the sabayon.
4 Melt the gelatine in a little raspberry purée, add to the rest of the purée, then refrigerate to allow to thicken a little.
5 Whisk the cream to soft peaks and gently fold in the thickened raspberry purée.
6 Fold the resulting raspberry cream and the sabayon together.
7 Pipe some of the resulting chocolate parfait mixture into the base of the 5.5 cm (2⅛ in.) spherical moulds.
8 Place a frozen lychee parfait sphere (from above recipe) into the centre of each chocolate parfait.
9 Put the tops of the spherical moulds on and fill with chocolate parfait.
10 Freeze, unmould, then place back in the freezer.

Spraying Chocolate

1 Melt the chocolate and cocoa butter together, then strain if necessary.
2 Place into a spray gun and, while still liquid but not hot, spray over the frozen parfait spheres.
3 Return the spheres to the freezer.

Caramelized Chocolate

1 Boil the water and sugar to 135°C (275°F).
2 Add the chocolate into the saucepan and whisk vigorously (the chocolate will look like sand).
3 Pour onto a Silpat® mat to cool.

Lychee Sorbet

1 Heat the water to 45°C (113°F), then add in the sugar and glucose syrup.
2 Heat to 85°C (185°F), allow to cool, then add in the purée with the rose water.
3 Churn in an ice cream machine according to the manufacturer's instructions.

Chocolate Garnish

1 Melt the white cocoa butter, flick onto an acetate sheet and allow to dry.
2 Melt the red cocoa butter, brush over the top of the white cocoa butter and allow to dry.
3 Brush with gold creative powder.
4 Place a thin layer of tempered chocolate on top. (To temper chocolate in a microwave, pour some callets of chocolate into a microwaveable plastic bowl, then melt at 800–1000W. Remove from the microwave every 15–20 seconds and stir well to ensure that the temperature is evenly distributed and no scorching occurs. Repeat until almost all the chocolate has melted; some small pieces of callet should still be visible in the bowl. NB The chocolate should not be above 34°C [93°F]. Remove from the microwave and stir well, until all the pieces of callet have disappeared and the liquid is even and slightly thickened. The chocolate is now tempered and ready to work with.)
5 Allow the garnish to dry a little, then cut into squares.
6 Place a light board on top, then put into the fridge and allow to set.

ASSEMBLING

Garnish Fresh raspberries

Place a square of chocolate garnish on top of each sphere, then a quenelle of lychee sorbet.
Draw a trail of caramelized chocolate around the sphere and add some fresh raspberries. You can also add any type of chocolate decoration (such as the chocolate swirl in the photo opposite).

CHOCOLATE AND CARAMEL SLICE

'This is a really luxurious chocolate mousse, which has a few different textures that make it exciting to eat,' Julie enthuses. 'I have done it as a plated dessert for this recipe, but it would be equally good as an afternoon tea pastry.'

MAKES 18   **DIFFICULTY** 4/5   **PREPARATION TIME** 5 hours (not including overnight maturation of the ice cream mixture)   **SPECIFIC EQUIPMENT** Digital candy thermometer; ice cream machine; cake tin (pan) (30 x 20 cm/11¾ x 7¾ in.); frame (30 x 20 cm/11¾ x 7¾ in.); piping (pastry) bag; acetate sheet

INGREDIENTS

For the Malted Barley Chocolate Ice Cream

Pearl barley 60 g | gen. 2 oz | gen. ¼ cup

Milk 250 g | 8½ fl oz | gen. 1 cup

Double (heavy) whipping cream (48% fat)
125 g | 4½ fl oz | ½ cup

1 vanilla pod (bean) (split, scraped, seeds reserved)

Caster (superfine) sugar 25 g | gen. ¾ oz | sc. 2 tbsp

Egg yolks 75 g | gen. 2⅓ oz | 5 tbsp

Malt extract 20 g | sc. ¾ oz | gen. 2 tbsp

Milk chocolate couverture (e.g. Papouasie 35.7%
by Cacao Barry) 75 g | gen. 2½ oz

INSTRUCTIONS

Malted Barley Chocolate Ice Cream

1   Place the pearl barley onto a tray and toast at 180°C (350°F) for 5 minutes, or until golden brown.

2   Bring the milk, cream and vanilla seeds to the boil with half the sugar and the toasted pearl barley.

3   Remove from the heat, place a lid on the saucepan and infuse for 40 minutes.

4   Strain the mixture, then bring back to the boil.

5   Whisk the other half of the sugar with the egg yolks and malt extract until fluffy and pale.

6   Once the milk has boiled, slowly pour it onto the egg yolk mixture and whisk.

7   Return to the pan and cook over a medium heat to 80°C (176°F), until it coats the back of a spoon.

8   Add in the chocolate, then strain.

9   Mature overnight in the fridge, then churn in an ice cream machine according to the manufacturer's instructions.

For the Chocolate Brownies – Triple Chocolate

Unsalted butter 185 g | 6½ oz

Dark chocolate couverture (e.g. Favorites Mi-Amère 58%
by Cacao Barry) 185 g | 6½ oz

Plain (all-purpose) flour 85 g | 3 oz | gen. ½ cup

Cocoa powder (e.g. Extra Brute by Cacao Barry) 40 g |
sc. 1½ oz | sc. ⅔ cup

3 large eggs

Light brown caster (superfine) sugar 275 g | 9¾ oz | 1⅓ cups

White chocolate buttons (e.g. Blanc Satin® 29.2%
by Cacao Barry) 50 g | 1¾ oz

Milk chocolate buttons (e.g. Lactée Supérieure 38.2%
by Cacao Barry) 50 g | 1¾ oz

For the Milk Chocolate and Caramel Mousse

Caster (superfine) sugar 130 g | 4½ oz | gen. ½ cup

Whipping cream (35% fat) [1] 255 g | sc. 9 fl oz | 1 cup (warm)

Pasteurised egg yolks 180 g | gen. 6¼ oz | ¾ cup

Gelatine (gold) 14 g | 7 sheets (softened in ice cold water,
with excess water squeezed out)

Milk chocolate couverture (e.g. Ghana 40.5%
by Cacao Barry) 460 g | 1 lb

Whipping cream (35% fat) [2] 900 g | 31½ fl oz | gen. 3½ cups

For the Feuilletine Crunch

Milk chocolate 55 g | sc. 2 oz

Praline paste 125 g | sc. 4½ oz | ½ cup

Pailleté feuilletine (chopped crêpes dentelles/
French crispy pancakes) 125 g | sc. 4½ oz | 1½ cups

For Pearled Chocolate Mousse Strip

Chilled mousse in piping/pastry bag (from previous recipe)

Chocolate pearls (to taste)

For the Espresso Caramel

Caster (superfine) sugar 50 g | 1¾ oz | sc. ¼ cup

Espresso coffee 2 shots

For the Dark Chocolate Glaze

Double (heavy) whipping cream (48% fat) 600 ml | 21 fl oz |
sc. 2½ cups

Dark chocolate couverture (e.g. Extra Bitter Guayaquil 64%
by Cacao Barry) 600 g | gen. 1 lb 5 oz

Unsalted butter 200 g | 7 oz (soft)

Chocolate Brownies – Triple Chocolate

1 Melt the butter and dark chocolate together, then cool.
2 Sift the flour and cocoa powder together three times.
3 Whisk the eggs and sugar together in a stand mixer to form a sabayon.
4 Fold in the cooled dark chocolate mixture.
5 Fold in the sifted flour and cocoa mixture.
6 Fold in the white chocolate and milk chocolate.
7 Prepare the cake tin (pan) by lining the bottom with a piece of waxed paper.
8 Pour the mixture into the tin (pan) and bake at 160°C (325°F) for 25 minutes.
9 Cool in the tin (pan), then transfer to the bottom of the frame.

Milk Chocolate and Caramel Mousse

1 Make a dry caramel from the sugar and allow it to foam.
2 Add the warm cream [1] in small additions to form a butterscotch sauce. NB Take care, as this will spit.
3 Whisk the egg yolks in a stand mixer until pale and fluffy.
4 Add the gelatine into the butterscotch sauce, then pour this onto the yolks while whisking.
5 Whisk to a sabayon, allowing to cool to 30°C (86°F).
6 Melt the milk chocolate and fold through the sabayon.
7 Semi-whip cream [2] and fold into the chocolate sabayon.
8 Pour 800 g (28 oz) on top of the brownie base in the frame (above recipe), then freeze.
9 Reserve 800 g (28 oz) at room temperature for assembling the cake.
10 Put the remainder of the mousse in the piping (pastry) bag and chill (this will be used for the pearled chocolate mousse strip below).

Feuilletine Crunch

1 Melt the chocolate and praline paste together, then fold in the pailleté feuilletine.
2 Spread between two sheets of silicone paper and roll to the desired thickness (3–4 mm/⅛ in.).
3 Leave to set in the freezer, then cut out to 30 x 20 cm (11¾ x 7¾ in.).

Pearled Chocolate Mousse Strip

1 Pipe thin lines of chocolate mousse – max. 9 cm (3½ in.) long – onto an acetate sheet, one line per cake.
2 Place some chocolate pearls onto a tray.
3 Turn the acetate sheet upside down and dip the strips into the pearls, which will adhere to the mousse.
4 Freeze.

Espresso Caramel

1 Make a dry caramel with the sugar, then deglaze the pan with the espresso coffee. NB Take care, as this will spit.
2 Allow to cool.

Dark Chocolate Glaze

1 Bring the cream to the boil.
2 Pour onto the chocolate and leave to settle for 2 minutes.
3 Mix well with a whisk or hand mixer, then add in the soft butter, trying to avoid getting too many bubbles in the mixture.
4 Use immediately.

ASSEMBLING

Garnishes Tempered chocolate curls, made by cutting a strip of acetate sheet, covering it with a thin layer of tempered chocolate, placing this into a curved mould to give it its shape, then allowing it to set

Take the brownie with its first chocolate mousse layer out of the freezer. Carefully insert the layer of feuilletine crunch. Top with the reserved 800 g (28 oz) of mousse and freeze again. Unmould from the frame, then cut into eighteen 9 x 3 cm (3½ x 1⅛ in.) slices, trimming and straightening the edges. Place onto a wire rack and glaze. Refrigerate to set. Garnish on the plate with a strip of pearled chocolate mousse, a chocolate curl and a quenelle of malted barley chocolate ice cream. Drizzle espresso caramel around the plate. You could also accompany each plate with fresh raspberries.

Luca Lacalamita

ITALY

Whisky as a perfume? Hold your thoughts for a moment. Italian head pastry chef Luca Lacalamita explains: 'I wanted to use a Longrow [Campbeltown single malt scotch] in a dessert, but I wanted to extract all the aromas and make the dessert without the actual whisky. It was a long project – almost two months to get it right – but the dessert was unique. All the aromas – smoke, caramel, vanilla, spices and malt – were in a whisky balloon glass, all in different textures, and the glass was served with a paper stick that had the whisky sprayed on. So the customer could eat the dessert while smelling the stick, thereby getting all the aromas of whisky but without ingesting any alcohol at all.'

This is the kind of captivating conceptual project that Luca develops with his team of five at the three-Michelin-starred Enoteca Pinchiorri in Florence. Luca's previous working experiences – whether with Gordon Ramsay in the UK; at Cracco-Peck in Milan, or Osteria Francescana in Modena; at El Bulli or Akelarre in Spain – have also shaped his predilection for new pairings that may be minimalist in form but are always deep in flavour.

'Before I went to join Massimo Bottura in Modena,' says Luca, 'he told me a quote that means a lot to me: "Once you have the technique in your hands, it's time to use your brains." We have a rule of four ingredients for a dessert. Once the components are satisfactory, we study the finish. This system provides some flexibility when we make new dishes, because we can keep changing elements of the plating or the order of the composition.' He goes on to note, 'I would describe myself as a translator because art and design are the most important factors in the pastry world, and a good pastry chef has to be the right link. We have to address all the senses because a customer has to understand everything we are doing.'

Customers and critics alike recognize and appreciate the exceptional drive on display. 'I remember one customer who came into the Enoteca just to have the dessert menu with wine pairing. In Italy this doesn't happen often,' recalls Luca. 'Then he asked for more. We made about twelve different desserts for him. He was ecstatic.' We would be for less.

www.enotecapinchiorri.com

WATER AND CHOCOLATE, THINKING ABOUT RICHARD SERRA

'We were thinking about the idealism of the sculptor Richard Serra,' Luca reminisces. 'We wanted to try and reproduce one of his works aesthetically. We transposed it with extreme ingredients – in this case, water and chocolate; two ingredients that will never work together – but this time we tried not to incorporate them together, but rather to let them co-exist.'

MAKES 8   **DIFFICULTY** 5/5   **PREPARATION TIME** 4 hours (not including freezing time for the marshmallow and granita or maturing time for the sorbet)   **SPECIFIC EQUIPMENT** Digital candy thermometer; acetate sheets; plain base shallow tray, ideally Plexiglas® (approx. 20 x 20 cm/7¾ x 7¾ in.); ice cream machine; Pacojet®, or small deep tray; Silpat® mat; sugar heat lamp, or hair dryer

INGREDIENTS

For the Iced Water Marshmallow

Sparkling water (e.g. Lauretana) [1] 168 g | sc. 6 fl oz | sc. ¾ cup

100% sugar syrup (ratio: 50 g/sc. 1¾ fl oz/3½ tbsp water
to 50 g/1¾ oz/¼ cup granulated white sugar)
38 g | 1¼ fl oz | 2½ tbsp

Gelatine (gold) 5.5 g | 2¾ sheets

Sparkling water (e.g. Lauretana) [2] 58 g | 2 fl oz | ¼ cup

For the Chocolate Sorbet

Sparkling water (e.g. Lauretana) 320 g | 11¼ fl oz | sc. 1⅓ cups

Granulated white sugar 50 g | 1¾ oz | ¼ cup

Sorbet stabilizer 3 g | sc. 1 tsp

Cocoa powder 15 g | ½ oz | 2 tbsp

Dark chocolate (e.g. Grand Cru Dark Baking Chocolate
Caraibe 66% by Valrhona) 70 g | 2½ oz

For the Water Granita

Granulated white sugar 20 g | sc. ¾ oz | 5 tsp

Sparkling water (e.g. Lauretana) 225 g | sc. 8 fl oz | sc. 1 cup

For the Water and Chocolate Sauce

Sparkling water (e.g. Lauretana) 130 g | 4½ fl oz | ½ cup

Glucose syrup 100 g | 3½ fl oz | gen. ¼ cup

Salt 1 g | gen. ⅛ tsp

Dark chocolate (e.g. Nyangbo 68% by Valrhona)
125 g | sc. 4½ oz

For the Chocolate Powder

Dark chocolate (e.g. Guanaja 70% by Valrhona) 100 g | 3½ oz

Liquid nitrogen

For the Chocolate Croquant

Sparkling water (e.g. Lauretana) 250 g | gen. 8¾ fl oz | 1 cup

Granulated white sugar 65 g | gen. 2¼ oz | ⅓ cup

Glucose syrup 19 g | ¾ fl oz | 1 tbsp

Dextrose 38 g | gen. 1¼ oz | 4 tbsp

Gellan low acyl 5 g | sc. ¼ oz | 1¼ tsp

Cocoa powder 50 g | 1¾ oz | sc. ½ cup

Salt 2.5 g | sc. ½ tsp

INSTRUCTIONS

Iced Water Marshmallow

1   Mix the water [1] and sugar syrup, then freeze.
2   Soak the gelatine in water [2], then heat to 40°C (104°F) to dissolve.
3   Start whipping the gelatine/water mixture, then slowly add the frozen water/syrup mixture.
4   Once whipped, spread the marshmallow on an acetate sheet-lined plain tray, use a flat bar to smooth the surface evenly, then freeze.
5   Once frozen, cut out rectangles 2 cm (¾ in.) wide and 7 cm (2¾ in.) long.
6   Reserve in the freezer.

Chocolate Sorbet

1   Boil the water, then add the sugar mixed with the stabilizer.
2   Slowly add the cocoa powder and chocolate, and blitz with an immersion blender.
3   Strain, then mature in the fridge for 8 hours.
4   Churn in an ice cream machine according to the manufacturer's instructions.

Water Granita

1   Mix and dissolve the sugar in a small amount of the water.
2   Blend together with the rest of the water, then freeze in a Pacojet® beaker and make frozen powder. Alternatively, if you do not have a Pacojet®, mix and dissolve the sugar in a small amount of the water; add this to the rest of the water and mix well; pour the mix into a small, deep tray; put the tray in the freezer at -20°C (-4°F) for at least 6 hours; use a fork to scrape the granita, then leave it in a small, sealed container in the freezer until ready for plating.

Water and Chocolate Sauce

1   Bring the water, glucose syrup and salt to the boil.
2   Add the chocolate and blitz with an immersion blender.
3   Strain, then reserve in the fridge.

Chocolate Powder

1   Freeze the chocolate in liquid nitrogen.
2   Promptly after freezing, blitz in a food processor, then leave in the freezer. NB Do not touch the chocolate with bare hands.

Chocolate Croquant

1   Boil the water, then add the sugar, glucose syrup and dextrose.
2   Add the gellan and cool to 70°C (158°F).
3   Blitz in a food processor, then add the cocoa powder and salt.
4   Make stencils by taking an acetate sheet and cutting out rectangles 11 cm (4⅜ in.) long and 2.5 cm (1 in.) wide.
5   Spread the croquant over the stencils on a Silpat® mat to make the rectangles (you will need 3–4 rectangles per serving).
6   Leave to dry at room temperature for 3 hours.
7   Bake in the oven at 160°C (325°F) for 6–8 minutes.
8   Leave to cool for 15 minutes.
9   Use a sugar heat lamp (or hair dryer) to gently re-heat the croquant rectangles so they can be shaped into 'waves' while warm (to aid the process, you can lay each croquant over a rod); ensure the croquant cools down for 5 minutes between each manipulation so that it is crunchy.
10 Once shaped, reserve cool in a sealed container and use the same day.

ASSEMBLING

Take the frozen marshmallows out of the freezer. Next, using a home-made rectangular stencil, smear four small rectangles of water/chocolate sauce on each plate. Sandwich frozen marshmallow between chocolate croquant waves, making a sort of 'mille-feuilles' with three to four layers. Place this in the middle of the plate. Sprinkle some chocolate powder inside the 'mille-feuilles' and some towards the edge of the plate. Place a quenelle of chocolate sorbet on the 'mille-feuilles', top with some granita, and serve.

BEETROOT PEACH

'The "peach" is a typical Italian pastry,' explains Luca. 'It is made out of a shortbread from Sicily/Messina that is dipped in Alkermes liqueur, giving it the colour of a peach, and in the middle there is an orange cream with chocolate. We have modernized this, giving more colour and flavour, thanks to the beetroot. We want to instil childhood memories, yet introduce a surprise with the textures.'

MAKES approx. 40   **DIFFICULTY** 3/5   **PREPARATION TIME** 1 day   **SPECIFIC EQUIPMENT** Piping (pastry) bag; dehydrator, or oven with low heat setting; digital candy thermometer

INGREDIENTS

For the Beetroot Meringue

60% sugar syrup (ratio: 100 g/3½ fl oz/sc. ½ cup water to 60 g/gen. 2 oz/gen. ¼ cup granulated white sugar) 62 g | gen. 2 fl oz | 4 tbsp

Versawhip 600K 7.5 g | ¼ oz | ½ tbsp

Beetroot juice 124 g | 4¼ fl oz | ½ cup (strained)

Xanthan gum 0.1 g | tip of tsp

Freeze-dried egg white powder 0.3 g | tip of tsp

For the Beetroot Jelly

Beetroot juice 100 g | sc. 3½ fl oz | sc. ½ cup (strained)

Agar agar 1.4 g | ½ tsp

60% sugar syrup 63 g | sc. 2¼ fl oz | gen. 4 tbsp

For the Yoghurt Ganache

Whipping cream (35% fat) 100 g | gen. 3½ fl oz | sc. ½ cup

White chocolate 160 g | sc. 5¾ oz

Yoghurt (full fat, e.g. Greek) 130 g | 4½ oz | gen. ½ cup

INSTRUCTIONS

Beetroot Meringue

1   Blend all the ingredients with a hand mixer, then leave to rest in the fridge for at least 2 hours.

2   Once rested, whip in a stand mixer (e.g. KitchenAid®) until firm.

3   Place in a piping (pastry) bag and form meringues of 3 cm (1⅛ in.) diameter.

4   Leave to dry for 16 hours in a dehydrator (or in an oven at 45°C/115°F; alternatively, if your oven does not go that low, 80–100°C/175–200°F for 4 hours).

5   Store the meringues in an airtight container with silica gel to prevent humidity, or you can keep them in the dehydrator at a low temperature (25-30°C/75-85°F) until needed.

6   Keep for a maximum of 2 days (the meringues must not become soft).

Beetroot Jelly

1   Put all the ingredients in a saucepan and bring to the boil.

2   Strain and put in a small container.

3   Leave to set in the fridge.

4   Once set, cut out cubes of 3 x 3 mm (⅛ x ⅛ in.).

Yoghurt Ganache

1   Bring the cream to the boil.

2   Make an emulsion with the white chocolate.

3   Let the mixture rest until it cools to 22°C (72°F), then mix in the yoghurt.

4   Place in the cleaned, re-used piping (pastry) bag and chill until a thick consistency has formed.

ASSEMBLING

Garnish Yoghurt powder

Pipe 6 g (¼ oz/1 tsp) of ganache onto one meringue, place a cube of beetroot jelly on the ganache, then finish the 'sandwich' with a second meringue. Dust with yoghurt powder, place on a plate and serve immediately, as the meringue will start to soften as soon as the ganache is added.

FROM THE LEMON TO THE LIMONCELLO

'This is a homage to the famous liqueur from Campania,' enthuses Luca. 'We imagined a lemon tree there and designed a dish that would incorporate the intensity of the lemon in all its integrity: the hearty flavour of the leaves, the aromatic compound of the tree (we used almond) and the sweetness (honey). The result is a new conceptual movement – you smell the limoncello from a perfume tester, but you taste a dessert without alcohol.'

MAKES 8   **DIFFICULTY** 4/5   **PREPARATION TIME** 4 hours (not including 36 hours for the lemon ice and 12 hours for the verbena madeleine)
SPECIFIC EQUIPMENT Vacuum food sealer and canister (e.g. Cryovac® or Sunbeam FoodSaver®); whipped cream siphon and two cartridges; 2 x plum cake moulds (each 10 cm/4 in. long, 4 cm/1⅝ in. wide, 6 cm/2⅜ in. deep); digital candy thermometer; 2 x piping (pastry) bags

INGREDIENTS

For the Lemon Water
Sparkling water 166 g | gen. 5¾ fl oz | sc. ¾ cup
Shaved rind of 1 lemon

For the Lemon Ice
(makes more than required, but a more manageable amount)
Sparkling water 100 g | 3½ fl oz | sc. ½ cup
Lemon water (from above recipe) 100 g | 3½ fl oz | sc. ½ cup
60% sugar syrup (ratio: 100 g/3½ fl oz/sc. ½ cup water to 60 g/gen. 2 oz/gen. ¼ cup granulated white sugar) 100 g | 3½ fl oz | sc. ½ cup
Gelatine (gold) 3 g | 1½ sheets (softened in ice cold water, with excess water squeezed out)

For the Verbena Madeleine
Milk 17 g | ½ fl oz | gen. 1 tbsp
Fresh verbena leaves 7 g | ¼ oz (chopped)
Unsalted butter 67 g | sc. 2½ oz
Icing (confectioner's) sugar 43 g | 1½ oz | ¼ cup
2 whole eggs
Honey 43 g | 1½ fl oz | 2 tbsp
Plain (all-purpose) flour 82 g | gen. 2¾ oz | gen. ½ cup (sifted)
Baking powder 3 g | 1 tsp
Verbena powder 5 g | sc. ¼ oz | 2½ tsp

For the Almond Milk
Sparkling water 800 g | 28 fl oz | 3⅓ cups
Unsweetened raw almond paste 130 g | 4½ oz | ½ cup

For the Almond Milk Granita
Almond milk (from above recipe)
Gelatine (gold) 3 g | 1½ sheets (softened in ice cold water, with excess water squeezed out)

For the Lemon Albedo Purée
(makes more than required, but a more manageable amount)
Water [1] 1 litre | sc. 35¼ fl oz | 4¼ cups
Granulated white sugar [1] 180 g | gen. 6¼ oz | sc. 1 cup
Lemon albedo (white pith beneath the yellow skin) 150 g | gen. 5¼ oz
Whipping cream (35% fat) 55 g | 2 fl oz | ⅕ cup
Lemon juice 25 g | gen. ¾ fl oz | 5 tsp
Granulated white sugar [2] 15 g | ½ oz | 1¼ tbsp
Water [2] 15 g | ½ fl oz | 3 tsp
Unsalted butter 15 g | ½ oz
Zest of 1 lemon

For the Honey Cookie
Unsalted butter 50 g | 1¾ oz (soft)
Granulated white sugar 25 g | gen. ¾ oz | 2 tbsp

INSTRUCTIONS

Lemon Water
1   Mix the water and the lemon rind, then place in the vacuum canister and seal.
2   Allow to infuse in the fridge for 24 hours.

Lemon Ice
1   Mix the water, lemon water and sugar syrup, and warm.
2   Melt the gelatine in the syrup mixture.
3   Place in a whipped cream siphon and charge with two cartridges.
4   Leave to rest in the fridge for at least 6 hours.
5   Line a shallow dish with plastic wrap and discharge the siphon contents into it.
6   Freeze for 6 hours, then cut out small cubes of 1.5 x 1.5 cm (⅝ x ⅝ in.).

Verbena Madeleine
1   Make a warm infusion with the milk and chopped verbena leaves.
2   Put the butter and sugar into a stand mixer with a paddle attachment and beat until pale.
3   Slowly add the eggs, and then the honey.
4   Add the flour, baking powder and verbena powder, then the infused milk.
5   Leave to rest in the fridge for at least 12 hours.
6   Bake in the cake moulds at 170°C (325°F) for 25–30 minutes, or until a skewer comes out clean.
7   Once baked, allow to cool on a wire rack.

Almond Milk
1   Bring the water and almond paste to the boil (the paste can be prepared by soaking raw almonds in water overnight, then draining and blitzing with a little fresh water).
2   Blend the boiled water and paste with an immersion blender, then strain.

Almond Milk Granita
1   Heat a small amount of the almond milk, dissolve the gelatine in it, then add it to the remainder of the milk.
2   Leave to set in the freezer until soft-frozen, then scrape with a fork.
3   Blend in a food processor until smooth, then reserve in the freezer.

Lemon Albedo Purée
1   Make a syrup by combining water [1] and sugar [1].
2   Put the albedo in the syrup and bring to the boil three times, starting from cold; leave to cool between the first two times; the third time, simmer for 35 minutes.
3   Strain, then immediately put the albedo into a food processor (it has to be hot to emulsify with the other ingredients); add the cream, lemon juice, sugar [2] and water [2], and blitz.
4   Cook the resulting mixture at 50°C (122°F) for 19 minutes.
5   Add the butter and lemon zest.
6   Place in a piping (pastry) bag and leave to rest in the fridge.

Honey Cookie
1   Put the butter, sugar and honey in a stand mixer with a paddle attachment and beat until pale and creamy.
2   Add the almond meal and plain (all-purpose) flour, and mix.
3   Spread the cookie on a plain surface to a thickness of 0.5 cm (³⁄₁₆ in.), then put in the fridge to firm up.
4   Cut out squares of 1 x 1 cm (⅜ x ⅜ in.), sprinkle over a silicone baking paper-lined tray, and bake at 160°C (325°F) for 8–10 minutes, or until golden.

Regular honey (ideally freeze-dried honey powder to help keep the cookie crunchy for a little longer and to preserve it from humidity) 25 g | sc. 1 fl oz | 3½ tsp

Blanched almond meal 50 g | 1¾ oz | gen. ½ cup

Plain (all-purpose) flour 50 g | 1¾ oz | ⅓ cup (sifted)

For the Verbena Gel

60% sugar syrup 90 g | 3½ fl oz | sc. ½ cup

Glucose powder 15 g | ½ oz | 1½ tbsp

Agar agar 2.2 g | ¾ tsp

Verbena water* 180 g | gen. 6¼ fl oz | ¾ cup

* Verbena Water

Fresh verbena leaves 100 g | 3½ oz

Water [1] (to boil verbena leaves)

Water [2] 200 g | 7 fl oz | gen. ⅘ cup

Vitamin C powder 0.5 g | gen. tip of tsp

Verbena Gel

1 Bring the sugar syrup, glucose powder and agar agar to the boil in a saucepan.
2 Leave to set in the fridge.
3 Use an immersion blender to blitz the mixture, then slowly add the verbena water (method similar to making a mayonnaise).
4 When the gel is smooth, put it in a piping (pastry) bag and leave it in the fridge.

* Verbena Water

1 Boil the verbena leaves in water [1] for 3 minutes.
2 At the same time, combine water [2] and the vitamin C in a bowl over ice.
3 Place the verbena leaves in the ice water and leave to rest for 5 minutes.
4 Pour the verbena leaves and ice water into a food processor.
5 Blitz until the verbena is totally dissolved and the water has an attractive green colour.

ASSEMBLING

Components/Garnishes Limoncello in a vaporization spray; perfume test paper

Cut each verbena madeleine into four long slices and place one slice on each plate. Pipe some verbena gel on top of the slices. Add three cubes of lemon ice, then cover with a layer of almond milk granita. Place some crushed honey cookie beside the cake (not shown in the photo below). Pipe two dots of lemon albedo purée on opposite sides of the plate. Spray limoncello over perfume test paper and place on the plate. You could also add lemon skin and bergamot skin confit garnishes.

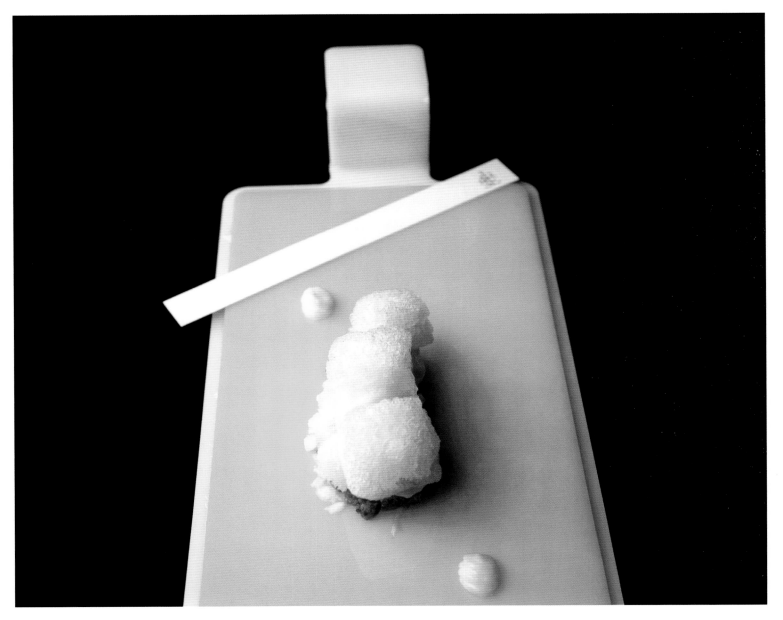

Marike van Beurden

HONG KONG

What chef Marike van Beurden excels at is the haute couture of pastry. If you ever have the chance to eat at Caprice restaurant, Four Seasons Hotel Hong Kong, you will see for yourself. Her desserts are exquisitely refined, their beauty masking the technical mastery on display and belying the gruelling production rate that such high-level cuisine imposes. Add the other pressures associated with working at a three-Michelin-starred restaurant, and managing an eclectic team, and you may deduce that one needs a commando mind-set. 'I would have loved to join the army,' Marike admits.

With the constant updating of the *à la carte*, chef's, lunch, weekend lunch, cake and birthday cake menus, as well as the pre-dessert and petit four selections, and, last but not least, the special menus for the festive seasons, 'it's a never-ending story', says Marike, but she loves it.

Born in the Netherlands, she grew up surrounded by gardens, which still inspire her today and which she translates into charmingly feminine desserts that borrow from classic flavours while being, as she playfully notes, 'pimped up'. This signature style has earned her prestigious prizes. 'My first competition was the Dutch Pastry Award, and the first year was a total disaster. My showpiece ended up on the floor before the jury could even see it. But, determined to show I could do better, the next time I entered I won the title!' She also recalls that 'the C3 of Valrhona was a dream come true, and getting the world title felt amazingly good'. In addition, Marike proudly represented the Netherlands at the 2013 World Chocolate Masters.

She is, nonetheless, quick to credit her success to others. 'My first full-time job was in a chocolaterie in Belgium with a very creative chef, Dominique Persoone. Then, moving to London, I worked in the pastry shop of Pierre Gagnaire, until I discovered his restaurant and longed to give it a try. The place where I started creating desserts on a regular basis was in the south of France. From there I moved on to work with Philippe Rigollot – an amazing opportunity. I can honestly say that I might not have reached the level I'm at now if it weren't for my time working with him.' Surely something that anyone who has the chance to work with Marike and her superlative creations would be equally swift to say about her.

www.fourseasons.com/hongkong | **www.marikevanbeurden.com**

POPCORN CHEESECAKE, BLACKCURRANT MERINGUE, RASPBERRY AND SOLLIÈS SORBET

'I love cheesecake, but prefer a lighter version; popcorn is my favourite "healthy snack"; and it was autumn at the time ... hence this creation,' Marike explains. 'Blackcurrant and raspberry were added for a fruity, colourful dessert. Design-wise, it's a coincidence of shapes one sees in daily life, combined with textures and colours.'

MAKES 8 **DIFFICULTY** 5/5 **PREPARATION TIME** 6–8 hours (but up to 24 hours if using a food dehydrator for drying the meringues)
SPECIFIC EQUIPMENT Piping (pastry) bag; desiccant; Thermomix® (preferred); digital candy thermometer; 8 x oval silicone moulds (each 7 x 4.8 cm/2¾ x 1⅞ in.); squeeze bottle; whipped cream siphon and two cartridges; 8 x small half-sphere silicone moulds (each 2 cm/¾ in. diameter); baking spray; Pacojet®, or ice cream machine

INGREDIENTS

For the Blackcurrant Meringue
Blackcurrant purée 56 g | 2 fl oz | ¼ cup
Water 19 g | gen. ½ fl oz | 4 tsp
Granulated white sugar 22 g | ¾ oz | sc. 2 tbsp
Egg white powder 8 g | ¼ oz | 3 tsp
Icing (confectioner's) sugar 44 g | 1½ oz | gen. ¼ cup

For the Popcorn Cheesecake
Cream cheese 250 g | gen. 8¾ oz | gen. 1 cup
Granulated white sugar 70 g | 2½ oz | ⅓ cup
Whole eggs 57 g | 2 oz | ¼ cup
Egg yolks 10 g | sc. ½ oz | gen. ½ tbsp
Whipping cream (35% fat) [1] 18 g | gen. ½ fl oz | 1 tbsp
Whipping cream (35% fat) [2] 240 g | sc. 8½ fl oz | 1 cup
Popcorn powder 12 g | sc. ½ oz | sc. ½ cup

For the Popcorn Crispy
White chocolate couverture (e.g. Ivoire 35% by Valrhona) 150 g | gen. 5¼ oz
Crispy rice 38 g | gen. 1¼ oz | gen. 1 cup
Popcorn powder 10 g | sc. ½ oz | ⅓ cup
Yoghurt powder 4 g | 1½ tsp

For the Raspberry Glazing
Granulated white sugar 188 g | sc. 6¾ oz | sc. 1 cup
Pectin NH 5 g | sc. ¼ oz | 2 tsp
Water 30 g | 1 fl oz | 2 tbsp
Raspberry purée 150 g | gen. 5¼ fl oz | gen. ½ cup
Glucose syrup 100 g | 3½ fl oz | gen. ¼ cup
Citric acid 1.5 g | ¼ tsp
Hot water 20 g | gen. ½ fl oz | 4 tsp
Red food colouring (to achieve desired colour)
Silver powder (to achieve desired colour)

For the Blackcurrant Tuile
Unsalted butter 37 g | gen. 1¼ oz
Granulated white sugar 75 g | gen. 2½ oz | gen. ⅓ cup
Blackcurrant purée 75 g | sc. 2¾ fl oz | ⅓ cup
Plain (all-purpose) flour 37 g | gen. 1¼ oz | ¼ cup (sifted)

INSTRUCTIONS

Blackcurrant Meringue
1 Whip all the ingredients together, then pipe into two sizes of dome on silicone baking paper.
2 Dry, preferably in a dehydrator for up to 24 hours, or in an oven at 90°C (195°F) for 6–8 hours.
3 Hollow the meringues out so they can be filled with berry jam (recipe opposite) immediately prior to serving.
4 Store in a sealed container with desiccant.

Popcorn Cheesecake
1 Combine the cream cheese, sugar, eggs, egg yolks and whipping cream [1], then cook, ideally in a Thermomix®, at 80°C (175°F) for 25 minutes.
2 Allow to cool down.
3 Whip cream [2] and add to the mixture, along with the popcorn powder.
4 Put in the oval moulds and top with popcorn crispy (recipe below).
5 Freeze, then unmould, and reserve frozen.

Popcorn Crispy
1 Melt the chocolate, then mix all the ingredients together.
2 Roll out between sheets of silicone baking paper to a thickness of 0.5 cm (³⁄₁₆ in.).
3 Leave to set in the fridge.
4 Once set, carefully cut into ovals slightly smaller than the oval moulds (from above recipe).

Raspberry Glazing
1 Mix some of the sugar with the pectin and water.
2 Start to heat up the raspberry purée with the rest of the sugar and the glucose syrup.
3 At 70°C (158°F) add the pectin mixture, then bring to the boil.
4 At the same time, dissolve the citric acid in the hot water.
5 Once the pectin/raspberry mixture is at a boil, remove from the heat, add the citric acid and skim off the foam.
6 Add some red food colouring and silver powder, then strain.
7 Use the mixture hot to glaze the cheesecakes once they are unmoulded but still frozen.
8 Reserve the remainder of the glaze in the squeeze bottle for plating.
9 Reserve the glazed cheesecakes in the fridge.

Blackcurrant Tuile
1 Soften the butter (without adding air) and mix in the sugar.
2 Warm to 30°C (86°F), then add the blackcurrant purée.
3 Once the mixture starts to become smooth, add the sifted flour.
4 Thinly smear the mixture over silicone baking paper that has been pre-cut into desired shapes, then bake at 150°C (300°F) for around 8 minutes, depending on the sizes and shapes chosen.
5 While still hot, shape as you wish (e.g. lie the tuiles over a rolling pin).
6 Peel off the baking paper once the tuiles have set.

For the Blackcurrant Espoumas

Blackcurrant purée 100 g | 3½ fl oz | ⅖ cup
Whipping cream (35% fat) 80 g | gen. 2¾ fl oz | ⅓ cup
Milk (3.5% fat) 20 g | gen. ½ fl oz | 4 tsp
Granulated white sugar 1.5 g | gen. ¼ tsp
Xanthan gum 0.5 g | tip of tsp

For the Raspberry Marshmallow

Granulated white sugar 55 g | sc. 2 oz | gen. ¼ cup
Trimoline (invert sugar) [1] 33 g | gen. 1 fl oz | sc. 1¾ tbsp
Raspberry purée 27 g | sc. 1 fl oz | gen. 1½ tbsp
Water 10 g | gen. ¼ fl oz | 2 tsp
Glucose syrup 25 g | gen. ¾ fl oz | sc. 1½ tbsp
Trimoline (invert sugar) [2] 27 g | gen. ¾ fl oz | gen. 1¼ tbsp
Gelatine (gold) 7 g | 3½ sheets (softened in ice cold water,
with excess water squeezed out)
Icing (confectioner's) sugar (to taste)
Raspberry powder (to taste)

For the Berry Jam

Frozen blackcurrants (e.g. Fruit'IQF by Capfruit) 125 g |
sc. 4½ oz | sc. 1 cup
Frozen raspberries (e.g. Fruit'IQF by Capfruit) 125 g |
sc. 4½ oz | gen. 1 cup
Granulated white sugar [1] 75 g | gen. 2½ oz | ⅓ cup
Pectin 5 g | sc. ¼ oz | 2 tsp
Granulated white sugar [2] 25 g | gen. ¾ oz | 2 tbsp

For the Forest Fruit Sorbet

Water 57 g | 2 fl oz | ¼ cup
Dried glucose powder 13 g | sc. ½ oz | sc. 1½ tbsp
(or replace with dextrose)
Dextrose powder 6.5 g | ¼ oz | 2 tsp
Granulated white sugar 41 g | sc. 1½ oz | gen. 3 tbsp
Sorbet stabilizer 0.7 g | a pinch
Fruits of the forest and red berry purée (e.g. Ravifruit)
225 g | 8 fl oz | sc. 1 cup

Blackcurrant Espoumas

1 Mix all the ingredients together with an immersion blender or Thermomix®.
2 Place in a whipped cream siphon and charge with two cartridges.
3 Reserve in the fridge.

Raspberry Marshmallow

1 Bring the granulated sugar, trimoline [1], raspberry purée, water and glucose syrup
to the boil.
2 Pour on top of trimoline [2] and the gelatine, then whip.
3 Prepare the small half-sphere moulds with baking spray and a dusting of icing
(confectioner's) sugar.
4 Pipe the mixture into the moulds and leave to set.
5 Prior to serving, roll the marshmallow in raspberry powder.

Berry Jam

1 Cook the frozen berries with sugar [1].
2 Mix the pectin and sugar [2], add to the previous mixture and bring to the boil.
3 Leave to cool and set.
4 Use to fill the hollowed-out meringues (recipe opposite) immediately prior to serving.

Forest Fruit Sorbet

1 Heat the water with the dried glucose powder and dextrose powder.
2 At 40°C (104°F) add the sugar mixed with the sorbet stabilizer.
3 Bring to the boil, then pour on top of the fruit purée.
4 Freeze in a Pacojet® beaker, or chill and churn in an ice cream machine according
to the manufacturer's instructions.

ASSEMBLING

Components/Garnishes Fresh figs; raspberry sauce (the remaining glaze); popcorn
(microwave salted); popcorn powder

Style as you wish, or as per Marike's plating (photo below).

MUM'S FLOWER GARDEN

'When I had to create a Mother's Day dessert, my own mother was of course my big inspiration,' confides Marike. 'She lives on lovely farmland in the Dutch countryside, so she's always out and about, working in her flower garden or fruit and veg patch. I've tried to recreate the feeling you get when you spend time there – the colourful flowers and the nice, fresh fruit. This is combined with my life in Hong Kong, hence some Asian citrus flavours.'

MAKES 8–10   **DIFFICULTY** 5/5   **PREPARATION TIME** 8 hours (+ 15–20 minutes' plating time for 8 people; NB the meringues may also be dehydrated overnight)   **SPECIFIC EQUIPMENT** Piping (pastry) bag and 'Mont blanc cream' nozzle (nozzle with many small holes) or very small round nozzle; desiccant; Silpat® mat; Thermomix® (preferred); 8–10 x rectangular silicone moulds (each 8 x 3 cm/3⅛ x 1⅛ in.); digital candy thermometer; spray gun; ice cream machine, or Pacojet®; squeeze bottle; whipped cream siphon and two cartridges; flower-shaped cutter (10-petal, 7 cm/2¾ in. diameter); 8–10 x half-sphere silicone moulds (each 4 ċm/1½ in. diameter); frame for plating (9 x 9 cm/3½ x 3½ in.); press block

INGREDIENTS

For the Meringue Citron

Lemon juice 110 g | 3¾ fl oz | sc. ½ cup
Granulated white sugar 100 g | 3½ oz | ½ cup
Egg white powder 13 g | sc. ½ oz | 2 tbsp
Icing (confectioner's) sugar 75 g | gen. 2½ oz | sc. ½ cup

For the Pistachio Shortbread

Unsalted butter 55 g | sc. 2 oz (room temperature)
Salt 2.5 g | sc. ½ tsp
Cassonade (unrefined moist brown sugar)
25 g | gen. ¾ oz | 2½ tbsp
Plain (all-purpose) flour 75 g | gen. 2½ oz | ½ cup
Baking powder 1 g | ¼ tsp
Cornflour (cornstarch) 12.5 g | sc. ½ oz | gen. 1 tbsp
Raw green pistachio purée (e.g. Capfruit)
20 g | sc. ¾ fl oz | gen. 1 tbsp
Chopped roasted pistachios 90 g | sc. 3¼ oz | ¾ cup

For the Pistachio Chantilly

Whipping cream (35% fat) 500 g | 17½ fl oz | 2 cups
Granulated white sugar 40 g | sc. 1½ oz | gen. 3 tbsp
Raw green pistachio purée (e.g. Capfruit)
75 g | 2½ fl oz | sc. ⅓ cup
Pistachios 25 g | gen. ¾ oz | 3 tbsp (very finely chopped)

For the Pistachio Biscuit

Egg whites 58 g | 2 oz | ¼ cup
Granulated white sugar [1] 25 g | gen. ¾ oz | 2 tbsp
Egg yolks 58 g | 2 oz | ¼ cup
Whole eggs 38 g | gen. 1¼ oz | 2½ tbsp
Granulated white sugar [2] 58 g | 2 oz | gen. ¼ cup
Plain (all-purpose) flour 15 g | ½ oz | 1¼ tbsp
Cornflour (cornstarch) 5 g | sc. ¼ oz | 1¼ tsp
Pistachio powder 48 g | sc. 1¾ oz | ⅓ cup
Almond meal 25 g | gen. ¾ oz | 4 tbsp

For the Calamansi and Violet Crémeux

Calamansi/lime purée (e.g. Capfruit) 100 g | 3½ fl oz | ⅖ cup
Water 25 g | gen. ¾ fl oz | 5 tsp
Whole eggs 100 g | 3½ oz | sc. ½ cup
Granulated white sugar 63 g | sc. 2¼ oz | sc. ⅓ cup
Gelatine (gold) 2.5 g | 1¼ sheets (softened in ice cold water,
with excess water squeezed out)
Unsalted butter 132 g | gen. 4½ oz (soft)
Egg whites 43 g | 1½ oz | sc. 3 tbsp
Violet aroma 7 drops

For the White Spray Coating of Frozen Crémeux

Cocoa butter 150 g | gen. 5¼ oz
White chocolate 150 g | gen. 5¼ oz
Titanium dioxide (enough to obtain a bright white colour)

For the Syrup for the Sorbet

Granulated white sugar 110 g | sc. 4 oz | gen. ½ cup
Ice cream stabilizer 2 g | gen. ½ tsp
Water 150 g | 5¼ fl oz | ⅔ cup
Dextrose 40 g | sc. 1½ oz | 4 tbsp

INSTRUCTIONS

Meringue Citron

1   Whip the lemon juice, granulated white sugar and egg white powder together.
2   Add the icing (confectioner's) sugar.
3   Pipe into dome shapes of different sizes on a silicone baking paper-lined tray.
4   Slowly dry in the oven at 80°C (175°F) for 6–8 hours, or ideally at 50°C (120°F) overnight.
5   Hollow the meringues out as much as possible so they can be filled with mara des bois and peach jam (recipe overleaf) prior to serving.
6   Store in a sealed container with desiccant.

Pistachio Shortbread

1   Mix all the ingredients, except for the chopped pistachios, together in a bowl.
2   Spread on a silicone baking paper-lined tray and bake at 160°C (325°F) for 15–20 minutes.
3   Once cooled down, remove the shortbread from the tray (it will crumble) and add the chopped pistachios.
4   Reserve in a sealed container.

Pistachio Chantilly

1   Whip the cream with the sugar.
2   Add the pistachio purée and very finely chopped pistachios.
3   Reserve in the fridge.

Pistachio Biscuit

1   Whip the egg whites with sugar [1].
2   Whip the egg yolks, eggs and sugar [2].
3   Mix the two together.
4   Sift the flour and cornflour (cornstarch) together, mix in with the pistachio powder and almond meal, then add to the egg mixture.
5   Work until a dough is formed.
6   Spread out to a thickness of 1 cm (⅜ in.) on a Silpat® mat.
7   Bake at 180°C (350°F) for 15 minutes.
8   Cool on a wire rack.
9   Once cool, cut into rectangles of 7 x 2.5 cm (2¾ x 1 in.).

Calamansi and Violet Crémeux

1   Cook the calamansi/lime purée, water, eggs and sugar to 82°C (180°F), ideally in a Thermomix®.
2   Add the gelatine and allow to cool to 35°C (95°F).
3   Mix in the butter.
4   Whisk the egg whites until light peaks form.
5   Fold the egg white meringue and the violet aroma into the purée mixture.
6   Put the resulting crémeux into the rectangular moulds (about 30 g/1 oz in each) and cover with a pistachio biscuit (from above recipe).
7   Freeze, then unmould, and reserve frozen.

White Spray Coating of Frozen Crémeux

1   Separately melt the cocoa butter and the chocolate.
2   Mix together with a blender, add the colouring, then strain.
3   Use a spray gun to spray the frozen crémeux (from above recipe) velvet white.
4   Reserve the coated crémeux in the fridge.

Syrup for the Sorbet

1   Mix a little of the sugar with the stabilizer.
2   Heat up the water with the dextrose and the remainder of the sugar.
3   Add the sugar/stabilizer to the dextrose mixture at 40°C (104°F) and bring to the boil.
4   Leave to cool to 50°C (122°F).

Mara des Bois and White Peach Sorbet

1   Mix the purées with the lemon juice, pour the warm syrup (from above recipe) on top, then stir.
2   Chill, then churn in an ice cream machine according to the manufacturer's instructions (or use a Pacojet®).
3   Spread out to a thickness of 1 cm (⅜ in.), then cut into 7 x 2 cm (2¾ x ¾ in.) bars.
4   Reserve in the freezer.

For the Mara des Bois and White Peach Sorbet

White peach purée (e.g. Capfruit) 250 g | 9 fl oz | 1 cup

Mara des bois strawberry purée (e.g. Capfruit)
250 g | 9 fl oz | 1 cup

Lemon juice 40 g | sc. 1½ fl oz | gen. 2½ tbsp

Syrup at 50°C/122°F (from above recipe)
250 g | gen. 8¼ fl oz | gen. 1 cup

For the Mara des Bois and Peach Jam

Frozen strawberries (e.g. Fruit'IQF by Capfruit)
125 g | sc. 4½ oz

White peach purée (e.g. Capfruit) 190 g | 6¾ fl oz | ¾ cup

Granulated white sugar [1] 50 g | 1¾ oz | ¼ cup

Granulated white sugar [2] 38 g | gen. 1¼ oz | gen. 3 tbsp

Pectin NH 4 g | 1½ tsp

Fresh peach brunoise (finely diced peaches) 100 g | 3½ oz

For the Mara des Bois Sauce

Granulated white sugar 30 g | 1 oz | 2½ tbsp

Pectin NH 2 g | sc. 1 tsp

Water 20 g | gen. ½ fl oz | 4 tsp

Mara des bois strawberry purée (e.g. Capfruit)
200 g | 7 fl oz | ¾ cup

For the Peach Siphon

White peach purée (e.g. Capfruit) 200 g | 7 fl oz | ¾ cup

Whipping cream (35% fat) 80 g | gen. 2¾ fl oz | ⅓ cup

Granulated white sugar 10 g | sc. ½ oz | 2½ tsp

Xanthan gum 0.5 g | tip of tsp

For the Sablé Flowers

Unsalted butter 90 g | sc. 3¼ oz (soft)

Icing (confectioner's) sugar 57 g | 2 oz | ⅓ cup

Salt 0.5 g | tip of tsp

Almond meal 18 g | gen. ½ oz | 3 tbsp

Vanilla powder 0.5 g | tip of tsp

Whole egg 34 g | gen. 1 oz | gen. 2 tbsp

Bread flour 150 g | gen. 5¼ oz | 1 cup

Sparkling food colouring powder (to achieve desired colour)

Mara des Bois and Peach Jam

1   Slowly heat the strawberries, peach purée and sugar [1] in a saucepan.
2   Mix sugar [2] with the pectin and add to the saucepan when it reaches 40°C (104°F), then boil everything together.
3   Allow to cool down.
4   Just before serving, mix 50 g (1¾ oz) of the jam with the fresh peach brunoise.

Mara des Bois Sauce

1   Mix the sugar and pectin together.
2   Add to the water and the mara des bois purée.
3   Bring to the boil, then remove from the heat after 1 minute.
4   Once cool, place in a squeeze bottle.

Peach Siphon

1   Mix all the ingredients together.
2   Place in a whipped cream siphon and charge with two cartridges.
3   Reserve in the fridge.

Sablé Flowers

1   Mix the butter with the icing (confectioner's) sugar and salt.
2   Add the almond meal and vanilla powder.
3   Add the egg and lastly the flour.
4   Gently mix until all the flour is combined (do not over-mix).
5   Leave to rest in the fridge, wrapped in plastic wrap.
6   Roll out the dough on a cold, flat surface to a thickness of 2 mm (1/16 in.), then use a flower cutter to cut out flowers (returning to the fridge or freezer as necessary to keep the dough firm).
7   Place the flowers in the half-sphere moulds (the petals will stick out of the moulds).
8   Bake at 160°C (325°F) for 8 minutes, then allow to cool down in the moulds.
9   Once cool, use a small brush to colour with sparkling food colouring powder.

ASSEMBLING

Components/Garnishes Pistachio powder; 'green grass' chocolate decorations made of tempered white chocolate with green food colouring powder, cut into strips; edible bourrache (borage) and purple delight flowers; lemon cress (baby lemon basil); wild strawberries, cut in half; green sugar rings made by melting isomalt sugar, adding green food colouring powder, cooling the mixture down slightly, using a utensil to pull out a thin strip and wrapping it quickly around a 9 cm (3½ in.) cylinder (e.g. a bottle), then cutting at the crossing point to create an open ring that can be positioned around the dessert (repeat as many times as servings)

Place the square frame on the first serving plate. Thinly pipe pistachio chantilly all over the base. Add some shortbread, which should then be pressed down. Remove the frame and repeat as many times as servings. Dust the shortbread with pistachio powder. Place a calamansi and violet crémeux in the middle, then 'green grass' chocolate on both sides. Fill up the meringues with the jam. Decorate each plate with the meringues, mara des bois sauce, edible flowers, lemon cress, halved wild strawberries, peach foam and green sugar rings. Place a sorbet slice on top of the calamansi and violet crémeux. Finally, fill the centre of each sablé flower with a dome of peach foam and place on the sorbet, along with half a wild strawberry.

NYANGBO | GINGER NYANGBO CHOCOLATE SHISO AND APPLE FOAM, DRUNKEN FROZEN CHOCOLATE, CRESS, SAKE AND COCOA SORBET

'This dessert was created when I was training on the amazing Hong Kong trails for the 100 km Oxfam Trailwalker race,' explains Marike. 'I wanted to work with Nyangbo 68% chocolate, which wasn't my favourite initially, but I regarded this as a challenge. The brief: combining the African chocolate with flavours from Asia. I chose Japan (sake, shiso and ginger), and some green apple for freshness. The design is inspired by the outdoors, forestry and woody chocolate landscape.'

MAKES 6 **DIFFICULTY** 5/5 **PREPARATION TIME** 6–8 hours (including 5+ hours for the marinated apples)
SPECIFIC EQUIPMENT Digital candy thermometer; 6 x square silicone moulds with central indent (each 6 x 6 cm/2⅜ x 2⅜ in.); piping (pastry) bag with narrow nozzle and 'Mont blanc cream' nozzle (nozzle with many small holes) or very small round nozzle; 2 x whipped cream siphons and four cartridges; paper coffee cups; 6 x small square silicone moulds (each 2 x 2 cm/¾ x ¾ in.), or small dome silicone moulds; toothpicks; Pacojet®, or ice cream machine; frame for plating (9 x 9 cm/3½ x 3½ in.); press block

INGREDIENTS

For the Marinated Apple
Fresh Fuji apple 100 g | 3½ oz
Ginger juice 100 g | 3½ fl oz | sc. ½ cup
Apple juice 25 g | gen. ¾ fl oz | gen. 1½ tbsp

For the Dark Chocolate Crumble
Unsalted butter 104 g | gen. 3½ oz
Granulated white sugar 180 g | gen. 6¼ oz | sc. 1 cup
Salt 8 g | ¼ oz | 1¼ tsp
1 small whole egg
Plain (all-purpose) flour 60 g | gen. 2 oz | sc. ½ cup (sifted)
Cocoa powder 52 g | 1¾ oz | sc. ½ cup

For the Brownie Biscuit
Dark chocolate (70%) 40 g | sc. 1½ oz
Unsalted butter 90 g | sc. 3¼ oz
Plain (all-purpose) flour 20 g | sc. ¾ oz | 4 tsp
Cocoa powder 7 g | ¼ oz | 1 tbsp
Whole eggs 80 g | gen. 2¾ oz | gen. ⅓ cup
Brown sugar 60 g | gen. 2 oz | sc. ⅓ cup
Granulated white sugar 60 g | gen. 2 oz | gen. ¼ cup

For the Confit Ginger
Candied/crystallized ginger (to taste)
Ginger juice (juice some fresh ginger)

For the Nyangbo and Ginger Crémeux
Milk 112 g | 3¾ fl oz | sc. ½ cup
Whipping cream (35% fat) 112 g | 4 fl oz | sc. ½ cup
Egg yolks 45 g | 1½ oz | 3 tbsp
Granulated white sugar 23 g | ¾ oz | 2 tbsp
Dark chocolate (e.g. Nyangbo 68% by Valrhona) 105 g | sc. 3¾ oz
Ginger juice 14 g | ½ fl oz | 1 tbsp

For the Chocolate Tuile
Unsalted butter 65 g | gen. 2¼ oz
Icing (confectioner's) sugar 65 g | gen. 2¼ oz | ⅔ cup
Egg whites 68 g | sc. 2½ oz | gen. ¼ cup
Plain (all-purpose) flour 58 g | 2 oz | gen. ⅓ cup
Cocoa powder 9 g | sc. ½ oz | gen. 1 tbsp

INSTRUCTIONS

Marinated Apple
1 Brunoise the apple (i.e. cut into small cubes), then mix with the ginger and apple juices.
2 Leave to infuse for at least 5 hours.

Dark Chocolate Crumble
1 Soften the butter, then mix with the sugar and salt.
2 Add the egg, then the sifted flour and the cocoa powder to achieve a very soft dough.
3 Spread out on a silicone baking paper-lined tray and bake at 170°C (325°F) for 25–30 minutes.
4 Leave to cool on a wire rack.
5 Once cool, blitz in a blender to form a fine crumble.

Brownie Biscuit
1 Melt the chocolate with the butter.
2 Sift the flour and cocoa powder together.
3 Whip the eggs with the brown and white sugar.
4 Add the melted chocolate/butter to the egg mixture.
5 Add the sifted powders.
6 Spread out on a silicone baking paper-lined tray and bake at 180°C (350°F) for 15–20 minutes.

Confit Ginger
1 Mix the candied/crystallized ginger with enough ginger juice to obtain a smooth paste.
2 Spread over the cooled brownie biscuit (from above recipe) and cut into 6 x 6 cm (2⅜ x 2⅜ in.) squares.

Nyangbo and Ginger Crémeux
1 Bring the milk and cream together to the boil.
2 At the same time, mix the egg yolks and sugar together until pale.
3 Combine the two mixtures.
4 Cook to 82°C (180°F), then strain.
5 Measure out 245 g (gen. 8½ oz) and pour, little by little, onto the chocolate to obtain a smooth ganache (use an immersion blender if necessary).
6 Add the ginger juice.
7 Put the resulting crémeux into the square silicone moulds with indents (about 50 g/1¾ oz in each).
8 Freeze.
9 Reserve a small amount of crémeux for the plating.

Chocolate Tuile
1 Mix all the ingredients together in a stand mixer until smooth.
2 Transfer to a piping (pastry) bag with a narrow nozzle.
3 Pipe in strips and bake for 6 minutes at 160°C (325°F).
4 Shape over a rolling pin or bottle immediately once out of the oven.

For the Microwave Cake

Egg whites 125 g | sc. 4½ oz | ½ cup
Blanched almond meal 75 g | gen. 2½ oz | gen. ⅘ cup
Icing (confectioner's) sugar 75 g | gen. 2½ oz | sc. ½ cup
Apple purée 40 g | sc. 1½ fl oz | gen. 2¼ tbsp
Egg yolks 40 g | sc. 1½ oz | gen. 2½ tbsp
Cocoa powder 20 g | sc. ¾ oz | 2¾ tbsp
Cornflour (cornstarch) 10 g | sc. ½ oz | 1 tbsp
Ginger juice 10 g | gen. ¼ fl oz | 2 tsp

For the Green Apple and Sisho Foam

Sisho leaves ('Japanese' mint) 20 g | sc. ¾ oz
Apple juice 88 g | 3 fl oz | 6 tbsp
Green apple purée 112 g | 4 fl oz | ⅗ cup
Granulated white sugar 4 g | 1 tsp
Ginger juice 2 g | ½ tsp
Xanthan gum 1.6 g | ¼ tsp

For the Chocolate Ginger Ravioli

Milk 100 g | sc. 3½ fl oz | sc. ½ cup
Dark chocolate (e.g. Nyangbo 68% by Valrhona)
20 g | sc. ¾ oz (melted)
Ginger juice 12 g | sc. ½ fl oz | ¾ tbsp
Water 170 g | 6 fl oz | sc. ¾ cup
Vegetable gelatine (e.g. Veggie Gel by Sosa) 10 g | sc. ½ oz |
approx. 3 tsp (or 2.5 g/sc. 1 tsp of agar agar)
Granulated white sugar 30 g | 1 oz | 2½ tbsp
Cocoa powder 10 g | sc. ½ oz | sc. 1½ tbsp

For the Cress, Sake and Nyangbo Ice Cream

Milk 150 g | gen. 5 fl oz | gen. ½ cup
Whipping cream (35% fat) 50 g | 1¾ fl oz | ⅕ cup
Trimoline (invert sugar) 15 g | gen. ½ fl oz | ¾ tbsp
Cocoa powder 2.5 g | 1 tsp
Granulated white sugar 35 g | 1¼ oz | 3 tbsp
Ice cream stabilizer 2.5 g | sc. 1 tsp
Dark chocolate (e.g. Nyangbo 68% by Valrhona) 28 g | 1 oz
Lemon cress (baby lemon basil) 25 g | gen. ¾ oz
Sake 33 g | gen. 1 fl oz | gen. 2 tbsp

For the Drunken Chocolate

Dark chocolate (e.g. Nyangbo 68% by Valrhona) (to taste)
Bacardi 151 ('frozen') (to taste)
Sparkling silver food colouring (to achieve desired colour)

Microwave Cake

1 Put all the ingredients in a food processor and mix until smooth.
2 Place in a whipped cream siphon, charge with two cartridges and shake vigorously.
3 Store at room temperature until ready for use (the cakes need to be cooked just before plating).
4 When ready for plating, microwave for 40–50 seconds on medium-high in disposable coffee cups, each filled half-way, with three holes previously punched in each base with a knife.

Green Apple and Sisho Foam

1 Blend the sisho leaves with the apple juice.
2 Add the apple purée, little by little, and blend until as smooth as possible.
3 Strain, mix in the other ingredients, then blend.
4 Place in a whipped cream siphon, charge with two cartridges and shake well.
5 Reserve in the fridge.

Chocolate Ginger Ravioli

1 Heat up the milk and mix with the melted chocolate.
2 Add the ginger juice and blend.
3 Put in the freezer in the small square moulds (or small domes); when nearly frozen, insert a toothpick into each, then allow to freeze completely.
4 In the meantime, make a dip by mixing the water, vegetable gelatine, sugar and cocoa powder while cold, bring to the boil, then allow to cool a little.
5 Once the moulds are frozen, unmould the ravioli and dip in the hot (but not boiling) dipping mixture two to three times, in quick succession.

Cress, Sake and Nyangbo Ice Cream

1 Heat the milk and cream with the trimoline and cocoa powder to 40°C (104°F).
2 Mix the sugar with the stabilizer, add to the saucepan and bring everything together to the boil.
3 Pour, little by little, on top of the chocolate to obtain a smooth mixture.
4 Leave to cool down.
5 Once cool, blend with the lemon cress and sake, then strain.
6 Process using a Pacojet® or ice cream machine according to the manufacturer's instructions.

Drunken Chocolate

1 Melt the chocolate at 45°C (113°F).
2 Place into a piping (pastry) bag with a 'Mont Blanc cream' nozzle.
3 Allow to cool down to 32°C (90°F), then pipe into the 'frozen' alcohol.
4 Roll in sparkling silver food colouring and serve immediately, as alcohol evaporates.

ASSEMBLING

Garnish Fresh sisho leaves

Place the square metal frame in the middle of the first serving plate. Spread a very thin layer of the reserved crémeux in this, then sprinkle chocolate crumble over it. Press down very well before removing the frame. Repeat as many times as servings. Place a crémeux square on top of each brownie, then place in the middle of the chocolate crumble. Fill up the central hole with marinated apples. Place ravioli and pieces of microwave cake on each plate. Just before serving, add drunken chocolate and green apple and sisho foam. Finish with a scoop of the ice cream and place swirls of chocolate tuile on top. Decorate both cake and tuile with fresh sisho leaves.

Michelle Gillott

UK

As a child, Michelle Gillott baked bread, cakes and pastries with her grandmother. Coming from Yorkshire, she swiftly progressed to good hearty dishes, but she longed to experiment further. She moved to Manchester, where she worked in a family-run hotel. Then, while studying for her NVQ Level 4 (the highest qualification in the UK for pâtisserie and confectionery specialists), she used her days off to learn more skills and also dedicated a whole year to sugar and chocolate work. 'I then landed my first head pastry chef job in a country-house hotel and went through a phase of trying to get as many elements on a dish as possible, based around three flavours,' Michelle recalls. 'Looking back, it felt as if I could – and wanted to – use all the skills I had.'

Her biggest influence was her next job, as head pastry chef and senior sous chef at the two-Michelin-starred Midsummer House restaurant in Cambridge, under chef Daniel Clifford. 'My dishes started out very complex and technical, and again there was a lot on the plate. Then I started eating out a lot more in restaurants around the world and, consequently, even if I still like to display a selection of textures on a dish, I prefer to keep things a little simpler,' she notes.

Currently working alongside Sosa's executive chef Jordi Puigvert Colomer as a consultant for the Home Chocolate Factory, Michelle runs demonstrations and her dishes are now heavily based around molecular gastronomy products. 'Having worked in establishments with no gadgets to one with all the mod cons, I've found it has only helped creativity, as there's so much more you can do,' she says. 'But for younger staff, who've only ever worked with mod cons, it can hinder in a big way. You need to know all the classics to have a good understanding of how to develop a dish. If something breaks, you have to know how to get through a service.'

Michelle is in fact addicted to the adrenaline that comes with hospitality. In addition to her corporate responsibilities, she juggles motherhood and working from home, creating bespoke cakes and chocolates and supplying a local chocolate shop and farmers' market, and she also teaches on a catering foundation course for young people with learning difficulties. This is dedication with a huge heart, and it translates into all Michelle's dishes.

http://chocolateshells1.com

CITRUS MERINGUE

'Combining two French classics – the citrus tart, which has always been a winner in any restaurant I've worked in, and floating islands – has resulted in something a little different and light,' notes Michelle.

MAKES 8 **DIFFICULTY** 4/5 **PREPARATION TIME** 4 hours (not including minimum 12 hours' drying time for the cannelloni) **SPECIFIC EQUIPMENT** Silpat® mat; metal or plastic tube (15 cm/6 in. long, 1 cm/⅜ in. diameter) or anything long and thin, as long as it is clean, such as cheap copper piping from the hardware shop, a cake dowel or a clean thick pen tube; ice cream machine; chinois (fine-mesh conical sieve/strainer); digital candy thermometer; 2 x piping (pastry) bags, one with small thin nozzle and one with large nozzle; 8 x ring moulds (each 7 cm/2¾ in. diameter); steamer tray; brûlée torch

INGREDIENTS

For the Orange Cannelloni

Orange purée (e.g. Boiron) 500 g | gen. 17¾ fl oz | 2 cups
Refined isomalt sugar (e.g. Sosa) 100 g | 3½ oz | gen. ½ cup
Optional but recommended: modified cornflour (cornstarch) (e.g. Ultra-tex or Gelcrem Hot by Sosa) 12 g | sc. ½ oz | gen. 1 tbsp

For the Orange Sherbet

Orange juice 350 g | 11¾ fl oz | sc. 1½ cups
Blood orange juice (or milk, if not using ice cream base) 150 g | 5 fl oz | gen. ½ cup
Caster (superfine) sugar 50 g | 1¾ oz | sc. ¼ cup
Lemon juice 5 g | sc. ¼ fl oz | 1 tsp
Ice cream base (e.g. Procrema 100 Cold by Sosa) 50 g | 1¾ oz | ½ cup

For the Passion Fruit Curd

7 egg yolks
Caster (superfine) sugar 60 g | gen. 2 oz | gen. ¼ cup
Double (heavy) whipping cream (40–45% fat) 300 g | 10½ fl oz | 1⅓ cups
Passion fruit juice 125 g | sc. 4½ fl oz | ½ cup
Gelatine (gold) 5 g | 2½ sheets (softened in ice cold water, with excess water squeezed out)
Unsalted butter 125 g | sc. 4½ oz (diced)

For the Steamed Grapefruit Meringue

Egg whites 250 g | gen. 8¾ oz | 1 cup
Egg white powder (e.g. Albumina by Sosa) 1.2 g | ½ tsp
Salt 0.6 g | tip of tsp
Lemon juice 5 g | sc. ¼ fl oz | 1 tsp
Grapefruit juice 10 g | gen. ¼ fl oz | 2 tsp
Caster (superfine) sugar 150 g | gen. 5¼ oz | sc. ¾ cup
Vodka (e.g. Marmalade by Chase Distillery) 22.5 g | ¾ fl oz | 1½ tbsp
Zest of ½ a large grapefruit

For the Crumble

Unsalted butter 63 g | sc. 2¼ oz
Caster (superfine) sugar 63 g | sc. 2¼ oz | gen. ¼ cup
Plain (all-purpose) flour 230 g | 8 oz | 1½ cups

For the Citrus Sauce

Orange juice 120 g | 4 fl oz | ½ cup
Grapefruit juice 120 g | 4 fl oz | ½ cup
Caster (superfine) sugar 50 g | 1¾ oz | sc. ¼ cup
Modified potato starch (e.g. Ultra-tex or Gelcrem Cold by Sosa) 12 g | sc. ½ oz | gen. 1 tbsp

For the Citrus Salad

1 orange
1 grapefruit
Chervil cress
Viola flowers
Freeze-dried passion fruit crispy (e.g. Sosa)

INSTRUCTIONS

Orange Cannelloni

1 Mix all the ingredients together.
2 Bring to the boil until thick and smooth.
3 Spread on a Silpat® mat.
4 Dry out in a dehydrator, or oven set to 80°C (175°F), until dry to the touch (approximately 6–8 hours, or overnight in an oven at a very low – 60°C/140°F – temperature).
5 Cut into rectangles 10 cm (4 in.) long and 4 cm (1⅝ in.) wide.
6 Roll the rectangles around a metal or plastic tube to achieve a cannelloni shape (the tube must be clean, dry and rubbed with a tiny amount of oil; any excess oil should be wiped off, otherwise it will prevent the drying process).
7 Remove the cannelloni from the tube, then place back in the dehydrator or oven until crisp (several hours).
8 Store in an airtight container in a cool place.
9 Fill with passion fruit curd (recipe below) just before serving.

Orange Sherbet

1 Blend all the ingredients together.
2 Leave to rest in the fridge for 3 hours.
3 Blend again, then churn in an ice cream machine according to the manufacturer's instructions.

Passion Fruit Curd

1 Whisk the egg yolks and sugar together until creamy and pale.
2 Bring the cream and juice to the boil, then pour little by little onto the egg yolk/sugar mixture while whisking.
3 Pour the resulting mixture onto the gelatine, then whisk in the diced butter until incorporated.
4 Pass through a chinois.
5 Cook in a plastic-wrapped tray in a bain-marie at 120°C (248°F) for 20–40 minutes, until a slight wobble is achieved.
6 Cool, then fill a piping (pastry) bag with a small thin nozzle and refrigerate until needed.

Steamed Grapefruit Meringue

1 Whisk the egg whites, egg white powder, salt, lemon juice, grapefruit juice and half the sugar by hand for 30 seconds to hydrate the egg white powder.
2 Whisk in a stand mixer until soft peaks form.
3 Add the remaining sugar and whisk until glossy.
4 Add the vodka, then fold in the grapefruit zest by hand.
5 Place the ring moulds on the steamer tray and pipe meringue mixture into each.
6 Steam at 70°C (158°F) for 4 minutes.
7 Remove from the heat and loosen by running a knife around the edge of each ring so as to gently unmould the meringues.
8 Gently blowtorch the meringues all over, then serve within half an hour for best results.

Crumble

1 Mix all the ingredients together until a crumble is formed.
2 Bake in a 180°C (350°F) oven until golden brown, then remove and leave to cool.

Citrus Sauce

1 Blend all the ingredients with an immersion blender until a smooth, shiny purée is achieved. Alternatively you can boil and reduce all the ingredients until the required consistency is achieved, but the sauce will be less fresh after boiling.

Citrus Salad

1 Cut the orange and grapefruit in half, then remove tiny individual sacs from the segments, ready to be mixed with the cress and flowers.
2 Mix in the freeze-dried passion fruit at the last minute to maintain crispness.

ASSEMBLING

Place a blowtorched steamed grapefruit meringue on each plate, add citrus sauce in dollops on top of the meringue, then build up the citrus salad. Add crumble to the side and top with a quenelle of orange sherbet. Finish with an orange cannelloni filled with passion fruit curd.

CHOCOLATE PISTACHIO AND CHERRY

'This recipe was taken from a pistachio brownie I once ate,' recalls Michelle. 'I decided to re-work it to fit a restaurant dessert.'

MAKES 10–15 **DIFFICULTY** 4/5 **PREPARATION TIME** 5 hours **SPECIFIC EQUIPMENT** Digital candy thermometer; acetate sheets (each 20 x 10 cm/7¾ x 4 in.); whipped cream siphon and one cartridge; ice cream machine; Silpat® mat, or oiled tray

INGREDIENTS

For the Tempered Chocolate Cannelloni
Dark chocolate (70%) 500 g | 1 lb 1½ oz
Optional: powdered metallic red food colouring
(e.g. Pavoni® Italia) (to achieve desired colour)

For the Pistachio Foam
Semi-skimmed milk 200 g | gen. 6¾ fl oz | sc. 1 cup
Double (heavy) whipping cream (40–45% fat)
250 g | 9 fl oz | 1 cup
4 egg yolks
Granulated white sugar 75 g | gen. 2½ oz | gen. ⅓ cup
Pistachio paste 50 g | 1¾ oz | 3 tbsp

For the Pistachio Powder
Pistachio paste 25 g | gen. ¾ oz | 1½ tbsp
Tapioca-based starch (e.g. Maltosec by Sosa)
30 g | 1 oz | 4 tbsp

For the Pistachio Sponge Cake
Pistachio meal 150 g | gen. 5¼ oz | 1½ cups
Polenta 25 g | gen. ¾ oz | 2½ tbsp
Plain (all-purpose) flour 25 g | gen. ¾ oz | 2 tbsp
Baking powder 2.3 g | ½ tsp
Zest of ¼ of a lemon
Olive oil 60 ml | 2¼ fl oz | 5 tbsp
Unsalted butter 100 g | 3½ oz (melted)
Caster (superfine) sugar 100 g | 3½ oz | sc. ½ cup
1½ whole eggs

For the Pliable Chocolate Ganache
Water 35 g | sc. 1¼ fl oz | sc. 2½ tbsp
Sorbitol 25 g | gen. ¾ oz | sc. 2½ tbsp
Agar agar 0.8 g | ¼ tsp
Dark chocolate (65%) 90 g | sc. 3¼ oz
Double (heavy) whipping cream (40–45% fat) 200 g |
7 fl oz | ⅘ cup
Glucose syrup 35 g | 1¼ fl oz | sc. 2 tbsp
Gelatine (gold) 2 g | 1 sheet (softened in ice cold water,
with excess water squeezed out)

For the White Chocolate Sorbet
Caster (superfine) sugar 150 g | gen. 5¼ oz | sc. ¾ cup
Water 500 g | 17½ fl oz | 2 cups
Glucose syrup 25 g | gen. ¾ fl oz | sc. 1½ tbsp
White chocolate 110 g | sc. 4 oz (chopped)

INSTRUCTIONS

Tempered Chocolate Cannelloni

1 Temper the chocolate by melting it to 50°C (122°F) in the microwave or over a pan of warm water, then cooling it to 28°C (82°F) by placing it over a bowl of ice water, then warming it to and keeping it at 32°C (90°F). NB Do not get any water in the chocolate or it will be unusable.

2 Spread a thin layer of the tempered chocolate halfway across the acetate sheets, along the short axis, creating a 10 x 10 cm (4 x 4 in.) square on each sheet. NB Ensure the sheets have no marks on them, as these will show on the finished product (sheets can be cleaned by rubbing with dry cotton wool).

3 Roll the acetate to form tight tubes with the chocolate on the inside, then secure with tape.

4 Leave to set in a cool place, ideally below 12°C (54°F), or in the fridge for 20 minutes.

5 Remove the tape (the acetate should peel off with ease), then paint with powdered food colouring (optional) and leave in a cool place until ready to plate up.

Pistachio Foam

1 Make pistachio custard by boiling the milk and cream together.

2 Whisk the egg yolks and sugar together.

3 Pour the boiled milk/cream mixture over the egg yolk/sugar mixture while whisking.

4 Return back to the pan and cook, stirring constantly, to 85°C (185°F), or until the custard coats the back of a spoon.

5 Remove from the heat and blend in the pistachio paste with an immersion blender.

6 Pass through a sieve (strainer) and chill.

7 Once cold, place into a whipped cream siphon, charge with one cartridge and shake well.

Pistachio Powder

1 Place the pistachio paste in a clean, dry bowl, stir in the tapioca-based starch (the more starch you add, the finer the powder), then store in a cool, dry place.

Pistachio Sponge Cake

1 Mix the dry ingredients and the lemon zest.

2 Separately, mix the olive oil and the melted butter together.

3 Whisk together the sugar and eggs, then fold in the oil mix, then fold in the dry mix.

4 Bake in a silicone baking paper-lined tray at 160°C (325°F) for 40 minutes.

Pliable Chocolate Ganache

1 Boil the water, sorbitol and agar agar, then put to one side.

2 Melt the chocolate to 32°C (90°F) to help with emulsification.

3 Boil the cream and glucose syrup, then add the gelatine.

4 Add the cream/glucose/gelatine to the chocolate in three additions.

5 Stir in the warm water/sorbitol/agar agar mixture.

6 Pour into a tray lined with plastic wrap and refrigerate.

White Chocolate Sorbet

1 Bring the sugar, water and glucose syrup to the boil to make a syrup.

2 Pour the syrup onto the chopped chocolate and gently stir until dissolved.

3 Chill, then churn in an ice cream machine according to the manufacturer's instructions.

For the Cherry Poached in Cherry Beer

Cherry beer 1 bottle (37.5 cl/12 ¾ fl oz)
Granulated white sugar 75 g | gen. 2½ oz | gen. ⅓ cup
Lemon juice 10 g | gen. ¼ fl oz | 2 tsp
Cherries 1 kg | gen. 2 lb (halved and de-stoned)
Chartreuse liqueur 25 ml | gen. ¾ fl oz | ⅛ cup

For the Cherry Semi-Gel

Agar agar 1.25 g | sc. ½ tsp
Cherry juice 125 g | sc. 4½ fl oz | ½ cup
Granulated white sugar 30 g | 1 oz | 2½ tbsp
Lemon juice 5 g | sc. ¼ fl oz | 1 tsp

For the Pulled Dark Chocolate Tuile

Fondant (e.g. Fondant Blanc Extra by Produits Marguerite, or Fondant Pâtissier by Caullet) 100 g | 3½ oz
Glucose syrup 100 g | 3½ fl oz | gen. ¼ cup
Dark chocolate (100% extra bitter preferred) 30 g | 1 oz (chopped)

Cherry Poached in Cherry Beer

1. Reduce the cherry beer by half, then add the sugar and lemon juice.
2. Sauté the cherries in a hot pan (no oil in the bottom).
3. Deglaze with the Chartreuse, then add the beer mixture.
4. Strain (reserve the cherries) and reduce the syrup to the required consistency.
5. Cool and return the cherries to soak in the syrup.

Cherry Semi-Gel

1. Mix all the Ingredients together and bring to the boil.
2. Remove from the heat and allow to cool and set.
3. Blitz with an immersion blender on high speed, then pass through a sieve (strainer).

Pulled Dark Chocolate Tuile

1. Mix the fondant and glucose syrup together in a pan, and bring to the boil.
2. Boil until 160°C (320°F) is reached, then remove from the heat and stir in the chopped chocolate.
3. Pour onto a Silpat® mat or oiled tray.
4. At this point the tuile can be pulled, using utensils, and cut with scissors into long thin strips.
   NB The mixture will be very hot; if it begins to cool, it will be difficult to pull, so put it in the oven for a few minutes to soften, but don't over-melt or the mixture will burn.

ASSEMBLING

Place cherry semi-gel on each plate. Add crumbles of pistachio sponge cake. Scatter a few beer-soaked cherries, and glaze the cherries with a little poaching syrup. Slice the pliable chocolate ganache into strips 1.5 cm (⅝ in.) wide; the thinner the better, as this will help with rolling and prevent cracking. Remove the ganache strips from the tray, lay flat and slice each strip to a length of 20 cm (7¾ in.); the depth will depend on how high the ganache set in the tray. Roll each strip into a pinwheel and place on each plate. Next fill the tempered chocolate cannelloni with pistachio foam. Scatter pistachio powder, and add a quenelle of white chocolate sorbet topped with a pulled dark chocolate tuile.

Experimental Exotica

A journey into the unconventional, but designed with a mastery that makes one exclaim: 'The future is here!' Visionaries, who are as much explorers, scientists and artists as they are pastry chefs, push the boundaries of the techniques and ingredients that are used in cooking and the way in which they are employed. This does not necessarily mean flaunting the most advanced food chemistry; most often it involves revisiting what already exists. What sounds impossible or unorthodox is systematically challenged, so that either your dessert is not what it seems or you cannot identify what it is by sight alone. Kitchens are turned into 'foodivore' labs, and all over the world pâtisserie addicts and cognoscenti tune in to follow each and every one of these chefs' breakthrough inventions. It is no surprise that most of these pioneers work for the top-rated restaurants at the forefront of culinary experimentation.

Alvaro Garrido

....

SPAIN

The label 'new pâtissier' applies to no one more than those independent chefs who pilot both the sweet and savoury sides of their menus. These chefs are usually visionaries who embrace the whole nature of food, and therefore feel free to swap ingredients and techniques from savoury cuisine to sweet, and vice versa. 'I'm a mixture of pastry chef and head chef, and this allows me to work with total creative freedom,' says Spaniard Alvaro Garrido. 'I describe myself primarily as a craftsman who loves to experiment with flavours, no matter whether salty or sweet. They are both conceptually the same.'

Alvaro states that his finest achievement to date has been the establishment of his restaurant, Mina, in the heart of Bilbao – a top destination today on any foodie's map. Mina welcomes customers into a warm room with ironwork on the windows, wooden beams and old stone walls; a historical, comforting décor that accommodates unashamedly contemporary dishes.

'To make a dessert, the first things I think of are the flavours, and then comes the artistic aspect, the composition. The true pleasure is when you're done and you see it all makes sense,' says Alvaro. 'My type of cuisine ensures that the flavours, engineered by the technique, create a magical experience in your mouth.' His alchemy might include red curry with dessert components, or the introduction of singular elements such as black garlic. He does not use many gadgets, as he focuses primarily on his products' core essence. He also practises sustainability, sourcing local goods that are in season.

'Every day the two worlds of savoury and sweet move closer together,' he states, 'though the field of pastry will always remain the most precise. Almost any ingredient can be used in pastry: it's just a matter of finding the right balance. My dishes almost always trigger appreciative feedback when they take a risk.' This is why he tries to keep up with and learn all the culinary trends, not in order to replicate what others are doing but to bring his own vocabulary and style up to date.

'Nowadays we're facing a paradoxical situation, in that we're all better cooks but with food going global we're losing the traditional, regional recipes and uniformity is looming.' Luckily we have Alvaro Garrido and Mina – a Biscay oasis of much-needed idiosyncrasy, recently and deservedly awarded its first Michelin star.

www.restaurantemina.es

SEA

'The idea behind this recipe is the image of having a taste of the sea in a dessert,' says Alvaro. 'A salty dessert? Impossible? No! Here seawater and seaweed complement other ingredients to make a balanced and fresh dessert.'

MAKES 8-10   DIFFICULTY 3/5   PREPARATION TIME 5 hours (not including dehydrating time for the seaweed)
SPECIFIC EQUIPMENT Dehydrator, or oven with low heat setting; ice cream machine; vacuum food sealer and canister (e.g. Cryovac® or Sunbeam FoodSaver®)

INGREDIENTS

For the Seaweed

'Sea lettuce' seaweed (one 7 x 7 cm/2¾ x 2¾ in. leaf per serving)
Egg white (to coat seaweed)
Granulated white sugar (to taste)

For the Lemon Ice Cream

Lemon juice 200 g | 6¾ fl oz | sc. 1 cup
Ice cream base (e.g. Procrema 100 Cold by Sosa) 50 g | 1¾ oz | ½ cup
Granulated white sugar 100 g | 3½ oz | ½ cup
Dextrose 25 g | gen. ¾ oz | gen. 2½ tbsp
Water 300 g | 10½ fl oz | 1¼ cups
Lemon peel confit 50 g | 1¾ oz

For the Sea Water Granita

Fresh water 150 g | 5¼ fl oz | ⅔ cup
Dextrose 40 g | sc. 1½ oz | 4 tbsp
Gelatine (gold) 2 g | 1 sheet (softened in ice cold water, with excess water squeezed out)
Micro-filtered sea water 100 g | 3½ fl oz | sc. ½ cup (can be found in a dietetics shop; alternatively use 3.5 g/⅛ oz sea salt to 100 g/3½ fl oz/sc. ½ cup water)

For the Lemon Cream

Granulated white sugar 70 g | 2½ oz | ⅓ cup
Whole eggs 70 g | 2½ oz | gen. ¼ cup
Unsalted butter 38 g | gen. 1¼ oz
Zest of 1 lemon
Juice of 1 lemon

For the Gin Soup

TPT sugar syrup (ratio: 1 part sugar to 1 part water) 100 g | 3½ fl oz | sc. ½ cup
London dry gin 150 g | 5¼ fl oz | ⅔ cup
Xanthan gum 0.7 g | ⅛ tsp

INSTRUCTIONS

Seaweed

1   Use a brush to coat the seaweed with egg white on both sides.
2   Sprinkle all over with sugar.
3   Put in a dehydrator (or fan oven) at around 60°C (140°F) for approximately 5 hours.
4   Store in a dry, sealed container.

Lemon Ice Cream

1   Blend all the ingredients together until smooth.
2   Strain, then chill for several hours.
3   Churn in an ice cream machine according to the manufacturer's instructions.

Sea Water Granita

1   Heat the fresh water with the dextrose.
2   Add the gelatine off the heat.
3   Mix with the sea/salt water.
4   Reserve in a plastic box in the freezer for at least 4 hours.

Lemon Cream

1   Mix all the ingredients together and cook in a bain-marie, whisking constantly until the mixture thickens.
2   Transfer to a sealed container and keep cool.

Gin Soup

1   Whisk all the ingredients together and put in a vacuum canister with vacuum seal to extract air bubbles.
2   Reserve cold in the fridge.
3   Strain before use.

ASSEMBLING

For each serving, spoon a mound of lemon cream into the centre of a shallow dish with a small central depression. Pour some gin soup around the lemon cream and place a spoonful of sea water granita on top. Add a quenelle of lemon ice cream. Cover with a seaweed leaf.

RED CURRY, BLACK GARLIC, YOGHURT AND CUCUMBER

'Oriental flavours, brought by foreign ingredients from savoury cuisine, suddenly make sense together in a dessert,' says Alvaro. 'At first, madras curry and black garlic seem unconventional in a dessert, but, thanks to yoghurt and cucumber, everything attains a cohesive balance.'

MAKES 8–10   **DIFFICULTY** 4/5   **PREPARATION TIME** 6 hours   **SPECIFIC EQUIPMENT** Digital candy thermometer; plum cake mould (1 litre/sc. 35¼ fl oz capacity, e.g. 23 x 8 x 7 cm/9 x 3⅛ x 2¾ in. L x W x H); vacuum food sealer, bag or canister (e.g. Cryovac® or Sunbeam FoodSaver®); ice cream machine

INGREDIENTS

For the Soufflé Glacé of Red Curry

Granulated white sugar [1] 100 g | 3½ oz | ½ cup

Water [1] 50 g | 1¾ fl oz | 3½ tbsp

6 egg yolks

Gelatine (gold) 7 g | 3½ sheets (softened in ice cold water, with excess water squeezed out)

Red curry powder 10 g | sc. ½ oz | 3½ tsp

Granulated white sugar [2] 65 g | gen. 2¼ oz | ⅓ cup

Water [2] 65 g | 2¼ fl oz | gen. ¼ cup

Egg whites 125 g | sc. 4½ oz | ½ cup

For the Yoghurt Powder Mix

Maltodextrin 100 g | 3½ oz | sc. 1 cup

Yoghurt powder 50 g | 1¾ oz | sc. ½ cup

For the Cucumber Jam

Cider vinegar 100 g | 3½ fl oz | sc. ½ cup

Honey 100 g | 3½ fl oz | 5 tbsp

Water 100 g | 3½ fl oz | sc. ½ cup

Peeled cucumber juice 100 g | 3½ fl oz | sc. ½ cup

Fresh cucumber 200 g | 7 oz (peeled and cubed 1 x 1 cm/⅜ x ⅜ in.)

Xanthan gum 1 g | sc. ¼ tsp

For the Cucumber Peel

Cucumber peel 15 g | ½ oz (cut very thick)

Granulated white sugar 15 g | ½ oz | gen. 1 tbsp

Salt 15 g | ½ oz | 2¼ tsp

Cider vinegar 10 g | gen. ¼ fl oz | 2 tsp

Fresh water (to clean cucumber filaments)

For the Black Garlic Ice Cream

Maltodextrin 18DE 75 g | gen. 2½ oz | sc. ¾ cup

Glucose powder 10 g | sc. ½ oz | 1 tbsp

Ice cream stabilizer 5 g | sc. ¼ oz | 1¼ tsp

Peeled black garlic 50 g | 1¾ oz

Milk 415 g | gen. 14 fl oz | 1¾ cups

INSTRUCTIONS

Soufflé Glacé of Red Curry

1 Make a syrup by heating sugar [1] and water [1] to 117°C (243°F).
2 Start whisking the egg yolks in a stand mixer.
3 Slowly pour the syrup over the yolks while beating.
4 Add the gelatine and the curry powder.
5 Whisk at high speed until the mixture cools down.
6 Separately, make a second syrup with sugar [2] and water [2].
7 When the syrup reaches 115°C (239°F), start whisking the egg whites in a stand mixer.
8 When the syrup reaches 121°C (250°F), pour it into the egg whites while slowly beating.
9 Beat on medium until thick and glossy.
10 Use a spatula to fold the red curry cream into the meringue until a mousse-like texture is achieved, then place in the rectangular plum cake mould and freeze.
11 Once frozen, cut individual rectangular pieces of 6 x 4 x 2 cm (2⅜ x 1⅝ x ¾ in.), then return to the freezer until ready to serve.

Yoghurt Powder Mix

1 Mix together the maltodextrin and yoghurt powder, then reserve.

Cucumber Jam

1 Make a syrup with the cider vinegar, honey and water.
2 Add the cucumber juice and mix thoroughly.
3 Add the cucumber cubes and mix.
4 Place in a vacuum bag or canister and vacuum seal, and leave to marinade for several hours.
5 Drain the liquid from the cubes, then add the xanthan gum to the liquid in a blender.
6 Place everything back in the vacuum bag or canister and re-vacuum to get rid of all the bubbles produced by the xanthan gum.

Cucumber Peel

1 Slice the thick cucumber peel into very fine filaments.
2 Put in a container and add the sugar, salt and cider vinegar.
3 Mix together and allow the filaments to macerate for 30 minutes.
4 Clean them with a little fresh water, then reserve.

Black Garlic Ice Cream

1 Mix the maltodextrin, glucose powder, stabilizer and garlic together, then add the milk.
2 Place in a blender, process until smooth, then mature for at least 2 hours in the fridge.
3 Return to the blender to mix before churning in an ice cream machine according to the manufacturer's instructions.

ASSEMBLING

Take a rectangular piece of soufflé glacé of red curry and coat with yoghurt powder mix *à la minute* before positioning to the left of each plate (spoon a little extra yoghurt powder mix over the soufflé). Place a spoonful of cucumber jam opposite, topped with a few cucumber filaments. Position a quenelle of black garlic ice cream between the two.

BANANA CREAM WITH VANILLA, COFFEE, BLACK OLIVES AND EARL GREY TEA

'The banana/vanilla/coffee combo sounds like a classic dessert, but we've increased the roasted flavours thanks to black olives and Earl Grey tea,' explains Alvaro. 'The positioning of each ingredient on the plate is also crucial, so that you can grab all the elements at the same time in one tablespoon, triggering an explosion of flavours in your mouth.'

MAKES 8–10 **DIFFICULTY** 4/5 **PREPARATION TIME** 6 hours **SPECIFIC EQUIPMENT** Ice cream machine, or Pacojet®; digital candy thermometer; Silpat® mat; whipped cream siphon and two cartridges; paper coffee cups with moderate wax lining

INGREDIENTS

For the Banana Cream with Vanilla
Whipping cream (35% fat) 356 g | 12½ fl oz | sc. 1½ cups
½ vanilla pod (bean) (split, scraped, both pod/bean and seeds reserved)
½ stick of cinnamon
Granulated white sugar 225 g | sc. 8 oz | 1⅛ cups
Water (to make syrup)
Ripe bananas 256 g | 9 oz (chopped)
Lyophilized powdered bananas 50 g | 1¾ oz | 6 tbsp
Antioxidant or lemon juice 7.5 g | ½ tbsp
Gelatine (gold) 4 g | 2 sheets (softened in ice cold water, with excess water squeezed out)

For the Black Olive Caramel
Fondant (e.g. Fondant Blanc Extra by Produits Marguerite, or Fondant Pâtissier by Caullet) 113 g | 4 oz
Glucose syrup 45 g | gen. 1½ fl oz | 2½ tbsp
Isomalt sugar 45 g | 1½ oz | sc. ¼ cup
Lyophilized powdered black olives 38 g | gen. 1¼ oz | gen. ⅓ cup

For the Earl Grey Tea Granita
Bottled water 500 ml | 17½ fl oz | 2 cups
Earl Grey tea leaves 15 g | ½ oz | 2 tbsp
Granulated white sugar 40 g | sc. 1½ oz | gen. 3 tbsp
Gelatine (gold) 2 g | 1 sheet (softened in ice cold water, with excess water squeezed out)

For the Siphon Coffee Cake
Egg whites 300 g | 10½ oz | 1¼ cups
Blanched almond meal 30 g | 1 oz | 5 tbsp
Granulated white sugar 35 g | 1¼ oz | 3 tbsp
Liquid instant coffee 25 ml | gen. ¾ fl oz | 5 tsp

INSTRUCTIONS

Banana Cream with Vanilla
1   Infuse the cream with the vanilla pod (bean) and seeds and the cinnamon over heat.
2   Make a syrup with the sugar and a little water (enough to achieve a sand-like texture).
3   Add the chopped banana and caramelize until golden.
4   Strain the hot infused cream and use to deglaze the banana. NB Take care, as it will spit.
5   Remove from the heat and stir in all the remaining ingredients.
6   Process with an immersion blender to form a smooth cream.
7   Strain, chill and churn in an ice cream machine according to the manufacturer's instructions (or freeze and Pacojet®).

Black Olive Caramel
1   Make a caramel with the fondant, glucose syrup and isomalt sugar to 160°C (320°F).
2   Remove from the heat and incorporate the powdered black olives.
3   Spread and leave to cool on a Silpat® mat.
4   Once cool, grind to a powder in a food processor, then sprinkle over the Silpat® mat.
5   Bake in the oven (no fan) at 180°C (350°F) for 8–10 minutes, then leave to cool.
6   Remove from the mat in pieces that are as large as possible and store in a sealed container.

Earl Grey Tea Granita
1   Heat the water to 80°C (176°F), then add the tea leaves and infuse off the heat, with the lid on, for 20 minutes.
2   Strain the infusion, then add the sugar and gelatine.
3   Stir well until all is combined.
4   Pour into a shallow dish and freeze.

Siphon Coffee Cake
1   Mix all the ingredients in a high-speed blender.
2   Transfer to a whipped cream siphon, charge with two cartridges, shake well and reserve in the fridge.
3   Pierce the bottom of a paper coffee cup with three holes, spray in the siphon contents to a depth of 4 cm (1⅝ in.) and cook in a microwave on medium for approximately 30–40 seconds.
4   Place upside down to cool, then unmould and use immediately.
5   Repeat as many times as servings.

ASSEMBLING

Place a quenelle of banana cream with vanilla on each shallow plate. Add two pieces of siphon coffee cake, one at each end of the quenelle. Spoon some Earl Grey tea granita on top (previously scraped with a fork as soon as taken out of the freezer). Finish with pieces of black olive caramel all over.

Fernando Rivarola

ARGENTINA

Fernando Rivarola's desserts are among the best edible tributes to and culinary ambassadors for his country, Argentina. His approach in favour of native produce, combined with his contemporary style, bear all the hallmarks of innovation and relevance on a plate. 'I work with many regional products, which foreign customers are intrigued by: raw materials as unique and unfamiliar as the Yacaratiá edible wood of Misiones province on Argentina's Mesopotámian coast; chayote, an interesting fruit from the Salta province in the northwest of the country; and special apples that are typical of Cipolletti in the Río Negro province of Patagonia,' he recounts. The list goes on, reading like a hedonistic travel brochure.

Fernando, who had been working in various kitchens around the world, joined forces with his girlfriend and sommelier Gabriela Lafuente around their shared passion for gastronomy and they launched El Baqueano restaurant in Buenos Aires, centred on sourcing the best meat from around the country. However, it was essential to design a dessert list as engaging as the main menu, and Fernando revelled in the task. He delights in the clashing of textures – cold/hot, crunchy/soft, hard/creamy – ultimately to transcend disparity in one ingredient-focused whole.

'My dishes are basically handcrafted using old-fashioned means of preparation, but I love the avant-garde as a reference to follow,' he explains. 'I work with a tasting menu, so I create between twenty-five and thirty-nine recipes a year. I love working with different versions of things, for example the texture of apples, and from there the dish can evolve into an interpretation for winter and summer, and every year we can come up with a different variant.' His dish 'The Apple (Version 2011)' (see p. 202) is a prime example of this exercise: jelly, sorbet, air and crisp are choreographed in a single ode to the fruit.

Had Fernando not become a chef, he would have been a lawyer – 'for the power of words,' he shares. Like any genuine passionate individual, he would ask his younger self, 'just as I keep asking my younger assistants: are you sure you are ready to sacrifice all that you love in life to become a true pastry chef?' All that you love? That sacrifice surely – and luckily for us – excludes the love of food.

http://restoelbaqueano.com | http://restoelbaqueano.blogspot.com

CHAYOTE, LEMON SOUP, CREAM CHEESE GEL, MISIONES YACARATIÁ WOOD AND CINNAMON ICE CREAM

'When we started working with regional products from different latitudes in Argentina,' explains Fernando, 'we discovered – almost by accident – the edible wood of the Yacaratiá tree. We were developing a dish to join the flagship products of the northwest and northeast, so we also thought of chayote, a botanical species akin to the pumpkin. The union of flavours is almost magical. This is now a signature dish in our restaurant.'

MAKES 4–6 **DIFFICULTY** 3/5 **PREPARATION TIME** 4 hours (not including cooling time for the chayote)
SPECIFIC EQUIPMENT Chinois (fine-mesh conical sieve/strainer); digital candy thermometer; ice cream machine; Silpat® mat, or silicone baking paper-lined tray

INGREDIENTS

For the Candied Chayote
(can be made in advance)
1 large fresh chayote (a.k.a. christophene or choko)
Granulated white sugar 500 g | 1 lb 1½ oz | 2½ cups
Water 500 ml | 17½ fl oz | 2 cups
Spices according to taste (cinnamon, cardamom, juniper berries, star anise, etc.)

For the Cinnamon Ice Cream
Milk 500 ml | 17½ fl oz | 2 cups
Whipping cream (35% fat) 100 ml | gen. 3½ fl oz | sc. ½ cup
Invert sugar 12.5 g | ½ fl oz | 1½ tsp
1½ cinnamon sticks
5 egg yolks
Granulated white sugar 125 g | sc. 4½ oz | gen. ½ cup
Ground cinnamon 7.5 g | ¼ oz | 3 tsp

For the Lemon Soup
2 whole eggs
Cornflour (cornstarch) 19 g | sc. ¾ oz | sc. 2 tbsp
Granulated white sugar 150 g | 5¼ oz | ¾ cup
Water 200 ml | 7 fl oz | sc. 1 cup
2 lemons juice and zest

For the Gelled Cream Cheese
Cream cheese 200 g | 7 oz | sc. 1 cup
Milk 25 g | gen. ¾ fl oz | 5 tsp
Agar agar 2 g | gen. ½ tsp

For the Almond Tuile
Granulated white sugar 60 g | gen. 2 oz | gen. ¼ cup
Unsalted butter 50 g | 1¾ oz
Milk 20 g | gen. ½ fl oz | 4 tsp
Glucose syrup 20 g | ¾ fl oz | 1 tbsp
Blanched almond meal 60 g | gen. 2 oz | sc. ¾ cup

INSTRUCTIONS

Candied Chayote
1 Place the fresh chayote in the oven, pre-heated to 180°C (350°F).
2 Leave to bake for 30 minutes, or until the skin begins to change to a light brown colour.
3 Cut lengthwise into four pieces, place in a bowl and cover with plastic wrap to allow to sweat.
4 Meanwhile, combine the sugar and water in a saucepan to make a syrup.
5 Bring to a low heat, dissolve the sugar and add the spices.
6 When the chayote reaches room temperature, remove the skin with a knife and cut into smaller portions.
7 Add the syrup and leave to cook for 2 hours over a low heat.
8 Leave to cool, then store in the syrup in an airtight jar.

Cinnamon Ice Cream
1 Bring the milk, cream, invert sugar and cinnamon sticks to the boil, then remove from the heat.
2 At the same time, hand-mix the egg yolks with the granulated sugar.
3 Pour some of the milk mixture onto the egg yolk/sugar mixture, stirring so the eggs do not scramble, then strain through a chinois back into the main saucepan.
4 Bring the whole back to 85°C (185°F) for 3 minutes, then remove from the heat.
5 Remove the cinnamon sticks, add the ground cinnamon and mix well.
6 Chill and then churn in an ice cream machine according to the manufacturer's instructions.

Lemon Soup
1 Beat the eggs and add the cornflour (cornstarch).
2 Add the sugar and water, and stir to dissolve.
3 Add the lemon juice and zest, and mix everything together.
4 Cook in a bain-marie, constantly whisking, until the mixture thickens a little.
5 Leave to cool in the fridge.

Gelled Cream Cheese
1 Mix all the ingredients together and heat to 85°C (185°F) for 5 minutes.
2 Smooth out into a shallow dish or frame, e.g. dimensions of 10 x 10 cm (4 x 4 in.).
3 Leave to cool in the fridge.
4 Once set, slice into the required number of pieces.

Almond Tuile
1 Bring the sugar, butter, milk and glucose syrup to the boil in a saucepan.
2 Remove from the heat, add the almond meal, then leave to cool.
3 Place in small spoonfuls onto a Silpat® mat or silicone baking paper-lined tray, spread into thin discs, and bake for 10 minutes at 175°C (350°F), or until uniformly golden brown.
4 Remove from the oven and lay each tuile over a rolling pin to create a curved shape (if the rolling pin is wooden, wrap it first with silicone baking paper).

ASSEMBLING

Components/garnishes Yacaratiá edible wood (a.k.a. wild papaya, from Argentina's Misiones province [see photo below left]; may be purchased ready-to-eat); mixed ground nuts (peanuts, walnuts, cashews, etc.)

Place some candied chayote in each soup dish. Add a gelled cream cheese slice and top with edible wood. Sprinkle with mixed ground nuts. Place a scoop of cinnamon ice cream to one side. To give volume to the top, garnish with an almond tuile. Pour in the lemon soup when ready to serve.

THE APPLE (VERSION 2011) | APPLE TEXTURES FROM VALLE DEL RÍO NEGRO, CIPOLLETTI CITY, ARGENTINA

'In 2008, we decided to make a dish with a single seasonal product that was also typically Argentinian,' explains Fernando. 'We opted for the green apple of Patagonia. The dish magically evolved, so we had different versions for subsequent years. These were created using various textures and temperatures, including gelatine, soup, hot and cold, foam, air, fresh apple, ice cream, pies, crunchy, candy, and more.'

MAKES 6   **DIFFICULTY** 3½/5   **PREPARATION TIME** 2½ hours (not including min. 10 hours' cooking time for the apple crisp)
SPECIFIC EQUIPMENT Digital candy thermometer; ice cream machine; fine muslin; whipped cream siphon and one cartridge

INGREDIENTS

For the Cider Jelly
Gelatine (gold) 10 g | 5 sheets (softened in ice cold water, with excess water squeezed out)
Cider (1 bottle) 750 ml | sc. 26½ fl oz | 3½ cups

For the Syrup Base for the Sorbet
Water 210 ml | sc. 7½ fl oz | sc. 1 cup
Dextrose 146 g | gen. 5 oz | sc. 1¼ cups
Granulated white sugar 90 g | sc. 3¼ oz | sc. ½ cup
Lemon juice 50 ml | 1¾ fl oz | sc. 3½ tbsp
Ice cream stabilizer 4 g | 1 tsp

For the Green Apple Sorbet
Green apples with peel 400 g | 14 oz
Acidulated water (to soak apples)
Syrup base (from above recipe)
Granulated white sugar 25 g | gen. ¾ oz | 2 tbsp
Water 25 ml | gen. ¾ fl oz | 5 tsp

For the Green Apple Air
Water 105 ml | gen. 3½ fl oz | sc. ½ cup
Granulated white sugar 120 g | 4¼ oz | gen. ½ cup
Lemon juice 25 ml | gen. ¾ fl oz | 5 tsp
Green apples with peel 250 g | gen. 8¾ oz
Gelatine (gold) 3 g | 1½ sheets (softened in ice cold water, with excess water squeezed out)
Soy lecithin 15 g | ½ oz | sc. 2 tbsp

For the Crunchy Fruit Syrup Base
Granulated white sugar 200 g | 7 oz | 1 cup
Water 200 ml | 7 fl oz | sc. 1 cup

For the Apple Crisp
1 medium green apple
Acidulated water (to soak apples)
Crunchy fruit syrup base (from above recipe)

INSTRUCTIONS

Cider Jelly
1   Mix the gelatine over a low heat with some of the cider, and stir until the gelatine dissolves.
2   Remove from the heat and add to the rest of the cider.
3   Freeze until the mixture sets, then reserve in the fridge.

Syrup Base for the Sorbet
1   Mix all the ingredients together and heat to 70°C (158°F) for no less than 5 minutes.

Green Apple Sorbet
1   Cut the apples into quarters and remove the seeds.
2   Immediately soak in the acidulated water to prevent rust.
3   Mix with the syrup base and the other ingredients.
4   Process in a food processor.
5   Chill and then churn in an ice cream machine according to the manufacturer's instructions.

Green Apple Air
1   Make a syrup with the water, sugar and lemon juice.
2   Put the syrup and the apples (cut into quarters, with seeds removed) into a food processor, and blitz.
3   Strain through fine muslin.
4   Add the gelatine and soy lecithin, and whisk vigorously.
5   Pour into a whipped cream siphon and leave to cool in the fridge.
6   Before serving, charge the siphon with one cartridge.

Crunchy Fruit Syrup Base
1   Make a syrup with the sugar and water.
2   Leave to cool before using.

Apple Crisp
1   Use a mandolin to divide the apple into approximately 25 slices, each 1 mm (⅟₁₆ in.) thick, immediately placing in the acidulated water to prevent rust.
2   Briefly soak in the crunchy fruit syrup base.
3   Place on a tray and bake at 60°C (140°F) for a minimum of 10 hours.

ASSEMBLING

Garnishes Double (heavy) cream, or mascarpone; fresh green apple strips

Cut the cider jelly into irregular pieces and place at the bottom of each dish. Add a spoonful of green apple sorbet on the side. Use the siphon to place green apple air around the jelly and the sorbet. Spoon dollops of cream or mascarpone here and there. Finally, garnish with apple crisps and strips of fresh green apple.

Florencia Rondón Strozzi

VENEZUELA

Meet the woman who 'gave birth' twice in one year. Metaphorically, that is. Florencia Rondón Strozzi delivered her son in 2009, the same year that she launched the culinary boutique Madame Blac in Caracas. 'All those months preparing recipes and taking vitamins for my pregnancy were the most emotional, anxiety-ridden and creative time of my life,' she confides.

Madame Blac (which offers an eclectic collection of *objets* as well as pastries) and Nolita restaurant (which opened in Bogotá, Colombia, in 2012) are just two of the recent ventures of GrupoMokambo, the company for which Florencia is head pastry chef and director. A graduate of the prestigious Culinary Institute of America, she defines herself foremost as a traditionalist. She does not shy away from repeating recipes, seeing this as a way to perfect her skills and pay homage to classics through her own interpretations.

'I am scared of highly complex or technical operations,' she admits, adding, 'It's not that I reject the benefits of technology, but I prefer to focus on the pleasure obtained from the harmony of flavours, and I like to keep in mind the importance of methodology.' She goes on to stress, 'I don't intend to surprise people because of the strange ingredients I use, but because of the taste of my pastry and what it might evoke in them; in other words, the most dazzling dish is not always the most tasty.'

This back-to-basics approach is paired with a phenomenal epicurean instinct and a faith in food as an integral part of culture and national heritage. She incorporates local flavours as bursts of spice, fruit and chocolate. 'I love to eat delicious food,' she says. 'I enjoy the colours and fragrances of the market; I'm excited by people remembering what they ate when they were children. The pleasure on their faces when they eat something they love has the power to transform a bad day into a day that is worth living.'

Florencia had long known that she wanted to become a pastry chef. 'I decided to quit university while my mother was abroad. When she came home and found out the news, she made a gesture that read as surprise and incomprehension, but also support and freedom,' Florencia recalls. 'Something that might be translated as, "OK then, but make sure you bake delicious cakes for my birthdays!"'

madameblac27@gmail.com

HIBISCUS FLOWER SOUP WITH ALMOND CRUMBLE AND YOGHURT ICE CREAM

'I was looking to make a light, fresh dessert,' says Florencia, 'but I'm against the use of artificial sweeteners. I therefore decided it was going to be a light dessert because of the absence of fat – as in the heavy cream, chocolate or butter that can be found in most desserts.'

MAKES 4 **DIFFICULTY** 2/5 **PREPARATION TIME** 4 hours **SPECIFIC EQUIPMENT** Straight-sided tray (28 x 28 cm/11 x 11 in., 1 cm/⅜ in. deep); digital candy thermometer; ice cream machine

INGREDIENTS

For the Hibiscus Flower Soup

Pectin 1 g | sc. ½ tsp

Granulated white sugar 35 g | 1¼ oz | 3 tbsp

Water 200 ml | 7 fl oz | sc. 1 cup

Hibiscus flower 15 g | ½ oz | ¼ cup

Santa Teresa Rhum Orange Liqueur 15 ml | ½ fl oz | 1 tbsp

For the Orange Gelée

Gelatine (gold) 35 g | 17½ sheets (softened in ice cold water, with excess water squeezed out)

50% orange reduction 100 g | 3½ fl oz | sc. ½ cup

Granulated white sugar 160 g | sc. 5¾ oz | sc. 1 cup

For the Almond Crumble

Granulated white sugar 25 g | gen. ¾ oz | 2 tbsp

Blanched almond meal 25 g | gen. ¾ oz | 4 tbsp

Plain (all-purpose) flour 25 g | gen. ¾ oz | 2 tbsp

Salted butter 25 g | gen. ¾ oz (cold, cut into chunks)

For the Yoghurt Ice Cream

Plain yoghurt 300 g | 10½ oz | sc. 1¼ cups

Granulated white sugar 40 g | sc. 1½ oz | gen. 3 tbsp

Dextrose 12 g | sc. ½ oz | 1¼ tbsp

Powdered milk 20 g | sc. ¾ oz | sc. 3 tbsp

INSTRUCTIONS

Hibiscus Flower Soup

1 Combine the pectin with approximately 20 g (sc. ¾ oz/5 tsp) of the sugar.

2 Place the water, hibiscus flower and remaining sugar in a saucepan and bring to the boil.

3 Simmer for 5 minutes, then remove the hibiscus flower.

4 Add the pectin/sugar mixture, leave to cook for 5 more minutes, then allow to cool.

5 Add the orange liqueur and keep refrigerated until ready to serve.

Orange Gelée

1 Melt the gelatine in a bain-marie.

2 Place the orange reduction and sugar in a saucepan and heat.

3 Add the gelatine, mix well and pour into the straight-sided tray.

4 Refrigerate for at least 2 hours.

Almond Crumble

1 Stir the sugar, almond meal and flour in a mixing bowl until well combined.

2 Add the cold butter chunks to the sugar/almond meal/flour mixture and rub in the butter with fingertips until the mixture resembles small crumbs.

3 Arrange on a silicone baking paper-lined tray and bake at 190°C (375°F) until deep golden brown.

Yoghurt Ice Cream

1 Place all the ingredients in a saucepan and cook to 82°C (180°F).

2 Chill as quickly as possible (ideally in a blast chiller), then churn in an ice cream machine according to the manufacturer's instructions.

3 Reserve in the freezer until needed.

ASSEMBLING

Components/Garnishes Strawberries and ideally blackberries, but can be replaced with blueberries and/or raspberries; dry rose petal powder; finely chopped peppermint leaves

Cut the strawberries and blackberries (or other fruits) into halves. Cut the orange gelée into four squares, then sub-divide into multiple cubes, each 1 cm (⅜ in.) square. Place the fruit, gelée and almond crumble in a soup dish. Add a scoop of yoghurt ice cream, and pour on the hibiscus flower soup. Finally, sprinkle some dry rose petal powder on the ice cream, and drop a few chopped peppermint leaves here and there.

COCONUT MOUSSE WITH PINEAPPLE AND PASSION FRUIT CONFITURE

'After my time with chef Yann Duytsche,' recalls Florencia, 'I made a version of one of his recipes called "Los Roques", after Venezuela's famous archipelago. I spiced it completely differently, but ultimately the Caribbean sea was still present.'

MAKES 6 amuse-bouche portions   **DIFFICULTY** 2/5   **PREPARATION TIME** 2 hours
SPECIFIC EQUIPMENT 6 x shot glasses

INGREDIENTS

For the Coconut Mousse

Coconut milk 175 g | 6 fl oz | ¾ cup
Granulated white sugar 18 g | gen. ½ oz | 1½ tbsp
Fresh grated coconut 10 g | sc. ½ oz | 2 tbsp
Gelatine (gold) 2.5 g | 1¼ sheets (softened in ice cold water, with excess water squeezed out)
White rum 7 g | ¼ fl oz | ½ tbsp
Whipping cream (35% fat) 75 g | sc. 2¾ fl oz | sc. ⅓ cup (whipped)

For the Pineapple and Passion Fruit Confiture

Pectin 1 g | sc. ½ tsp
Granulated white sugar 40 g | sc. 1½ oz | gen. 3 tbsp
Fresh pineapple 112 g | 4 oz
Passion fruit pulp 8 g | ¼ oz | ½ tbsp
Fresh grated ginger 2.5 g | ½ tsp

INSTRUCTIONS

Coconut Mousse

1 Combine the coconut milk, sugar and grated coconut in a saucepan and bring to the boil.
2 Remove from the heat and add the gelatine.
3 Pour into a mixing bowl set on ice water and leave to cool.
4 Stir in the rum.
5 Fold in the whipped cream.
6 Set aside until ready to assemble.

Pineapple and Passion Fruit Confiture

1 Combine the pectin with one-third of the sugar.
2 Cut the pineapple into cubes.
3 Place the pineapple, passion fruit pulp, grated ginger and remaining sugar in a saucepan.
4 Cook on a medium-low heat for about 15 minutes.
5 Add the pectin/sugar mixture and stir to combine.
6 Keep cooking for 5 more minutes.
7 Leave to cool.

ASSEMBLING

Garnishes Fresh coconut shavings; 6 lychees

Take six shot glasses of your choice and use a spoon to fill them with half the confiture. Top with coconut mousse, then leave to refrigerate for at least 1 hour, or until the desserts set. Pour on the rest of the confiture, then decorate with the coconut shavings and a lychee cut into quarters.

Janice Wong
·······················
SINGAPORE

A humble little berry inspired this inventive, Singapore-based dessert visionary. 'I had an epiphany when I was at a strawberry farm in Melbourne. I remember holding these fresh strawberries, which I'd just hand-picked. The moment I placed one in my mouth I felt that I wanted to become a pastry chef. I've never looked back.' So says Janice Wong, who has apprenticed at Les Amis, Thomas Keller's Per Se, Grant Achatz's Alinea alongside Alex Stupak, Will Goldfarb's Room 4 Dessert (see also p. 256) and Wylie Dufresne's WD-50. She is now owner and head chef of 2am:dessert bar (a modern venue where one can taste her philosophy first-hand); head artist/chef of the 2am:experience (a gallery showcasing edible art); and founder of the 2am:lab (a think-tank that explores every aspect of food).

Her business résumé is full of initiatives. 'I try to think out of the box, which is fairly risky most of the time. I'm a chef, artist and dessert architect, who designs sweets not only on a plate but on any surface I can think of.' As she recalls: 'When I created an event for the launch of my book, I envisioned a completely unique theme for my four hundred guests by creating seven edible art pieces, including a marshmallow ceiling and gumdrop walls. Guests had the chance to interact with the pieces, and these kept evolving as the guests ate them, but at the end of the day they still remained as a piece of art.'

Janice's book title, 'Perfection in Imperfection', echoes the way she describes the style of her desserts: 'perfectly imperfect'. Her destructured compositions combine both free-flowing pictorial creativity and scientific questioning. In fact, Janice works closely with professionals from various industries to understand and thus exploit to the fullest the physics and chemistry of each ingredient.

The erudition at play is counterbalanced by a sense of poetry, as in her exploration of colours. She has extended the 'Shades of...' series in her book with three exclusive recipes for us. 'I love working with one shade of a colour, as without this handicap you don't realize how many unique flavour pairings you can get out of it,' she explains. 2am is no longer just a time; it is also the best place to eat edible art.

www.2amdessertbar.com | www.2amexperience.com | http://2amlab.org

SHADES OF YELLOW | ORANGE POPPY SEED CAKE, YUZU WHITE CHOCOLATE GANACHE, LEMON ZAT

'Working with colour can be challenging, especially if it's just a shade of a colour,' admits Janice, 'but one can find amazing food pairings with such restrictions. This recipe started out with the pairing of yuzu, lemon and popcorn, which I found to be delicious, then I focused on the taste and textures, finally achieving a refreshing, zesty, light-textured dessert.'

MAKES 10   **DIFFICULTY** 4/5   **PREPARATION TIME** 3–4 hours (not including 3–4 days' fermentation time for the pomelo syrup and overnight drying time for the marshmallow)   **SPECIFIC EQUIPMENT** 3 x piping (pastry) bags; digital candy thermometer; Silpat® mat; small half-sphere silicone mould sheet (with up to 20 cavities, each cavity 3 cm/1⅛ in. diameter)

INGREDIENTS

For the Lemon Zat

Whipping cream (35% fat) 150 ml | sc. 5½ fl oz | gen. ½ cup
Milk 80 ml | gen. 2¾ fl oz | ⅓ cup
Lemon juice 30 ml | 1 fl oz | 2 tbsp
Fermented pomelo syrup* 25 ml | gen. ¾ fl oz | 5 tsp
Caster (superfine) sugar 20 g | sc. ¾ oz | 1½ tbsp
Cornflour (cornstarch) 4 g | sc. 1 tsp
Xanthan gum 0.6 g | ⅛ tsp
Gelatine (gold) 2.5 g | 1¼ sheets (softened in ice cold water, with excess water squeezed out)

* Fermented Pomelo Syrup

Pomelo dices (without skin or pith) 200 g | 7 oz
Water 250 ml | gen. 8¾ fl oz | 1 cup
Granulated white sugar 50 g | 1¾ oz | ¼ cup

For the Lemon Marshmallow

Granulated white sugar 150 g | gen. 5¼ oz | ¾ cup
Trimoline (invert sugar) [1] 50 g | 1¾ fl oz | 2½ tbsp
Water 200 ml | 7 fl oz | sc. 1 cup
Trimoline (invert sugar) [2] 62 g | 2¼ fl oz | gen. 3 tbsp
Gelatine (gold) 9 g | 4½ sheets (softened in ice cold water, with excess water squeezed out)
Lemon essence 2 drops
Yellow food colouring 2 drops
Icing (confectioner's) sugar/cornflour (cornstarch) mixture

For the Yuzu White Chocolate Ganache

Whipping cream (35% fat) 88 ml | gen. 3 fl oz | ⅓ cup
Yuzu juice 37 ml | gen. 1¼ fl oz | 2½ tbsp
White chocolate 250 g | gen. 8¾ oz

For the Yuzu Calamansi Sauce

Yuzu juice 103 ml | gen. 3½ fl oz | gen. ⅖ cup
Calamansi juice 112 ml | sc. 4 fl oz | sc. ½ cup (if calamansi cannot be found, lemon juice may be used)
Glucose syrup 187 g | gen. 6½ fl oz | gen. ½ cup
Trimoline (invert sugar) 46 g | gen. 1½ fl oz | 2¼ tbsp
Agar agar 5 g | sc. ¼ oz | sc. 2 tsp

For the Orange Poppy Seed Cake

Whole egg 45 g | 1½ oz | 3 tbsp
Granulated white sugar 45 g | 1½ oz | sc. ¼ cup
Whipping cream (35% fat) 25 g | gen. ¾ fl oz | sc. 1½ tbsp
Orange juice 35 ml | 1¼ fl oz | sc. 2½ tbsp
Plain (all-purpose) flour 45 g | 1½ oz | gen. ¼ cup
Baking powder 1 g | ¼ tsp
Poppy seeds 2 g | ½ tsp
Unsalted butter 15 g | ½ oz (melted)

Dipping Mixture

White chocolate 75 g | gen. 2½ oz
Cocoa butter 37 g | gen. 1¼ oz

INSTRUCTIONS

Lemon Zat

1 Heat the cream, milk, lemon juice, pomelo syrup and sugar in a saucepan.
2 Add the cornflour (cornstarch) and xanthan gum.
3 Whisk over heat until the mixture slightly thickens, then add the gelatine.
4 Strain, then place in a piping (pastry) bag and store in the fridge.

* Fermented Pomelo Syrup

1 Mix all the ingredients together in a bowl and leave outdoors, covered with cloth, for about 3–4 days (depending on the weather).
2 Taste the mixture every morning and evening until you detect a little acidity/zestiness.

Lemon Marshmallow

1 Boil the sugar, trimoline [1] and water to 109°C (228°F) to form a syrup.
2 Put trimoline [2] and the gelatine in the bowl of a stand mixer, and gradually whisk in the syrup until soft peaks form.
3 Add the lemon essence and food colouring.
4 Transfer into a piping (pastry) bag and pipe immediately onto a Silpat® mat in small mounds varying in size from 2 to 4 cm (¾–1⅝ in.).
5 Leave to dry overnight at room temperature.
6 The next day, toss in the icing (confectioner's) sugar/cornflour (cornstarch) mixture.

Yuzu White Chocolate Ganache

1 Bring the cream and yuzu juice to the boil, then pour over the white chocolate.
2 Leave to rest for 1 minute, then stir gently in one direction from the centre.
3 Stir until well incorporated, but do not over-stir.
4 Store in a piping (pastry) bag in the fridge.

Yuzu Calamansi Sauce

1 Place all the ingredients in a saucepan and heat while stirring thoroughly.
2 Strain, then leave to cool.
3 Once cooled, blitz with an immersion blender and store in the fridge.

Orange Poppy Seed Cake

1 Whisk the egg and sugar to ribbon stage.
2 Add the cream and orange juice.
3 Fold in the flour, baking powder and poppy seeds, then add the melted butter last.
4 Pour the batter into the small half-sphere moulds (about three-quarters full).
5 Bake at 180°C (350°F) for 10-12 minutes, then allow to cool.
6 Coat in white chocolate and cocoa butter dipping mixture (recipe below).

Dipping Mixture

1 Melt the white chocolate and cocoa butter together in a bain-marie.
2 Use at around 25°C (77°F).

ASSEMBLING

Garnish Popcorn powder

Place lemon marshmallows on each plate. Pipe on yuzu white chocolate ganache and lemon zat. Drizzle yuzu calamansi sauce around the plate. Add dipped orange poppy seed cake. Sprinkle with two teaspoons of popcorn powder.

SHADES OF BROWN | RED MISO BAVAROIS, MANGOSTEEN BARK, SORBET, SALTED PEANUT FOAM

'I've always loved working with all the parts of a fruit or vegetable, and mangosteen happened to be in season,' says Janice. 'Taking the skin and peel, I made a crunchy tuile for the balance of texture in this dessert. The flavours of miso caramel with mangosteen also make for a bold combination.'

MAKES 10   **DIFFICULTY** 4/5   **PREPARATION TIME** 3–4 hours (not including 5 hours' maturation time for the sorbet)
SPECIFIC EQUIPMENT Silpat® mat; digital candy thermometer; sorbet maker; whipped cream siphon and two cartridges

INGREDIENTS

For the Mangosteen Bark

Mangosteen pith 150 g | gen. 5¼ oz
Water 60 ml | 2 fl oz | ¼ cup
Balsamic vinegar 25 ml | gen. ¾ fl oz | 1¾ tbsp
Yuzu juice 50 ml | 1¾ fl oz | sc. 3½ tbsp
Icing (confectioner's) sugar 40 g | sc. 1½ oz | 4 tbsp

For the Mangosteen Sorbet

Caster (superfine) sugar 100 g | 3½ oz | sc. ½ cup
Ice cream stabilizer 4 g | 1 tsp
Water 120 g | 4 fl oz | ½ cup
Glucose syrup 50 g | 1¾ fl oz | sc. 3 tbsp
Fresh mangosteen purée 500 g | gen. 17¾ fl oz | 2 cups

For the Red Miso Caramel Bavarois

Whipping cream (35% fat) [1] 100 ml | gen. 3½ fl oz | sc. ½ cup
Milk 100 ml | 3½ fl oz | sc. ½ cup
Egg yolks 45 g | 1½ oz | 3 tbsp
Granulated white sugar [1] 62 g | gen. 2 oz | sc. ⅓ cup
Cornflour (cornstarch) 10 g | sc. ½ oz | 1 tbsp
Granulated white sugar [2] 72 g | 2½ oz | gen. ⅓ cup
Water 10 ml | sc. ½ fl oz | 2 tsp
Gelatine (gold) 6 g | 3 sheets (softened in ice cold water, with excess water squeezed out)
Red miso 25 g | gen. ¾ oz | 1½ tbsp
Whipping cream (35% fat) [2] 200 ml | 7 fl oz | ⅘ cup

For the Peanut Foam

Whipping cream (35% fat) 180 ml | gen. 6¼ fl oz | ¾ cup
Milk 180 ml | 6¼ fl oz | ¾ cup
Smooth peanut butter 165 g | 5¾ oz | ⅔ cup
Fine sea salt 2.5 g | ½ tsp (reduce or omit if using salted peanut butter)
Gelatine (gold) 1.5 g | ¾ sheet (softened in ice cold water, with excess water squeezed out)

For the Soy Jelly

Caster (superfine) sugar 35 g | 1¼ oz | sc. 2¾ tbsp
Water 50 ml | 1¾ fl oz | 3½ tbsp
Soy sauce (normal) 75 ml | gen. 2½ fl oz | 5 tbsp
Gelatine (gold) 2 g | 1 sheet (softened in ice cold water, with excess water squeezed out)

INSTRUCTIONS

Mangosteen Bark

1 Blend the mangosteen pith with the water until smooth.
2 Add the balsamic vinegar, yuzu juice and sugar, and blend until smooth.
3 Spread thinly on a Silpat® mat and dehydrate at 120°C (250°F) for 20 minutes.
4 Peel off the Silpat® mat while still in the oven and mould into the desired shape.
5 Store in a sealed container in a dry place.

Mangosteen Sorbet

1 Mix the sugar and stabilizer together.
2 Combine the water, glucose syrup and sugar/stabilizer mixture in a saucepan and heat to 85°C (185°F).
3 Add the mangosteen purée, then strain the mixture.
4 Leave to rest in the fridge for 5 hours before churning in a sorbet maker according to the manufacturer's instructions.

Red Miso Caramel Bavarois

1 Make an anglaise sauce by boiling cream [1] and the milk; at the same time, whisk the egg yolks with sugar [1] and the cornflour (cornstarch); temper in the hot liquid, then return to the stove on a low heat to thicken, stirring constantly.
2 Make a caramel by boiling sugar [2] and the water until the caramel is slightly burnt.
3 Slowly pour the caramel into the anglaise and continue whisking. NB Take care, as it will bubble vigorously.
4 Add the gelatine.
5 Add the red miso and mix well.
6 Strain the mixture, then leave to cool.
7 Lightly whip cream [2] and fold in the cooled mixture.
8 Reserve in the fridge.

Peanut Foam

1 Bring the cream and milk to the boil.
2 Pour over the peanut butter and incorporate well.
3 Add the salt (if using).
4 Add the gelatine.
5 Mix well, then allow to cool slightly.
6 Pour into a whipped cream siphon and charge with two cartridges.
7 Reserve in the fridge.

Soy Jelly

1 Heat the sugar, water and soy sauce.
2 Add the gelatine.
3 Strain into a container and reserve in the fridge.

ASSEMBLING

Style as you wish.

SHADES OF WHITE&BLACK | COOKIES AND CREAM, CHOCOLATE SHORTBREAD, VANILLA WOBBLE, GUMMY, CHOCOLATE MOUSSE

'I've always loved black and white,' confides Janice. 'White is a colour that has lost its colours, and black is a colour that has lost its colours in itself. The combination also reminds me of my childhood sweet, cookies and cream. Creating my own version, I put together a simple dessert with textures reminiscent of my past, such as gummies and chocolate mousse.'

MAKES 10   **DIFFICULTY** 4/5   **PREPARATION TIME** 4–5 hours   **SPECIFIC EQUIPMENT** Digital candy thermometer;
Silpat® mats; rectangular moulds recommended (e.g. 7.5 x 2.5 x 2.5 cm/2⅞ x 1 x 1 in. L x W x H), but can be any shape
or size; piping (pastry) bag

INGREDIENTS

For the Chocolate Shortbread

Plain (all-purpose) flour 70 g | 2½ oz | ½ cup
Cocoa powder 12 g | sc. ½ oz | 4 tsp
Icing (confectioner's) sugar 33 g | gen. 1 oz | 3 tbsp
Unsalted butter 77 g | 2¾ oz (soft)
Dark chocolate (70%) 30 g | 1 oz (melted)
Treacle 6 g | sc. ¼ fl oz | 1 tsp

For the Vanilla Gummy

Boiling hot water 15 ml | ½ fl oz | 1 tbsp
Gelatine (gold) 20 g | 10 sheets (softened in ice cold water, with excess water squeezed out)
Glucose syrup 90 g | 3¼ fl oz | ¼ cup
Caster (superfine) sugar 130 g | 4½ oz | gen. ½ cup
Water 90 g | 3 fl oz | ⅓ cup
Vanilla vodka 50 ml | 1¾ fl oz | 3½ tbsp
White and black food colouring (to achieve desired colour)

For the Vanilla Wobble

Milk 100 ml | 3½ fl oz | sc. ½ cup
Whipping cream (35% fat) 600 ml | 21 fl oz | sc. 2½ cups
2 vanilla pods (beans) (split, scraped, both pods/beans and seeds reserved)
Caster (superfine) sugar 20 g | sc. ¾ oz | 1½ tbsp
Gelatine (gold) 8 g | 4 sheets (softened in ice cold water, with excess water squeezed out)

For the Earl Grey Chocolate Mousse

Whipping cream (35% fat) [1] 200 g | 7 fl oz | ⅘ cup
Earl Grey tea 25 g | gen. ¾ fl oz | 5½ tbsp
Dark chocolate (72%) 150 g | gen. 5¼ oz
Caster (superfine) sugar 70 g | 2½ oz | sc. ⅓ cup
Water 25 g | gen. ¾ fl oz | 5 tsp
1 small whole egg
Egg yolks 50 g | 1¾ oz | sc. 3½ tbsp
Whipping cream (35% fat) [2] 50 g | 1¾ fl oz | ⅕ cup

INSTRUCTIONS

Chocolate Shortbread

1   Sift the flour, cocoa powder and sugar together.
2   Beat the soft butter and melted chocolate together, then add in the dry ingredients.
3   Add the treacle.
4   Spread on a silicone baking paper-lined tray to form a 10 x 10 cm (4 x 4 in.) square, 2 cm (¾ in.) deep.
5   Leave to rest in the fridge for 1 hour.
6   Bake at 165°C (325°F) for 25–30 minutes.

Vanilla Gummy

1   Add the boiling hot water to the gelatine, then reserve.
2   Heat the glucose syrup, sugar and water to 135°C (275°F), then add the previous mixture.
3   Add the vanilla vodka.
4   Pour onto several Silpat® mats to form a thin, continuous layer and mix in white and black food colouring in a disorderly fashion.
5   Once set, reserve in the fridge.

Vanilla Wobble

1   Combine the milk, cream, vanilla pods (beans) and seeds, and the sugar in a saucepan and heat to 80-90°C (176–194°F) (just enough for the sugar to melt).
2   Add in the gelatine and mix well, then strain.
3   Leave to set in moulds in the fridge.
4   Once set, unmould and wrap each vanilla wobble with a thin sheet of vanilla gummy (from above recipe), reserving the remainder of the vanilla gummy for plating up.

Earl Grey Chocolate Mousse

1   Cold-infuse cream [1] with the Earl Grey tea for several hours (or reduce this to approximately 1 hour by using a quick vacuum marinading system).
2   Strain the mixture and reserve the cream.
3   Melt the chocolate, then cool to 45°C (113°F).
4   Make a syrup with the sugar and water, and boil it until it reaches 125°C (257°F).
5   Whisk the egg and egg yolks in the bowl of a stand mixer to a foamy consistency, then slowly pour in the syrup.
6   Continue whisking until the mixture doubles in volume.
7   Whip the Earl Grey-infused cream [1] to a soft peak consistency.
8   Whip cream [2], add to the melted chocolate and stir in quickly.
9   Combine the chocolate and Earl Grey cream mixtures together.
10 Fold in the egg yolk mixture until well combined.
11 Reserve in a piping (pastry) bag in the fridge.

ASSEMBLING

Component Whipped 35% fat whipping cream (200 g/7 fl oz/⅘ cup)

Transfer a thin sheet of vanilla gummy onto each plate. Place a vanilla wobble, wrapped in its gummy, on the plate. Pipe on two mounds of Earl Grey chocolate mousse and cover each with a tablespoon of whipped cream. Place pieces of chocolate shortbread around the plate.

Leonor de Sousa Bastos

PORTUGAL

'Less is more', as in less culinary convolution and more authentic simplicity. This gives you a glimpse into what Portuguese prodigy Leonor de Sousa Bastos is all about. The result? Addictive desserts that are the antithesis of over-the-top and calorie-laden. 'Pastry is something that makes me vibrate,' she says. 'I like the joyful connotation of desserts; the association between cake and party, between sweet and desire – so much so that it becomes extremely difficult for me to define any moment of inspiration. I've reached the point where I interpret the simplest word or the most trivial situation as pastry. It's in my blood!'

While Leonor's passion may verge on obsession, it also serves a rational cause. She is striving to 'democratize pastry'. Her blog, Flagrante Delícia, is acclaimed for doing precisely that. She has blazed a trail through the somewhat conservative Portuguese pastry industry, with even *The New York Times* applauding her work. 'Pastry can still be underestimated in comparison to mainstream cooking, so many chefs don't understand the need to have an expert on the subject within a restaurant,' she claims. 'I also deplore the fact that in Portugal chefs don't usually give creative freedom to pastry chefs. Instead of having two worlds functioning in harmony, it seems that one is serving the other.' Not for much longer, if Leonor's multi-disciplinary ventures are anything to go by.

As a writer, pastry consultant, workshop instructor, contributor to magazines and TV programmes, and owner of a dessert bar/restaurant in downtown Oporto, Leonor has racked up an impressive list of achievements, especially considering she only embarked on her journey in 2006. 'As a freshman at law school, I used to feel that I was condemning myself to spending the rest of my life toiling in a profession that wouldn't make me happy,' she confides. 'I was already spending more time cooking than studying, to the point that I used to fall asleep while reading recipe books. The turning point coincided with the first time I really fell in love. Love has this ability to make us believe that anything is possible. In just three months, I had quit law school and enrolled in Palma de Mallorca as a culinary student.' Let us praise love, for it has brought us a refreshing and dynamic pastry talent!

www.leonordesousabastos.com | www.flagrantedelicia.com

AZEITÃO CHEESE PANNA COTTA, BANANA JAM, GUAVA FOAM, BANANA BRÛLÉE AND PÃO-DE-LÓ CROUTONS

'The combination of cheese and/or banana/quince jam/pão-de-ló [sponge cake] is very traditional,' says Leonor. 'I've put the ingredients together, but with lighter textures. The creamy, soft Azeitão, similar in flavour to the famous Queijo da Serra, is made from sheep's milk curdled with cardoon thistle. Instead of quince jam, I've used guava, which is used to make *goiabada*, a Brazilian guava jelly that is very popular in Portugal. I've also used Madeira bananas, which are smaller, firmer and sweeter than the common banana.'

MAKES 4   DIFFICULTY 3/5   PREPARATION TIME 4 hours   SPECIFIC EQUIPMENT Acetate sheets; whipped cream siphon and one cartridge; brûlée torch; cake tin (pan) (20 cm/ 7¾ in. diameter)

INGREDIENTS

For the Madeira Banana Jam
Madeira bananas 250 g | gen. 8¾ oz (peeled)
Light brown sugar 45 g | 1½ oz | 3½ tbsp
Ground nutmeg 0.56 g | ⅛ tsp
Unsalted butter 20 g | sc. ¾ oz (melted)

For the Azeitão Cheese Panna Cotta
Whipping cream (35% fat) 100 g | gen. 3½ fl oz | sc. ½ cup
Skimmed milk 40 g | gen. 1¼ fl oz | sc. 3 tbsp
Azeitão cheese, with rind discarded 100 g | 3½ oz
(if you cannot source Azeitão cheese – its consistency is
dense with no air holes, and its texture buttery soft and
creamy to firm – you could substitute a high-quality
Camembert, double-cream Brie or St André)
Granulated white sugar 40 g | sc. 1½ oz | gen. 3 tbsp
Gelatine (gold) 2 g | 1 sheet (softened in ice cold water,
with excess water squeezed out)

For the Guava Foam
Frozen guava pulp 300 g | 10 fl oz | gen. 1 cup
Granulated white sugar 35 g | 1¼ oz | 3 tbsp
Gelatine (gold) 4 g | 2 sheets (softened in ice cold water,
with excess water squeezed out)

For the Banana Brûlée
2 Madeira bananas
Lemon juice (to taste)
Light brown sugar (to taste)

For the Pão-de-ló
Unsalted butter (to grease cake tin/pan)
Egg yolks 140 g | sc. 5 oz | gen. ½ cup
Egg whites 70 g | 2½ oz | sc. ⅓ cup
Granulated white sugar 120 g | 4¼ oz | gen. ½ cup
Water 15 ml | ½ fl oz | 1 tbsp
Plain (all-purpose) flour 50 g | 1¾ oz | ⅓ cup
Baking powder 2.5 g | gen. ½ tsp

INSTRUCTIONS

Madeira Banana Jam
1 Pre-heat the oven to 220°C (425°F).
2 Cut the bananas lengthwise and place them on a silicone baking paper-lined tray.
3 Sprinkle with the sugar and nutmeg, then drizzle with the melted butter.
4 Bake until golden brown and candied (about 20–25 minutes).
5 Remove from the oven and purée in a food processor until smooth and fine.
6 Cover with plastic wrap and refrigerate until completely cold.

Azeitão Cheese Panna Cotta
1 Prepare two food-safe acetate tubes, 2 cm (¾ in.) diameter and 30 cm (11¾ in.) long, and seal one end of each tube very securely with plastic wrap (use tape).
2 Bring the cream, milk, rindless cheese and sugar to the boil in a saucepan.
3 Remove from the heat and add the gelatine, stirring well.
4 Pour the mixture inside the acetate tubes in vertical position, with the sealed ends at the bottom.
5 Cover the opposite ends with plastic wrap, then refrigerate, maintaining the vertical position.
6 Once the panna cotta is firm (about 1 hour), freeze until completely solid.

Guava Foam
1 Put half the pulp and all of the sugar into a pan and bring to the boil.
2 When the mixture begins to boil, remove from the heat and add the gelatine, stirring until completely dissolved.
3 Add the remaining pulp and stir until smooth.
4 Strain with a fine sieve (strainer).
5 Place in a whipped cream siphon, charge with one cartridge and shake vigorously.
6 Refrigerate for at least 1–2 hours before serving.

Banana Brûlée
1 Cut rectangles of banana 2 x 1 x 1 cm (¾ x ⅜ x ⅜ in.).
2 Sprinkle with lemon juice and refrigerate.
3 Sprinkle with sugar and caramelize with a brûlée torch just before serving.

Pão-de-ló
1 Pre-heat the oven to 220°C (425°F).
2 Grease the cake tin (pan) with butter and line with silicone baking paper, leaving a margin of paper out of the pan of approximately 6 cm (2½ in.).
3 Beat the egg yolks and egg whites with the sugar in a stand mixer at medium speed until they have tripled in volume and the mixture has become whitish (15 minutes).
4 Add the water, while mixing, and continue to beat for approximately 5 minutes.
5 Sift the flour with the baking powder and add to the egg mixture, folding gently with a spatula.
6 Pour the mixture into the cake tin (pan) and bake for about 20 minutes, or until a toothpick inserted in the centre of the cake comes out clean.
7 Remove from the oven and leave to cool completely on a wire rack before unmoulding.
8 Once cooled, pre-heat the oven to 180°C (350°F).
9 Cut approximately 28 cubes of pão-de-ló, measuring 1 x 1 x 1 cm (⅜ x ⅜ x ⅜ in.).
10 Place on a baking tray and bake for about 5 minutes, or until the croutons are golden brown.

ASSEMBLING

Place a spoonful of Madeira banana jam on each plate. Take the panna cotta out of the freezer, remove the acetate and cut each tube into two equal parts. Place one half over the banana jam. Serve with guava foam, banana brûlée rectangles and pão-de-ló croutons.

WHITE FIGS WITH PORT WINE AND RASPBERRY CARAMEL, RASPBERRIES, COCOA CRUMBLE, CARAMEL AND 70% CHOCOLATE GANACHE WITH TAVIRA FLEUR DE SEL

'Figs, port wine, raspberries, caramel, chocolate and sea salt blend perfectly,' says Leonor. 'Port is an excellent wine for desserts, as well as being emblematic of my city. The creamy dark chocolate is seasoned with fleur de sel from Tavira, giving the dish a perfect balance.'

MAKES 5   **DIFFICULTY** 3/5   **PREPARATION TIME** 2 hours (not including 4 hours' setting time for the ganache)
SPECIFIC EQUIPMENT Digital candy thermometer

INGREDIENTS

For the Caramel and 70% Chocolate Ganache
Dark chocolate (70%) 90 g | sc. 3¼ oz
Egg yolks 50 g | 1¾ oz | sc. 3½ tbsp
Milk 50 g | sc. 1¾ fl oz | sc. 3½ tbsp
Whipping cream (35% fat) 200 g | 7 fl oz | ⅘ cup
Light brown sugar 50 g | 1¾ oz | 4 tbsp

For the Cocoa Crumble
Plain (all-purpose) flour 20 g | sc. ¾ oz | 4 tsp
Granulated white sugar 25 g | gen. ¾ oz | 2 tbsp
Cocoa powder 5 g | sc. ¼ oz | sc. 1 tbsp
Unsalted butter 25 g | gen. ¾ oz

For the Port Wine and Raspberry Caramel
Granulated white sugar 40 g | sc. 1½ oz | gen. 3 tbsp
Tawny port wine 25 g | gen. ¾ fl oz | 5 tsp
Fresh raspberries 25 g | gen. ¾ oz
Whipping cream (35% fat) 25 g | gen. ¾ fl oz | sc. 1½ tbsp
Salted butter 10 g | sc. ½ oz

INSTRUCTIONS

Caramel and 70% Chocolate Ganache
1 Finely chop the chocolate, place in a bowl and set aside.
2 Mix the egg yolks with a small amount of milk.
3 Mix the remaining milk and cream in a saucepan, and bring to the boil.
4 Place the sugar in a heavy-bottomed saucepan and bring to a medium heat until caramelized.
5 Gradually pour the hot milk/cream over the caramel, mixing constantly until a homogeneous mixture is achieved.
6 Pour the hot milk/cream with caramel over the egg mixture, stirring constantly.
7 Strain the mixture and bring back to the boil until thickened (until it reaches 85°C/185°F).
8 Remove from the heat and pour over the chocolate, stirring constantly until the mixture becomes smooth and shiny.
9 Refrigerate for about 4 hours, or until fully set.

Cocoa Crumble
1 Pre-heat the oven to 180°C (350°F).
2 Place the flour, sugar and cocoa powder in a small food processor.
3 Add the butter and 'pulse', just enough to mix all the ingredients.
4 Refrigerate for 30 minutes, then spread on a tray.
5 Bake for 15 minutes, or until golden brown.
6 Remove from the oven and allow to cool completely on a wire rack.
7 Place in a food processor and blitz to a fine crumb.
8 Store in an airtight container.

Port Wine and Raspberry Caramel
1 Place the sugar in a heavy-bottomed saucepan and bring to a medium heat to make a light brown, dry caramel at 130°C (266°F).
2 Add the port wine and the raspberries, then immediately reduce the heat and stir to let all the alcohol evaporate and to achieve a lump-free texture. NB Cover hands and arms to avoid injury due to caramel splashes.
3 Add the cream, stir well and simmer for about 1 minute.
4 Add the butter and mix until smooth.
5 Remove from the heat and strain.
6 Refrigerate (the texture should be that of a fluid, thick toffee).

ASSEMBLING

Components/Garnishes Approx. 4–5 small white figs (150 g/gen. 5¼ oz); extra virgin olive oil (20 g/¾ fl oz/sc. 2 tbsp); approx. 10 raspberries (30 g/1 oz/¼ cup); Tavira fleur de sel (Portuguese sea salt: 2.5 g/½ tsp)

Cut the figs into quarters, then each quarter into two halves. Place in a bowl with the olive oil and mix well. Heat a frying pan and lightly brown both sides of the figs. Remove from the heat and set aside. Place cocoa crumble, figs and fresh raspberries on each plate. Drizzle port wine and raspberry caramel mostly on the figs. Make two small quenelles of chocolate ganache and place on each plate (the simplest way to make a ganache quenelle is to dip a spoon into hot water, which will give the desired glossy texture). Sprinkle Tavira fleur de sel on the ganache.

Pamela Yung
....
USA

When one thinks about cutting-edge cuisine, what may come to mind is molecular jargon and visions of test tubes and kitchen syringes. To Pamela Yung, former pastry chef at ISA in Brooklyn, New York, this definition is rather narrow. In her case, an unconventional pantry and the treatment of its contents (burning, fermenting, ageing) usher new, deep flavours into her desserts, creating a surprising and texturally rich experience.

Notably, Pamela has no formal training. She acquired her skills the hard way: by diving head-first into the business. 'I interviewed with Chef Will Goldfarb (see p. 256) to open Room 4 Dessert as an "apprentice". Impulsively, I gave up an ambitious design job in Detroit to work long hours for hardly any pay. It was certainly a naïve move, but I don't regret it. Years later, I spent some time staging in European kitchens. This taught me about patience and sacrifice. I realized that this isn't simply a job; it's a way of life I have chosen. I had a real sense of freedom after Europe.'

Unrestricted by rules, Pamela starts the ideation of a dessert with the product. Talented farmer and friend Dan Machin, for example, supplied the most delicious root vegetables in the thick of a New York winter, when most pastry chefs adhere to apples, pears, nuts and chocolate. Pamela's mind was spinning. Tapping into traditional techniques from the savoury kitchen, such as preserving, drying and use of a wood-burning oven, she discovered a whole new spectrum of flavours to exploit for her desserts.

Her latest project is one entrenched in the community in which she and her boyfriend, Jose Ramirez-Ruiz, live – Brooklyn. *Chez Jose* is a pop-up concept run out of a tiny coffee shop, where the couple prepare intimate, creative, vegetable-centric dinners, using Machin's products and dairy and butter from farmer friends Cowbella. Pamela has also launched a small CSB ('community-supported bakery'), preparing naturally leavened sourdough boules for local bread fanatics.

Of her desserts' savoury-sweetness, she comments, 'I really believe in striking a balance; that desserts shouldn't just be a compilation of sugars, fats and creams. They should be a natural continuation of the savoury courses, creating a satisfying finish on a sweet note.' And that is just what Pamela delivers.

goodbreadisback@gmail.com | Dan Machin: http://loneacre.wordpress.com | www.cowbella.com

GRAPEFRUIT CURD, PISTACHIO, MATCHA, LIME

'This dessert brings bright and intense flavours to the dead of winter,' notes Pamela. 'Winter in New York is the citrus season, and the white grapefruit can be incredible. Everyone loves a citrus curd, and this one is paired with a creamy and salted lime sherbet and a matcha and pistachio *streusel*, combining dried herbs from past seasons.'

MAKES 24 **DIFFICULTY** 4/5 **PREPARATION TIME** See below each step **SPECIFIC EQUIPMENT** Baking tray (33 x 23 cm/13 x 9 in.; 2.5 cm/1 in. high); digital candy thermometer; chinois (fine-mesh conical sieve/strainer); squeeze bottle; ice cream machine; cheesecloth (if making own mascarpone); piping (pastry) bag with small, round nozzle

INGREDIENTS

For the Grapefruit Curd
Time: 30 minutes (preparing)
Juice of approx. 2 white grapefruit 260 g | gen. 8¾ fl oz | gen. 1 cup
Zest of white grapefruit from fruit juiced above
Granulated white sugar 200 g | 7 oz | 1 cup
Salt a pinch
Whole eggs 300 g | 10½ oz | gen. 1⅓ cups (whisked)
Gelatine (gold) 8 g | 4 sheets (softened in ice cold water, with excess water squeezed out)
Unsalted butter 375 g | 13¼ oz (room temperature)

For the Moss
Time: 10 minutes (mixing) + 15–20 minutes (baking) + 5 minutes (mixing moss)
Matcha Crumble
Plain (all-purpose) flour 63 g | sc. 2¼ oz | sc. ½ cup
Blanched almond meal 63 g | sc. 2¼ oz | ¾ cup
Granulated white sugar 50 g | 1¾ oz | ¼ cup
Japanese matcha powder 7 g | ¼ oz | 1½ tbsp
Salt 0.75 g | ⅛ tsp
Unsalted butter 69 g | sc. 2½ oz (soft)
Finishing the 'moss'
Matcha crumble (from above recipe)
Halved toasted pistachios 100 g | 3½ oz | 1 cup
Salt (to taste)
Japanese matcha powder (to taste)
Dried ground parsley (to taste)
Dried ground lemon verbena (to taste)
Citric acid (to taste)
Lime zest and juice (to taste)

For the Parsley Fluid Gel
Time: 10 minutes (preparing) + waiting time
Parsley juice (parsley leaves + water + ice) 100 g | 3½ fl oz | sc. ½ cup
Water 100 g | 3½ fl oz | sc. ½ cup
Granulated white sugar 25 g | gen. ¾ oz | 2 tbsp
Agar agar 2.25 g | ¾ tsp
Salt (to taste)
Lemon juice (to taste)

For the Lime Sherbet
Time: 20 minutes (preparing) + at least 6 hours (maturing)
Water 250 g | gen. 8¾ fl oz | 1 cup
Granulated white sugar 250 g | gen. 8¾ fl oz | 1¼ cups
Milk 250 g | 8½ fl oz | gen. 1 cup
Fresh lime juice 250 g | 8½ fl oz | gen. 1 cup
Salt (generous)

INSTRUCTIONS

Grapefruit Curd

1   Line the baking tray with plastic wrap, ensuring minimal wrinkles.
2   Heat the juice, zest, sugar and salt in a bain-marie until the sugar dissolves.
3   Temper in the whisked eggs, then return to the bain-marie.
4   Cook until thickened, whisking constantly.
5   Add the gelatine, then when dissolved sit over an ice bath.
6   When the mixture reaches 40°C (104°F), add the butter and use an immersion blender to combine.
7   Once combined, strain through a fine-mesh sieve (strainer) into the lined tray and leave to set in the fridge on a flat surface.
8   Once set, place in the freezer and chill until firm enough to slice and move cleanly, but still flexible.
9   Divide into 24 strips with a long, warm knife.

Moss
Matcha Crumble

1   Mix all the dry ingredients well, then add the soft butter.
2   Distribute the butter well by hand, rubbing the mixture through your hands so it resembles crumbs (not too large or too fine).
3   Bake at 165°C (325°F) for 12 minutes.
4   Remove and allow to cool.
Finishing the 'moss'
5   As soon as the matcha crumble is cool, combine with all the other ingredients to create a 'moss' effect/appearance.

Parsley Fluid Gel

1   Make parsley juice by puréeing fresh parsley leaves with a tiny bit of water and a few pieces of ice, then strain through a chinois set over an ice bath.
2   Bring the water, sugar and agar agar to the boil in a small saucepan for 2 minutes.
3   Strain and cool slightly, whisking in the cold parsley juice before it sets.
4   Once set, purée in the blender until smooth, then pass through the chinois.
5   Season with salt and lemon juice as needed.
6   Store in a squeeze bottle, chilled.

Lime Sherbet

1   Make a syrup with the water and sugar.
2   Once cool, add the milk and lime juice.
3   Season liberally with salt (you should be able to taste the salinity).
4   Mature in the fridge for a minimum of 6 hours.
5   Churn in an ice cream machine according to the manufacturer's instructions.

Grapefruit Confit

1   Halve and juice the grapefruit, then strain the juice to remove the seeds and pulp.
2   Blanch the grapefruit rinds four times to remove some of the bitterness.
3   Cook in water until tender (1–2 hours).
4   Strain, then clean with a sharp knife, removing most of the pith.
5   Return to the saucepan and add the sugar and grapefruit juice, in equal measure, until covered.
6   Cook slowly on a low heat until translucent and glossy.
7   Leave to cool in the cooking syrup.
8   Cut into small cubes and store in the syrup.

For the Grapefruit Confit

(makes more than required, but a more manageable amount)

Time: 1 hour (preparing) + 2–3 hours (cooking)

2 white grapefruit (rinds and juice)

Granulated white sugar (to taste)

For the Mascarpone

Time: 2-4 hours (the mascarpone can also be bought ready-made)

Double (heavy) whipping cream (83% fat)
920 g | sc. 33½ fl oz | 1 qt

Ascorbic acid 2.6 g | 1 tsp

Salt (to taste)

For the Lime Salt

Time: 5 minutes (preparing)

Zest of 3 limes

Maldon salt (sea salt flakes) (to taste)

Mascarpone

1   Heat the cream In a bain-marie to 68°C (154°F).

2   Add the ascorbic acid and immediately remove from the heat, stirring constantly.

3   Add salt to taste.

4   Hang in cheesecloth until the desired texture is achieved (pipeable; not too dense, nor too loose).

5   Fill a piping (pastry) bag with a small, round nozzle.

Lime Salt

1   Mix the lime zest and Maldon salt.

2   Dehydrate slightly so that the mixture is not sticky but the colour remains bright.

ASSEMBLING

Garnish Japanese matcha powder

Arrange an arc of grapefruit curd on each 25.5 cm (10 in.) round white plate. Pipe on mascarpone to one side, and spoon matcha mixture at one end of the curd. Garnish with dots of parsley fluid gel and grapefruit confit. Dust the plate lightly with matcha powder. Add a quenelle of lime sherbet and season with lime salt.

GRILLED CELERIAC, MALT, ESPRESSO, SEVILLE ORANGE

'One winter I worked at the Michelin-starred In De Wulf, nestled on the border of Belgium and France,' recalls Pamela. 'We served a grilled celeriac soup with bacon, beer and cheese. The warmth of the char lent great character to the naturally sweet celeriac. I wanted to use it in a dessert. My first instinct was to pair it with something dark and bitter: espresso. Then those wintry flavours needed some lightness: I used intense Seville orange and bright Lisbon lemon. The red wine sauce is a reminder of the late-night glass of Lambrusco I often enjoyed after work. The malt is an homage to the original soup with its beer – a true Belgian pairing.'

MAKES 24   **DIFFICULTY** 4/5   **PREPARATION TIME** See below each step   **SPECIFIC EQUIPMENT** Mandolin (ideally deli meat slicer); Silpat® mats; spray bottle; chinois (fine-mesh conical sieve/strainer); digital candy thermometer; ice cream machine; piping (pastry) bag with No. 124 petal nozzle; box grater

INGREDIENTS

For the Celeriac Chips

Time: 2 days (preparing and drying)

1 large celeriac

Simple syrup (ratio: 1 part sugar to 1 part water)
(to mist celeriac)

Icing (confectioner's) sugar (to taste)

Celery salt (to taste)

For the Espresso Ice Cream

Time: 1 day (soaking and reducing) +

30 minutes (preparing) + 8 hours (maturing)

For the Espresso Milk

Milk 500 g | 17 fl oz | gen. 2 cups

Whipping cream (35% fat) 250 g | 8¾ fl oz | 1 cup

Coarsely cracked whole espresso beans 75 g | gen. 2½ oz | 1 cup

For the Ice Cream

Espresso milk (from above recipe)

Ground espresso 8 g | ¼ oz | 1¼ tbsp

Granulated white sugar 80 g | gen. 2¾ oz | ⅖ cup

Maltodextrin 50 g | 1¾ oz | ½ cup

Glucose powder 31 g | 1 oz | 3 tbsp

Non-fat dried milk powder 50 g | 1¾ oz | ½ cup

Glucose syrup 61 g | 2¼ fl oz | sc. 3½ tbsp

Whole eggs 92 g | 3¼ oz | sc. ½ cup

Espresso reduction (slowly reduced from 150 g/5¼ fl oz/⅔ cup
fresh-brewed espresso) 50 g | 1¾ fl oz | sc. 3½ tbsp

Fresh-brewed espresso 50 g | sc. 1¾ fl oz | sc. 3½ tbsp

For the Grilled Celeriac Cream

Time: 2 hours (preparing)

For the Celeriac Purée

Approx. 1 large celeriac 400 g | 14 oz (peeled and cut into
0.5 cm/¼ in. slices)

Milk 400 g | gen. 13½ fl oz | sc. 1¾ cups

Whipping cream (35% fat) 200 g | 7 fl oz | ⅘ cup

For the Grilled Celeriac Milk

Milk 300 g | 10¼ fl oz | 1¼ cups

Whipping cream (35% fat) 150 g | sc. 5½ fl oz | gen. ½ cup

Grilled celeriac purée (from above recipe)

For the Cream

Iota carrageenan 6 g | ¼ oz | 1½ tsp

Locust bean gum 1 g | ¼ tsp

Granulated white sugar [1] 10 g | sc. ½ oz | 2½ tsp

Grilled celeriac milk (from above recipe)

5 egg yolks

Granulated white sugar [2] 66 g | gen. 2¼ oz | ⅓ cup

Salt (to taste)

For the Grated Malt Sucrée

Time: 8 minutes (preparing)

Plain (all-purpose) flour 100 g | 3½ oz | ⅔ cup

Granulated white sugar 90 g | sc. 3¼ oz | sc. ½ cup

Salt 7.5 g | ¼ oz | gen. 1¼ tsp

Dark roast malt powder 7.5 g | ¼ oz | 1 tbsp

Malted milk powder 2.5 g | sc. 1 tsp

Light roast malt powder 7.5 g | ¼ oz | 1 tbsp

Unsalted butter 100 g | 3½ oz (soft)

INSTRUCTIONS

Celeriac Chips

1 Peel the celeriac, then slice using a mandolin (or deli meat slicer) to a thickness of 1 mm (¹⁄₁₆ in.).

2 Lay the slices flat (without touching) on baking trays lined with Silpat® mats.

3 Allow to dry at room temperature until slightly curled (12–24 hours). NB The chips will shrink significantly; rearrange them on the mats to accommodate more pieces.

4 Use a spray bottle to mist with the simple syrup.

5 Sift the icing (confectioner's) sugar on top, and season lightly with celery salt.

6 Dry in a 120°C (250°F) oven (no fan) for 30–60 minutes until crunchy.

7 Once cool, store in an airtight container, ideally with some silica gel desiccant.

Espresso Ice Cream

Espresso Milk

1 Combine the milk, cream and espresso beans, and allow to cold-infuse overnight.

2 Strain through a chinois, pressing lightly with the back of a ladle to squeeze out the liquid from the beans.

Ice Cream

3 Heat the espresso milk, while whisking in the ground espresso.

4 Mix the sugar, maltodextrin, glucose powder and milk powder together in a bowl.

5 At 25°C (77°F) add the glucose syrup to the milk mixture, then follow with the above sugar mixture, whisking constantly.

6 At 65°C (149°F) temper in the eggs and cook to 72°C (162°F), whisking constantly.

7 Hold at 72°C (162°F) for 5 minutes, then strain through a chinois and chill over ice.

8 Once cold, add the espresso reduction and the fresh-brewed espresso.

9 Mature for 8 hours.

10 Churn in an ice cream machine according to the manufacturer's instructions.

Grilled Celeriac Cream

Celeriac Purée

1 Grill (broil) the celeriac slices on both sides until charred thoroughly.

2 Heat the milk and cream together.

3 Infuse the celeriac and simmer until cooked through and very soft to the touch.

4 Purée in a blender, then pass through a chinois.

Grilled Celeriac Milk

5 Combine the milk, cream and 600 g (21 oz/2½ cups) of the celeriac purée in a saucepan.

6 Heat to 70°C (158°F), whisking constantly to avoid burning.

7 Immediately after the mixture reaches 70°C (158°F), pour it in a blender. NB The iota carrageenan and locust bean gum from the recipe below will need this temperature to hydrate properly.

Cream

8 Combine the iota carrageenan, locust bean gum and sugar [1] (this is to prevent clumping when they are added into the liquid medium).

9 Pour 1 kg (35 fl oz/4 cups) of grilled celeriac milk into a blender on a low-medium speed, enough to create a vortex.

10 Add the egg yolks, one at a time.

11 Add sugar [2].

12 Add the iota carrageenan/locust bean gum/sugar mixture (the cream will visibly thicken).

13 Increase the blender speed to ensure everything is well distributed.

14 Pass through a chinois and allow to cool completely and set.

15 Once thoroughly chilled, pulse in a food processor or with an immersion blender until smooth and creamy.

16 Fill a piping (pastry) bag fitted with a No. 124 petal nozzle and reserve chilled.

Grated Malt Sucrée

1 Mix all the dry ingredients, then incorporate the soft butter until a dough is formed.

2 Freeze in small portions, together with a box grater.

3 Grate, using the medium-coarse holes of the frozen box grater. NB Work quickly, otherwise the dough will soften and melt (you want the sucrée to look a bit like grated cheese).

4 Keep the mixture frozen.

For the Seville Orange Confit

Time: 4–5 hours (preparing + simmering)

2 Seville oranges (for juice and rind)

Water (to simmer orange rinds)

Granulated white sugar (to make cooking syrup)

Glucose syrup (to make cooking syrup)

For the Lemon Granita

Time: 10 minutes (preparing)

Water 400 g | 14 fl oz | 1¾ cups

Granulated white sugar 125 g | sc. 4½ oz | gen. ½ cup

Gelatine (gold) 1.25 g | ⅝ sheet (softened in ice cold water, with excess water squeezed out)

Freshly squeezed lemon juice 250 g | 8½ fl oz | gen. 1 cup

For the Coffee-Malt

Time: 3 minutes (preparing)

Dark chocolate malt (most often found at beer brewing supply stores)

Coffee beans (to taste)

For the Red Wine Sauce

Time: 3 hours (preparing)

Red wine 250 g | gen. 8¾ fl oz | 1 cup

Port wine 250 g | gen. 8¾ fl oz | 1 cup

Glucose syrup (to achieve desired consistency)

Seville Orange Confit

1 Halve and juice the oranges, then strain the juice to remove seeds and pulp.

2 Blanch the orange rinds 3-4 times to soften the bitterness.

3 Simmer the rinds for 1-2 hours in water, stirring occasionally, until softened (a cake tester should pass through without resistance) but still with a bite.

4 Strain, then clean with a sharp knife, removing most of the pith.

5 Cook with equal parts sugar and orange juice, and add 10% as much glucose syrup, to cover (you want a light simmer).

6 Remove from the heat when the fruit is translucent and glossy.

7 Leave to cool in the cooking syrup.

8 Julienne, and store in the syrup.

Lemon Granita

1 Heat half of the water to dissolve the sugar and gelatine.

2 Chill, then whisk in the remaining water and lemon juice.

3 Freeze, agitating every 30 minutes until frozen.

4 Scrape with a fork.

Coffee-Malt

1 Coarsely crush some dark chocolate malt and coffee beans in a mortar and pestle.

Red Wine Sauce

1 Reduce the red wine and port wine slowly until syrupy.

2 Blend in a blender on low speed, adding glucose until the sauce drops on a plate without oozing.

ASSEMBLING

Pipe the grilled celeriac cream in an undulating pattern on each 25.5 cm (10 in.) round white plate. Place a few pieces of orange confit on top. Sprinkle grated malt sucrée in one corner and place a quenelle of espresso ice cream on top. Add coffee-malt, and follow with lemon granita. Garnish with celeriac chips and splatters of red wine sauce.

SUNCHOKE, CHESTNUT, 'DIRT'

'This is an homage to the humble and under-appreciated sunchoke,' says Pamela. 'Working at In de Wulf in Belgium gave me a deep respect and love for these knobbly roots. They often arrived caked in layers of mud (the best way to store them, otherwise they begin to dry out) and required repeated rinses and scrubbings, so I made a dessert-y version of "dirt" here. The sweetness of chestnut also seemed to make a lot of sense. Then dried black trumpet mushrooms gave a unique texture and earthiness, hinting at the root vegetable origins of the dish.'

MAKES 12 **DIFFICULTY** 4/5 **PREPARATION TIME** See below each step **SPECIFIC EQUIPMENT** Whipped cream siphon and three cartridges; digital candy thermometer; piping (pastry) bag; chinois (fine-mesh conical sieve/strainer); ice cream machine; wood-burning oven, or chestnut roasting pan; brûlée torch

INGREDIENTS

For the Caramelized Sunchoke Cream
Time: 1½ hours (preparing purée) + 15 minutes (cream)

For the Purée
Whole sunchokes (Jerusalem artichokes) 250 g | gen. 8¾ oz
Brown (unsalted) butter (to cook sunchokes)
Milk (to achieve desired consistency)

For the Cream
Caramelized sunchoke purée (from above recipe)
Milk 250 g | 8½ fl oz | gen. 1 cup
Granulated white sugar 30 g | 1 oz | 2½ tbsp
Salt (to taste)
Gelatine (gold) 2.85 g | 1⅖ sheets (softened in ice cold water, with excess water squeezed out)

For the Whipped Yolks
Time: 7 minutes (preparing)
Fresh egg yolks 90 g | sc. 3¼ oz | gen. ⅓ cup
Salt a pinch
Granulated white sugar 75 g | gen. 2½ oz | gen. ⅓ cup
Water 20 g | gen. ½ fl oz | 4 tsp

For the Sunchoke Sorbet
Time: 1½ hours (preparing)
For the White Sunchoke Purée
Sunchokes 250 g | gen. 8¾ oz (approx. 350 g/ sc. 12½ oz unpeeled)
Ascorbic acid (to preserve colour)

For the Sorbet
Sunchoke cooking liquid (from above recipe) 63 g | 2 fl oz | ¼ cup
Glucose syrup 42 g | 1½ fl oz | sc. 2½ tbsp
Granulated white sugar 17 g | ½ oz | sc. 1½ tbsp
Trimoline (invert sugar) 7 g | ¼ oz | 1 tsp
Gelatine (gold) 1.1 g | ½ sheet (softened in ice cold water, with excess water squeezed out)
Salt (to taste)
Citric acid (to taste)
White sunchoke purée (from above recipe)

INSTRUCTIONS

Caramelized Sunchoke Cream
Purée
1. Cut the sunchokes into smaller pieces (the more surface area for caramelization, the more intense the flavour).
2. Prepare the butter by heating it in a wide-bottomed saucepan on medium until golden brown; use a whisk to scrape the most flavoursome brown bits off the bottom of the pan, then remove from the heat and cool.
3. Arrange the sunchokes in a single-layered wide rondeau over a generous helping of the brown butter.
4. Allow to caramelize slowly over medium heat, flipping the sunchokes from time to time to ensure even browning on as much of the surface area as possible.
5. Finish in a 160°C (325°F) oven until cooked through and slightly dehydrated (evaporating some of the water will concentrate the flavour).
6. Make a purée loosened with some milk but still quite thick; in the process, use the milk to bring the amount back up to 250 g (gen. 8¾ fl oz/gen. 1 cup).

Cream
7. Heat the purée, milk, sugar and salt.
8. Add the gelatine.
9. Cool the entire mixture over an ice bath.
10. Fill a whipped cream siphon and charge with three cartridges.
11. Keep chilled until ready for use.

Whipped Yolks
1. Use a stand mixer to whip the egg yolks with a pinch of salt to ribbon stage.
2. Make a syrup with the sugar and water and heat to 121°C (250°F).
3. Slowly drizzle the syrup into the yolks (as you would in making an Italian meringue).
4. Fill a piping (pastry) bag.

Sunchoke Sorbet
White Sunchoke Purée
1. Clean, peel and thinly slice the sunchokes so that only the white part is retained.
2. Keep the pieces in cold water with a pinch of ascorbic acid to avoid oxidation.
3. Cook rapidly in boiling water until soft.
4. Strain, reserving the reduced cooking liquid.
5. Purée the sunchokes until smooth, then pass through a chinois over an ice bath.

Sorbet
6. Make a sorbet syrup with the reserved cooking liquid by heating it and dissolving the glucose syrup, sugar, trimoline and gelatine.
7. Season with a healthy amount of salt and a touch of citric acid.
8. Strain, chill to room temperature, then whisk into 250 g (gen. 8¾ oz/gen. 1 cup) of the purée.
9. Churn in an ice cream machine according to the manufacturer's instructions.

For the Roasted Chestnut Ice Cream
Time: 1 hour (preparing) + 1 day (infusing and maturing)

For the Infused Milk

Fresh chestnuts 250 g | gen. 8¾ oz
Milk 375 ml | gen. 12½ fl oz | gen. 1½ cups
Whipping cream (35% fat) 125 ml | 4½ fl oz | ½ cup

For the Ice Cream

Infused milk (from above recipe) weight will be slightly less than 500 g | 17 fl oz
Glucose syrup 63 g | 2 fl oz | 3½ tbsp
Granulated white sugar 50 g | 1¾ oz | ¼ cup
Trimoline (invert sugar) 38 g | gen. 1¼ oz | 2 tbsp
Non-fat dry milk powder 25 g | gen. ¾ oz | ¼ cup
Fresh egg yolks 48 g | sc. 1¾ oz | gen. 3 tbsp

For the 'Dirt'
Time: 30 minutes (preparing)

For the Black Cocoa Cookie

Plain (all-purpose) flour 52 g | 1¾ oz | ⅓ cup
Granulated white sugar 30 g | 1 oz | 2½ tbsp
Black cocoa powder 7 g | ¼ oz | 1 tbsp
Dutch process cocoa powder 5 g | sc. ¼ oz | sc. 1 tbsp
Black trumpet mushroom powder* 4 g | 2 tsp (dehydrated trumpets, powdered finely in a spice grinder)
Bicarbonate of soda (baking soda) 0.5 g | tip of tsp
Salt 1.8 g | gen. ¼ tsp
Unsalted butter 44 g | 1½ oz (soft)

Finishing the 'Dirt'

Black cocoa cookie (from above recipe) 100 g | 3½ oz | ¾ cup
Black trumpet mushroom powder* 20 g | sc. ¾ oz | 4 tbsp
Ground espresso 7 g | ¼ oz | 1 tbsp
Dried black olives 7 g | ¼ oz | approx. 4 (coarsely pounded)
Cocoa nibs 7 g | ¼ oz | 1 tbsp (broken)
Coffee beans 7 g | ¼ oz | 1½ tbsp (broken)
Black cocoa powder 5 g | sc. ¼ oz | sc. 1 tbsp
Muscovado sugar (to taste)
Salt (to taste)
Truffle oil (to taste; or use grated fresh black truffle)

Roasted Chestnut Ice Cream

Infused Milk

1 Wipe the chestnuts clean with a towel, then score them.
2 Roast the chestnuts in a wood-burning oven or chestnut roasting pan over a high flame until dark, fragrant and burnt (the chestnuts will crackle and open).
3 Heat the milk and cream to a simmer.
4 Infuse the chestnuts overnight in the milk/cream mixture.
5 Strain out the chestnuts, peel them and remove the meat.
6 Purée in a food processor, then set aside.
7 Use the infused milk to make an ice cream base (recipe below).

Ice Cream

8 Heat the infused milk.
9 Add in the glucose syrup, sugar, trimoline and milk powder, whisking well.
10 Temper in the egg yolks and cook until thick enough to coat the back of a spoon (78°C/172°F).
11 Strain over an ice bath.
12 Once fully chilled, use an immersion blender to add in the chestnut purée (from above recipe).
13 Mature for at least 6 hours in the fridge, then churn in your ice cream machine according to the manufacturer's instructions.

'Dirt'

Black Cocoa Cookie

1 Combine all the ingredients, except the soft butter, in a stand mixer with a paddle attachment.
2 Add in the butter and paddle until a dough can be made by pressing the mixture between two fingers.
3 Roll out thinly on silicone baking paper.
4 Bake at 180°C (350°F) for 12–15 minutes.
5 Allow to cool, then process in a food processor to a fine crumb.

Finishing the 'Dirt'

6 Mix the black cocoa cookie crumbs with all the other ingredients until the mixture resembles dirt and tastes sweet, salty and earthy.

*** Dehydrated black trumpet mushrooms should be easy to find in gourmet stores, but here is how to make your own from fresh black trumpet mushrooms (3–4 hours):**

1 Rinse mushrooms well in cold water to remove any debris.
2 Pat dry with towels and arrange in a single layer on silicone baking paper-lined trays.
3 Dry in a 100°C (200°F) oven until crispy and shrunken.
4 Store in a cool, dry place, tightly covered.
5 To use in this recipe, powder finely in a spice grinder.

ASSEMBLING

Components/Garnishes Crème fraîche (in a piping/pastry bag); dehydrated trumpet mushrooms; Maldon salt (sea salt flakes)

Pipe some whipped yolk into the base of each small bowl, then blowtorch to caramelize lightly. Follow with a dot of crème fraîche. Sprinkle dehydrated trumpet mushroom pieces on top. Follow with a small amount of sunchoke sorbet. Place a round scoop of roasted chestnut ice cream on top of the sunchoke sorbet and season with a little Maldon salt. Place dried trumpet mushroom pieces on top of the ice cream. Finish by dispensing a mound of caramelized sunchoke cream on top, covering all the previous ingredients. Sprinkle the top of the cream with the 'dirt'. Serve promptly.

Pierre François Roelofs

AUSTRALIA

Picture this: 'Dessert Evenings'. Doesn't the title alone conjure up bright days ahead? One chef and his team of five orchestrate a menu composed of intriguing desserts that spellbind the senses. You have to be in Melbourne, Australia, and you have to look out for Pierre François Roelofs, the genius founder of these epicurean rendezvous. 'I am completely independent and free to do exactly what I want to do, which is to focus on my desserts. My ambition is to continue what I'm doing. I don't need to answer to business partners or compromise on my vision,' states Pierre. 'I can spend 95% of my time creating, preparing and serving dishes and only 5% focusing on running the business. The purity and simplicity of the Dessert Evenings is incredibly important to me, and I wouldn't compromise it for anything.'

For a patron, there is little more satisfying than putting oneself in the hands of an expert who devotes his expertise exclusively to your care, and with Pierre this is exactly what you get. 'I've always been very driven, disciplined and organized. I'm also very honest with myself and constantly assess my professional output. I take what I do very seriously,' he shares.

The range of his ingredients appears unconventionally broad – grains and pulses (rye, chickpeas, quinoa, amaranth, brown rice, polenta, couscous, barley) and vegetables (beetroot, celery, carrot, parsnip, pumpkin, potato) – but this is not for shock or novelty value, but rather for the openness and fluidity of Pierre's concept. 'Logic dictates that some ingredients will never make sense in a dessert context, but each element is a carefully considered addition to bring a desired dimension and to influence the eating experience in some way,' he explains.

'The organic nature of my presentation also creates mystery and surprise. Nothing is completely evident or obvious. Different ingredients and preparations remain hidden or unidentified, only revealing themselves when eaten, producing an authentic, exciting, modern, expressive and gastronomic dessert.' Incredibly, considering his highly sophisticated pâtisserie, Pierre says that 'a food dehydrator is the only "gadget" in my kitchen at the moment; it definitely has less equipment in it than that of a keen home cook!' His is a true talent without artifice.

www.pierreroelofs.com

HIBISCUS, BERRIES, BUBBLEGUM

'Every pastry chef loves using berries because of their exquisite colour, flavour, and of course huge popularity!' laughs Pierre. 'Hibiscus, like many other floral flavours, goes very well with raspberries and strawberries. I've also tried to do something a little different with berries by pairing them with the familiar yet unexpected taste of bubblegum.'

MAKES 10   **DIFFICULTY** 5/5   **PREPARATION TIME** 10 hours (not including 48 hours' drying time for the strawberry paper and 24 hours' drying time for the meringue)   **SPECIFIC EQUIPMENT** Silpat® mats, or silicone baking paper; food dehydrator (or fan oven set to the lowest possible temperature, with door left ajar and drying times shortened); desiccant; 2 x piping (pastry) bags; 3 x squeeze bottles (preferred, but spoons may also be used for plating); shallow tray (10 x 16 cm/4 x 6¼ in.)

INGREDIENTS

For the Strawberry Paper
Fresh strawberries 200 g | 7 oz | 1½ cups
Icing (confectioner's) sugar 50 g | 1¾ oz | 5 tbsp
Juice of ½ a lemon

For the Bubblegum Meringues
(can be made several days in advance)
Egg white powder 7.5 g | ¼ oz | 3 tsp
Water 53 g | 1¾ fl oz | 3½ tbsp
Granulated white sugar 40 g | sc. 1½ oz | gen. 3 tbsp
Bubblegum flavour (to taste)
Red food colouring (optional)

For the Strawberry Cheesecake Purée
(can be made 1 day in advance)
Cream cheese 200 g | 7 oz | sc. 1 cup
Caster (superfine) sugar 75 g | gen. 2½ oz | ⅓ cup
1 whole egg
Cornflour (cornstarch) 10 g | sc. ½ oz | 1 tbsp
Semi-dried strawberries* approx. 200 g | 7 oz | 1 cup
Lemon juice 10 ml | gen. ¼ fl oz | 2 tsp

* For the Semi-Dried Strawberries
(can be made 1 day in advance)
Fresh strawberries 400 g | 14 oz | 3 cups
Icing (confectioner's) sugar 50 g | 1¾ oz | 5 tbsp
Juice of 1 lemon

For the Strawberry Gel
(can be made 1 day in advance)
Fresh strawberries 200 g | 7 oz | 1½ cups
Agar agar 2 g | gen. ½ tsp
Caster (superfine) sugar 35 g | 1¼ oz | sc. 2¾ tbsp
Juice of ½ a lemon

For the Blueberry Gel
(can be made 1 day in advance)
Blueberries 200 g | 7 oz | gen. 1½ cups
Caster (superfine) sugar 50 g | 1¾ oz | sc. ¼ cup
Lemon juice 12.5 ml | sc. ½ fl oz | sc. 1 tbsp
Agar agar 2 g | gen. ½ tsp

INSTRUCTIONS

Strawberry Paper
1   Purée the ingredients and spread thinly onto Silpat® mats, or silicone baking paper.
2   Dehydrate in a food dehydrator at 35°C (95°F) until crispy (approximately 48 hours).
3   Store in an airtight container with desiccant.

Bubblegum Meringues
1   Mix the egg white powder, water and sugar, and allow to sit for 1 hour before whisking to a firm meringue.
2   Add the bubblegum flavour to taste and red food colouring if desired.
3   Pipe to desired size and dehydrate in a food dehydrator at 35°C (95°F) until completely dry and crunchy (approximately 24 hours).
4   Store immediately in an airtight container with desiccant.

Strawberry Cheesecake Purée
1   Whisk the cream cheese and sugar until soft.
2   Slowly add the egg, followed by the cornflour (cornstarch).
3   Bake in a bain-marie in the oven at 150°C (300°F) for 25 minutes until set, then leave to cool.
4   Add the semi-dried strawberries and use a food processor to blend into a purée.
5   Add the lemon juice and mix well.
6   Place in a piping (pastry) bag with a plain nozzle.
7   Serve at room temperature.

* Semi-Dried Strawberries
1   Halve the strawberries, mix well with the sugar and lemon juice, then drain.
2   Dehydrate in a food dehydrator at 45°C (115°F) until the desired texture is achieved (approximately 8 hours); this will make about 200 g (7 oz/1 cup) for the cheesecake purée recipe above.
3   Serve at room temperature.

Strawberry Gel
1   Purée the strawberries and pass through a sieve (strainer).
2   Combine with the agar agar and sugar, and bring to the boil.
3   Pour into a metal tray and leave to cool completely.
4   Once cool, blend into a smooth gel, then add the lemon juice.
5   Place in a squeeze bottle and refrigerate until needed.

Blueberry Gel
1   Purée the blueberries and pass through a sieve (strainer).
2   Combine with the other ingredients and bring to the boil.
3   Cool completely before blending into a smooth gel.
4   Place in a squeeze bottle and refrigerate until needed.

For the Blackberry Gel (can be made 1 day in advance)

Fresh blackberries 175 g | 6 oz | gen. 1 cup
Granulated white sugar 75 g | gen. 2½ oz | gen. ⅓ cup
Whipping cream (35% fat) 125 g | 4½ fl oz | ½ cup
Milk 125 g | 4¼ fl oz | gen. ½ cup
Agar agar 3.6 g | sc. 1¼ tsp
Xantham gum 0.5 g | tip of tsp
Juice of ½ a lemon

For the Hibiscus Jelly (can be made 1 day in advance)

Water 163 g | 5¾ fl oz | ⅔ cup
Granulated white sugar 38 g | gen. 1¼ oz | gen. 3 tbsp
Dried hibiscus flowers 10 g | sc. ½ oz | 3 tbsp
Gelatine (gold) 4 g | 2 sheets (softened in ice cold water, with excess water squeezed out)

For the White Chocolate and Raspberry Crumble (can be made several days in advance)

White chocolate 100 g | 3½ oz
Powdered freeze-dried raspberries 25 g | gen. ¾ oz | ½ cup
Salt a small pinch
Tapioca maltodextrin approx. 100 g | 3½ oz | sc. 1 cup

For the Black Tapioca Pearls

Black tapioca pearls 100 g | 3½ oz | ⅔ cup
Water 1000 g | sc. 35¼ fl oz | 4¼ cups (for boiling)

Blackberry Gel

1 Purée the blackberries and pass through a sieve (strainer).
2 Combine with the other ingredients, except the lemon juice, and bring to the boil.
3 Pour into a metal tray and leave to cool completely.
4 Once cool, blend into a smooth gel, then add the lemon juice.
5 Place in a squeeze bottle and refrigerate until needed.

Hibiscus Jelly

1 Boil the water and sugar, and pour over the dried hibiscus flowers.
2 Steep until the desired strength is achieved.
3 Strain, then add enough water to achieve 200 ml (6¾ fl oz/gen. ¾ cup).
4 Add the gelatine and dissolve.
5 Leave to set in the shallow 10 x 16 cm (4 x 6¼ in.) tray.

White Chocolate and Raspberry Crumble

1 Melt the white chocolate.
2 Add the powdered raspberries and salt, and mix well.
3 Slowly add the maltodextrin until a crumble-like texture is achieved.

Black Tapioca Pearls

1 Cook the tapioca pearls in boiling water until soft and chewy (approximately 30 minutes).
2 Rinse and store in cold water at room temperature.

ASSEMBLING

Garnishes Freeze-dried raspberry pieces (20 g/sc. ¾ oz/⅔ cup); fresh blueberries (400 g/14 oz/gen. 2⅔ cups); fresh raspberries (400 g/14 oz/3¼ cups)

Style as you wish.

PARSNIP, LICORICE, LEMON, CHICORY

'Parsnip isn't normally seen in desserts, even though it's relatively sweet. I think it makes the best purée of all!' says Pierre. 'Licorice is a flavour that is so distinctive and divisive. Lemon brings acidity and keeps the taste buds stimulated. Chicory has a deep, earthy, slightly bitter flavour that is quite intriguing. I love the idea of allowing all these different properties to play off one another to create something harmonious.'

MAKES 10 **DIFFICULTY** 5/5 **PREPARATION TIME** 8 hours (not including 48 hours' preparation time for the lemon sour cream and 24 hours' drying time for the meringues) **SPECIFIC EQUIPMENT** Coffee filter paper suitable for filtering deep-fryer oil (similar to coffee filters, but much more robust); conical sieve (strainer); 2 x piping (pastry) bags with plain nozzles; food dehydrator (or fan oven set to the lowest possible temperature, with door left ajar and drying times shortened); desiccant; squeeze bottle (preferred, but a spoon may also be used for plating); digital candy thermometer; tray (30 x 15 cm/11¾ x 6 in.)

INGREDIENTS

For the Lemon Sour Cream (can be made 1 day in advance)
Full-fat sour cream 200 g | 7 oz | sc. 1 cup
Icing (confectioner's) sugar 100 g | 3½ oz | sc. ⅔ cup
Juice and zest of 1 lemon

For the Chicory Meringues (can be made 1 day in advance)
Egg white powder 7.5 g | ¼ oz | 3 tsp
Water 53 g | 1¾ fl oz | 3½ tbsp
Light brown sugar 40 g | sc. 1½ oz | 4 tbsp
Chicory essence (liquid chicory extract) (to taste; can be substituted with coffee and chicory essence)

For the Chicory Gel (can be made 1 day in advance)
Chicory essence 25 g | gen. ¾ fl oz | 5 tsp
(or coffee and chicory essence)
Brown sugar 75 g | gen. 2½ oz | sc. ½ cup
Whipping cream (35% fat) 150 g | sc. 5½ fl oz | gen. ½ cup
Milk 150 g | gen. 5 fl oz | gen. ½ cup
Agar agar 3.6 g | sc. 1¼ tsp
Xanthan gum 0.5 g | tip of tsp
Salt 0.5 g | tip of tsp

For the Shortcrust Crumbs
Soft flour (cake flour) 125 g | sc. 4½ oz | ⅘ cup
Unsalted butter 75 g | gen. 2½ oz
Salt 4 g | gen. ½ tsp
Ice cold water 38 ml | gen. 1¼ fl oz | 2½ tbsp

For the Parsnip Purée (can be made 1 day in advance)
Approx. 3 medium parsnips (outer flesh) 300 g | 10½ oz
Milk 650 g | sc. 22¼ fl oz | 2¾ cups
Whipping cream (35% fat) 100 g | gen. 3½ fl oz | sc. ½ cup
Unsalted butter 100 g | 3½ oz
Caster (superfine) sugar 25 g | gen. ¾ oz | sc. 2 tbsp
Salt 2.5 g | sc. ½ tsp

For the Parsnip Milk
Cooking milk (from above recipe)
Salt and sugar (to taste)

For the Licorice Parfait (can be made several days in advance)
Milk 250 ml | gen. 8¾ fl oz | gen. 1 cup
Licorice sweets 100 g | 3½ oz (chopped)
Whipping cream (35% fat) 200 ml | 7 fl oz | ⅘ cup
5 egg yolks
Caster (superfine) sugar 125 g | sc. 4½ oz | gen. ½ cup
Water 50 ml | 1¾ fl oz | 3½ tbsp
Gelatine (gold) 4 g | 2 sheets (softened in ice cold water, with excess water squeezed out)

INSTRUCTIONS

Lemon Sour Cream
1 Mix all the ingredients.
2 Place the mixture in a coffee filter paper-lined conical sieve (strainer).
3 Leave in the cold for two days.

Chicory Meringues
1 Mix the egg white powder, water and sugar, and sit for 1 hour before whisking to a firm meringue.
2 Add chicory essence to taste.
3 Pipe into desired shape and dehydrate in a food dehydrator at 35°C (95°F) until completely dry and crunchy (approximately 24 hours).
4 Store immediately in an airtight container with desiccant.

Chicory Gel
1 Combine all the ingredients and bring to the boil.
2 Cool completely before blending into a smooth gel.
3 Place in a squeeze bottle and refrigerate until needed.

Shortcrust Crumbs
1 Crumb the flour, butter and salt, then add the water and mix until smooth.
2 Roll into a 'sausage' shape, wrap in plastic wrap and refrigerate overnight.
3 Cut into slices about 2 cm (¾ in.) thick and bake at 220°C (425°F) until golden brown (approximately 20 minutes).
4 Allow to cool, then place in a food processor and blend until a fine crumb is achieved.

Parsnip Purée
1 Peel, core and chop the parsnips (reserve the peel).
2 Gently cook in the milk until soft (approximately 35 minutes).
3 Strain, reserving the cooking milk.
4 Blend smooth with enough of the milk to obtain a purée.
5 Add the cream, butter, sugar and salt, then pass through a sieve (strainer).
6 Cool and place in a piping (pastry) bag with a plain nozzle.

Parsnip Milk
1 Strain the remaining cooking milk from the parsnip purée (from above recipe).
2 Season to taste with salt and sugar.
3 Reserve cold.

Licorice Parfait
1 Heat the milk and chopped licorice sweets, simmer until soft, then blend and pass through a sieve (strainer).
2 Semi-whip the cream.
3 Whisk the egg yolks in a stand mixer.
4 Mix the sugar with the water and boil to 121°C (250°F).
5 Pour the sugar syrup over the egg yolks and whip until cold.
6 Add the licorice paste to the egg yolks and mix gently.
7 Add the gelatine, fold in the cream, then pour into a plastic wrap-lined tray.
8 Freeze overnight.
9 Remove from the tray and cut into 2 x 2 cm (¾ x ¾ in.) squares.
10 Return to the freezer until required.

For the Lemon Marshmallow
(can be made 1 day in advance)
Gelatine powder 14 g | ½ oz | gen. 1 tbsp
Lemon juice [1] 60 ml | gen. 2 fl oz | 4 tbsp
Granulated white sugar 200 g | 7 oz | 1 cup
Glucose syrup 80 ml | 2¾ fl oz | gen. ¼ cup
Lemon juice [2] 30 ml | 1 fl oz | 2 tbsp
Salt 1 g | gen. ⅛ tsp

For the Toasted Golden Linseeds
(can be made 1 day in advance)
Linseeds 50 g | 1¾ oz | ⅓ cup
Grapeseed oil 1.25 ml | ¼ tsp
Salt a small pinch

For the Parsnip Peel Crisps
Parsnip peel (from parsnip purée recipe)
Grapeseed oil (to fry parsnip peel)
Salt (to taste)

Lemon Marshmallow
1 Mix the gelatine powder and lemon juice [1].
2 Heat the sugar, glucose syrup, lemon juice [2] and salt to 121°C (250°F).
3 Pour the sugar syrup over the gelatine mixture and whisk until light and fluffy.
4 Transfer to the 30 x 15 cm (11¾ x 6 in.) tray, previously lined with plastic wrap then lightly oiled.
5 Working quickly, spread the mixture evenly.
6 Leave to set in the fridge for at least 1 hour before cutting into 1 x 1 cm (⅜ x ⅜ in.) squares.
7 Serve at room temperature.

Toasted Golden Linseeds
1 Mix the linseeds with the grapeseed oil.
2 Roast at 150°C (300°F) for 25 minutes.
3 Cool on a paper towel.
4 Season lightly with salt and store in an airtight container.

Parsnip Peel Crisps
1 Place the reserved parsnip peelings in a food dehydrator at 35°C (95°F) for 1 hour.
2 Deep-fry in grapeseed oil at 180°C (356°F) until golden brown.
3 Season with salt.
4 Use immediately.

ASSEMBLING

Garnishes Fresh dill fronds; finely sliced licorice sweets

Style as you wish.

PISTACHIO, GINGER, RUM, CEREALS

'This dish highlights my love of using cereals and grains in desserts,' says Pierre. 'The combination of ginger and rum is a classic one and goes well with the nutty, earthy flavours provided by the grains and couscous. The addition of pistachio adds contrasts in taste and colour.'

MAKES 10   **DIFFICULTY** 5/5   **PREPARATION TIME** 8 hours (NB the hung ginger yoghurt needs to be made several days in advance)
SPECIFIC EQUIPMENT Muslin cloth (or coffee filter paper suitable for filtering deep-fryer oil – similar to coffee filters, but much more robust); squeeze bottle (preferred, but a spoon may also be used for plating); whipped cream siphon and two cartridges; non-metallic dariole moulds (or disposable paper cups); 2 x piping (pastry) bags with plain nozzles

INGREDIENTS

For the Hung Ginger Yoghurt
(should be made several days in advance)
Greek yoghurt 500 g | 1 lb 1½ oz | 2 cups
Icing (confectioner's) sugar 75 g | gen. 2½ oz | sc. ½ cup
Finely puréed candied ginger 100 g | 3½ oz | ¼ cup

For the Rum Gel (can be made 1 day in advance)
White rum (e.g. Mount Gay) 200 ml | 7 fl oz | sc. 1 cup
Water 50 ml | 1¾ fl oz | 3½ tbsp
Caster (superfine) sugar 50 g | 1¾ oz | sc. ¼ cup
Agar agar 2.7 g | sc. 1 tsp

For the Pistachio Instant Sponge
(can be made 1 day in advance and stored in the fridge)
2 egg yolks
1 whole egg
Icing (confectioner's) sugar 25 g | gen. ¾ oz | 2½ tbsp
Milk 50 ml | 1¾ fl oz | sc. 3½ tbsp
Unsweetened pure pistachio paste 25 g | gen. ¾ oz | 1½ tbsp
Soft flour (cake flour) 50 g | 1¾ oz | ⅓ cup
Salt 1 g | gen. ⅛ tsp

INSTRUCTIONS

Hung Ginger Yoghurt

1 Mix all the ingredients together.
2 Hang in muslin cloth (or coffee filter paper) for two days, in the cold.
3 Place in a piping (pastry) bag with a plain nozzle.

Rum Gel

1 Combine all the ingredients.
2 Bring to the boil.
3 Pour into a metal tray, then leave to cool completely.
4 Once cool, blend into a smooth gel.
5 Place in a squeeze bottle and refrigerate until needed.

Pistachio Instant Sponge

1 Whisk together the egg yolks, egg and sugar, then add the milk followed by the pistachio paste, flour and salt, mixing well.
2 Pass through a sieve (strainer).
3 Pour into a whipped cream siphon, charge with two cartridges and put in the fridge.
4 Shake well before using, then discharge the mixture into a lightly oiled dariole mould (or small microwave-proof paper cup), filled to two-thirds.
5 Cook on full power in the microwave for approximately 30 seconds (cooking time depends on each microwave; start with a 15-second burst to assess the cooking time required).
6 Leave to rest for 30 seconds before removing the sponge from the mould.
7 Repeat as many times as servings.

For the Ginger Ale Jelly
(can be made 1 day in advance)

Natural ginger ale 175 g | gen. 6 fl oz | ¾ cup

Caster (superfine) sugar 25 g | gen. ¾ oz | sc. 2 tbsp

Gelatine (gold) 4 g | 2 sheets (softened in ice cold water,
with excess water squeezed out)

For the Rum Bubbles
Rum Bubble Mixture

White rum (e.g. Mount Gay) 200 ml | 7 fl oz | sc. 1 cup

Water 50 ml | 1¾ fl oz | 3½ tbsp

Caster (superfine) sugar 50 g | 1¾ oz | sc. ¼ cup

Sodium alginate 2.5 g | ¾ tsp

Calcium Chloride Solution

Water 1000 g | sc. 35¼ fl oz | 4¼ cups

Calcium chloride 6.5 g | ¼ oz | 2 tsp

For the Pistachio Crème
(can be made 1 day in advance)

Milk 125 g | 4¼ fl oz | gen. ½ cup

Whipping cream (35% fat) 125 g | 4½ fl oz | ½ cup

Caster (superfine) sugar 38 g | gen. 1¼ oz | 3 tbsp

1 whole egg

3 egg yolks

Cornflour (cornstarch) 25 g | gen. ¾ oz | 2½ tbsp

Unsweetened pure pistachio paste 50 g | 1¾ oz | 3 tbsp

For the Assorted Puffed Grains
(can be made 1 day in advance)

Puffed Kamut khorasan wheat, spelt, millet and
bran flakes 90 g | sc. 3¼ oz

Grapeseed oil (to roast grains and bran flakes)

Salt (to taste)

For the Roast Pumpkin Seeds
(can be made 1 day in advance)

Pumpkin seeds (kernels) 33 g | gen. 1 oz | ¼ cup

Pumpkin oil 5 ml | sc. ¼ fl oz | 1 tsp

Salt (to taste)

For the Roasted Couscous

Couscous 100 g | 3½ oz | gen. ½ cup

Boiling water 100 ml | 3½ fl oz | sc. ½ cup

Salt (to taste)

Ginger Ale Jelly

1 Gently warm the ginger ale and sugar, then dissolve the gelatine.

2 Leave to set in a shallow tray or container in the fridge.

Rum Bubbles
Rum Bubble Mixture

1 Blend all the ingredients with an immersion or jug blender, then allow to rest for at least 1 hour before using so that no bubbles remain.

Calcium Chloride Solution

2 Blend the water and calcium chloride well.

For the Rum Bubbles

3 While both mixtures can be made one day in advance, the bubbles themselves need to be made just before serving. Place individual small spoonfuls of the rum bubble mixture on the surface of the calcium chloride solution and allow a skin to form on the undersurface of each (this will take approximately 30 seconds). Insert the spoon carefully into each and gently push down into the solution so it rounds up to form a ball ('bubble'). Remove the bubbles with a spoon and carefully rinse in water before serving.

Pistachio Crème

1 Bring the milk, cream and sugar to the boil.

2 Whisk the egg, egg yolks and cornflour (cornstarch) together until smooth.

3 Add one-third of the milk mixture to the egg mixture, mix well and put back in the saucepan.

4 Return to the stove and cook out until firm.

5 Add the pistachio paste and mix well.

6 Allow to cool completely before blending smooth.

7 Place in a piping (pastry) bag with a plain nozzle.

8 Serve at room temperature.

Assorted Puffed Grains

1 Combine the grains and bran flakes with a tiny amount of grapeseed oil and roast at 150°C (300°F) until crunchy and full of flavour (approximately 20 minutes).

2 Leave to cool, season lightly with salt, then store in an airtight container.

Roast Pumpkin Seeds

1 Mix the pumpkin seeds with the pumpkin oil and salt.

2 Gently roast at 120°C (250°F) for approximately 10 minutes until crunchy.

3 Leave to cool on a paper towel, then store in an airtight container.

Roasted Couscous

1 Roast the couscous in a dry saucepan until golden brown.

2 Add the boiling water and cover straight away.

3 Leave to steam for 10 minutes.

4 Stir through with a fork to fluff up the couscous.

5 Season lightly with salt and leave to cool to room temperature before serving.

ASSEMBLING

Garnishes Lemon balm shoots (1 punnet); chervil shoots (1 punnet); Iranian pistachio slivers (25 g/gen. ¾ oz/3 tbsp); finely sliced candied ginger pieces (50 g/1¾ oz/⅓ cup)

Style as you wish.

Rosio Sanchez

DENMARK

When one considers the two dominant creative directions at the forefront of the pastry revolution – authenticity and experimentation – American-born Rosio Sanchez encapsulates the best of both. On the one hand, she was exposed to the finest in technologically advanced/experimental chemistry pastry techniques when she worked as pastry sous chef at WD-50 in New York. 'It was a defining moment in my career,' she recalls. 'Being able to work in Wylie Dufresne's kitchen opened my eyes to a whole new way of thinking about food. Everything was questioned and no idea was too impossible to attempt. I also don't think I would be the strong person I am today if it hadn't been for Alex Stupak's guidance and his tenacity for creativity.' On the other hand, Rosio now promotes the authenticity-driven methodology of extreme seasonality and foraging for local produce, under the patronage of René Redzepi of Noma in Copenhagen, the restaurant that helped propel modern Nordic cuisine into the stratosphere, or at least the No. 1 position in the 'World's 50 Best Restaurants' ranking.

'When it comes to producing dishes,' says Rosio, 'we always start with a product that is in season and go from there. Capturing the purest essence of the product and then taking it to another level is our main goal.' And this is precisely what Rosio excels at. Her low-sugar desserts prominently feature savoury ingredients, which challenges old-school convention yet intriguingly excites: potato, carrot, Jerusalem artichoke, cucumber, hay, bitters, fresh cheese, grilled pear and pine, juniper and rhubarb have all played a part in her kitchen. She has undoubtedly developed a highly accurate palate and an exceptional ability to balance flavours and understand ratios, but her sheer determination also makes her a creative powerhouse. 'We push for one dessert a month, and the recipes that I collect from working on those desserts far exceed how many actually make it onto the menu,' she says. It may come as no surprise to know that Rosio has found her one and only vocation. 'The truth is I can't see myself doing anything else. In this field, there are always new flavours to explore and techniques to discover.'

http://noma.dk

POTATO AND PLUMS

'Being successful at creating a delicious potato dessert that actually tasted of potato was the inspiration,' explains Rosio.

MAKES 6–8   DIFFICULTY 4/5   PREPARATION TIME 3 hours (not including max. 2 days for preparation of the plums)
SPECIFIC EQUIPMENT Vacuum food sealer, bag and canister (e.g. Cryovac® or Sunbeam FoodSaver®); digital candy thermometer; potato ricer; Silpat® mat; whipped cream siphon and one cartridge; muslin cloths

INGREDIENTS

For the Potato Stock
5 large baking potatoes
Salt (to taste)

For the Bintje Potatoes
Peeled Bintje potatoes 400 g | 14 oz (an alternative to the Bintje potato may be used, but it should not be too starchy or waxy)

For the Potato Mash
Egg yolks 60 g | gen. 2 oz | ¼ cup
Milk 60 g | 2 fl oz | ¼ cup
Reduced potato stock (from previous recipe) 130 g | 4½ fl oz | ½ cup
Granulated white sugar 25 g | gen. ¾ oz | 2 tbsp
Invert sugar 20 g | ¾ fl oz | 1 tbsp
Riced Bintje potatoes (from above recipe) 400 g | 14 oz
Unsalted butter 170 g | 6 oz
Salt (to taste)

For the Plum Stone Foam
Peeled plum kernels (from large plums) 30 g | 1 oz | 3 tbsp (crack the seeds of plums open with a hammer; inside are plum kernels, which have a thin skin that should be peeled before use)
Granulated white sugar 40 g | sc. 1½ oz | gen. 3 tbsp
Milk 100 g | sc. 3½ fl oz | sc. ½ cup
Whipping cream (35% fat) 400 g | 14 fl oz | gen. 1½ cups

For the Prunes
Plums (large) 300 g | 10½ oz

For the Prune Compote
Prune flesh (from above recipe) 120 g | 4¼ oz | ¾ cup
Plum aquavit (Scandinavian liqueur) 80 g | 2¾ fl oz | ⅓ cup
Brown sugar 30 g | 1 oz | sc. 2½ tbsp

For the Plum Sauce
For the Plum Juice
Frozen plums 500 g | 1 lb 1½ oz
For the Plum Reduction
Frozen plums 500 g | 1 lb 1½ oz
For the Plum Sauce
Plum juice (from previous recipe) 70 g | sc. 2½ fl oz | 4¾ tbsp
Plum reduction (from above recipe) 35 g | sc. 1¼ fl oz | 2 tbsp
Water 85 g | 3 fl oz | 5¾ tbsp

INSTRUCTIONS

Potato Stock
1 Wash the potatoes and cut into smaller pieces.
2 Put into a saucepan, cover with water and simmer for 1 hour.
3 Strain, discard the potatoes, reduce down the liquid and season with salt.

Bintje Potatoes
1 Cut the potatoes into equal-size pieces and seal in a vacuum bag.
2 Cook the potatoes in a water bath at 72°C (162°F) for 45 minutes.
3 Remove the bag and cool in ice water (this cuts down the starch so the mash will not be sticky).
4 Place the bag in boiling water until the potatoes are tender.
5 Once cooked, put the potatoes through the potato ricer to ensure an even consistency.
6 Place in a plastic container and reserve until required.

Potato Mash
1 Heat the egg yolks, milk, potato stock, granulated sugar and invert sugar without boiling to form a custard, while constantly stirring.
2 Add the riced potatoes and the butter, and stir together over heat.
3 Pass through a fine sieve (strainer), then season with salt.
4 Use a spatula to spread onto the Silpat® mat to a thickness of 2 mm (⅟₁₆ in.), then freeze.
5 Once frozen, cut into long, thin strips (batons).
6 Reserve in a container in the freezer until required.

Plum Stone Foam
1 Blend the plum kernels with the sugar and milk until smooth.
2 Pour into a vacuum canister, add the cream, seal and leave to infuse overnight.
3 The next day, strain and reserve the liquid (the plum kernels can also be kept and reused).
4 Pour the liquid into a whipped cream siphon, charge with one cartridge and shake well.
5 Set aside in the fridge.

Prunes
1 Wash the plums, then dry them off.
2 Put them in the oven and dehydrate them at 60°C (140°F) until they look like prunes (approximately 10–12 hours).

Prune Compote
1 Cook the prune flesh with the aquavit.
2 Add the brown sugar when the alcohol has boiled off.
3 Allow to cool down, ensuring there are bits of prunes in the compote to give texture.

Plum Sauce
Plum Juice
1 Hang the frozen plums in muslin and drain the juice off.
Plum Reduction
2 Hang the frozen plums in muslin and drain the juice off.
3 Cook the juice down to a syrup.
For the Plum Sauce
4 Mix all the ingredients together and keep cold.

ASSEMBLING

Measure out 15 g (½ oz/1 tbsp) of the prune compote and spread on each plate so that it isn't completely flat. Carefully but quickly place potato batons on top of the compote so that they are straight but not completely vertical. Place plum sauce in between the gaps of the batons. Finish with a generous dollop of the plum stone foam off to the side.

BROWN CHEESE AND SLOE BERRIES

'The first time I came across fresh sloe berries, I knew I had to try and use them in a dessert to show everyone how great they are,' enthuses Rosio. 'It made sense to pair the flavour with the caramel notes found in Norwegian brown cheese.'

MAKES 12–14   DIFFICULTY 4/5   PREPARATION TIME 6-8 hours (not including time needed to freeze each component sufficiently so it can be punched out into shapes, or 12 hours' infusion time for the kernel cream)   SPECIFIC EQUIPMENT Thermomix®; offset spatula; chocolate funnel dispenser; Silpat® mats; circle cutter (2.5 cm/1 in.); fine-mesh sieve (strainer) (e.g. Superbag®); vacuum food sealer and canister (e.g. Cryovac® or Sunbeam FoodSaver®)

INGREDIENTS

For the Brown Cheese Ganache
Whipping cream (35% fat) 200 g | 7 fl oz | ⅘ cup
Brown cheese 225 g | sc. 8 oz (a brown Scandinavian whey cheese)
Egg yolks 50 g | 1¾ oz | sc. 3½ tbsp
Milk 400 g | gen. 13½ fl oz | sc. 1¾ cups
Brown sugar 50 g | 1¾ oz | 4 tbsp
Iota carrageenan 2 g | ½ tsp
Gelatine (gold) 6 g | 3 sheets (softened in ice cold water, with excess water squeezed out)

For the Sloe Berry (Blackthorn Berry) Gel
Sloe berry juice 500 g | 17½ fl oz | 2 cups
Apple vinegar 60 g | 2 fl oz | 4 tbsp
Agar agar 8 g | ¼ oz | gen. 1 tbsp
Granulated white sugar 50 g | 1¾ oz | ¼ cup
Gelatine (gold) 5 g | 2½ sheets (softened in ice cold water, with excess water squeezed out)
Whey (liquid and acidic) 250 g | gen. 8¾ fl oz | 1 cup (NB Noma hangs yoghurt in cheesecloth and collects the whey)

For the Kernel Cream
Peeled plum kernels 50 g | 1¾ oz | 5 tbsp
(crack the seeds of plums open with a hammer; inside are plum kernels, which have a thin skin that should be peeled before use; alternatively use raw almonds)
Milk 50 g | sc. 1¾ fl oz | sc. 3½ tbsp
Granulated white sugar 40 g | sc. 1½ oz | gen. 3 tbsp
Whipping cream (35% fat) 450 g | 15¾ fl oz | gen. 1¾ cups

For the Blackberry Shortbread
TIPO 00 flour 180 g | gen. 6¼ oz | gen. 1¼ cups
(plain/all-purpose flour may also be used)
Blanched almond meal 110 g | sc. 4 oz | gen. 1¼ cups
Icing (confectioner's) sugar 90 g | sc. 3¼ oz | gen. ½ cup
Unsalted butter 110 g | sc. 4 oz (melted)
Grapeseed oil 100 g | 3¾ fl oz | ½ cup
Freeze-dried blackberries 150 g | gen. 5¼ oz | 5 cups

For the Sloe Berry Juice
Frozen sloe berries 600 g | gen. 1 lb 5 oz
Brown sugar (to taste)

INSTRUCTIONS

Brown Cheese Ganache
1   Combine all the ingredients, except the iota carrageenan and gelatine, in a Thermomix® on medium speed, and bring the mixture to beyond 84°C (183°F).
2   When the Thermomix® mixture reaches the desired temperature, gently add in the iota and allow the mixture to combine for a good minute before adding in the gelatine.
3   Use an offset spatula to check a small amount of the mixture to make sure that the iota has been hydrated and is beginning to gel.
4   Once ready, strain the mixture to catch any of the spices usually present in brown cheese.
5   Transfer the mixture to a chocolate funnel dispenser and carefully pour over as many Silpat® mats as needed, then freeze.
6   Once frozen, punch out 2.5 cm (1 in.) discs and store in the freezer.

Sloe Berry (Blackthorn Berry) Gel
1   Combine the sloe berry juice with the vinegar, agar agar and sugar, and bring to the boil.
2   After a few minutes add the gelatine, then pour into a flat dish to set.
3   Once set, transfer to a high-speed blender and blitz with the whey until completely smooth.
4   Pass through a fine-mesh sieve (strainer).
5   Use the offset spatula to spread a thin layer evenly on top of a few Silpat® mats, then freeze.
6   Punch out the same size discs as for the brown cheese ganache.

Kernel Cream
1   Blend the kernels (or raw almonds) with the milk and sugar until a chunky, purée-like consistency is achieved.
2   Combine with the cream.
3   Vacuum seal in a canister for about 12 hours in the cold.
4   Pass through a fine-mesh sieve (strainer).
5   Whip to a stiff cream.

Blackberry Shortbread
1   Combine all the ingredients, except the grapeseed oil and freeze-dried blackberries.
2   Bake on a silicone baking paper-lined tray at 160°C (325°F) for about 20 minutes, or until lightly golden brown.
3   Allow to cool, then transfer to a Thermomix® and blend until the crumble becomes a thick purée.
4   Add the oil, followed by the freeze-dried blackberries.
5   Use the offset spatula to spread on top of a Silpat® mat and freeze.
6   Punch out the same size discs as for the brown cheese ganache and sloe berry gel.

Sloe Berry Juice
1   Blend the frozen sloe berries, then pass through a fine-mesh sieve (strainer).
2   If necessary, add brown sugar to sweeten a little (equivalent 15 Brix).

ASSEMBLING

Place half a tablespoon of the whipped kernel cream at the bottom of each bowl. Spoon approximately three tablespoons of sloe berry juice over the top. In no particular order, but all facing the same way, arrange three brown cheese ganache discs, four blackberry shortbread discs and seven sloe berry gel discs on top of the cream.

PEAR 'TREE'

'At Noma we really love a good grilled pear,' notes Rosio. 'Complementing that with a light parfait, and seeing the connection of trees with pears, is where we got the inspiration for this dish.'

MAKES 4   **DIFFICULTY** 4/5   **PREPARATION TIME** 4 hours (including time to freeze the parfait completely so that it can be carved into shape, but not including overnight infusing time if making own pine oil)   **SPECIFIC EQUIPMENT** Vacuum food sealer, bag and canister (e.g. Cryovac® or Sunbeam FoodSaver®); steam oven, or food steamer; digital candy thermometer; small melon ball scoop; grill (broiler)/barbecue; Thermomix®; muslin cloth (if making own pine oil); mandolin   **NOTE: THIS RECIPE CONTAINS PINE ESSENTIAL OIL**

INGREDIENTS

For the Pear Sauce

Very ripe, peeled Clara Frijs pears (or any very sweet pear)
125 g | sc. 4½ oz

Pear liqueur (e.g. pear aquavit) 2.5 g | ½ tsp

Citric acid 0.5 g | tip of tsp (or squeeze of lemon juice)

For the Grilled Pear (this should take about 15 minutes, depending on the pear)

2 ripe Clara Frijs pears

Grapeseed oil 1.6 g | gen. ¼ tsp

Thyme oil 25 g | 1 fl oz | 2 tbsp

For the Herbs

20 small verbena leaves

20 top shoots of lemon thyme

20 tops of bronze fennel

Heather 0.5 g | 1 tsp

For the Aerated Pine Parfait
(makes more than required, but a more manageable amount)

Egg yolks 68 g | sc. 2½ oz | gen. ¼ cup

Water 45 g | 1½ fl oz | 3 tbsp

Spruce pine shoots 10 g | sc. ½ oz

Fresh spruce pine 19 g | sc. ¾ oz

Icing (confectioner's) sugar 5 g | sc. ¼ oz | ½ tbsp

Caster (superfine) sugar 17 g | ½ oz | 3½ tsp

Gelatine (gold) 2 g | 1 sheet (softened in ice cold water, with excess water squeezed out)

Whipping cream (35% fat) 64 g | 2¼ fl oz | ¼ cup

Salt 0.25 g | a tiny pinch

* For Pine Oil

Vegetable or olive oil

Blanched and dried spruce pine needles

INSTRUCTIONS

Pear Sauce

1   Vacuum the peeled pears with the pear liqueur in a bag.

2   Use a steam oven or food steamer to steam the pears at 100°C (212°F) for 10 minutes.

3   Blitz with a blender on high speed until the pear purée is smooth.

4   Pass through a fine sieve (strainer), season with citric acid (or lemon), then chill.

Grilled Pear

1   Peel the pears, cut them in half, remove any seeds with a small melon ball scoop, cut the core and middle string away, and remove a portion from the bottom so that each pear can stand upright on its own.

2   Brush the cut surfaces with a little grapeseed oil.

3   Place the pears on a very warm grill (broiler) and allow to barbecue until a layer of char has formed.

4   The pears are ready to come off the grill (broiler) when they are slightly tender to the touch and feel as if they have been cooked thoroughly.

5   Place the pears in a thyme-oiled container and keep airtight to allow them to steam a little.

6   Reserve in a warm area, around 60°C (140°F).

Herbs

1   Pick all the herbs and flowers, and refresh in ice water if required.

2   Reserve in a container on moist paper towel and keep cold.

Aerated Pine Parfait

1   Place the egg yolks, water, spruce pine shoots and fresh spruce pine in a Thermomix®.

2   Blend at medium speed until the mixture reaches 84°C (183°F).

3   Once thickened to a sabayon-like consistency, pass through a fine sieve (strainer).

4   Put back into the Thermomix® together with the icing (confectioner's) sugar and caster (superfine) sugar.

5   Blend again to dissolve the sugars, then add the gelatine.

6   Transfer the mixture to a stand mixer and whip on high speed using a whisk attachment.

7   Leave to cool, and meanwhile whip the cream to medium peaks.

8   Fold the pine mixture into the whipped cream, along with the salt.

9   For every 125 g (sc. 4½ oz) of parfait mix, add 20 g (¾ fl oz) of pine oil* and pour into a small (0.7 litre/gen. 24½ fl oz) vacuum canister.

10 Aerate the parfait by vacuuming until the mixture reaches the top of the canister (or the device automatically stops)

11 Freeze for a minimum of 2 hours.

* Pine Oil

1   Use 1 part oil to 2 parts needles, or enough to make a dense purée (if using a Thermomix®, it is better to do a big batch – ratio of 500 g/19 fl oz oil to 1 kg/gen. 2 lb needles – otherwise the mixture will not blend). NB Wear gloves when handling dried needles, as they are sharp.

2   Purée until steam starts to escape from the blender, but do not purée too finely.

3   Vacuum seal in a canister overnight to infuse.

4   The next day, hang in a muslin cloth to drain and collect the oil.

ASSEMBLING

Components Thyme oil (6.5 g/¼ fl oz/2 tsp); unripe pear; juniper salt

When the aerated pine parfait is frozen enough, carve out 15 g (½ oz) portions and set aside. Take some of the pear sauce and add a small amount of thyme oil (just enough to create a swirled effect). Use about two tablespoons to sauce each plate with a circular pattern. Take the pears out of their container and remove the charred 'skin'. Slice a crudité of unripe pear with a mandolin so that the slice fits perfectly over the grilled pear. Dress with the herbs and place on the sauced plate, followed by the parfait seasoned with juniper salt.

Sarah Jordan

....

USA

Sarah Jordan's desserts bear all the hallmarks of theatrical stage set-ups, with their depth of field, harmonious colours and contrasting textures. 'I like food to look like "food-scapes",' she states. 'I like to make sure components are placed in the way they are supposed to be.'

Irish-born Sarah was raised in a family of food lovers, who were very supportive when she decided to move to America. 'I've always been very independent and I've always enjoyed cooking,' she says. 'Once in the States, I interned in the restaurant I was working at doing pastry. That was what I enjoyed the most and I crossed over full-time.' Now head pastry chef for BOKA and GT Fish & Oyster, both of the BOKA restaurant group in Chicago, Sarah revels in intuitive experimentation – 'sometimes it can be a childhood favourite which evolves into a composed fine dining dish' – and in keeping things moving while maintaining core pleasures – 'I have access to new technology, such as immersion circulators and Cryovac® machines, which are nice to have, but you can always find an alternative method. This is an industry where you are always learning, and if you're not you're doing something wrong.'

A female in a male-dominated industry, Sarah prides herself on her drive and assertiveness, but she also recognizes the importance of teamwork. 'I think it's important to be adaptable to any circumstance, whether that means being a quick problem solver or not taking yourself too seriously.' She points out, 'I usually taste my recipes numerous times with the chefs, the savoury cooks and my pastry team. If we don't like it, I won't serve it.'

With a predilection for citrus, in particular yuzu and Meyer lemons for their refreshing quality and versatility – 'pair citrus with black cardamom,' she hints – Sarah has come a long way from her teen years of improvisational 'jazz baking'. She is now one of the most exciting designers of contemporary pastry, though one who is careful not to bewilder customers with too much radical innovation. 'At GT Fish & Oyster my salted caramel tart, which is based on a banoffee pie, has had people cry over it,' she recounts. 'And at BOKA I did my version of a childhood favourite, pavlova. We have regular customers who will call a couple of days ahead specifically to order it'. Sentiments we all can understand...

www.bokachicago.com | http://gtoyster.com

KEY LIME PIE

'When I started working at GT Fish & Oyster, the previous pastry chef had a key lime pie on the menu,' recalls Sarah. 'I took it off when I changed the menu, but customers kept requesting it, so this was my version of an old American classic.'

MAKES 8 DIFFICULTY 3½/5 PREPARATION TIME 2 hours (not including preferred overnight resting period for the graham cracker crumbs) SPECIFIC EQUIPMENT Digital candy thermometer; 8 x traditional low wide ramekins (each 9 cm/3½ in. diameter, 3 cm/1⅛ in. high); candy or digital thermometer; piping (pastry) bag with size 11 round nozzle; brûlée torch

INGREDIENTS

For the Key Lime Curd

9 egg yolks
Granulated white sugar 205 g | 7¼ oz | 1 cup
Key lime juice 150 ml | 5 fl oz | gen. ½ cup
Unsalted butter 114 g | 4 oz

For the Marshmallow Fluff

Egg whites 80 g | gen. 2¾ oz | ⅓ cup
Salt 2.5 g | sc. ½ tsp
Vanilla extract 2.5 ml | ½ tsp
Gelatine (gold) 4 g | 2 sheets (softened in ice cold water, with excess water squeezed out)
Hot water 60 ml | 2 fl oz | ¼ cup
Granulated white sugar 184 g | 6½ oz | sc. 1 cup
Glucose syrup 84 g | sc. 3 fl oz | sc. ¼ cup
Water 60 ml | 2 fl oz | ¼ cup

For the Graham Cracker Crumbs

Whole wheat flour 114 g | 4 oz | ¾ cup
Plain (all-purpose) flour 57 g | 2 oz | gen. ⅓ cup
Salt 1 g | gen. ⅛ tsp
Bicarbonate of soda (baking soda) 0.5 g | ⅛ tsp
Cinnamon 2 g | ¾ tsp
Unsalted butter 28 g | 1 oz (soft)
Granulated white sugar 50 g | 1¾ oz | ¼ cup
Molasses 22 g | ½ fl oz | 1¼ tbsp
Hot water 6 ml | sc. ¼ fl oz | gen. 1 tsp
½ a whole egg
Honey 50 g | 1¾ fl oz | sc. 2½ tbsp

INSTRUCTIONS

Key Lime Curd

1 Combine the egg yolks, sugar and key lime juice in a medium-sized glass bowl.
2 Heat a medium saucepan, fill with hot water and bring to the boil.
3 Place the glass bowl on top of the saucepan to make a bain-marie, and whisk frequently.
4 Cook the mixture at 74–77°C (165–170°F) until it thickens.
5 Remove from the bain-marie and begin to whisk in the butter until fully incorporated.
6 Divide the curd between the ramekins and allow to cool in the fridge.

Marshmallow Fluff

1 Whip the egg whites, salt and vanilla extract in the bowl of a stand mixer on low speed until frothy.
2 Dissolve the gelatine in the hot water and slowly stream down the side of the stand mixer bowl.
3 Turn the speed to medium and continue to whip.
4 Meanwhile, in a small saucepan, cook the sugar, glucose syrup and water very slowly, measuring the temperature with a candy or digital thermometer and ensuring there are no sugar granules on the side of the pan. NB Do not stir the sugar mixture when cooking; swirl the pan now and then to ensure it is cooking evenly.
5 When the sugar mixture reaches 116°C (240°F), remove from the heat and slowly stream down the side of the bowl into the egg white mixture.
6 Once all the sugar is added, turn the speed to high and whip until stiff peaks form.
7 Remove the resulting marshmallow from the bowl and place in a piping (pastry) bag fitted with a size 11 round nozzle.
8 Refrigerate until ready to use.

Graham Cracker Crumbs

1 Sift together the whole wheat flour, plain (all-purpose) flour, salt, bicarbonate of soda (baking soda) and cinnamon.
2 Cream the soft butter and the sugar in the bowl of a stand mixer with a paddle attachment on medium speed for 3 minutes.
3 Combine the molasses and hot water, then add to the butter and sugar.
4 Scrape down the sides of the bowl and add the egg on low speed.
5 Add the honey to the mixture, followed by the sifted dry ingredients.
6 Mix until the dry ingredients are just incorporated.
7 Remove the dough from the mixer, shape into a tube, wrap in plastic wrap, then refrigerate for at least 1 hour, or preferably overnight.
8 Slice the dough about 3 mm (⅛ in.) thick and lay out on a silicone baking paper-lined tray.
9 Bake at 180°C (350°F) for 10 to 12 minutes (but allow to cook thoroughly), then leave to cool.
10 Once cool, place in a food processor and pulse until the cookies are broken down into crumbs.

ASSEMBLING

Components Translucent pâtes de fruit (ready-bought)

Place each curd-filled ramekin in the centre of a larger plate. Pipe marshmallow onto the curd and the base plate, as desired. Brûlée the marshmallow mounds with the brûlée torch. Place graham cracker crumbs on and around the marshmallow mounds. Finally, decorate with translucent pâtes de fruit as desired.

PINEAPPLE

'We got some new equipment at BOKA, which made this dish possible,' explains Sarah. 'I wanted it to be simple in flavour profile, but a little more complicated when it came to the execution.'

MAKES 10–12 **DIFFICULTY** 4/5 **PREPARATION TIME** 3 hours (not including overnight maturing time for the sorbet)
SPECIFIC EQUIPMENT Vacuum food sealer and bag (e.g. Cryovac® or Sunbeam FoodSaver®); digital candy thermometer; ice cream machine; blender (Vita-Prep®/commercial equipment enables extremely smooth purée to be made; household processors may not be powerful enough to achieve the same result, but the taste will not be affected); whipped cream siphon and two cartridges; disposable paper coffee cups with moderate wax lining (non-metallic dariole moulds may also be used)

INGREDIENTS

For the Saffron Braised Pineapple
1 sweet, ripe pineapple
Water 118 g | 4 fl oz | ½ cup
Salt a pinch
Saffron a pinch

Pineapple Long Pepper Sorbet
Pineapple purée 1 kg | gen. 2 lb | 5 cups
10 peppercorns
Water 250 g | gen. 8¾ fl oz | 1 cup
Glucose syrup 100 g | 3½ fl oz | gen. ¼ cup
Granulated white sugar 150 g | gen. 5¼ oz | ¾ cup
Sorbet stabilizer 8 g | ¼ oz | 2 tsp

For the Yuzu Coconut Fluid Gel
Coconut milk 400 g | gen. 13½ fl oz | 1¾ cups
Yuzu juice 100 g | 3½ fl oz | ½ cup
Granulated white sugar 50 g | 1¾ oz | ¼ cup
Agar agar 6 g | ¼ oz | 2 tsp
1 vanilla pod (bean) (split, scraped, both pod/bean
and seeds reserved)

For the Microwave Sponge Cake
Whole eggs 400 g | 14 oz | 1¾ cups
Egg yolks 150 g | gen. 5¼ oz | sc. ⅔ cup
Granulated white sugar 150 g | gen. 5¼ oz | ¾ cup
Salt 5 g | sc. ¼ oz | sc. 1 tsp
Coconut purée/cream 175 g | 6¼ fl oz | sc. ¾ cup
Unsalted butter 100 g | 3½ oz (melted)
Plain (all-purpose) flour 100 g | 3½ oz | ⅔ cup

For the Candied Sesame Seeds
Granulated white sugar 66 g | gen. 2¼ oz | ⅓ cup
Black sesame seeds 144 g | 5 oz | 1⅛ cups

INSTRUCTIONS

Saffron Braised Pineapple
1 Remove the top and bottom of the pineapple and cut away the skin.
2 Cut into 10 x 2.5 cm (4 x 1 in.) rectangles, about 1 cm (½ in.) thick, reserving the trimmings.
3 Place the trimmings in a small to medium saucepan with the water and a pinch of salt and saffron, bring to the boil, simmer for 10 minutes, then purée until smooth.
4 Place the rectangles of pineapple in vacuum bags, together with the purée, and seal.
5 Place the sealed bag in a water bath at 75°C (167°F) for 45 minutes.
6 Remove from the water bath and allow to cool.
7 Reserve for plating.

Pineapple Long Pepper Sorbet
1 Heat up the purée, add the peppercorns, then remove from the heat, cover and allow to steep for 1 hour before removing the peppercorns.
2 Combine the water, glucose syrup and most of the sugar in a medium saucepan.
3 Mix the remaining sugar with the sorbet stabilizer.
4 Bring the water mixture to the boil, stirring every so often.
5 Once boiling, add the sugar/stabilizer mixture, then return to the boil.
6 Once boiled, remove from the heat and whisk in the pineapple purée.
7 Allow to cool, then refrigerate overnight.
8 Churn in an ice cream machine according to the manufacturer's instructions.

Yuzu Coconut Fluid Gel
1 Combine the coconut milk, yuzu juice and sugar in a small saucepan.
2 Whisk together, then add the agar agar.
3 Continue whisking for 2 minutes to hydrate the agar agar.
4 Place over a medium heat, add the vanilla pod (bean) and seeds, and bring to the boil.
5 Once boiled, strain into a container.
6 Place the container in an ice bath and allow the mixture to set fully.
7 Once set, run through roughly with a knife and place in a blender.
8 Process until very smooth.

Microwave Sponge Cake
1 Combine the whole eggs, egg yolks, sugar and salt in a blender on low speed.
2 Slowly add the coconut purée/cream and the melted butter.
3 Add the flour and process for 1 minute.
4 Pour the cake batter into a container and refrigerate for at least 1 hour.
5 Pour into a whipped cream siphon, charge with two cartridges and shake vigorously.
6 Keep refrigerated until ready to use.
7 Discharge the batter from the siphon into a disposable 55 g (sc. 2 oz) plastic or paper cup whose bottom has been pierced with three holes.
8 Fill with batter to halfway up the side, then cook in a microwave on medium power for about 30–40 seconds.
9 Sit upside down to cool, then unmould and use immediately.
10 Repeat as many times as servings.

Candied Sesame Seeds
1 Cook the sugar to 118°C (244°F).
2 Add the sesame seeds.
3 Stir the mixture (it will begin to crystallize), then remove from the heat and allow to cool.

ASSEMBLING

Garnishes Fresh coconut slices; micro mint leaves; glacé pineapple

Style as you wish.

Will Goldfarb
....

BALI

The sky is no longer the limit for Will Goldfarb. 'I look forward to space exploration through pâtisserie!' he cries. In his work, a plethora of flavoursome and textural layers become apparent behind the somewhat formal simplicity of the outer appearance. Calling Will's style 'deconstructive' would not be entirely in line with his perfectionism. While his creations may share the disassembled, staged, random appearance of deconstructionism, each element is in fact precisely positioned and created to enhance a solid underlying narrative.

'I work with an ingredient, a technique, a philosophy, and use solitude; I love to transmit my ideas into dessert. "Experiential" is how I would describe my pastry style,' he notes. His worldwide ascension reads like an ambitious road map, the starting point of which was a challenge. 'I knew this was what I wanted to do the minute somebody told me I should try something else, since I didn't have the "gift" for it,' he recalls. 'Later, at El Bulli, shortly after I was told I would be doing pastry instead of savoury, I bought Albert Adrià's first book and I realized I was home.' This pivotal moment was followed by acclaimed endeavours such as Room 4 Dessert in New York and Will's current position at KU DE TA in Bali.

Notwithstanding his success as a chef, Will is also an entrepreneur who strives to share his knowledge with others. He launched Willpowder in 2005, a one-stop shop for obtaining – in small quantities – what were once secret ingredients or items impossible for most amateurs to find. The list reads like something from a chemist's laboratory: hydrocolloid products for emulsification, spherification, gelification, and more. A fine incentive to have us experimenting at home, not that we could ever match the profusion of Will's creativity.

All of his inventiveness and skill, however, serve a higher agenda: fashioning 'tasty food'. 'My desserts are flavourful and savoury rather than saccharine. Inedible garnishes, sameness, austerity and technique in place of deliciousness anger me,' he states. Having said that, one of Will's great strengths is no doubt his ability not to take himself too seriously. 'I'm still hoping to make the ATP (Association of Tennis Professionals) tour, though the trouble is I've never been very talented at tennis. That said, I bet Roger Federer's financier cakes aren't very good!'

www.willpowder.com | www.kudeta.net

LONELINESS TRANSFORMED FROM ANXIETY INTO CALM 'This dish has taken many forms since it was first inspired by one of Ayako Suwa's food creations during a class at Janice Wong's 2am:lab,' says Will. 'Tending to lean in the direction of my emotions, the dessert began as an expression of discord and moved towards resolution. The harmony and resolution of two solitudes bordering, protecting and saluting each other allows the dish to be called love in the most Rilkean fashion.'

MAKES 12–20 **DIFFICULTY** 4/5 **PREPARATION TIME** 6 hours (not including 6 hours' resting time for the praline cashew sponge, or 6 hours' drying time for the mango petals) **SPECIFIC EQUIPMENT** Whipped cream siphon and two cartridges; paper coffee cups (230 ml/8 fl oz volume); immersion blender with a flat disc aeration beater (e.g. Bamix®); acetate sheets, or silicone baking paper

INGREDIENTS

For the Praline Cashew Sponge
Praline cashew 100 g | 3½ oz
Egg whites 104 g | gen. 3½ oz | ⅖ cup
Egg yolks 67 g | sc. 2½ oz | gen. ¼ cup
Granulated white sugar 67 g | sc. 2½ oz | ⅓ cup
Plain (all-purpose) flour 17 g | ½ oz | sc. 1½ tbsp

For the Bitter Cocoa Yoghurt
Water 100 g | 3½ fl oz | sc. ½ cup
Granulated white sugar 40 g | sc. 1½ oz | gen. 3 tbsp
Whipping cream (35% fat) 10 g | gen. ¼ fl oz | ½ tbsp
Raw cocoa powder (e.g. Big Tree) 40 g | sc. 1½ oz | sc. ⅖ cup
Greek yoghurt (well hung) 100 g | 3½ oz | sc. ½ cup

For the Cream Bubbles
Whipping cream (35% fat) 250 g | 8¾ fl oz | 1 cup
Milk 125 g | 4¼ fl oz | gen. ½ cup
Water 87.5 g | 3 fl oz | 6 tbsp
Sugar syrup 37.5 g/1¼ fl oz/2½ tbsp water + 37.5 g/gen. 1¼ oz/gen. 3 tbsp granulated white sugar
Sucrose ester (e.g. Willpowder) 5 g | sc. ¼ oz
1 piece cardamom (seeds only)
1 vanilla pod (bean) (split, scraped, both pod/bean and seeds reserved)
1 whole piece torch ginger flower

For the Mango Petals
Passion fruit juice 200 g | 6¾ fl oz | sc. 1 cup
Mango purée 200 g | 7 fl oz | ¾ cup
Sugar syrup 50 g/1¾ fl oz/3½ tbsp water + 50 g/1¾ oz/¼ cup granulated white sugar
Sodium alginate (medium viscosity) (e.g. Willpowder) 2.8 g | ¾ tsp

INSTRUCTIONS

Praline Cashew Sponge
1 Mix all the ingredients in a high-speed blender.
2 Pass through a fine-mesh sieve (strainer).
3 Fill a whipped cream siphon, charge with two cartridges and shake for 2 minutes.
4 Allow to rest for 6 hours.
5 Pierce 3 small holes in the bottom of each paper coffee cup that will be used (one cup per serving).
6 Spray 20 g (sc. ¾ oz) of base into each cup.
7 Microwave individually at 1000 watts for approximately 30–40 seconds.
8 Sit upside down until cool.
9 Unmould and use immediately.

Bitter Cocoa Yoghurt
1 Bring the water, sugar, cream and cocoa powder to the boil.
2 Reduce the mixture to a syrup.
3 Allow to cool.
4 Mix with the yoghurt.
5 Reserve cold.

Cream Bubbles
1 Bring all the ingredients to the boil.
2 Mix well with an immersion blender.
3 Pass through a fine-mesh sieve (strainer).
4 Reserve warm.
5 Foam *à la minute* with an immersion blender with a flat disc aeration beater.

Mango Petals
1 Mix all the ingredients in a high-speed blender.
2 Pass through a fine-mesh sieve (strainer).
3 Spread onto acetate (or silicone baking paper), previously cut into the shape of petals.
4 Dry at 43°C (110°F) for 3 hours.
5 Flip over and dry for another 3 hours.
6 Reserve dry.

ASSEMBLING

Style as you wish.

SKINNY BLANQUETTE, BOYS - SIMPLY FRAUGHT WITH SIGNIFICANCE

'During my silent meditations on the life-giving coconut,' recalls Will, 'I toyed with the notion of the "fat blanket" of the artist Joseph Beuys, which we reconfigured with no little irony. At the same time, outraged by my own pretentiousness, I felt compelled to refer to the laughable representation of Boomer Petway and his agent Ultima Sommerville – with her catchphrase *du jour*, "fraught, simply fraught, with significance" – from Tom Robbins's book, *Skinny Legs and All*.'

MAKES 12 **DIFFICULTY** 4/5 **PREPARATION TIME** 3 hours (not including 24 hours' preparation time for the coconut bacon, or 4–6 hours' dehydrating time for the coconut water wafer) **SPECIFIC EQUIPMENT** Vacuum food sealer and bag (e.g. Cryovac® or Sunbeam FoodSaver®); digital candy thermometer; acetate sheets, or silicone baking paper; dehydrator, or oven with low heat setting; silica gel; tray (20 x 40 cm/7¾ x 15¾ in.)

INGREDIENTS

For the Coconut Bacon

Coconut flesh 150 g | gen. 5¼ oz (crack a fresh young coconut in half and scrape the flesh out in strips)

Kecap manis (Indonesian soy sauce) 125 g | gen. 4 fl oz | 6½ tbsp

1 kluwak nut (crushed)

Honey 25 g | sc. 1 fl oz | 3½ tsp

Water 25 g | gen. ¾ fl oz | 5 tsp

Extra virgin olive oil 25 g | sc. 1 fl oz | 2¼ tbsp

Xanthan gum (e.g. Willpowder) 0.2 g | tip of tsp

Smoke powder 1 g | ½ tsp

For the Coconut Water Wafer

Coconut water 350 g | gen. 12¼ fl oz | sc. 1½ cups

Egg whites 90 g | sc. 3¼ oz | gen. ⅓ cup

Icing (confectioner's) sugar 60 g | gen. 2 oz | 6 tbsp

Xanthan gum (e.g. Willpowder) 2.5 g | ½ tsp

3 kaffir lime leaves

1 piece lemongrass

For the Coconut Milk Turbo Fluid Gel

Fresh coconut milk 700 g | 24 fl oz | 3 cups

Whipping cream (35% fat) 200 g | 7 fl oz | ⅘ cup

Milk 100 g | sc. 3½ fl oz | sc. ½ cup

Granulated white sugar 100 g | 3½ oz | ½ cup

Gellan F (low acyl) (e.g. Willpowder) 4 g | gen. 1 tsp

Ultratex 8 tapioca starch (e.g. Willpowder) 10 g | sc. ½ oz | 4 tsp

For the Coconut Cake

Unsalted butter 175 g | 6 oz

Granulated white sugar 230 g | 8 oz | 1⅛ cups

2½ whole eggs

Fresh grated coconut 150 g | gen. 5¼ oz | gen. 1 cup

Plain (all-purpose) flour 160 g | sc. 5¾ oz | gen. 1 cup

Bicarbonate of soda (baking soda) 5 g | sc. ¼ oz | ¾ tsp

Coconut rum 25 g | gen. ¾ fl oz | 5 tsp

Fresh coconut milk 150 g | gen. 5 fl oz | sc. ¾ cup

INSTRUCTIONS

Coconut Bacon

1 Mix all the ingredients well, then vacuum seal in a bag.
2 Cook in a water bath at 75°C (167°F) for 2 hours.
3 Strain and dry the coconut for 24 hours at 43°C (110°F).
4 Reserve dry.

Coconut Water Wafer

1 Mix all the ingredients in a high-speed blender.
2 Pass through a fine-mesh sieve (strainer).
3 Whip at high speed until light and fluffy.
4 Spread wafer-thin on lightly oiled acetate sheets, or silicone baking paper.
5 Dehydrate at 43°C (110°F) for 4–6 hours.
6 Reserve dry with silica gel.

Coconut Milk Turbo Fluid Gel

1 Bring all the ingredients, except the tapioca starch, to the boil.
2 Pass through a fine-mesh sieve (strainer), then leave to set.
3 Mix in a high-speed blender, then add the tapioca starch.
4 Strain again, then reserve cold.

Coconut Cake

1 Cream the butter and the sugar.
2 Add the eggs, then the coconut.
3 Alternate a flour/bicarbonate of soda (baking soda) mix and a rum/coconut milk mix to make a homogeneous mass.
4 Put on the tray and bake covered at 160°C (325°F) for 1 hour.

ASSEMBLING

Garnishes Coconut sorbet (optional); coconut palm sugar with cinnamon (e.g. Big Tree Farms); coconut oil powder; kemangi leaves/lemon basil

Style as you wish.

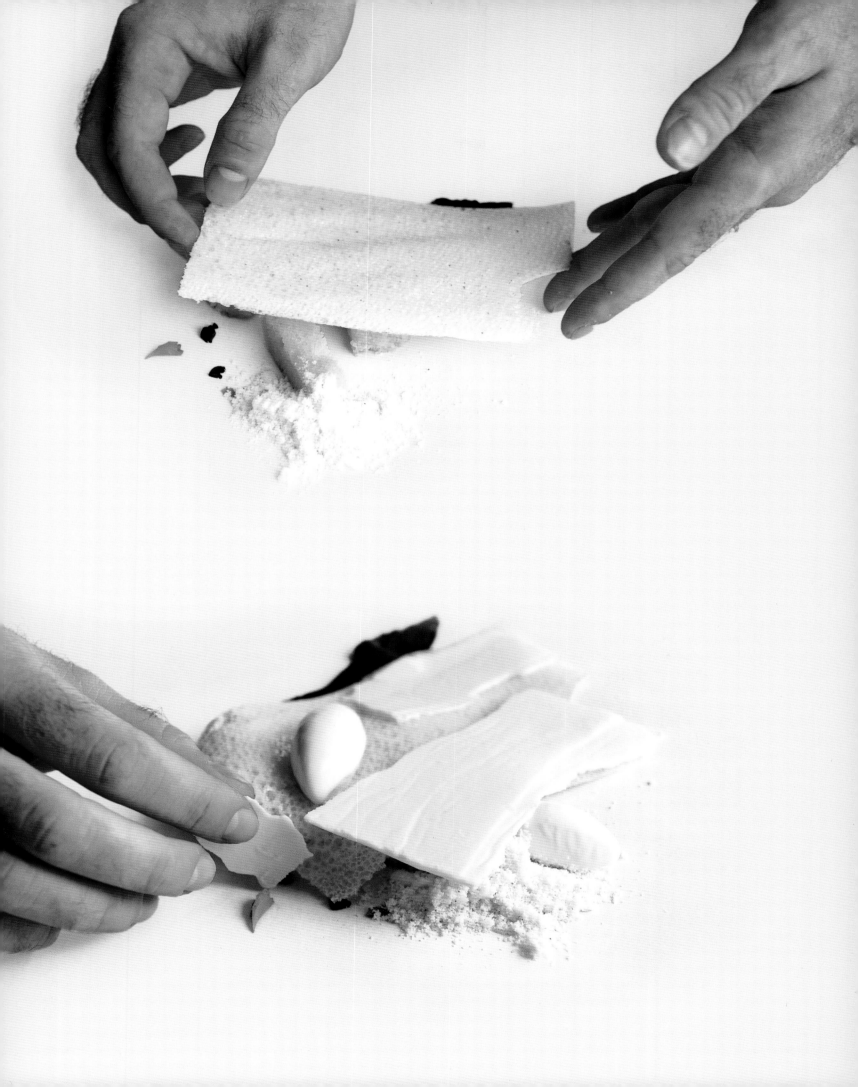

SUGAR REFINERY V. 2012 SPRINGTEMPS

'This dish tells a story,' explains Will. 'The story takes one through space, time and history, along the great Gaussian coordinates towards the relativity of taste. The flavours and textures of this simple and elegant mille-feuilles can only be "made in Bali".'

MAKES 6–12 **DIFFICULTY** 4/5 **PREPARATION TIME** 4–5 hours **SPECIFIC EQUIPMENT** Piping (pastry) bag with size 11 and 5 nozzles; blast chiller (or regular freezer); vacuum food sealer and bag (e.g. Cryovac® or Sunbeam FoodSaver®); acetate sheets (4 x 9 cm/1⅝ x 3½ in.); sorbet maker

INGREDIENTS

For the Crumbly White Chocolate Palm Sugar Leaf
Raw white chocolate (e.g. Big Tree Farms) 150 g | gen. 5¼ oz
Ginger palm sugar (e.g. Big Tree Farms) 150 g | gen. 5¼ oz | 1 cup

For the Walnut Tuile
Unsalted butter 30 g | 1 oz
Walnut oil 10 g | sc. ½ fl oz | 2 tsp
Walnut purée 50 g | 1¾ fl oz | 4 tbsp
Tapioca maltodextrin (e.g. Willpowder) 5 g | sc. ¼ oz | 1½ tsp
Icing (confectioner's) sugar 30 g | 1 oz | 3 tbsp
Egg whites 30 g | 1 oz | 2 tbsp
Plain (all-purpose) flour 35 g | 1¼ oz | 3 tbsp

For the Caramel Cream
Granulated white sugar 106 g | 3¾ oz | ½ cup
Whipping cream (35% fat) 360 g | gen. 12½ fl oz | sc. 1½ cups
Iota carrageenan (e.g. Willpowder) 0.76 g | ¼ tsp
Kappa carrageenan (e.g. Willpowder) 0.14 g | tip of tsp

For the Muscovado Granite
Water 250 g | gen. 8¾ fl oz | 1 cup
Muscovado sugar 83.3 g | 3 oz | gen. ½ cup
Methylcellulose F50 (e.g. Willpowder) 0.66 g | ¼ tsp
Gelatine (gold) 2.5 g | 1¼ sheets (softened in ice cold water, with excess water squeezed out)

For the Espresso Caramel
Granulated white sugar 125 g | sc. 4½ oz | gen. ½ cup
Hot espresso coffee 250 g | gen. 8¾ fl oz | 1 cup
1 kluwak nut (crushed)

For the Sorbet Mangosteen
Glucose syrup 80 g | 2¾ fl oz | sc. ¼ cup
Water 130 g | 4½ fl oz | ½ cup
Granulated white sugar 112 g | 4 oz | gen. ½ cup
Sorbet stabilizer (e.g. Willpowder custom-blend) 3 g | sc. 1 tsp
Lychee purée 300 g | sc. 10¾ fl oz | sc. 1¼ cups (very cold)
Mangosteen purée 700 g | 25 fl oz | 2¾ cups (very cold)

INSTRUCTIONS

Crumbly White Chocolate Palm Sugar Leaf
1   Melt the white chocolate in a bain-marie, then mix in the sugar.
2   Roll out thinly between layers of silicone baking paper and cut into desired shapes.
3   Reserve cold.

Walnut Tuile
1   Use a food processor (cutting blade) to mix all the ingredients, reserving the flour for last and folding it in by hand.
2   Roll out thinly between two pieces of silicone baking paper, then remove the top paper sheet and bake at 160°C (325°F) until deep tanning occurs.
3   While still warm, quickly cut into desired shapes; alternatively you may par-bake, cut and then finish baking them to avoid stress fractures.

Caramel Cream
1   Strongly caramelize the sugar.
2   At the same time, heat the cream and use to deglaze the caramel. NB Take care, as this will spit.
3   Boil the caramel mixture with the iota and kappa carrageenans.
4   Shear (i.e. mix) for 2 minutes with an immersion blender.
5   Strain, then leave to set in the fridge for 2–4 hours.
6   Whip at high speed in a stand mixer.
7   Reserve in the fridge in a piping (pastry) bag with a size 11 nozzle.

Muscovado Granite
1   Boil the water and the sugar together.
2   Sprinkle in the methylcellulose, then add the gelatine.
3   Set in a blast chiller (or, if using a normal freezer, double the amount of gelatine and freeze until set, which will take 2–6 hours).
4   Vacuum seal and keep cold for 2–4 hours.
5   Mix with an immersion blender and whip over high speed until fluffy as can be (may be finished in a stand mixer with whisk attachment).
6   Pipe onto the acetate sheets with a size 5 nozzle, roll into tubes, blast chill and reserve frozen.

Espresso Caramel
1   Make a caramel with the sugar and deglaze with the espresso.
2   Add the crushed kluwak nut and reduce (approximately 1 hour on low heat).
3   Strain before using.

Sorbet Mangosteen
1   Make a sorbet syrup with all the ingredients, except the fruit purées, taking care to mix the stabilizer in well, then bring to the boil.
2   Allow the syrup to cool, then mix well with the very cold purées.
3   Churn immediately in a sorbet maker according to the manufacturer's instructions.

ASSEMBLING

Place espresso caramel at the bottom of each plate (not visible in the photo opposite). Build the rest of the dish as you wish, preferably alternating layers of the cream/sorbet/granite textures with the tuile/leaf, like a deconstructed mille-feuilles.

Wonderland Confections

Here are awe-inspiring cakes created for important occasions. The sugar-paste masters behind these edible sculptures will design the cake of your dreams, whether for that intimate 'I do' moment or for a special gathering with family and friends. They will listen to your story, capture your predilections and ensure they contribute to one of the best days of your life. These chefs are not your usual celebration cake designers, churning out cute birthday numbers with a pink ballerina for girls and a blue car for boys, or red roses on black icing for Valentine's Day. These sculptors display a more extravagant, and yet more subtle, repertoire. They revel in brilliant miniaturism, playful festivity and the sheer artistry of what can be achieved with simple ingredients. Their creations are so exquisite that you may not wish to slice and share, but you will be very glad you did.

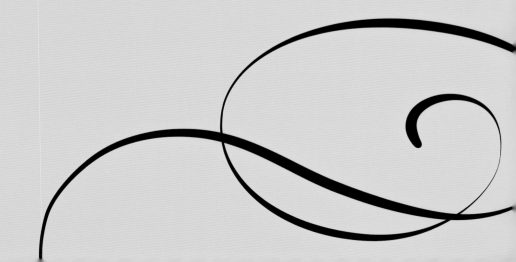

Bobbette & Belle

CANADA

When Steve and Katherine got married, one question kept being asked: who made the superb wedding cake? The elegant tiers of sugar-paste flowers that became the centrepiece of the reception are a speciality of Bobbette & Belle, a.k.a Allyson Bobbitt and Sarah Bell, the two high priestesses of tasteful cakes, big and small.

'What makes us passionate about what we do is being able to elevate a classic. Something as simple as a carrot cake can become someone's favourite dessert if it's baked from scratch with the freshest ingredients and a true understanding of balanced flavours,' they say. 'There are a lot of ready-made sweets for consumers out there but so much is mass-produced, using non-natural ingredients, that people have lost touch with how great home-baked desserts really are. Our entire business is built on trying to reignite the love of truly excellent pastry.'

The pair's combined backgrounds include a science degree, a pastry diploma, teaching experience, a brief stint as a banker and another as a portrait artist. What may seem a mixed bag of jobs has actually produced an invaluable knowledge bank that has helped them turn their business into a multi-faceted powerhouse. In addition Sarah reports, 'Allyson has a natural-born salty tooth and I have a sweet tooth. I head straight for cupcakes and macarons, while Allyson prefers croissants and scones. If anything, the difference in our palates helps us to create a wide array of sweets that are appealing to most people.'

Their store in Toronto's Leslieville is a perfect rendition of their creative style. Stylish and pretty, with white wood and lots of flowers and pastels, it is the sort of place you expect Audrey Hepburn to enter at any moment. Now Allyson and Sarah plan to expand, bolstered by their frequent contributions to wedding magazines, their much-watched baking segments on a national TV show and their sagacious business model.

'We operate our specialty cake design service like a fashion house, with a more affordable "prêt-a-porter" range and with the ultimate made-to-order "haute couture" category,' they say. 'Because our pastry shop stemmed out of an events-based business, we've learned to put the customer first. We still strive to be innovative but we never want to alienate our core customers.' And it works. The brides and grooms keep returning – for baby showers, christenings, birthdays, Christmas... All hooked on Bobbette & Belle for life.

www.bobbetteandbelle.com

ALICE IN WONDERLAND CAKE

'In our bakery there are lots of customers that become regulars but, when it comes to high-end, custom-designed cakes, true regulars are rare and a real treat to work with. Once you've created a beautiful custom cake for someone, a level of trust develops, and as an artist you can really flex your creativity. Such was the case for an Alice in Wonderland-themed wedding shower for which we were commissioned to create a cake. The bride-to-be and her family had ordered many designer cakes from us in the past, but the bride had never had one made for herself. We wanted to deliver something spectacular that she would fall in love with.

Our inspiration started with a hand-painted, Alice-themed teapot that would be used as the centrepiece of each table. We decided to recreate the teapot as an edible version and to top it off with a sugar figurine of the White Rabbit. We tried to capture as many details as possible, such as his pocket watch, umbrella and even tiny eyeglasses. The bottom half of the cake consisted of two tiers of hand-painted Wonderland backgrounds and detailed sugar figurines of Alice and the Cheshire Cat. The added benefit of including sugar figurines is that, although they are edible, they harden over time and can be kept as beautiful mementoes.

The bride's mother supplied us with her daughter's favourite Lewis Carroll quote and we painted it around the lower tiers of the cake. In order to add a final touch of whimsy, we created colourful sugar mushrooms, a checkerboard base and falling playing cards reminiscent of the Queen of Hearts.

The cake was a huge hit. Being able to be a part of the most important moments of clients' lives is the most fulfilling part of our work, and that kind of human connection is what really spurs on our creativity.'

RED VELVET CAKE

'Red velvet cake is a must-have at our bakery. Over the last few years it has gained in popularity as a flavour both for a wedding cake and a cupcake. We find that people who are usually divided when it comes to what they like better – vanilla or chocolate – come together, and both really love red velvet! Who doesn't adore the drama and surprise of cutting into a rich red cake? We've added sour cream to increase the moistness and softness. And pairing it with our cream cheese buttercream is amazing. Unlike a traditional frosting, our buttercream is rich in flavour but light in texture and not too sweet. It's a new way to present the classic red velvet cake.'

MAKES 1 cake (3 x round 20 cm/7¾ in. cake layers); serves 12   **DIFFICULTY** 1/5   **PREPARATION TIME** 2–3 hours
SPECIFIC EQUIPMENT Round cake tin (pan) (20 cm/7¾ in. diameter); digital candy thermometer

INGREDIENTS

For the Cake

Soft flour (cake flour) 230 g | 8 oz | 1½ cups
Baking powder 3.5 g | sc. 1 tsp
Bicarbonate of soda (baking soda) 3.5 g | ½ tsp
Salt 3.5 g | gen. ½ tsp
Cocoa powder 30 g | 1 oz | gen. ¼ cup
Unsalted butter 88 g | gen. 3 oz (room temperature)
Granulated white sugar 225 g | sc. 8 oz | 1⅛ cups
2 whole eggs
1 egg yolk
Buttermilk 90 g | gen. 3 fl oz | gen. ⅓ cup
Sour cream 85 g | 3 fl oz | ⅓ cup
Red food colouring (to achieve desired colour)
Vanilla extract 5 ml | 1 tsp

For the Cream Cheese Swiss Meringue Buttercream

Caster (superfine) sugar 120 g | 4¼ oz | gen. ½ cup
2 egg whites
Unsalted butter 250 g | gen. 8¾ oz (soft)
Vanilla extract 5 ml | 1 tsp
Plain cream cheese 125 g | sc. 4½ oz | gen. ½ cup (soft)

INSTRUCTIONS

Cake

1   Preheat the oven to 180°C (350°F).
2   Lightly grease and line the bottom of the round cake tin (pan) with silicone baking paper.
3   In a bowl, sift together the flour, baking powder, bicarbonate of soda (baking soda), salt and cocoa powder, then set aside.
4   Use a stand mixer with a paddle attachment to beat together the butter and sugar for 2–3 minutes until light and fluffy.
5   In a separate bowl, whisk together the eggs and egg yolk, then slowly add to the butter/sugar mixture on low speed.
6   In a small bowl, whisk together the buttermilk, sour cream, red food colouring and vanilla extract. NB Food colouring brands differ in concentration levels, so simply add colouring until the batter takes on a medium-red hue; the colour will continue to develop during baking.
7   On low speed, add one-third of the sifted dry ingredients to the beaten egg/sugar mixture and mix until the dry ingredients are just barely incorporated.
8   Add half of the red liquid mixture and continue on low speed until thoroughly combined.
9   Stop the mixer, scrape down the sides, then add another one-third of the dry ingredients and mix until completely incorporated.
10 Add the remainder of the liquid ingredients and mix well.
11 Remove the bowl from the mixer and add the remaining one-third dry ingredients by hand.
12 Pour into the cake tin (pan).
13 Bake for a maximum of 55–60 minutes. NB Depending on your oven it could take less time, so start checking the cake at 40 minutes; as soon as it springs back when you press the middle, or an inserted toothpick comes out clean, the cake is ready to be removed from the oven.
14 Once the cake has cooled in the tin (pan) for about 10 minutes, knock it out onto a wire rack and cool completely to room temperature.

Cream Cheese Swiss Meringue Buttercream

1   Mix the sugar and egg whites together in a heatproof bowl.
2   Put the bowl over a bain-marie and whisk continuously until the sugar dissolves (the temperature should reach around 60°C/140°F).
3   Remove from the heat and transfer contents into the bowl of a stand mixer.
4   Whisk for 3–4 minutes on high speed, or until the mixture is bright white and does not move in the bowl.
5   Divide the softened butter into eight blocks.
6   Reduce the speed of the mixer to medium, ensure the bowl is cool to the touch so that the butter does not melt when added, then start adding butter, one block at a time, waiting for each block to mix thoroughly.
7   After five blocks have been added the mixture may look curdled, but keep adding the butter slowly, as the mixture will come back together.
8   Keep mixing for another 4–5 minutes.
9   Add the vanilla extract.
10 Slowly add the softened cream cheese in chunks and mix until well incorporated.

ASSEMBLING

Slice the cake into three even discs. Set the first layer on a serving plate. Using a spatula, add a good-size dollop of buttercream and spread until it is evenly distributed out to the edges of the cake. Repeat with the second layer. Set the third layer on top and spread the remaining buttercream on the sides and top of the entire cake until there is no red velvet left showing. Reserve in the fridge. Slice and enjoy!

Bonnae Gokson

HONG KONG

When America's wedding event guru, Colin Cowie, lists you on his website and introduces you as Queen of Confectionery in Asia, you know you must have elevated pastry craft to a whole new level. The Queen B – B for Bonnae Gokson – is a Hong Kong entrepreneur and style icon, whose primary background is in high fashion and luxury. 'I stem from a retailing family. My grandfather founded the best-known department store in Shanghai in the 1930s and my sister, Joyce Ma, was the doyenne of fashion in the East, introducing Hong Kong and Asia to most of the top brand names in the world,' Bonnae explains. 'Besides my pastry business, I remain a consultant for the fashion, lifestyle and hotel industries.'

Bonnae's business drive has enabled her to establish the most sought-after network of retail hotspots in the city: the roof-top SEVVA, the bespoke Ms B's Cakery and the cool C'est La B café-bars. Her unique stylish vibe is imprinted through all her ventures. 'I'm really blessed that, with travel, I've had lots of exposure to all parts of the world. It means I can envision a unique confectionery concept for Hong Kong,' she says.

Best known for her feather-light cakes with reduced sugar recipes, Bonnae succeeds in balancing simplicity and prettiness with extravagance and humour. As well as catering for birthdays and weddings, she has been called on for corporate events by many fashion brands and hip membership clubs for their own signature cakes.

'I'm actually not a chef, and I don't bake either,' admits Bonnae. 'You may say I'm like a conductor of an orchestra. I use my skilled chefs' hands to execute my ideas. There has been non-stop positive press coverage from all over the world, and it's still going strong. I'm very humbled by this, as, not having gone to pastry school, I have created something different. Just thinking out of the box, where there are no rules or formulas to bind me, has brought me to where I am today.'

Bonnae, with her signature butterflies, has raised the benchmark of the cake industry in Hong Kong not only by imposing the highest standards but also by introducing glamour, and thereby lifting the world of pastry to stratospheric new heights.

www.sevva.hk | www.msbscakery.hk

Love at first bite...

'HOW DEEP IS YOUR LOVE' CAKE

'Hong Kong, being one of the most exciting cities in the world, has its fair share of incredible, memorable events. One of the many that my cakery and I have been involved in was the fabulous two-day wedding of celebrity singer/songwriter Coco Lee and her Canadian businessman beau, Bruce Rockowitz. The wedding was rumoured to have cost US$15 million, and some of the most famous personalities from all over the world, such as Alicia Keys, Bruno Mars, Jackie Chan, Steve Wynn and Tommy Hilfiger, were among the many who attended.

From years back in my fashion days, when I was Regional Chief of Image and Communications for Chanel Asia-Pacific, I had chosen and groomed a celebrity for our fashion campaign of the season. What karma was it that, years later, she calls up and wants me to design her wedding cake! When we met up, Coco was very sweet to tell me that she trusted my taste and that she'd leave it up to me to design the cake for her. She did, however, have two tearsheets from magazines that she liked, which were quite classic in style, with lots of flowers surrounding each tier.

Her other criteria were a massive venue, which turned out to be a movie studio, and the fact that the entire site would be transformed into the lookalike of New York's former club, Studio 54. The cake had to be so tall that guests would be able to view it from far away, as the stage would be for artists who'd flown in from the US to perform. Her chosen bridesmaids' colours were soft lilac, and she liked the idea of a bit of bling!

With three months' notice, my sugar-flower workshop and I set to work on colour palettes of the most beautiful blooms, from wild roses and tuberoses to lilies of the valley, orchids and pansies. It took a few hundred hours to hand-make

each petal for the finished artworks, and they turned out to be exquisitely delicate and fine. Colours were from softest pinks to nudes, to soft violets and champagne cream tones. There must have been thousands of stems that I ended up arranging for many hours in a small room in the film studio, which I also shared with Fergie and The Black Eyed Peas!

The cake was six tiers – 9 feet tall, with a base cake diameter of 3 feet. Just on fondant alone, without the sugar flowers, we used over 400 pounds of sugar. Each tier had pretty lace imprints, which also took many sleepless nights to stencil and carve to perfection. The ultimate touch was to place thousands of moonstone Swarovski crystals at different points of the lacework.

Transporting the tiers to the film studio was no joke, and arranging each sugar-flower stem was quite a task, but the cake looked sublime. I had also designed the foot-tall cake topper to be "CB", the wedding couple's initials, in glittering moon-stone Swarovskis. In the wee hours of the morning, while the workers were still assembling the interior and setting up the sound and lighting, the challenge was to figure out how they would lift this humungous work-of-art "wow" piece to the middle of the stage, where it needed to remain a surprise. I was almost in tears thinking that so many days and nights of dedication might be wasted if the cranes that were lifting this 700-pounder dropped it in the middle of transporting it from one corner of the huge studio to another.

After the suspense and drama of that night I returned home to get some rest until the big day. When I arrived as a guest the next evening, the magic of the night and the entertainment was like an Oscar award party but probably more fun. Sadly we can't show the cake in this book, but it was a show-stopper and received so much applause for its breathtaking beauty as it twinkled under the lights.'

MARIE ANTOINETTE'S CRAVE

'I've been travelling to Paris since I was young, and I wanted to create something with a regal French appeal. Watercolour macarons were my first idea, then a light, soft cake. Pistachio chiffon came to mind, and from there I meditated on what Marie Antoinette might have loved. Something decadent to go with whipped cream, like rose petal jam to enhance sweet, fresh raspberries. Being a queen, she would also have something precious, like edible metallic dragée beads. Finally, a topper of sugar-spun cotton candy. *Voilà!* A creation fit for any queen.'

MAKES 1 cake (15 cm/6 in. diameter); serves 6–8 **DIFFICULTY** 3/5 **PREPARATION TIME** 4½ hours (not including 1½ hours' cooling time) **SPECIFIC EQUIPMENT** Cake tin (pan) (15 cm/6 in. diameter, 10 cm/4 in. high); Silpat mat®, or silicone baking paper-lined tray; piping (pastry) bags with medium, round nozzles

INGREDIENTS

For the Pistachio Sponge Cake

Soft flour (cake flour) 100 g | 3½ oz | ⅔ cup
Baking powder 4.5 g | gen. 1 tsp
Pistachio paste (or ground pistachio) 30 g | 1 oz | 2 tbsp
Water 50 ml | 1¾ fl oz | 3½ tbsp
Vegetable oil 30 ml | gen. 1 fl oz | 2½ tbsp
Green food colouring 2 drops
4 egg yolks
Granulated white sugar [1] 50 g | 1¾ oz | ¼ cup
5 egg whites
Cream of tartar 0.8 g | ⅛ tsp
Granulated white sugar [2] 60 g | gen. 2 oz | gen. ¼ cup

For the Macaron Shells
(makes 80 pieces)

Blanched almond meal 85 g | 3 oz | 1 cup
Icing (confectioner's) sugar 150 g | gen. 5¼ oz | sc. 1 cup
Egg whites 70 g | 2½ oz | sc. ⅓ cup
Cream of tartar 0.7 g | sc. ⅛ tsp
Caster (superfine) sugar 18 g | gen. ½ oz | gen. 3½ tsp
Various food colourings and essences a few drops:
pink (strawberry essence), orange (mango essence),
yellow (lemon essence), green (pandan essence),
purple (taro essence), white (vanilla essence)

INSTRUCTIONS

Pistachio Sponge Cake

1   Preheat the oven to 185°C (350°F) and line the cake tin (pan) with silicone baking paper.
2   In a bowl, sift together the flour and baking powder, then set aside.
3   In another bowl, dilute the pistachio paste (or ground pistachio) with the water, vegetable oil and food colouring, then set aside.
4   In the bowl of a stand mixer, whisk the egg yolks while slowly adding in sugar [1] until the mixture becomes pale and creamy, then set aside.
5   In the bowl of the stand mixer, whisk the egg whites and cream of tartar on medium-high speed until they become foamy.
6   Slowly add sugar [2] into the foamy egg whites, then raise the mixer speed to high and beat until they are white and shiny and hold medium stiff peaks.
7   Gently fold the beaten egg whites, in two lots, into the beaten egg yolks until uniform.
8   Gently fold in the flour/baking powder, in two lots, and combine until almost homogeneous.
9   Add some of the resulting mixture into the pistachio mix and combine well.
10 Pour back into the remaining whole mixture and gently combine until completely homogeneous.
11 Pour the resulting batter into the cake tin (pan) and bake at 185°C (350°F) for 30–35 minutes, or until an inserted skewer comes out clean and the cake surface springs back when pressed.
12 Immediately invert the cake tin (pan) onto a wire rack and allow to cool completely.

Macaron Shells

1   In a bowl, combine the almond meal and icing (confectioner's) sugar, and sift.
2   In the bowl of a stand mixer, whisk the egg whites and cream of tartar on medium speed until foamy, then slowly add in the caster (superfine) sugar.
3   Raise the mixer speed to high and beat until white, shiny and holding medium stiff peaks.
4   Add one-third of the almond/sugar mixture, fold to combine by hand, and repeat with two more additions until all the ingredients are incorporated.
5   Divide the mixture into as many colour and flavour combinations as desired.
6   Fold a few drops of desired colouring and flavouring essence into each mixture.
7   Place each mixture into a piping (pastry) bag fitted with a medium, round nozzle.
8   Pipe rounds of 2 cm (¾ in.) and 3 cm (1⅛ in.) on a Silpat® mat, or silicone baking paper-lined tray; tap the bottom of the mat/tray a few times to flatten the tops and even out the surface.
9   Preheat the oven to 140°C (275°F).
10 Let the macarons sit and dry for 20 minutes or more, until their tops form a slight skin.
11 Place in the preheated oven and bake for 12–15 minutes, or until set.
12 Cool completely before removing from the tray and transferring to a wire rack.

ASSEMBLING

Components/Garnishes 35% fat whipping cream (700 g/24½ fl oz/sc. 3 cups); caster (superfine) sugar (50 g/1¾ oz/sc. ¼ cup); rose petal jam; fresh raspberries (175 g/6 oz/gen. 1 cup); candy pearlettes (multicoloured metallic dragées); strawberry chocolate curls; pink cotton candy floss

Unmould the pistachio sponge cake and cut into four even discs. In the bowl of a stand mixer, whip the cream and sugar with a whisk attachment on medium speed until soft peaks form. Spread rose petal jam onto the first layer of cake, then top generously with fresh raspberries. Place the second layer on top and spread with a good amount of whipped cream. Repeat the third layer with rose petal jam and raspberries. Finish with the last layer. Cover the entire cake with the remaining whipped cream, then chill in the fridge for 15 minutes. Place macaron shells on the cake to create a spontaneous, prettily coloured pattern. Fill in gaps with candy pearlettes. Serve on a cake platter, with strawberry chocolate curls sprinkled around the base. Adorn with pink cotton candy floss.

Emily Miranda
....
USA

There are rare cakes that call for a big reveal, as when heavy velvet curtains are raised before a play begins. Emily Miranda's sugar-paste sculptures are of that kind. 'My goal is always to create cakes that are magnificent, decadent spectacles. I love the challenge of replicating nature in the medium of sugar paste, creating temporary tableaux of wonder and delight,' declares Emily.

She has always gravitated towards the arts, having studied metalsmithing and graduated with several diplomas in painting and sculpture. 'I always knew I would be an artist of some sort. I started out as a painter and have turned out to be a sculptor who makes cakes and jewelry,' she says. She has also worked for over ten years as a decorative painter, creating elaborate faux finishes in high-end apartments in and around New York City. It was through this line of work that her love of the decorative arts emerged and her eye was educated.

'The first time I glimpsed the creative possibilities of cake was when I was living in Maine and was hired to make a cake for the oldest member of the town's founding family,' she explains. 'With the help of a friend who ran a bakery, I made sheet pans of carrot cake and built up a topographical map of the island the town was on, complete with almond sliver forests, whirlpools of icing and towering cake sea monsters.' From this early success, Emily could have exploited the niche and developed a business, but she soon realized that a full-time venture could not be an option. 'I accepted I would never be fully compensated for my time if I wanted to remain uncompromising with my vision, so I ended up making cakes as a labour of love.'

She spends hours researching her commissioners' passions and life stories, and her cakes remain made-to-measure and unique. 'My favourite part is the actual constructing; the carving and building of the figures,' Emily shares. 'Sugar paste is an amazing medium. It's silky smooth and elastic, yet dries hard in minutes to hold a thin, delicate shape. I would someday love to create a rambling, table-wide narrative installation - an encyclopedic "Ode to the Museum of Natural History".' What an appetizing celebration of flora and fauna that would be!

www.emilymirandastudio.com

GARY'S CAKE

'Gary Graham is a fashion designer in New York City. I'm a fan and was thrilled when he asked me if I'd like to sell my jewelry in his store. His idea was to have a launch event which would coincide with his annual holiday party. We decided to make a cake as the centrepiece. Gary wanted it to have a relationship to the decorations he had planned for his holiday window display: deconstructed Diet Coke cans. The inspiration references I get from a client are the most important starting point, but Gary's minimal, abstract idea had me stumped.

When the cans were finally cut and strung, I rushed over to see them. They were sparkling pinwheels – silver, black and red whirlygigs. The cans had been cut and flattened, twisted and stretched into new geometric shapes. They were strung as dangling, glittering ornaments, which swayed and twirled in the ambient air. I was inspired. But I had never made an abstract cake before. Clearly no images were going to be appropriate for Gary's cake; it needed to be about shape, geometry, festivity, movement, sparkle. But how to represent this in a cake?

The first thing was to choose a structure, an overall shape. A low, flat cake wouldn't work, and a classic tiered cake felt too bulky in the spirit of those lighter-than-air dancing cans. I thought of mimicking the structure of the columns of cans themselves. There were three or four suspended on each long wire. What if the cake layers were somehow suspended on a central shaft?

After much brainstorming, I developed a plan to use a long ½-inch round pipe that would go through a hole in the table. The pipe would extend about 4 feet above the table, and the different cake layers would be suspended using rings that tightened around the pipe using set screws at adjustable heights.

I decided to make four separate "moments", which would all be different. The palette was black, gold, white and silver – the colours of Gary's holiday collection. Only one layer would be the actual cake (it only needed to feed about sixty), but I wanted every element to be edible. Gary had requested a gluten-free cake, so I decided on flourless chocolate. It would have a black ganache coating and be speckled with sparkly silver balls, to match one of Gary's showpiece dresses.

I wanted the top to look like a Christmas tree star, or a fireworks explosion. I bought 50 "stems" of rock candy and stuck them, in symmetrical formation, into a Styrofoam ball coated with silver royal icing.

For the bottom, I heated black licorice stems so a wire could be inserted into each core, with wire left sticking out on both ends. I bent the licorice into half moons and inserted the wire ends into a gold royal icing-covered Styrofoam hexagon.

The last challenge was the "moment" that would be second to the top. At first I couldn't figure it out. I wanted it to be jagged, rigid, spiked – like the folds of the Coke cans on Gary's whirligig. But what edible material was stiff and sturdy enough to be "threaded" on the pipe? What was malleable enough for me to create the shapes I wanted? Finally it hit me: sugar cookies! I plotted a star design and stayed up all night making thick cookies in various sizes. In the morning I iced them with white royal icing, iced small cookie spacers in gold to go in between, did a test, then packed the whole thing up for delivery.

The assembly went smoothly, and the event went even better. People broke off the tips of the stars and nibbled on them all evening; the rock candy lollipops were plucked and circulated; and someone discovered that if you took two licorice pieces out you could wire the ends together and make a bangle. People were not only eating, but wearing them! My first interactive cake! It was a smashing success.'

CYNTHIA'S CAKE

'Cynthia's daughter contacted me only two weeks before the wedding. Her mother was in China and had charged her with finding a cake. She had seen some other cakes of mine on a blog, then remembered me again when she saw my jewelry in Gary Graham's store, where she was picking up her mother's wedding dress. Even though two weeks is short notice for me, it was only for ten people and I agreed.

To begin a cake, I usually ask the client for a list of twenty of their favourite things. From this, I make my own list of the images and ideas that fit together and most inspire me, and then I begin to conjure the cake's narrative tableau.

I learned that the groom's favourite cake of mine was "Marissa's Cake", a floral still-life featuring a large parrot tulip. So parrot tulips made my list, as did spring-time flowers (it was May). Cynthia's daughter then told me that the logo for her mother's Chinese porcelain importing company was a peony. A giant peony began to form in my mind as the centrepiece. She also told me that Cynthia's dog was named Poppy. I imagined a red poppy with a red-and-white striped peony, like the parrot tulip from "Marissa's Cake".

So I had a giant red-and-white striped peony, a red poppy and some parrot tulips (I imagined them in a peachy pink), but what was the structure? After many failed sketches, I asked Cynthia's daughter to send me anything she could think of that might give me ideas to complete the narrative. She sent me images from a show that Cynthia had recently curated. Two images jumped out: a Chinese scholar stone and a white "drip" painting by artist Roxy Paine. I had found my solution! The flowers would "grow" out of a sugar-paste scholar stone, and I would "paint" the cake stand with successive layers of royal icing to build up drips (every

three hours or so for two days). The whole composition, while remaining very spare and simple, would be texturally complex and very personal to Cynthia.

The giant peony was made up of thirty-six petals. Each one was rolled through a pasta machine, pressed in a rubber peony petal mould to give lifelike veins, cut with an X-Acto knife while still on the mould, shaped by being draped over crumpled Saran wrap (cling film), then adjusted into a lifelike position and left to dry for 30–40 minutes. Each petal was then hand-"striped" with a tiny brush dipped in red food colouring, first on one side and left to dry, then on the other. Each individual petal was then glued with watered-down sugar paste to the centre point made of wire. I had to hold each petal in my hand for one minute before I could set it down to dry completely, which took 30–40 minutes. When all the petals were glued and dried, I reinforced the joints by painting layers of white royal icing on them. If this is not done, then petals this thin will often break under their own weight.

The poppy would have only four petals, so they had to be perfect: the simpler the flower, the more pressure to get the gesture of each element exactly right. These petals were made just like the peony's, then glued onto the sugar-paste poppy centre (at the end of a royal icing-covered floral wire) and painted with an adjusted red food colouring mix to get the undulating shades of "poppy red" just right.

The tulips ended up being small and mostly in bud form. The process for making them was the same as above, except that the petals needed to be worked into shape as they began to dry in my hands (about 10 minutes). This was necessary in order to get that curled-under "toothy" look that young parrot tulip petals have. They were painted with different shades of pale yellow over the pink sugar paste to give them a luminous peachy glow, and then they were striped with light green. The cake was a huge success ... and not one petal broke!'

Resources

Speciality brands used by most pâtissiers featured in this book

Albert y Ferran Adrià www.albertyferranadria.com

Big Tree Farms http://bigtreefarms.com

Cacao Barry www.cacaobarry.com

Capfruit www.capfruit.com

Felchlin www.felchlin.com

Ravifruit www.ravifruit.com

SOSA www.sosa.cat

Valrhona www.valrhona.com

Willpowder http://willpowder.com

Worldwide suppliers of equipment and ingredients, recommended by the pâtissiers themselves, and many offering online services as well as store outlets

ARGENTINA

Ingredients and utensils

Doña Clara (bakery products, ingredients and utensils), Avenida Corrientes 2561, Buenos Aires www.donaclara.com.ar

GastroBaires (kitchenware, and cooking and baking equipment), Avenida Jujuy 1591, Buenos Aires www.gastrobaires.com

Online for ingredients

Lodiser (raw materials for industrial and professional confectioners, ice cream manufacturers and chocolatiers) www.lodiser.com.ar

Yacaratiá Delicatessen (edible wood) www.yacaratiadelicatessen.com

AUSTRALIA/NEW ZEALAND

Creative/DIY accessories

Barnes: stores in Sydney, Melbourne and Brisbane, Australia www.barnes.com.au

Ingredients and utensils

Chef's Armoury: stores in Sydney and Melbourne, Australia www.chefsarmoury.com

Chef's Warehouse, 111–115 Albion Street, Surry Hills, Sydney, NSW 2010, Australia http://chefswarehouse.com.au

The Essential Ingredient: stores in various locations across Australia www.essentialingredient.com.au

Fresh As (freeze-dried fruits), 7A/43A Linwood Ave, Mt Albert, Auckland, New Zealand http://fresh-as.com

Friends of the Earth (packaging-free organic grains, pulses, flour, spices, teas, dairy products, etc.), 312 Smith Street, Collingwood, Melbourne, VIC 3066, Australia www.melbourne.foe.org.au/?q=co_op/home

The Red Spoon Company, 461 Liverpool Rd, Strathfield, Sydney, NSW 2135, Australia www.redspooncompany.com

Royal Nut Company (nuts, dried fruits, spices, grains, etc.), 204–206 Albion Street, Brunswick, VIC 3056, Australia www.royalnutcompany.com.au

CANADA

Utensils

Nella Cucina, 876 Bathurst Street, Toronto, ON M5R 3G3 www.nellacucina.ca

FRANCE

Ingredients

G. Detou, 58 rue Tiquetonne, 75002 Paris http://gdetou.com

La Grande Épicerie du Bon Marché, 38 rue de Sèvres, 75007 Paris www.lagrandeepicerie.com

Heratchian Frères, 6 rue Lamartine, 75009 Paris www.traiteurheratchian.fr

Izraël: L'Épicerie du Monde, 30 rue François Miron, 75004 Paris

Kioko (Japanese ingredients and utensils), 46 rue des Petits Champs, 75002 Paris www.kioko.fr

La Maison du Miel (honey products), 24 rue Vignon, 75009 Paris www.maisondumiel.com

Saveurs de l'Aventure (spices and gourmet food), 1 avenue du Marché, 44500 La Baule www.saveursdelaventure.com

La Tête dans les Olives (olive oil products), 2 rue Sainte Marthe, 75010 Paris www.latetedanslesolives.com

Workshop ISSé (Japanese ingredients), 11 rue Saint-Augustin, 75002 Paris www.workshop-isse.fr

Online for ingredients, utensils and books

Cerf Dellier www.cerfdellier.com

La Cocotte: own products sold in many locations worldwide www.lacocotte.net

Coin Cuisine, 110 rue du Théâtre, 75015 Paris www.coin-cuisine.com

E. Dehillerin, 18/20 rue Coquillière, 75001 Paris www.e-dehillerin.fr

Kitchen Bazaar: stores in Paris and all other major French cities www.kitchenbazaar.fr

Librairie Gourmande, 92/96 rue Montmartre, 75002 Paris www.librairiegourmande.fr

Lydia SAS, 20 Place du Forum, 51100 Reims/La Cuisine à Lydia,
55 rue du Commerce, 51350 Cormontreuil www.facebook.com/
pages/La-Cuisine-à-Lydia/ 164479703620908
Meilleur du Chef
www.meilleurduchef.com/cgi/mdc/l/fr/boutique/index.html
Mora, 13 rue Montmartre, 75001 Paris www.mora.fr
Zôdio (stores in various French cities) www.zodio.fr

HONG KONG

Ingredients and utensils
Complete Deelite, 2 Fl. On Lan Centre, 11–15 On Lan Street, Central,
Hong Kong http://completedeelite.com
Foodtalk (mainly for savoury goods): several stores across Hong Kong
www.foodtalk.com.hk
I ♥ Cake www.ilovecake.hk

ITALY

Ingredients
Caffè Sicilia (nuts and dried fruits), Corso Vittorio Emanuele,
Noto, Sicily
Giachi (Frantoio olive oil), Via Campoli, 31, Mercatale Val di Pesa,
50024 Florence http://giachioleari.it
Mercato di San Lorenzo (fresh fruits and herbs), Florence

Ingredients and utensils
Dolci Fai Da Te, Via Luigi Settembrini, 100, 80138 Naples
www.dolcifaidate.com
Lady Chef (mainly utensils and tableware), Centro Commerciale
Vulcano Buono, Porta Capri, 80035 Nola www.ladychef.net

JAPAN

Utensils
All the shops along Kappabashi Dougu Street
www.kappabashi.or.jp/en/index.html

PORTUGAL

Ingredients
Casa Lourenço (smoked meat, cheese, olive oil, wine, etc.),
Rua Bonjardim, 417, 4000-125 Porto
http://casalourenco.com.pt/pt
A Favorita do Bolhão (dried fruits and nuts, spices, tea, wine, honey,
etc.), Rua Fernandes Tomás, 783, 4000-218 Porto
A Pérola do Bolhão (dried fruits and nuts, spices, tea, wine, honey,
etc.), Rua Formosa, 279, 4000-252 Porto

Utensils
Vista Alegre Atlantis (tableware), Rua das Carmelitas, 40,
4050-161 Porto www.vistaalegreatlantis.com

SINGAPORE

Ingredients and utensils
Cold Storage: several supermarkets across Singapore
www.coldstorage.com.sg

FairPrice: several supermarkets across Singapore
www.fairprice.com.sg
Phoon Huat (baking and dessert ingredients, and baking accessories):
several stores across Singapore www.phoonhuat.com
Traditional Chinese medical halls to be found in Chinatown

SPAIN

Utensils
Utilcentre, Calle Joan Armengol, 08770 Sant Sadurní d'Anoia
http://utilcentre.com

SWEDEN

Ingredients and utensils
Bagaren och Kocken, Ängsvaktaregatan 4, 416 52 Gothenburg
http://bagarenochkocken.se
Cajsa Warg: stores in Stockholm www.cajsawarg.se
Chokladfabriken: stores in Stockholm
www.chokladfabriken.com/baking-your-own.html
Cordon-Bleu, Vasagatan 48, 111 20 Stockholm http://cordon-bleu.se
Sundquist: showroom at Flygfältsgatan 16A, 423 37 Torslanda
www.sundquist.se
Urban Deli, Nytorget 4, 116 40 Stockholm www.urbandeli.org

UK

Books
Books for Cooks, 4 Blenheim Crescent, London W11 1NN
www.booksforcooks.com

Online for ingredients and utensils
HB Ingredients www.hbingredients.co.uk
Home Chocolate Factory www.homechocolatefactory.com
Keylink www.keylink.org
Squires Kitchen www.squires-shop.com
Vantage House www.vantagehouse.com

USA

Books, ingredients and utensils
The Brooklyn Kitchen, 100 Frost Street, Brooklyn, NY 11211
www.thebrooklynkitchen.com
Chef Rubber: showroom at 6627 Schuster Street, Las Vegas,
NV 89118 http://chefrubber.com
Economy Candy, 108 Rivington Street, New York, NY 10002
www.economycandy.com
JB Prince, 36 East 31st Street, New York, NY 10016
www.jbprince.com
Kalustyan's, 123 Lexington Ave., New York, NY 10016
http://www.kalustyans.com
N.Y. Cake, 56 West 22nd Street, New York, NY 10010
www.nycake.com
Sur La Table: stores in various locations across the USA
www.surlatable.com

Online for ingredients
Terra Spice Company http://terraspice.com

Picture Credits

a = above; b = below; l = left; r = right

p. 4 Photo courtesy of Janice Wong.

p. 7 Photo courtesy of Barry Callebaut.

p. 8 Photo courtesy of Marike van Beurden.

THE NEW CLASSICS

Andrea Reiss: all photos pp. 12, 13, 14, 15, 17 & 18–19 by David Reiss (www.davidreiss.com.au).

Arnaud Delmontel: pp. 20, 21 al, bl & br by Guillaume Murat (http://guillaumemurat.com); pp. 21 ar, 23 & 24 by Laurent Fau (www.studiodesfleurs.com).

Bernard Heberle: pp. 26, 27, 29 & 30 by Hidekazu Kurumiya (www.kurumiya750.com); p. 31 by Drazen Tomic.

Christophe Roussel: pp. 32 & 35 by Pascal Lattes (www.thuries magazine.fr); pp. 33 & 37 by Patrick Gérard (pgphot@wanadoo.fr).

Gontran Cherrier: all photos pp. 38, 39, 41, 42–43 & 45 by David François (www.galloismontbrunfabiani.fr/photographer/david-françois).

Luca Ori: pp. 46, 47, 48 & 51 courtesy of Ivano Zinelli Fotografo (www.ivanozinelli.com); p. 49 by Drazen Tomic; p. 50 by Olivier Dupon.

Martin Isaksson: pp. 52, 53, 54, 57 & 58 by Axel Engelberth (www.axelengelberth.se); p. 56 by Drazen Tomic.

Nadège Nourian: all photos pp. 60, 61, 62, 64–65 & 66–67 courtesy of Nadège Nourian.

Nathaniel Reid: all photos pp. 68, 69, 70, 73 & 74 by Erik Kellar (http://erikkellar.com).

Pasquale Marigliano: pp. 76, 77, 78–79, 81 & 82–83 by Francesco La Marca (www.francescolamarca.it); p. 80 by Olivier Dupon.

Ronny Latva: pp. 84, 85, 86 & 88 by Axel Engelberth (www.axelengelberth.se); p. 89 by Drazen Tomic.

Sébastien Gaudard: all photos pp. 90, 91, 92 & 95 by Michaël Adelo (www.adelo.book.fr).

Sébastien Ordioni: all photos pp. 96, 97, 98–99 & 101 courtesy of Le Macaron Bleu (http://lemacaronbleu.fr).

Shigeru Nojima: pp. 102, 103, 104, 107 & 108 by Hidekazu Kurumiya (www.kurumiya750.com); p. 106 by Olivier Dupon.

Siang Yee: all photos pp. 110, 111, 112 & 115 by Audrey and Mok (http://audreyandmok.com).

ART ON A PLATE

Anna Polyviou: pp. 118, 119, 121 & 123 by James Morgan (www.morgan-photo.com); p. 124 by Drazen Tomic; pp. 126–27 by Nicole Jones (http://nicolejonesphotos.blogspot.com.au).

Antonio Bachour: all photos pp. 128, 129, 130 & 133 courtesy of Antonio Bachour.

Carmelo Sciampagna: pp. 134, 135, 136–37, 139 & 141 courtesy of Carmelo Sciampagna; p. 138 by Drazen Tomic.

Douce Steiner: all photos pp. 142, 143, 144–45 & 147 by Michael Wissing (www.michael-wissing.de).

John Ralley: all photos pp. 148, 149, 151, 152 & 155 by Thomas Walk and Patrick Stevenson (www.hoboincognito.com).

Julie Sharp: all photos pp. 156, 157, 159, 160, 161, 162 & 163 courtesy of Barry Callebaut (www.barry-callebaut.com).

Luca Lacalamita: all photos pp. 164, 165, 166, 169 & 171 by Roberto Quagli (www.studioquagli.com).

Marike van Beurden: pp. 172, 173 al, bl, br & 175 courtesy of Marike van Beurden; pp. 173 ar & 180 Four Seasons Hotel Hong Kong (www.fourseasons.com/hongkong); pp. 176 & 178 by Louis Chong (www.louischong.com); p. 181 by Drazen Tomic.

Michelle Gillott: all photos pp. 182, 183, 184 & 187 by Andreas Beck (www.karohemd.co.uk).

EXPERIMENTAL EXOTICA

Alvaro Garrido: all photos pp. 190, 191, 193, 194, 195 & 197 by Victor H. Antón Baigorri (http://vicugo.com).

Fernando Rivarola: all photos pp. 198, 199, 200, 201 & 203 courtesy of Fernando Rivarola.

Florencia Rondon: pp. 204, 205, 206 & 209 by Gabriela Medina (http://gabrielamedina.com/food.asp); p. 208 by Drazen Tomic.

Janice Wong: p. 210 by Kai Lian (http://lightedpixelspixies.com/category/kai-lian); pp. 211, 212, 214–15 & 216–17 courtesy of Janice Wong.

Leonor de Sousa Bastos: all photos pp. 218, 219, 220–21 & 223 by Miguel Coelho (http://miguelcoelho.com).

Pamela Yung: pp. 224, 228 & 230 by Melissa Hom (www.melissahom.com); pp. 225, 227 & 233 by Emilie Baltz (www.emiliebaltz.com).

Pierre François Roelofs: all photos pp. 234, 235, 237, 239 & 240–41 courtesy of Pierre François Roelofs.

Rosio Sanchez: all photos pp. 242, 243, 244, 247 & 248 by Hannah Grant (www.hannahgrant.com).

Sarah Jordan: all photos pp. 250, 251, 253 & 254 by Eric Kleinberg (www.facebook.com/ebkphoto).

Will Goldfarb: all photos pp. 256, 257, 259, 261 & 263 by Mertha Kurnia (www.kudeta.net).

WONDERLAND CONFECTIONS

Bobbette & Belle: pp. 266, 267 ar & 268 a by Jon Thorpe (www.jonthorpe.com); pp. 267 al & 269 courtesy of Bobbette & Belle; p. 267 bl by Donna Griffith (www.donnagriffith.com); pp. 267 br, 268 bl & br, & 270 by Tara McMullen (http://taramcmullen.com).

Bonnae Gokson: p. 272 by Van Hai; pp. 273, 274, 275 & 277 by A. Chester Ong.

Emily Miranda: pp. 278, 279 al & br, 280, 281, 282 & 283 by Adam Klimaszewski (www.adamklimaszewski.com); p. 279 ar & bl courtesy of Emily Miranda.

p. 288 by Drazen Tomic.

Image quality control by Helen Brooke
www.maverickdesigntribe.com.au

Acknowledgments

First and foremost I would like to thank my publisher, editor and the entire team behind this project. You have accompanied me book after book, and I could not wish for a better team.

This particular publication has represented a great learning curve. Each recipe has been formatted for consistency, translated where need be, investigated, dissected, questioned and ultimately tested by a team of three amateurs to ensure that the dishes can be replicated by non-professionals. A special mention is therefore due to Denise King and Mark Wilsher for your tremendous help in thoroughly testing some of the 89 recipes presented. Simply put: without you, the task would have verged on the impossible. A special and grateful mention also to my parents, who have been patient supporters and even diligent tasters on a few testings.

Thank you to Antonio C. Miari for translating and liaising with the Italian pastry talents featured in the book: I am very grateful to you for your efficiency and friendliness. Thank you also to Maria Teresa Brigazzi-Percossi Papi (www.percossipapi.com) for ultimately introducing me to Antonio. Thanks are also due to Meiko Ishii for all your help in ensuring that the book includes great Japanese representation.

Last but not least, thank you to all the chefs who embarked with me on this journey. Your time is packed and precious, but you were always helpful and available to my numerous requests. The outcome is a joyful celebration of pastry in all its splendour. Sharing your secrets and signature best-sellers, and opening up your kitchens and workshops, has made the subject matter of this book all the more approachable. We very much look forward to tasting your future concoctions, and we hope you will continue to bring pastry and desserts to the forefront of the culinary world.